Exclusion and Discrimination:
Concepts, Perspectives and Challenges

Exclusion and Discrimination

Concepts, Perspectives and Challenges

Edited by

YAGATI CHINNA RAO
SUDHAKARA KARAKOTI

KANISHKA PUBLISHERS, DISTRIBUTORS
NEW DELHI-110 002

KANISHKA PUBLISHERS, DISTRIBUTORS
4697/5-21 A, Ansari Road, Daryaganj
New Delhi-110 002
Phones : 2327 0497, 2328 8285
Fax : 011-2328 8285
E-mail: kanishka_publishing@yahoo.co.in

Exclusion and Discrimination:
Concepts, Perspectives and Challenges

First Published 2010

ISBN 978-81-8457-224-7

PRINTED IN INDIA

Published by Madan Sachdeva for Kanishka Publishers, Distributors, 4697/5-21A, Ansari Road, Daryaganj, New Delhi-110 002, Typeset by Sunshine Graphics, Delhi, and Printed at Rajdhani Printers, Delhi.

In honour of

- *Professor* Romila Thapar
- *Professor* T.K. Oommen
- *Professor* Ghanshyam Shah
- *Professor* Abhijit Sen
- *Professor* S.K. Thorat
- *Professor* Zoya Hasan

Foreword

The concept of 'social exclusion' is made popular by social scientists that are broadly influenced by European training or Anglo-Saxon education. The term was used and popularized by economists like Amartya Sen, (the noble laureate with an Indian passport) in the academic discourse. It is a direct import from the European Union. In fact, Amartya Sen himself has noted the origin of the concept as European, particularly its French connection in his Asian Development Bank Lecture on social exclusion in 2000. It is strange that none of the social scientists who has been discussing about social exclusion has referred to the Indian version. There are several conceptual infirmities in understanding the European 'social exclusion' as deprivation. The concept in its European form talks about groups of people or individuals including a social people. Yet, the concept intriguingly evades the economic process in the capitalist West that has 'alienated' these individuals or groups of people from mainstream. The historical process of alienation which is inherent in the western economic system has not been explicitly discussed. They have however recognized the menace of exclusion and created special ministries to deal with it in Europe.

Social exclusion in India is a value. It has been cultivated as a norm both in public and private life of people from time immemorial. Therefore, the European concept of social exclusion has several limitations in applying it to Indian conditions. In fact, the nature of exclusion was long recognized in India and a constructive policy was declared by Ram Manohar Lohia. It is pertinent on the centenary year of Lohia to remember what he said about it. In his article in "The Two Segregations of Caste and Sex" in 1953, he said that, "I am convinced that the two segregations of caste and woman are primarily responsible for this decline of the spirit. These segregations have enough power to kill all capacity for adventure and joy...... All war on poverty is a sham, unless it is at the same time, a conscious and sustained war on these two segregations." It was Ram Manohar Lohia who in his 1950 Banaras speech for the first time brought the 85 per cent proportion of 'Women, Harijans, Sudras, depressed Muslims and Christians and Adivasis' in our total population. He went on to say that in the four decisive fields, namely politics, army, trade and high government jobs, they are less than 10 per cent. Until the imbalance is set right, neither the caste system will vanish nor will new life be generated in the country'. Thus, Lohia has proposed 60 to 70 per cent of reservation in government services. He has also proposed in the meeting to allocate more than sixty percent of the seats to backward castes in the socialist party. He said that it is through these constructive programmes, the destruction of caste and thus segregations will disappear.

There are very few studies elaborating the concept of social exclusion with Indian experiences. Hundreds of studies are being published now to validate the European concept with Indian categories. Several decades after Babasaheb Ambedkar's studies on caste and Scheduled Caste Commission reports scholars are trying to prove through empirical studies that there is untouchability, discrimination and deprivation. But, none of these studies has looked at the caste system as a 'compulsive exclusion' originated in pre-historic times due to alien invasions of hordes of uncivilized clans destroying the settled culture and civilization of natives. It is these hordes of sinecure aliens who had created structures to physically distance the natives to interact with them lest they get absorbed. These structures must have been reviewed and reorganized when new hordes are added or new regions are enslaved. It is to provide legitimacy to these arrangements a gigantic corpus of religious scriptures; incarnations, laws etc. are created to continue the hegemony of the alien. It is said that these structures have been utilized by the colonial rulers and it is still in vogue American characters. The physical distance of social exclusion was not a part of Sen's concept of social exclusion and so were the studies by Indian and European social scientists. The rules of segregation or social exclusion were so cruel that any infringement of the code was brutally suppressed. It is alive today. A media report on March 22, 2010 reported that the hut of a dhobi in Nellore, not an untouchable in Andhra, but an OBC, was burnt as it is on the north east of upper caste habitations and it is bad omen as per Brahminical Sutras. Around the same time, the scholars and learned professors of

Jawaharlal Nehru University opposed the proposal to provide affirmative action to Scheduled Castes and Tribes in teaching posts. It is also reported that those who were opposing the proposal were not academically qualified to hold their present positions in the university. I, cite these examples to show that social exclusion in India is not only physical but cerebral and emotional. The ingenuity of Indian abstract minds are so creative that they keep on innovating new forms of exclusion as India is progressing and integrating with rest of the world.

It is in this context, a group of young scholars have discussed some of these issues in the present volume on "Exclusion and Discrimination: Concepts, Perspectives and Challenges." They are not trying to reinvent the wheel like the mainstream scholars. They have provided insolent ideas, concepts and experiences from their own lives and from their exposure to discrimination and exclusion. Therefore, it is easy to identify the background of the writer even without reading the name and social milieu that she/he belongs. Interestingly there are one or two pieces that justify caste system based on the virulent material posted by fundamentalists on the net. It is said in one of the papers that the caste system is based on the planetary configuration at the time of birth of a person. One need not get surprised with such formulations even in 2010 as there are permanent structures in the country repeating the thousand years old social norms, customs, codes and beliefs as religious and holy practices. They are now using people's money and state patronage with the support of ICT and global networks. This is the greatest boon of globalization to Indian mind set. Interestingly, the Indian mind set and American mind set corroborate each other here. The mind set is so creative that they can occupy the extreme right to the extreme radical positions with a hidden agenda to keep the hegemony of superiority of birth. Similarly, the rhetoric of untouchability, humiliation and discrimination is found to be not so diversified in the writings of the victims despite of new data and theories. None of the writers have challenged the veracity of the concept of exclusion developed in the market mould. It is the market that excludes communities like the Adivasis and some dalit groups who are still in a non-monetized economy and therefore at a disadvantage in terms of trade in the exchange of goods and services in India. Sen has recognized the exclusion of social groups in the labour market and others. But he has justified the market by saying that it is due to other factors that they are discriminated.

There are 19 papers in the volume divided into four parts. There are papers from scholars from North East, Kerala, on conversions, Education, judiciary and also an agenda against social exclusion in a democratic polity. There are endeavours to bring Marxian concepts to interrogate caste equating it as race. The concept of dalit is once again discussed as a wider term to absorb all social categories of oppressed as originally developed by Mahatma Phooley. But, the recent empirical experience show that no backward caste person either as some untouchables in North India (Dhobi, Nai etc.,) or the low service castes in the south are willing to call themselves as Dalit. In fact, there were attempts by some scholars to use both Dalit and bahujan concepts simultaneously to distinguish the OBCs from untouchable Dalits. This has not enriched the academic discourse, though some religious groups must have benefited by this categorization. This has helped them to bring all converts under one umbrella for political support. The paper on conversions has elaborated the Indian meaning of dalit conversions. It has brought out a very interesting historical event to show that the upper castes started converting to Christianity only when the missionary Robert De Nobili practiced untouchability and Brahminical customs and traditions in 1606. It means that the metaphysical rhetoric of Christian brotherhood is far from empirical reality once it is grounded in India. I remember a very influential upper caste Christian intellectual branding one of our colleagues as anti-Christian when he has raised the issue of discrimination and physical exclusion in the church. The St. Stephen's College episode in Delhi about the Dalit red herring to overcome an internal crisis is whispered in the Dalit corridors even today. Similar episodes are also pouring in from Punjab Dehras, Muslims practicing untouchability and so on.

The papers on education and literacy among adivasis and scheduled castes have provided new insights into the problem. The experiences of Kerala, as a universal literate state has a portent story of how reservations are not followed in the recruitment of teachers in government aided schools. It is a case to be taken seriously in the ensuing reforms in education. It is not Kerala that has the highest literacy rate today among scheduled castes but it is Mizoram a north eastern Indian state. Similar experiences from Orissa, Tamil Nadu and other experiments are illuminating in the book.

Social exclusion today is practiced more in economic opportunities than in social interactions as the Adivasis and scheduled castes are slowly getting educated and enlightened. There are very few studies to show that once the dalits are converted to Buddhism, Christianity, Islam, Sikh or other faiths or parties or formations they are treated differently than before. Nor are there studies to prove that the militancy and mobilization have increased after the conversions. On the other hand, it is increasingly proved that it is the native Indian untouchables and adivasis who are divided and further fragmented on the basis of religion, language, region, ideology, political party and so on. Therefore, it is easy for the crafty to perpetuate the age old norms of social exclusion based on the fragmentation of the natives. It is time that the oppressed and historically excluded groups should realize this and come together to prove that they are more inclusive than the oppressors or perpetrators. This requires lot of energy, persuasion and above all intellectual inputs. I hope, the attempts made by these young scholars in the volume will pave the way for a new beginning in the studies on social exclusion in India.

PROF. K.S. CHALAM

14 April 2010
New Delhi

Preface

In 2002, Professor Prabhat Patnaik, the then Dean, School of Social Sciences, Jawaharlal Nehru University, appointed a committee consisting of Professor Romila Thapar (Chairperson), Prof. T.K. Oommen, Prof. Ghanshyam Shah, Prof. Abhijit Sen, Prof. S.K. Thorat and Prof. Zoya Hasan (Convenor) to see the possibility and feasibility to study exclusion and discrimination. The committee recommended the introduction of a school-level programme with focus on discrimination and exclusion on the basis of caste, tribe and religion. Consequently a Programme for the Study of Discrimination and Exclusion (PSDE) was launched in 2005. Some of the principal objectives of PSDE are: to document and explain discrimination and exclusion of the Scheduled Castes, Scheduled Tribes and minorities in Indian society; to collate and generate more information and facts on the experiences and outcomes of discrimination and conditions and process of exclusion of members of these groups and to engage in detailed analysis of the socio-economic data generated by government agencies and assessment of the effective performance of equalizing measures. Followed by this the University Grants Commission under the stewardship of Professor S.K. Thorat established Centre(s) for Study of Social Exclusion and Inclusive Policy (CSSEIP) in thirty-five universities across the country to support research on the issues of social exclusion and inclusive policy.

Dozens of studies are available on these themes originated and owes either to Europe or US. Few available studies on Indian patterns of exclusion or discrimination are limited to disciplines of economics and public health. The conventional subjects/Departments/Centres of social sciences have rarely focused on these themes of research. In recognition of the absence of specialized research or focus on these themes in mainstream disciplinary genres, these specialized centres of CSSEIPs have been established. Given the emerging significance of the framework and the specific disciplinary orientation of these new and innovative programmes/centres, there is a need to relate to the social exclusion and discrimination with Indian experiences to the general discourses in the west. It is hoped that this volume is only a modest beginning on these lines.

Originally, these essays were invited for a "young social scientists' workshop on discrimination and exclusion", which for many reasons, could not be held. From the idea of workshop to making of this monograph, we owe to many friends and colleagues who have in several ways helped us in this endeavour. It may not be possible to name all, but we will fail in our duty if we do not mention some of them, who have been extremely helpful. First of all we acknowledge all the contributors of this volume, who enthusiastically responded to our invitation and patiently reworked on their drafts. We are profusely thankful to Prof. K.S. Chalam, who despite his hectic schedule, kindly accepted our request to write the foreword. We are thankful to Prof. Pralay Kanungo (Honorary Director, PSDE) for his support and to Dr. Priyadarshini Vijaisri (CSDS) and Raja Sekhar Vundru (IAS) for their valuable comments on earlier drafts of the papers. We also thank Avinash Kumar and Dr. Sugadan for their editorial inputs. Md. Asif Equbal and Girender Singh provided us the secretarial and logistic support and finally we thank Madan Sachdeva and Vivek Chaturvedi of Kanishka Publishers for bringing out the volume in such a short time span.

All the usual disclaims are applicable.

Yagati Chinna Rao
Sudhakara Karakoti

24 April 2010
New Delhi

Contents

Contributors

Yagati Chinna Rao, Associate Professor, Programme for the Studies on Discrimination and Exclusion, School of Social Sciences, Jawaharlal Nehru University, New Delhi.

V. Ravindra Sastry, Professor, Department of Political Science, Osmania University, Hyderabad.

G. Ram Reddy, Assistant Professor, Department of Political Science, Osmania University, Hyderabad.

Shura Darapuri, Associate Professor, Centre for the Study of Social Exclusion and Inclusive Policy, Babasaheb Bhimrao Ambedkar University, Lucknow.

Netrapal Singh, Assistant Professor, Department of History, Motilal Nehru College, Delhi University, Delhi.

Pragati Burman, Research Scholar, Centre for Historical Studies, School of Social Sciences, Jawaharlal Nehru University, New Delhi.

Chunnu Prasad, Centre for Political Studies, School of Social Sciences, Jawaharlal Nehru University, New Delhi.

N. William Singh, Assistant Professor, Department of Sociology, Mizoram University, Mizoram.

Rabindra Kumar, Associate Professor, Department of Sociology, Indira Gandhi National Open University (IGNOU), New Delhi.

M. Poornima, Research Scholar, Centre for the Study of Law & Governance, Jawaharlal Nehru University, New Delhi and is also a Junior Research Fellow, National Council of Educational Research and Training, New Delhi.

Sunil Babu, Assistant Professor, Department of Economics, Delhi University, Delhi and is also with Centre for Economic Studies and Planning, School of Social Sciences, Jawaharlal Nehru University, New Delhi.

Sudhakara Karakoti, Doctoral Research Fellow, Centre for the Study of Law & Governance, Jawaharlal Nehru University, New Delhi.

Pankaj Deep, Centre for Political Studies, School of Social Sciences, Jawaharlal Nehru University, New Delhi.

L. David Lal, Research Scholar, Department of Political Science, Delhi University, Delhi.

Jagannath Ambagudia, Lecturer, National Law University of India, Bangalore.

Raghunath Prasad Saket, Lecturer, Laxmi Bai College, Delhi University and is also with Centre for Economic Studies and Planning, Jawaharlal Nehru University.

Suresh Babu G.S., Assistant Professor, Department of Sociology, University of Jammu, Jammu and Kashmir.

Pallavi Bahar, Reseach Scholar, Centre for the Study of Law & Governance, Jawaharlal Nehru University, New Delhi.

Vikash Kumar, Research Scholar, School of International Studies, Jawaharlal Nehru University, New Delhi

Shailaja Menon, Lecturer, Department of History, Janki Devi Memorial College, Delhi University, Delhi.

Avinash Kumar, Junior Researcher with the Religious and Development Programme, University of Birmingham, UK and Indian Institute of Dalit Studies, New Delhi. He is also a Research Scholar, Department of Political Science, Jamia Milia Islamia.

Introduction

In social sciences literature, there is a general agreement on the core features of social exclusion, its principal indicators, and the way it relates to poverty and inequality. Social exclusion is the denial of equal opportunities to some groups in a society by some dominant groups, which leads to the inability of the affected/excluded individual to participate in the basic political, economic and social functions within the society. Recent developments in social science disciplines enable us to better comprehend the meanings and manifestations of the concept of social exclusion, and its applicability to caste and ethnicity-based exclusion in our country. Accordingly, in social sciences literature, the concept of social exclusion-essentially refers to the processes through which groups are wholly or partially excluded from full participation in the society in which they live. It emphasises two crucial dimensions involving the notion of exclusion, namely the "societal institutions" (of exclusion), and their "outcomes" (in terms of deprivation). To understand the dimensions of exclusion, it is necessary to explore the societal interrelations and institutions, which lead to the exclusion of certain groups and deprivation in multiple spheres-civil, cultural, political, and economic. Thus, for a broader understanding of the concept of exclusion, the insights into the societal processes and institutions of exclusions are as important as the outcome in terms of deprivation for certain groups.

Amartya Sen, therefore, refers to various meanings and manifestations of social exclusions, particularly, with respect to the causes or the processes of discrimination and deprivation in a given society. Thus, exclusion could occur through direct exclusion, violating fair norms of exclusion (that is unfavourable exclusion), or through inclusion, but under unfavourable conditions, again violating fair norms of inclusion (that is unfavourable inclusion), or through deliberate government policies (that is active exclusion), and through unintended attempts and circumstances (passive exclusion), or exclusion caused through the inability of some persons to relate to other persons (constitutive relevance).[1] Mainstream economists have further elaborated on the concept of discrimination that operates particularly through markets. Social exclusion can indeed arise in a variety of ways, and it is important to recognise the versatility of the idea and its reach.

In India, exclusion is embedded in societal interrelations and institutions that exclude, discriminate, isolate, and deprive some groups on the basis of their identities like caste and ethnicity. The nature of exclusion revolving around the caste system particularly needs to be discerned and conceptualised.

The fundamental characteristics of the caste system such as fixed civil, cultural, and economic rights for each caste, with restrictions for change imply "forced exclusion" of one caste from the rights of other castes, or from undertaking the occupations of other castes.[2] Exclusion and discrimination in civil, cultural, and particularly in economic spheres such as occupation and employment, is therefore, internal to the system, and a necessary outcome of its governing principles. In the market economy framework, the occupational immobility would operate through restrictions in various markets such as land, labour, credit, other inputs, and services necessary for any economic activity. Labour being an integral part of the production process of any economic activity, would obviously become a part of market discrimination.[3]

Unlike most societies, the caste system in India does not recognise the individual and his/her distinctiveness as the center of the social purpose. In fact, for the purpose of rights and duties, the unit of the Hindu society is not an individual (even the family is not regarded as a unit in the Hindu society except for the purposes of marriages and inheritance). The primary unit in the Hindu society is caste, and therefore, the rights and privileges (or the lack of them) of an individual are on account of he/she being a member of a particular caste. Also, due to differential ranking, and the hierarchical nature of the caste system, the entitlements to various rights become narrower and narrower as one goes down in hierarchical ladder in the caste system. The fundamental features of the caste system, namely fixed social, cultural and economic rights for each caste by birth, with restrictions on change, have created manifold forms of exclusion and marginalisation.

A section of Dalits continue to pursue traditional caste occupations such as weaving, tanning, shoe-making along with agriculture. The capitalist system has opened avenues for those whose skills are marketable. In urban areas, the Dalits are employed in the organised and unorganised sectors; they are petty shopkeepers, small entrepreneurs and white-collar workers mainly in the public sector. But the number of such persons is very small. The recent report of the National Commission for Enterprises in the Unorganised Sector indicates the extent of marginalisation of the weaker sections in the economy. Informal workers, who have no employment, work or social security, now constitute 92 per cent of the total workforce and discrimination is reinforced by one's social identity, rural location and low or no education.[4] A perusal of the report makes it clear that a substantial number of these workers fall into the category of the Dalits and Tribals.

Thus, the evidence points to both change and continuity from the past. Significant changes that have taken place have created greater inclusion and lessened social and economic marginalisation of the Dalits post-Independence atleast when one compares with pre-Independence times. But these changes have occurred only in some parts of the country and impacted only a small portion of the marginalised lot. The vast majority of these people in the countryside still routinely suffer exclusion in public and private life and, being illiterate and poor, remain on the margins of the society. Paradoxically, this is happening despite the *social deepening* of democracy in the recent past. Only very recently the academia has turned its attention to this subject.

Given the complexity and crucial relevance of these issues to many a group of people, the discipline assumes greater significance. Moreover, establishing these social exclusion programmes[5] as part of the curriculum in various institutions holds the promise of more specialised knowledge to overcome the challenges posed to the governments and other stakeholders, especially in the post-colonial era. Even if the governmental action is tardy, as it often is, such knowledge matters, because exclusion from the domain of knowledge has got the means of preserving exclusion.

This volume is a compilation of 19 chapters and has been divided into four thematic parts: 'Concepts and Theories';

'Perspectives on Exclusion and Discrimination'; 'Exclusion and Discrimination in Education'; and 'Facing the Challenges'.

The first chapter by Y. Chinna Rao deals with the nuances and concepts centered around the exclusion and discrimination, its emergence and applicability along with the human rights situation with special reference to Scheduled Castes, social exclusion in relation to human rights situation and exclusion of Scheduled Castes and scheduled tribes in higher education in the post-colonial India. The second chapter entitled 'Exclusion and Exploitation: A Conceptual Understanding' by V. Ravindra Sastry and G. Ram Reddy, argues that according to Marxists like D.D. Kosambi, in societies like ours, caste plays the role of class struggles, which in turn is the result of the varying caste structures. But the liberals argue that the contentions in our society can't just be based on class but other factors as well. It is agreed that human society is characterised by one vertical division or other and that this division is the basis for exclusions. The paper argues that the search for a common identity is itself exclusion, as it involves exclusion of someone else from that identity. It is a common perception that throughout the history there are identifiable perpetrators of exclusion. Exclusion leads to exploitation both social as well as economic. The underlying cause of all economic denial and furtherance of social division is maintenance of political hegemony which in turn facilitates exploitation at the social and economic levels. This then becomes a vicious cycle from which both the excluded as well as the exploited have no hope of breaking out. The cause for the emergence of this process in our society is the caste system and the logic it firmly embeds into the minds of one and all. What is of consequence to this paper is the fact that there are perceptions of exclusions within the groups that are considered cohesive. Because the topography of our society today firmly suggests that there is no one pattern of exclusion and exploitation. As in a causal chain where a cause is also an effect, those who are excluded are also a part of the process of exclusion. It is only this realisation that can help identify the true cause and nature of exploitation rather than the construct of the meek versus the mighty, which at best can only provide a partial picture and that too a distorted one. The way to eliminate exclusions lies in correctly understanding what it is in the first place.

The next chapter 'Social Inclusion and Social Justice: A Historical Perspective' by Shura Darapuri argues that the

'Dharmashastras' could be held responsible for the "exclusion" of the Dalits in our country as they sanctify the caste system. The fact is that the Dalits have been relentlessly asserting themselves and protesting against their 'exclusions' in varying degrees and forms much before our governments realised the need for 'inclusive policies' to bring about social justice. The efforts for social inclusion of the excluded groups is evident at various junctures of history. The Bhakti Movement was also an effort towards inclusion exclusively of the upper castes. The social reformers of the early nineteenth century, particularly the Christian missionaries to some extent, also geared up to attack 'exclusion' ascribed by the Brahminical Hinduism and the caste system. They were also aware of the nature of the pre-colonial protest movements such as the 'Vaishnava' cults and hence some of the ideas of the Bhakti tradition were embedded into the preaching of these Christian missionaries. The educational and socio-religious efforts of these missionaries also contributed immensely to a new awakening amongst the 'excluded' sections, especially the Dalits. Traditional or the pre British India may be regarded on the whole as a religious society, while modern India experienced steadily increasing secularisation since her conquest by Britain. She further seeks to indicate that the widespread desire for inclusion during this period among the marginalized groups comes from an unusual source namely, the Census operations. The Census authenticated their inclusion, and erased though in imperfect manner, their remotest semblance to exclusion. Therefore, history is witness to the assertions made by the Dalits themselves in protest against their 'exclusions' much before the 'inclusive policies' that the successive governments since Independence have tried to bring about.

"The Constitution of India: An Antidote to the Manu Smriti Remedies to Caste and Poverty' by Netrapal Singh deals with the fundamental problems of our nation—caste and poverty. It attempts to trace and interlink the historical origin of the menacing caste structures and diabolic dance of poverty of the millions. The salient features of the Manu Smriti have been highlighted to understand the context, as practiced among the Brahmin-Bania-Thakurs trilogy- and dominates public life. It notes how the Fundamental Rights and the Directive Principles in the Constitution can cure the problems of caste and poverty. Mahatma Phule, Chhatrapati Shahuji Maharaj and especially Babasaheb Ambedkar's contribution in the making of the Constitution has been highlighted to understand the historical and present contexts to implement the Constitutional guarantees.

This chapter is followed by 'Caste Oppression, Economic Discrimination and Poverty among Scheduled Castes in India' by Sudhakara Karakoti and Raghunath Prasad Saket which argues that historically, the Scheduled Castes faced various kinds of exclusion, discrimination, denial and oppression. The paper attempts to make a link between the high incidence of poverty and caste-based economic discrimination with special reference to the Scheduled Castes. In the sphere of education, they are traditionally restricted from acquiring knowledge that can help them unshackle their fetters. In the economic sphere, they are restricted from gaining wealth and are condemned to work for the upper castes. In the social sphere, they are restricted from participating in social and cultural activities. The first part of this paper deals with discrimination based on official macro level data. While the second part presents some empirical evidences on economic discrimination, captured by a few micro level studies. The analysis is based on the data from the National Sample Survey (NSS) for employment/unemployment, land ownership, occupational patterns and poverty, and the Rural Labour Enquiry Report to understand the lives of the daily wage labour households.

The next chapter 'Discrimination and Humiliation: The Uttar Pradesh Experience' by Sudhakara Karakoti and Pragati Burman, deals mainly with untouchability. It poignantly draws attention to the condition of the Scheduled Castes in many areas of the country as living in degraded conditions in juxtaposition to the oppressive castes whose social mores find nothing unusual and unbecoming in their social thinking and behaviour. For them it is a divinely ordained injunction and hence to be practiced with impunity. It further adds that the vulnerable condition of the Scheduled Castes who are denied even the basic human rights, is also conflated by the discriminatory practices of the Muslims. The Dalits are formally excluded from mainstream religion and educational institutions, and are a pariah in the entire sanctified universe of the so-called "Dwijas."

Chunnu Prasad in the next chapter titled 'Dalits, Democracy and Exclusive Policies: A Case of Scheduled Castes of Arunachal Pradesh' argues that Arunachal is in fact dominated by the

Scheduled Tribes. The Tribals constitute a separate endogamous community with their own territory, customs and traditions and are extremely different from other tribal communities elsewhere in the country. This Northeastern state has approximately 6,000 thousand Scheduled Caste population who suffer from duel backwardness, one as a general Scheduled Caste and the other arising from the general regional backwardness. These people are even denied of their basic fundamental rights and suffer from discrimination and exclusion by both the State Government as well as the other local population of the state. The paper also focuses on the various issues related to the people who, despite being residents of this state over a period of time, their constitutional rights are never recognised not are given option to lead a dignified life. It also focuses on the various constitutional provisions related to the SCs/STs in general and those living in Arunachal Pradesh in particular.

The next chapter entitled "Chinki": Is it a Racial Category or a Vilification Tag?' by N. William Singh focuses on the North-eastern region, one of the most under-developed regions of the country. The region has many syndromes of underdevelopment/backwardness in terms of regional disparities, poor roads and rail connectivity, pitiable infrastructure, multitudes of well-armed insurgent groups mingling illegitimately with the legitimate administration of many of these seven North-eastern states. Most importantly, these states lack basic amenities like drinking water, electricity and healthcare facilities among others. More exasperating is the fact that every nook and corner of these states dot Para-military forces and plain-clothed policemen. However, the primary objective of this paper is not to illustrate these disturbing issues but to thematise another burning issue, the citizens of this region minority racial status, which is a fact and not just a claim. It unravels multiple interlocking layers of social discriminations and social exclusions, especially in the northern regions. The term "Chinki" embodies the cultural denigration of specific ethnic communities and uses it to trace the emerging new form of informal and mocking tag in society across spaces ascribed to the people of North-east. It is argues that such mocking and vilification tag is an overt signifier of an existing form of racial exclusion and discrimination.

The next chapter 'From Hindu Untouchables to Dalit Christians: Conversion and Social Exclusion' by L. David Lal engages with the dimensions surrounding conversion in case of the Dalit Christians. The plights of the Dalit Christians continue to be marginalised. Here, in fact along with the civil society, state institutions, the Church also in specific way determines the process and nature of exclusion. Rabindra Kumar in his paper entitled 'Systematic Exclusion of the Dalits' sociologically locates the varied forms of exclusions resulting into stigmatisations of communities excluded from the mainstream society. It accounts the experiences of systematic exclusion inbuilt in the hierarchical social system, which excludes the Dalits from interaction and access to social resources through social arrangements, normative value systems and customs.

The third part on education and exclusion features G.S. Suresh Babu's paper 'Emerging Challenges of Equality: Private Educational Sector in Kerala' contextualised in the backdrop of critique of Kerala model of development focussing on educational institutional policies. In this context, this paper makes an attempt to analyse the elusive attitude of aided educational institutions towards affirmative policies reflecting on how this failure poses a new challenge to the highly celebrated Kerala model of development on the one hand, and the market-oriented unaided educational sector in the state on the other. Since a large share of public expenditure has gone in feeding the aided educational institutions in the state over the years, it also questions the very basis of arguing these institutions as private enterprises.

Pankaj Deep, in his chapter 'Politics of Tribal Education and Governance: The Orissa Experience' focuses on the continued marginalised of Tribals in Orissa and critiques the model of governance by specifically mapping the larger consequences through evaluations of the educational policies. The next chapter 'Social Exclusion and Elementary Education: A Case Study of Scheduled Tribes' by Sujit Kumar Choudhary notes the extent of social exclusion of the Scheduled Tribe children in elementary education and argues for a comprehensive policy response to address the various barriers they face to access education. It reviews the underlying causes of their disadvantaged status, linking these to elementary education. The paper concludes that for social policy to adequately respond to social exclusion in elementary education, a holistic approach is needed which should address the structural and basic causes of these problems in a context-specific and comprehensive manner. Further 'Combating Social Exclusion in Education: Re-examining the 'Inclusive' Framework of Accommodation'. by Jagannath Ambagudia deals with the dynamics of exclusion and inclusion and despite the welfare state policy of education it plays a complex and sometimes contradictory role. Thus, while on one hand, public schooling often serves as an effective vehicle for overcoming marginalization and enhancing inclusion into citizenship, work and other spheres of social participation on the other, it is often seen to perpetuate the socio-economic disparities, as well as the forms of discrimination based on gender, age, health, residence and minority status. It also explores various constraints, which contribute to the exclusion of Tribals from the formal educational process in Orissa. The basic premise as put in by the author is the inability of the existing educational policies/inclusive policies and programmes to encompass the complex social reality within a single framework and are, therefore, unable to bridge the gap between policy and practice.

The next chapter on 'Poverty, Social Exclusion and Basic Education: The Tamil Nadu Experience' by M. Poornima, delineate the specific of exclusionary nature of poverty retarding growth and development of an individual. Poverty is often seen as a reflection of inequality as some sections of the society are deprived of their basic needs and rights. Thus empowerment or combating social exclusion necessitates eradication of poverty by creating opportunities and access to resources and promotion of egalitarian ethos. This paper brings out the issues of poverty, exclusion and development, highlighting the strategic importance of basic education in eradicating poverty and move towards sustainable development. It discusses the capability approach and human rights-based approach in particular, which talks about the importance of empowering the poor through education so that their voices can be heard.

Pallavi Bahar in her chapter on 'Indian Judiciary and Problems of the Poor: Where Do the Marginalised Find a Place?' brings in the legal dimensions and on the cumulative notions of justice. The challenges of accessibility of these arrangements to all citizens, the procedural constraints, results in the procedures of courts as slow and expensive, that only the poor and weaker sections excluded from the scope of securing basic rights.

Vikas Kumar in his chapter on 'Disability, Inclusiveness and PRIs' enages with a very critical domain of the exclusion, the disabled.

It brings to the fore increasing population of the disabled in the country, constituting almost 6-7 per cent of the total population, their political representation is almost abysmal, simultaneously with lack of any attempt to gather authentic data of their political participation and representation. It suggests that their political participation at the grassroots level, especially in leadership roles, could be one of the major respites from their dilapidated condition. In the light of various national and international commitments it is imperative to study the basic lacuna in the governmental and societal approach to these people, as also to find out what are the hindrances in the way of political their empowerment at par with other sections of the society. In the aftermath of world wide disability rights movement, this paper also seeks to find out whether the Panchayati Raj Institutions are truly and practically inclusive and what could be the possible models for ensuring greater participation of persons with disabilities in the process of governance?

Shailaja Menon in her paper entitled 'The Rhetoric of Exclusive Development' critically focuses on as the title indicates the specific mode of development and the varied forms of exclusion that it reproduces. It weaves in crucial aspects involved in the process that of rights of communities over resources, sustainable development, and the coercive nature of state couched in the neo rhetoric participatory of development. It argues that the development as a concept and ideology is a protean, multi-dimensional process leading to a desired and desirable change brought about by a participatory process, which makes them self-reliant. Thus, rather than a linear view, it has to be viewed in terms of the different environmental needs of the people, i.e. in a non-linear perspective. The paper succinctly notes that such visionary ideas are only a footnote in our country's development planning now.

The last chapter by Avinash Kumar on 'Tacking Social Exclusion the Indian Way: Democracy, Development and Citizenship' traces the marginalisation of the Muslims and the Dalits constituting nearly one-third of the population. Tracing the different trajectories of exclusion of the communities, in the colonial and post-colonial periods it argues for a special attention and designing specific strategies of inclusion into mainstream society. The chapter draws from the Sachar report,[6] besides dealing with the experiences of discrimination faced by the Scheduled Castes in the job market, on the basis of the IIDS's study.

NOTES AND REFERENCES

1. For details see Amartya Sen, *Social Exclusion: Concept, Application, and Scrutiny*, (Manila: Asian Development Bank, 2000).
2. B.R. Ambedkar, "The Hindu Social Order – Its Essential Features", in Vasant Moon (ed.), *Dr. Babasaheb Ambedkar's Writings and Speeches*, (Bombay: Government of Maharashtra, 1987), vol. 3, pp. 1-34.
3. Sukhadeo Thorat, "Caste, Ethnicity, and Religion: An Overview Paper on Exclusion/Discrimination and Deprivation", Concept paper for DFID, New Delhi, (May 2003); also see his other writings on this theme including "Caste, Social Exclusion and Poverty Linkages: Concept, Measurement and Empirical Evidence", 2005, mimeo (2007).
4. It was established in September 2004, as part of the Common Minimum Programme of the UPA Government to examine the condition of workers in the unorganized sector, see National Commission for Enterprises in the Unorganized Sector, Government of India August 2007: 'Introduction'.
5. In 2002, Professor Prabhat Patnaik, the then Dean of School of Social Sciences, Jawaharlal Nehru University, mooted the idea and a committee consisting of Prof. Romila Thaper (Chairperson), Prof. T.K. Oommen, Prof. Ghanshyam Shah, Prof. S.K. Thorat, Prof. Abhijit Sen and Prof. Zoya Hasan (Convener), recommended the introduction of a school-level programme in an interdisciplinary and comparative framework with a focus on discrimination and exclusion on the basis of caste, tribe and religion. As a result, the Programme for the Study of Discrimination and Exclusion (PSDE) was launched in 2005. Later on the University Grants Commission under the chairmanship of Professor S.K. Thorat, specialised departments were established under the name of the Centre for Study of Social Exclusion and Inclusive Policy in 13 universities during 2006-07 and another 22 universities during 2007-08.
6. *Social, Economic and Educational Status of the Muslim Community of India: A Report*, (New Delhi: Prime Minister's High Level Committee, 2006).

PART–I

CONCEPTS AND THEORIES

1
Social Exclusion in India: Concepts and Context

Y. CHINNA RAO

The term "social exclusion" is so evocative, ambiguous, multidimensional and expansive that it can be defined in many different ways. Yet the difficulty of defining exclusion and the fact that it is interpreted differently in different contexts at different times can be seen as a theoretical opportunity.[1] Rather than putting forward a single definition of exclusion, it is interesting to understand the disputes surrounding the term "exclusion" and its usage in different contexts, by tracing the history of the idea and decoding the multiple meanings of the term in a variety of national contexts.

In Europe, the term "social exclusion" emerged in the late twentieth century as a key concept among analysts and policy-makers seeking to understand and formulate directives of approaches to alleviate some of the negative social effects of economic restructuring. Thus, the term has an evident appeal for politicians and policy analysts. In Western Europe, those meanings are embedded in the emergence of the term in French political rhetoric and the specific institutional history of the European Union. The term, social exclusion was originally coined in France in 1974 to refer to various categories of people who were unprotected by social insurance at the time but labeled as "social problems" identified as—"mentally and physically handicapped, suicidal people, aged invalids, abused children, substance abusers, delinquents, single parents, multi-problem households, marginal, asocial persons and other social 'misfits."[2] However, in the 1980s, this stigmatizing and narrow view of social exclusion was superseded as the term became central to French debates about the nature of the neo poverty associated with technological change and economic restructuring.[3] Social exclusion in this context was not simply equated with poverty, but was broadened to refer to a process of social disintegration, in the sense of a progressive rupture of the relationship between the individual and society, which was occurring due to increasing long-term unemployment, particularly focused on unskilled workers and immigrants, the inability of young people to enter the labour market, greater family instability and isolated single-member households, increasing numbers of homeless people, and rising tensions and periodic violence in the low-cost housing settlements on the periphery of cities (*banlieues*). This dissipation of the social fabric of society seemed to be a consequence of the result of long-term process of transformations in the structure and organization of economic life.

Addressing social exclusion requires a holistic approach which promotes involvement of excluded populations in community life, ensures access to all basic services, promotes behavioural change, increases income, and addresses other key elements of exclusion.[4] Discrimination is clearly a particular kind of exclusion and it can take on either an active or passive form. Active exclusion through discrimination will see agents systematically refusing to hire or accept the participation of members of a social group despite their formal qualifications (or even over-qualification), while routinely favoring members of groups who are equally or even less qualified. The consequences of discrimination can lead to deprivation indirectly, through passive discrimination in which discouragement and lower self-confidence results in poor performance, or through direct routes that limit access to income or education that is mobility enhancing.

In social science literature there is general agreement on the core features of social exclusion, its principal indicators, and the way it relates to poverty and inequality. Social exclusion is the denial of equal opportunities imposed by certain groups of society upon others which leads to inability of an individual to participate in the basic political, economic and social functioning of the society. The developments in social science literature indeed enable us to comprehend the meanings and manifestations of the concept of social exclusion, and its applicability to caste and ethnicity-based exclusion in India. The manner in which it has been developed in social science literature, the concept of social exclusion, thus, essentially refers to the processes through which groups are wholly, or partially, excluded from full participation in the society in which they live. It emphasizes two crucial dimensions involving the notion of exclusion, namely the "societal institutions" (of exclusion), and their "outcome" (in terms of deprivation). In order to understand the dimensions of exclusion, it is necessary to explore the societal interrelations and institutions, which lead to exclusion of certain groups and deprivation in multiple spheres - civil, cultural, political, and economic. Thus, for a broader understanding of the concept of exclusion, the insight into the societal process and institutions of exclusion are as important as the outcome in terms of deprivation for certain groups. Amartya Sen[5] therefore refers to various meanings and manifestations of social exclusion, particularly, with respect to the causes or the processes of discrimination and deprivation in a given society. Exclusion could occur through direct exclusion, violating fair norms of exclusion (that is, unfavorable exclusion), or through inclusion, but under unfavorable conditions, again violating fair norms of inclusion (that is unfavorable inclusion), or through deliberate government policies (that is, active exclusion), and through unintended attempts and circumstances (passive exclusion), or exclusion caused through inability of some persons when compared to other persons (constitutive relevance). The mainstream economists have further elaborated the concept of discrimination that operates particularly through markets. Social exclusion can indeed arise in a variety of ways, and it is important to recognize the versatility of the idea and its reach.

Social Exclusion in Indian Context

In India, exclusion is embedded in societal interrelations and institutions that exclude, discriminate, isolate, and deprive some groups on the basis of group's identities like caste and ethnicity. The nature of exclusion revolving around the caste system particularly needs to be understood and conceptualized. The fundamental characteristics of caste system fixed civil, cultural, and economic rights for each caste, with restrictions for change implying "forced exclusion" of one caste from the rights of other caste, or from undertaking the occupations of other castes.[6] Exclusion and discrimination in civil, cultural, and particularly in economic spheres such as occupation and labour employment, is therefore, internal to the system, and a necessary outcome of its governing principles. In the market economy framework, the occupational immobility would operate through restrictions in various markets such as land, labour, credit, other inputs, and services necessary for any economic activity. Labour being an integral part of the production process of any economic activity, would obviously become a part of market discrimination.[7]

In the light of the above, the caste and untouchability-based exclusion and discrimination can be categorized in the economic, civil, cultural, and political spheres as the exclusion, and the denial of equal opportunity in economic spheres would necessarily operate through markets and non-market transactions and exchange. Firstly, exclusion can be practiced through the denial in labour market in hiring for jobs; in capital market through the denial of access to capital; in agriculture land market through the denial in sale and purchase or leasing of land; in input market through the denial in sale and purchase of factor inputs; and in consumer market through the denial in sale and purchase of commodities and consumer goods.[8] Secondly, discrimination can occur through what Amartya Sen would describe as "unfavorable inclusion", namely through differential treatment in terms and conditions; of contract, one of them would reflect in discrimination in the prices charged and received by discriminated groups. This can be inclusive of the price of factor inputs, and consumer goods, price of factors of production such as wages for labour, price of land or rent on land, interest on capital, rent on residential houses, charges or fees on services such as water and electricity. Discriminated groups can get lower prices for the goods that they sell, and could pay higher prices for the goods that they buy, as compared with the market price or the price paid by other groups. Thirdly, exclusion and discrimination can occur in terms of access to social needs supplied by the government or public institutions, or by private institutions in education, housing and health, including common property resources like water bodies, grazing land, and other land of common use and Fourthly, a group (particularly the untouchables) may face discrimination from participation in certain categories of jobs (the sweeper being excluded from inside household jobs), because of the notion of purity and pollution of occupations, and engagements in so-called unclean occupations.

To Sum Up

1. In the civil and cultural spheres, the untouchables may face

discrimination and exclusion in the use of public services like public roads, temples, water bodies, and institutions delivering services like education, health and other public services.

2. In the political spheres, the untouchables can face discrimination in use of political rights, and in participation in decision-making process.
3. Due to the physical (or residential) segregation, and social exclusion on account of the notion of untouchability (or touch-me-not-sum), they can suffer from a general societal exclusion.
4. Since there is societal mechanism to regulate and enforce the customary norms and rules of the caste system, the untouchables generally can face opposition in the form of social and economic boycott, violence, and act as a general deterrent to their right to development.

Social Exclusion and Human Rights Situation

Reviewing the effectiveness of policies and programmes in addressing social exclusion relates to the discussion on human development and human rights. Put simply, development approaches from the 1950s to the 1980s primarily focused on social and economic development as an outcome of the development process and were less concerned with civil and political rights. During this period, government policy and the community development were also less concerned with the quality of the process by which the outcomes were achieved.[9] In contrast, the human rights-based approach to development recognizes both the achievement of a desirable outcome and the establishment of an adequate process to achieve and sustain that outcome. Participation, local ownership, empowerment, and sustainability are essential characteristics of a high-quality process.[10] A rights based approach is based on principles that emphasize accountability of those with obligations to realize, for instance, the rights of children; the universality of rights; the indivisibility and interdependence of rights; and also the principle of the best interests of the child and taking into account the views of the child. The state and the other 'duty-bearers' (e.g. parents and teachers) have obligations to fulfill these rights. As rights-holders, children are entitled to demand that the duty-bearers meet their respective obligation to respect, protect and fulfill their rights.[11]

This approach necessitates a broader perspective in addressing the issue of social exclusion, and also highlights the importance of focusing on both achieving the desired outcome (i.e. all children in school) and following an inclusive and participatory process. Similar to the broader recognition that poverty is not merely a lack of income but rather a condition of living in various forms of deprivation, . social exclusion is not only a development issue, but is also a human rights issue and therefore requires a more comprehensive and process-oriented response.

Historically, the caste system classified people by their occupation and status. Each caste had a specific place in the hierarchy of social status.[12] However, since the Nineteenth century, the link between caste and occupation has become less rigid as it became easier for people to change occupations. This change has accelerated with the economic boom which has taken place in India since the early 1990s. In the recent past, the European Parliament had taken a resolution on the human rights situation of the Dalits in India. It mentioned that the National Human Rights Commission of India has reported that the implementation of the Scheduled Castes and Scheduled Tribes (Prevention of Atrocities) Act remains very unsatisfactory, and it even has published numerous recommendations to address this problem.

Untouchability is prohibited under the Constitution of India. To give effect to this Article, parliament enacted the Untouchability (Offences) Act, 1955, based on Article 17- Abolition of Untouchability has scope over the entire country and its provisions are implemented by the respective State Governments and the Union Territories and coordinated by the Government of India. The Act provides penalties for enforcing untouchability or any disability arising thereof – preventing a person from entering a place of public worship and offering prayers or taking water from sacred tank, well or spring. To make the provisions of this Act more stringent, the Act was amended in 1976 and was also renamed the Protection of Civil Rights Act, 1955 [PCR Act]. Under the Act, the Government of India also notified the PCR Rules, 1977, to carry out the provisions of this Act. As cases of atrocities on Scheduled Castes/Scheduled Tribes were not covered under the provisions of PCR Act, 1955, parliament passed another Act in 1989, to take measures to prevent the atrocities committed against them. This Act, known as the Scheduled Castes and the

Scheduled Tribes (Prevention of Atrocities) Act, 1989, became effective from January 30, 1990. For carrying out the provisions of this Act the Government of India notified the SCs and the STs (Prevention of Atrocities) Rules, 1995 on March 31, 1995. Based on the provisions of the Scheduled Castes and the Scheduled Tribes (Prevention of Atrocities) Act, 1989, caste-based atrocities committed against the members of the Scheduled Caste and the Scheduled Tribes are an offence punishable under the law. Offences under the PCR Act are cognizable as well as non-compoundable. The number of cases registered under PCR Act is an indication of the continued perpetuation of untouchability, violation of human rights, committing atrocity and discrimination.

A recent study on untouchability in rural India,[13] covering 560 villages in 11 states, found that public health workers refused to visit Dalit homes in 33 per cent of villages, Dalits were prevented from entering police stations in 28 per cent of villages, Dalit children had to sit separately while eating in 38 per cent of government schools, Dalits did not get mail delivered to their homes in 24 per cent of villages, and Dalits were denied access to water sources in 48 per cent of villages because of segregation and untouchability practices. Another record shows that 27 officially registered atrocities are being committed against Dalits every day, police often prevent Dalits from entering police stations, refuse the registration of cases by Dalits and regularly resort to the practice of torture against Dalits with impunity. And despite the fact that many Dalits do not report crimes for fear of reprisals by the dominant castes, official police statistics averaged over the past 5 years show that 13 Dalits are murdered every week, 5 Dalits' homes or possessions are burnt every week, 6 Dalits are kidnapped or abducted every week, 3 Dalit women are raped every day, 11 Dalits are beaten every day and a crime is committed against a Dalit every 18 minutes.[14]

Untouchability in schools has contributed to far higher drop-out[15] and illiteracy levels for Dalit children are higher than those of the general population. This 'gap of illiteracy' between Dalits and non-Dalits has hardly changed since India's independence and literacy rates for Dalit women remaining as low as 38 per cent in rural India.[16] About half of India's Dalit children are undernourished, 21 per cent are 'severely underweight' and 12 per cent die before their fifth birthday.[17]

It is seen that Andhra Pradesh tops the list in terms of reported cases, while UP and Bihar where one third of the country's Dalits live report very little. The data needs to be taken with much caution since many of these practices are considered part of the existing social rules and norms and are accepted even by the Dalit community as owing to their 'lower' social and economic status. Cases also go unreported owing to the dependency of Dalit communities for their livelihood and the fear of backlash by the perpetrators as they hold social, economic and institutional power in the area. Dalit victims also do not receive any support from the police or administration to register human rights violation against them. From its review with various State Governments, the SC and ST Commission viewed that "a large number of cases of atrocities go unregistered, mainly because of reluctance on the part of police officers to register the cases..."[18]

In addition to the PCR Act, crimes against Dalits are also registered under the SC/ST Prevention of Atrocities Act, 1989 and other sections of the Indian Penal Code (IPC). At all India level, 25,093 cases in 1999, 25,455 in 2000 and 33,501 in 2001 are registered. This is an annual average of 28,016 crimes. It is inferred from the data that during the period of 1999-2001, the most intolerant states as far as crimes against the Dalits are concerned were Uttar Pradesh, followed by Rajasthan, Madhya Pradesh and Andhra Pradesh respectively. It is strange that UP and Rajasthan show a very small record of cases registered under PCRA in the same years. West Bengal consistently claims that there is no practice of untouchability in the state.

The ActionAid Study explored Dalits' access to basic public services that may not be directly related to the state. As is evident from the study, by far the most prevalent practice of untouchability in this realm was related to the denial of access to water resources – a little less than half (48.4%) of the villages surveyed reported the presence of this practice in some form or the other.

The notions of purity and pollution have been particularly resilient in relation to drinking water sources. The study also confirmed the fact and found that persistent conflicts were reported with regard to drinking water. While complete denial of access to a particular water source (well, tank, tube-well and so on) designated as upper caste was quite common, what was even more common was the imposition of differential behaviour on Dalits. In over one-third (about 36%) of the villages surveyed, the Dalits were denied entry into village shops. This usually meant that the Dalits were not allowed to come up to the counter like other customers, but were made to wait outside or at some distance from the shop. In about one-thirds of the villages, the teashops discriminated against the Dalits by asking them to be seated separately and by widespread practice of the two-glass system. The social status of the castes providing services such as washermen and barbers is dependent on their denying the services to Dalits. Such denial of services to Dalits is always demanded by non-Dalits. Discrimination by washermen and barbers was found to be present in as many as 47 per cent of the villages.

These can be seen in times of emergency and disaster response as reported in the time of Tsunami. Dalits were forced to huddle in a corner and be invisible when relief and aid came, were not allowed to use the water tanks or toilets provided by aid agencies. In many places, dominant castes actively prevented Dalits from accessing food brought by organizations and would serve the spoilt and left over rice the next day after fresh supplies reached them.

One could see the parallel and simultaneous debate on human rights in the Universal Declaration of Human Rights with a commitment to a new world order. Despite India taking a leading role in the formation of the League of Nations and the UN, the anti-caste and anti-untouchability movements within the country did not find any mention in this historical global document as a 'source of discrimination' nor 'Dalits' in the 'Victims of discrimination'. It is further surprising to note that India brought the issue of the discrimination of 'people of India' origin in South Africa in 1946. Dalits' topic did not come into the purview or debate or discourse of building universal human rights mechanisms. Caste is not listed in the UN treaties like International Convention on the Elimination of all forms of Racial Discrimination (ICERD), International Covenant on Civil and Political Rights (ICCPR), Convention on the Elimination of all forms of Discrimination Against Women (CEDAW) or Convention on the Rights of the Child (CRC) and the specificity of caste dimension affecting over 200 million people in Asia was often overshadowed by other dimensions of discrimination and the Dalit concerns did not inform UN Human Rights discourse for many decades.[19] It is the responsibility of both the state and the civil society to see that the Dalits and tribes, like rest of the population, lead their lives with dignity and without fear. Dalit human rights will remain a dream as long as their material conditions are not improved. They continue to be unambiguously at the disadvantaged level as group as a whole.

Social Exclusion and Higher Education

The Government of India set up an interim University Grants Commission by a resolution and began to function from the last week of December 1953; it came to existence formally through an Act of Parliament only in November 1956. India became Republic in 1950 by adopting a new Constitution, in which reservations for SCs and STs were incorporated. Therefore, the Government should have directed and the UGC should have adopted the reservation policy at least from 1956, if not from 1953. On the contrary, the UGC went on reiterating that no reservations should be made available to SCs and STs for appointments particularly to the posts of teachers in Universities and its affiliated Colleges.[20] However, for the first time after more than two daces of its existence, in 1975 in its meeting,[21] agreed, in principle to provide reservations to SCs and STs for recruitment only at the level of Lecturers with a condition that not to operate reservation on a roster system and also not to carry forward reserved posts.

The Committee of Vice-Chancellors of central universities gave recommendations for implementation of reservations,[22] which were not in consonance with the spirit of reservation policy. However, UGC accepted the same and insisted not to operate roster system and not to carry forward the reserved posts from year to year basis.[23] By doing so, the UGC almost gave free hand to the universities to implement the reservations the way they wanted. It gave indirect encouragement to implement the reservations detrimentally. We shall see in the next section. how these institutions responded in the process of fulfilling the constitutional mandate and their apathy towards social justice, There are three types of Universities in India, i.e., Central Universities, State Universities and Deemed (to be) Universities. Out of 20 Central Universities, 18 Universities get both development (Plan) and maintenance (non-plan) assistance from the University Grants Commission. And the remaining two Universities, Indira Gandhi National Open University, New Delhi and Central Agricultural University, Imphal are directly funded by the Ministry of Human Resource Development and Ministry of Agriculture, Government of India respectively. Regarding Aligarh Muslim University, Banaras Hindu University, University of Delhi, University of Hyderabad, Jamia Millia Islamia, Jawaharlal Nehru University, North-Eastern Hill University, Pondicherry University, Visva-Bharati University, Assam University, Tezpur University, Nagaland University, Mizoram University, Babasaheb Bhimrao Ambedkar University, Maulana Azad National Urdu University, University of Allahabad, Manipur University and Mahatma Gandhi Antarrashtriya Hindi University, let us give a schematic look at the manner in which these 18 Central Universities are working in the process of appointments and delivering their institutional responsibilities.

Representation of SC and ST in Teaching Positions (As on 31.03.2006)

Post	*Total Sanctioned Posts*	*Occupied by the General Category*	*Vacant*	*Filled by Scheduled Castes*	*Short-fall of SCs*	*Filled by Scheduled Tribes*	*Short-fall of STs*
Professor	1430 (100%)	1248 (87.27%)	154 (10.77%)	11 (0.77%)	204 (14.23%)	17 (1.18%)	91 (6.38%)
Reader	2592 (100%)	1875 (72.34%)	657 (25.35%)	29 (1.11%)	360 (13.89%)	31 (1.19%)	169 (6.31%)
Lecturer	4189 (100%)	1932 (46.60%)	1917 (45.75%)	192 (4.58%)	436 (10.42%)	148 (3.53%)	166 (3.97%)
Selection Grade/ Senior Lecturer	_	640	_	37 (5.78%)	59 (9.22%)	40 (6.25%)	8 (1.25%)
Others*	554 (100%)	_	_	11 (1.58%)	72 (13.02%)	2 (0.36%)	40 (7.14%)

Source: Compiled from the information furnished by the Central Universities to the UGC.

This category was not defined, but seems to include posts like the part-time teachers, and non-teaching research staff.

In these 18 Central Universities total sanctioned teaching posts are 8765 consisting of 1430 Professors, 2592 Readers and 4189 Lecturers. However, the existing strength of faculty members is only 6588, leaving 1177 total posts lying vacant. Out of present strength of 6588, Professors are 1276, Readers 1935 and Lecturers 2272. Thus, presently 154, 657 and 1917 posts of Professors, Readers and Lecturers respectively are lying vacant in Central Universities. When thousands and thousands of youth armed with degrees are roaming on roads in search of jobs and many already in service waiting for promotions, it is quite disturbing to see the posts lying vacant in such large numbers. There might be academic and even non-academic constraints of Universities, but non-filling of vacancies would likely to adversely affect the national agenda of empowerment of disprivileged sections of the society, particularly Scheduled Caste and Scheduled Tribe communities.

The representation of SCs and STs in teaching posts in Central Universities can be seen in a recent study[24] mentioned in the table. Out of sanctioned 1430 posts of Professors, 1248 have been occupied by the General Category faculty members. However, only 11 and 17 Professors belong to SCs and STs respectively. Numerically it comes to be less than one Professor of SC and ST per University. Only five universities have one Professor who belongs to SC community. In other words, no Professor who belongs to SC is on the rolls of 13 Universities. The universities without SC Professor include Banaras Hindu University, Pondicherry University, Jamia Millia Islamia, North Eastern Hill University and Allahabad University. The University of Delhi, one of the oldest with faculty strength of 1086, has just one Professor from SC category. Vishwa Bharati University with total 655 teachers also has one Professor from SC. The other universities such as University of Hyderabad, JNU and Assam University have two, three and four SC Professors respectively.

In case of Scheduled Tribes, their percentage of representation in posts of Professors is also quite low (1.18%). It will not be out place to point that out of 17 Professors who belong to STs, 12 are placed in two universities, that too from North-Eastern regions of the country. From remaining five Professors of STs, three are in JNU and one each in DU and Vishwa Bharati University. Surprisingly, 13 central universities do not have even a single Professor of ST community. The same case may be seen in respect of Readers positions, as it is evident in the table.

Until recently there is no provision of reservations at the level of Professors and Readers in the central universities, unlike the State universities. This fact is always used to justify the lower representation of SCs and STs at the level of Professor and Reader. It means whenever and wherever the reservation is applicable, SCs and STs are given due representation as prescribed in the guidelines of the Government. Since the reservation in teaching positions in the central universities is given only at the level of Lecturer, it will be interesting to see its implementation in recruitment at the Lecturer level. Indeed it is quite disappointing to note. It is only 4.58 per cent of Scheduled Castes and 3.53 per cent of Scheduled Tribes filled so far, whereas the constitutional mandate is 15 per cent and 7.5 per cent respectively. In other words, there should have been 629 and 314 Lecturers of SC and ST category respectively. Instead, only 192 SCs and 148 STs have been appointed till March 2003. On the other hand, 1932 posts of Lecturers have been occupied by the general category candidates and 1917 posts are lying vacant. Four central universities do not have any Lecturer belonging to SC category, and three universities have no Lecturer from ST category.

Concluding Remarks

The question remains as to why the Scheduled Castes and Scheduled Tribes have poor access to all resources which directly and indirectly determine the level of income and capabilities to secure other sources of income? Why the ownership of agricultural land and non-land capital assets is low compared with non-SC/ST? Why are the unemployment rates high particularly among the SC compared with non-SC/ST? Why are the daily wage earnings of SC/ST in non-farm activities low compared with non-SC/ST? Why the literacy rate and education level are much lower when compared with non SC/ST?

Given the complexity and crucial relevance of these issues to large groups of people, the issue we are presently discussing, assumes great significance. The establishment of social exclusion programmes of study in various institutions holds promise of more specialized knowledge to overcome the challenges posed to government, especially in the post-colonial era. Even if government action is tardy, as it often is such knowledge matters, because exclusion from the domain of knowledge has got the means of preserving exclusion.

---

* An earlier version of this paper was delivered as 'Valedictory Address' at SOCIAL EXCLUSION IN INDIAN SOCIETY: THE RESPONSE OF STATE AND CIVIL SOCIETY held at Dr. Ambedakar Center for Social Justice, University of Mumbai (14–15 March 2008).

Table-A
Cases Registered Under the PCR Act in 2000 and 2002

Sl. No.	State/UT	Number of Cases Registered During the Year 2002*	Number of Cases Registered in 2000**
1.	Andhra Pradesh	343	284
2.	Karnataka	101	95
3.	Maharashtra	41	98
4.	Pondicherry	18	-
5.	Madhya Pradesh	07	27
6.	Orissa	07	00
7.	Himachal Pradesh	03	-
8.	Jharkhand	02	-
9.	Tamil Nadu	02	103
10.	Rajasthan	01	00
11.	Delhi	01	-
12.	Bihar	-	06
13.	U.P.	-	18
	All India	526	631

Source

* Annual Report on the Protection of Civil Rights Act, 1955 for the Year 2002 (Twenty Second Report) Government of India, Ministry of Social Justice and Empowerment.

** *Crime in India, 1999-2001*, National crime Records Bureau, Ministry of Home Affairs, Government of India.

Table-B
Incidences of Violation of Civil Rights and Atrocities Against the SCs in India, 1999-2001

Sl.	State/India	Incidence of Total Crime 1999	2000	2001	Average of 3 yrs	% of Crime to All India	Rate per Lakh	Rank
1.	Andhra Pradesh	1749	1582	2933	2088	7.5	2.8	06
2.	Assam	07	11	06	08	0.0	0.0	15

Contd...

Sl.	State/India	Incidence of Total Crime 1999	2000	2001	Average of 3 yrs	% of Crime to All India	Rate per Lakh	Rank
3.	Bihar	820	741	1303	955	3.4	1.2	11
4.	Gujarat	1781	1332	1242	1452	5.2	2.9	05
5.	Haryana	121	117	229	156	0.6	0.7	12
6.	Himachal Pradesh	54	52	110	72	0.3	1.2	10
7.	Karnataka	1277	1329	1621	1409	5.0	2.7	07
8.	Kerala	514	467	499	493		1.8	1.5
9.	Madhya Pradesh	4667	4631	4212	4503	16.1	7.5	02
10.	Maharashtra	605	489	625	573	2.0	0.6	13
11.	Orissa	772	793	1734	1100	3.9	3.0	04
12.	Punjab	39	34	134	69	0.2	0.3	14
13.	Rajasthan	5623	5190	4892	5235	18.7	9.3	01
14	Tamil Nadu	883	1296	2336	1505	5.4	2.4	08
15.	Uttar Pradesh	6122	7330	10732	8061	28.8	4.9	03
16.	West Bengal	00	00	10	03	0.0	0.0	16
	All India	25093	25455	33501	28016	100	2.7	

Source: All these figures represent the number of cases registered under the Protection of Civil Rights Act, 1955 and SC/ST Prevention of Atrocities Act, 1989. For details see *Crime in India, 1999-01*, National Crime Records Bureau, Ministry of HomeAffairs.

Table-C

Denial of Access to Basic Public Services

(Forms/Sites Arranged in Decreasing Order of Incidence; Pooled Data from 11 States)

Forms/Sites of Untouchability Practice	Percentage of Villages where Form is Practiced	No. of Villages where Form is Practiced	Total Surveyed Villages
Denied access to water facilities	48.4	255	527
No entry into villages shops	35.8	186	519
No access to restaurants/hotels	25.6	92	359

Contd...

Forms/Sites of Untouchability Practice	*Percentage of Villages where Form is Practiced*	*No. of Villages where Form is Practiced*	*Total Surveyed Villages*
No entry into private health centre/clinic	21.3	74	348
No access/entry to public transport	9.2	41	447
No entry/seating in Cinema Halls	3.2	6	187

Villages where status of practice is ambiguous are excluded. Total surveyed villages exclude villages where relevant institution/site is absent.

Source: Action Aid, People's Report on Untouchability in Rural India.

Table-D

Discriminatory Treatment in Public Services

(Forms/Sites Arranged in Decreasing Order of Incidence; Pooled Data from 11 States)

Forms/Sites of Untouchability Practice	*Percentage of Villages where Form is Practiced*	*No. of Villages where Form is Practiced*	*Total Surveyed Villages*
Denied barbers' services	46.6	229	491
Denied washermen's services	45.8	194	424
Separate seating in restaurants/hotels	32.7	144	441
Separate utensils in restaurants/hotels	32.3	145	449
Denied carpenter's services	25.7	117	455
Tailor will not take measurements	20.8	96	462
Potter will not sell pots	20.5	75	365
Untouchability during transactions in shops	18.5	87	470
No seating/last entry in public transport	12.8	57	444
Discriminatory treatment in private clinics	8.7	24	276

Villages where status of practice is ambiguous are excluded. Total surveyed villages exclude villages where relevant institution/site is absent.

Source: Action Aid, People's Report on Untouchability in Rural India.

Table-E
Discriminatory Restrictions on Public Behaviour
(Forms/Sites Arranged in Decreasing Order of Incidence; Pooled Data from 11 States)

Forms/Sites of Untouchability Practice	*Percentage of Villages where Form is Practiced*	*No. of Villages where Form is Practiced*	*Total Surveyed Villages*
Ban on marriage processions on roads	47.4	229	483
Forced to stand in front of upper caste men	25.6	136	532
Ban on festival processions on public roads	23.8	114	478
Cannot wear new/ 'bright' clothes	19.0	101	531
Cannot use umbrellas in public roads	16.7	82	490
Cannot wear dark glasses, smoke etc.	13.7	66	481
Cannot use chappals on public roads	10.6	47	443
Cannot use bicycles on public roads	7.1	32	448

Villages where status of practice is ambiguous are excluded. Total surveyed villages exclude villages where relevant institution/ site is absent

Source: Action Aid, People's Report on Untouchability in Rural India.

Table-F
State Wise Incidences of Crime-Caste Discrimination and Atrocities Against Scheduled Castes in India, 2000

State/UT	*Murder*	*Hurt*	*Rape*	*Kidnap & Abd.*	*Dac-oity*	*Rob-bery*	*Arson*	*PCR Act*	*POA Act*	*Other Offences*
Andhra Pradesh	29	323	53	9	2	0	8	284	529	345
Bihar	4	244	17	5	2	3	12	6	220	228
Karnataka	10	13	14	2	0	0	1	95	1073	10
Kerala	7	126	65	0	1	0	4	0	146	118
Madhya Pradesh	45	798	289	26	5	8	27	27	539	2867
Maharashtra	2	16	49	4	1	2	5	98	128	184
Orissa	14	47	6	0	0	0	3	0	147	158

Contd...

State/UT	Murder	Hurt	Rape	Kidnap & Abd.	Dacoity	Robbery	Arson	PCR Act	POA Act	Other Offences
Punjab	0	4	8	2	0	0	0	0	13	3
Rajasthan	48	153	128	13	1	3	49	0	454	4341
Tamil Nadu	12	654	17	1	0	1	0	103	418	90
Uttar Pradesh	302	761	346	163	23	65	142	18	2683	2096
All-India	473	3139	992	225	35	82	251	631	6350	10440

Table–G
Cases Registered Under Various Crimes on Scheduled Castes and Tribes

Type of Cases	*1991*	*1999*	*2000*
Total cases	8029	115878	116131
Cases disposed off	-	8673	12956
Conviction cases	125	700	982
Acquittal cases	1367	7420	11605
Cases pending	6537	107204	100891
Percentage Share in Total Cases	*1991*	*1999*	*2000*
Cases disposed off	-	7.48	11.16
Conviction cases	1.56	0.60	0.85
Acquittal cases	17.03	6.40	9.99
Cases pending	81.42	92.51	86.88

Source: National Commission for Scheduled Castes and Scheduled Tribes, Sixth Report, 1991, 1999-2000 and 2000-01.

NOTES AND REFERENCES

1. W.B. Gallie, "Essentially contested concepts", in *Aristotelian Society Proceedings*, (No. 56, 1956), cited in Hillary Silver "Reconceptualizing social Disadvantage: Three paradigms of social exclusion" in Gerry Rodgers, Charles Gore and Jose B. Figueiredo (eds.), *Social Exclusion: Rhetoric, Reality, Responses*, (Geneva: International Institute for Labour Studies, International Labour Institute, 1995), pp. 57-80.
2. Hillary Silver "Reconceptualizing social Disadvantage: Three paradigms of social exclusion" *ibid.* p. 63. Also see Hillary Silver, *Social Solidarity*

and Social Exclusion: Three Paradigms, (Geneva: International Institute for Labour Studies, 1994), Discussion Paper Series, No. 69, p. 18.
3. Charles Gore *et.al.*, "Introduction: Markets, Citizenship and Social Exclusion", in Gerry Rodgers, Charles Gore and Jose B. Figueiredo (eds.), *Social Exclusion, op. cit.*, pp. 1-2.
4. Robert Jenkins and Eimar Barr, "Social Exclusion of Scheduled Caste Children from Primary Education in India", (New Delhi: UNICEF, 2006), mimeo, p. 16.
5. Amartya Sen, *Social Exclusion: Concept, Application, and Scrutiny*, (Manila: Asian Development Bank, 2000).
6. B.R. Ambedkar, "The Hindu Social Order – Its Essential Features", in Vasant Moon (ed.), *Dr. Babasaheb Ambedkar Writings and Speeches*, (Bombay: Government of Maharashtra, 1987), vol. 3, pp. 1-34.
7. Sukhadeo Thorat, "Caste, Ethnicity, and Religion: An Overview Paper on Exclusion/Discrimination and Deprivation", Concept paper for DFID, Delhi, (May 2003); also see his other writings on this theme including "Caste, Social Exclusion and Poverty Linkages: Concept, Measurement and Empirical Evidence", 2005, mimeo.
8. S.K. Thorat, "Caste, Untouchability and Economic and Market Discrimination: Theory, Concept and Consequences", *Artha Vighyan*, Journal of Gokhale Institute of Politics and Economics, Vol. XLIII, Nos. 1-2, (2001). Also see, S.K. Thorat and R.S. Deshpande, "Caste and Labour Market Discrimination", *Indian Journal of Labour Economics*, Conference special number, (November, 1999); S.K. Thorat, "On Economic Exclusion and Inclusive Policy", *The Little Magazine*, Vol. VI, Nos. 4-5, (2006).
9. Urban Jonsson, *Human Rights Approach to Development Programming*, (Nairobi: Eastern and Southern Africa Regional Office, UNICEF, 2003), p. 4.
10. *Ibid.*, p. 45.
11. United Nations Children's Fund, *Human Rights based Approach to Programming*, (New York: UNICEF, 2002).
12. Ghanshyam Shah, Harsh Mander, Sukhadeo Thorat, Satish Deshpande and Amita Baviskar, *Untouchability in Rural India*, (New Delhi: Sage, 2006), p. 19.
13. For details of a recent study conducted in 560 districts spread over 11 states across the country, see Ghanshyam Shah, Harsh Mander, Sukhadeo Thorat, Satish Deshpande and Amita Baviskar, *Untouchability in Rural India, op. cit.*
14. For details see *Crime in India, 2005*, http://ncrb.nic.in/crime2005/home.htm
15. These drop-outs are in fact not 'drop-outs' put often are 'push-outs' from the institutions of learning due to biases of caste/untouchability.
16. *Census of India 2001*.

17. *National Family Health Survey*, Ministry of Health and Family Welfare, 1998-99 (recent past survey available), Chapter VI, p. 187.
18. The National Commission for Scheduled Castes and Scheduled Tribes, (Sixth Report, 1999-2000 and 2000-01, (New Delhi, 2002), p. ii.
19. Annie Namala, *Dismantling Caste Based Discrimination: Report on Descent Based Discrimination and Access to Rights*, (New Delhi, 2006), p. 13.
20. Kavita A. Sharma, *50 Years of University Grants Commission*, New Delhi, 2003, p. 119.
21. This historic meeting held on 14-15 July, 1975, the detailed of this meeting got formulated and became a policy in the same year. UGC D.O.No. F.1-46/46(CP), August 26/29, 1975.
22. See UGC D.O. No. F.1-46 (CP), September 8/10, 1976. Also see R.K. Kale, "Reservation for SC and ST in Central Universities: Is it a Failure of Will or Efforts?" *University News*, Vol. 44, No. 48, (27 November – 03 December 2006), pp. 92-105.
23. UGC D.O. No. F.7-3/83 (SCT), April 19/30, 1983.
24. R.K. Kale, "Reservations for SC and STs in Central Universities: Is it a Failure of Will or Efforts", *University News*, Vol. 44, No. 48, (27 November–03 December 2006), p. 94.

2

Exclusion and Exploitation: A Conceptual Understanding

V. RAVINDRA SASTRY AND G. RAM REDDY

According to Karl Marx, all human history is history of class struggles. Much has been said and written about this famous statement of Marx. The issue has not been resolved to anyone's satisfaction. The most common argument against Marx has been that it cannot be demonstrated that all societies have clear-cut class formations and classes actually engage with each other from adversarial positions. Following from this argument, Marxists from India armed with D.D. Kosambi's perspective argued that in societies like India, caste plays a class role. The struggles in Indian society have thus been characterized as those emanating from caste structures. As against Marxist and other leftist oriented philosophies, the liberals argued that contentions in society cannot be based in class alone and that there are other factors that lead to discords in society. Irrespective of the shades that one chooses to base one's argument in, it is generally agreed that it is true that human society is characterized by some kind of a vertical division or another and that this division is the basis for exclusions. When people actively engage in the process of finding commonalities they also necessarily end up finding difference. The difference often gets exaggerated or is exaggerated deliberately when people are mobilized on the basis of commonality. A bold and controversial statement can be made here. All attempts at forging commonality are necessarily based in the motive of demonstrating that something is also not common. This essentially means that the search for a common identity is also to exclude someone else from that identity.

A simple case in point can be seen in the politics of Independent India and the Mandal Commission issue in particular. It is argued that the then Prime Minister of the country Mr. Vishwanath Pratap Singh brought the Mandal Commission report into the open and tried implementing it so as to counter the threat that was posed to him by the Deputy Prime Minister Mr. Devi Lal. It is well known that Devi Lal tried to mobilize farmers on the basis of an identity that was exclusive to farmers,[1] V.P. Singh's response was to consolidate votes by bringing together Dalits, Scheduled Tribes, Other Backward Classes (OBCs) and Muslims onto one platform on the basis of one identity constituted on the basis of the fact that these were sections of Indian society that had been subject to exploitation traditionally by the upper castes. This argument was articulated earlier by Dr. Ambedkar. The Bharatiya Janata Party (BJP) took this opportunity to push forward its agenda of Hindutva, wherein all Hindus of the country were called to unite against religions and cultures that had been brought to India by various different invaders. The antagonists of this argument have suggested that even the culture of Hindus is one that found its entry into the country through invasions carried out by the Aryans.

Much has been said since then. The BJP and the historians who are allied with it have tried to construct a theory of the Aryans as being indigenous people of the country by using various sources. Remote sensing satellite pictures have been used in conjunction with radio-carbon dating to demonstrate the existence of the river Saraswati which has otherwise been considered to be mythical. Elaborate arguments have been presented to show that Aryan civilization was born on the banks of this river. The protagonists of the Aryan invasion theory have used other forms of evidence in order to demonstrate the veracity of their argument that Aryans were also invaders. There is as yet no final outcome of this contention. There may never be. That has little consequence or relevance to this paper. What is of relevance is the fact that efforts such as these exist. And they form the basic framework for all activities aimed at exclusion.

This is also the time to look into the veracity of the commonly held perceptions that throughout history there are identifiable perpetrators of exclusion. It is very common to hear the idea that there are identifiable sections of Indian society that started the process of exclusion and its resultant concomitant, exploitation. All exclusion is considered by this argument, to be aimed at exploitation which is both social and economic. The purpose behind all economic denial and furtherance of social division is that of maintenance of political hegemony which in turn facilitates exploitation at the social and economic levels. This then is the vicious cycle from which the excluded and the exploited have no hope of breaking out. The argument is very correct in its larger construct. However, by remaining only at that level of examination one tends to miss out on the finer and smaller details that are equally crucial in the understanding of the process of exclusion and exploitation. The above picture tends to portray the players in this act as constant and unchanging. The story is therefore considered as valid today as it was a few thousand years ago. This is the part that needs re-examination. While it is undoubtedly true that the construction of Indian society like most others is based in power relations, what needs to be examined is the nature of power and the ways and means in which it is used and towards what ends. Avoiding details at the micro level could lead to a misleading picture. When one sees the moon in its entirety the indentations on it are almost insignificant. It is only when one takes a closer look at it that the true nature of the moon becomes evident. The same can be said of the earth. Views from outer space tend to show the earth as a blue planet. Only closer examination shows all the non-blue aspects.

Power and its existence have been constant in Indian society. But the nature and means of its exercise may have changed. This is perhaps due to the changing nature of Indian society. One of the most striking aspects of Indian society has been the persistence of age old social concepts, practices and institutions. Here it becomes necessary to distinguish between causes of origin and causes of persistence. One may often arrive at erroneous conclusions if the lines of that difference are obliterated or blurred out. The manifestations of exclusion and practices that have led to it in the first place are myriad. It would be beyond the scope of this paper to explore all of them, even provided one has identified them all in the first place. It is therefore relevant to examine one aspect of Indian and Hindu society that stands out strikingly and therefore has been the subject of much discussion. Caste is the variable that has troubled, fascinated and frustrated social scientists by defying complete apprehension and consequently complete clarity as well.

It can be argued without fear of contradiction that the origins of the caste system have been lost in the mists of time. The number of reasons that have been put forth as causes of its origin, range from the cosmological to the social. Confounding the problem is the fact that caste has irrefutably become a political variable as well from the twentieth century onwards. Mohandas Karamchand Gandhi saw caste as everyman's natural calling.[2] In his view, it is possible to see the existence of all four hues or varnas of the caste system in one family alone. For him a society that is based in caste was not divided vertically but simply horizontally. Caste for him was a social function that was based in one's natural ability. The four varnas simply reflected different abilities without in anyway hinting at the superiority or the inferiority of one against the others. "The object of the *Varna* is to prevent competition and class struggle and class war. I believe in the *Varna* system because it fixes the duties and occupations of persons."[3] This he saw as being an integral part of the inviolable Sanatana Hindu Dharma which manifests itself in the ordering of the cosmos. The vertical division of Hindu society into categories of superiority and inferiority was due to the chicanery of Brahminism and he sought to actively differentiate Sanatana Dharma from Brahminical religion. Gandhi's idea of social reform was not about abandoning Hinduism but it was more a return to Sanatana Dharma by relinquishing the corruptions brought into Hinduism by Brahminical religion and thinking.

> The caste system is a natural order of society. In India it has been given a religious coating. Other countries not having understood the utility of the caste system, it existed only in a loose condition and consequently those countries have not derived from caste system the same degree of advantage which India has derived. These being my views I am opposed to all those who are out to destroy the caste system.[4]

Ambedkar did not accept this line of thinking. He saw no possibility of caste as *varna* or any kind of horizontal social organization. Right from its inception, the caste system was an integral part of the Hindu religion created solely for the purpose of social exploitation, and therefore for him, caste was *jaati*. Ambedkar cited endogamy as the evidence for an argument of caste as *jaati* and this according to him provided sufficient reason to believe that certain tasks were menial while others were exalted and the system of endogamy was cleverly designed to make certain people menial and leave them on the peripheries of society forever. Power relations for him were an integral part of all Hindu society and the elimination of the category of the heathen solely depended upon leaving the fold of Hinduism. He saw in Buddhism an alternative and egalitarian system of society as opposed to Hindu society. Anything less than the total abandoning of Hindu principles was only going to lead to the perpetuation of atrocities based in the principle of exclusion.

> The Hindus often complain of the isolation and exclusiveness of a gang or a clique and blame them for anti-social spirit. But they conveniently forget that this anti-social spirit is the worst feature of their own Caste System. One caste enjoys singing a hymn of hate against another caste as much as the Germans enjoyed singing their hymn of hate against the English during the First World War-I. The literature of the Hindus is full of caste genealogies in which an attempt is made to give a noble origin to one caste and an ignoble origin to other castes. The Sahyadrikhand is a notorious instance of this class of literature.[5]

In the same article, he further argues about the fact that Hindu religion and the system of castes that it produced were mainly premised in a form of life which was ultimately against the notion of a cohesive society.

> This anti-social spirit is not confined to caste alone. It has gone deeper and has poisoned the mutual relations of the sub-castes as well. In my province the Golak Brahmins, Deorukha Brahmins, Karada Brahmins, Palshe Brahmins, and Chitpavan Brahmins all claim to be sub-divisions of the Brahmin caste. But the anti-social spirit that prevails between them is quite as marked and quite as virulent as the anti-social spirit that prevails between them and other non-Brahmin castes. There is nothing strange in this. An anti-social spirit is found wherever one group has "interests of its own" which shut it out from full interaction with other groups, so that its prevailing purpose is protection of what it has got. This anti-social spirit, this spirit of protecting its own interests, is as much a marked feature of the different castes in their isolation from one another as it is of nations in their isolation. The Brahmin's primary concern is to protect "his interest" against those of the non-Brahmins, and the non-Brahmins' primary concern is to protect their

> interests against those of the Brahmins. The Hindus, therefore, are not merely an assortment of castes, but are so many warring groups, each living for itself and for its selfish ideal. There is another feature of caste which is deplorable. The ancestors of the present-day English fought on one side or the other in the Wars of the Roses and the Cromwellian War. But the descendants of those who fought on the one side do not bear any animosity – any grudge – against the descendents of those who fought on the other side. The feud is forgotten. But the present-day non-Brahmins cannot forgive the present-day Brahmins for the insult their ancestors gave to Shivaji. The present-day Kayasthas will not forgive the present-day Brahmins for the infamy cast upon their forefathers by the forefathers of the latter. To what is this difference due? Obviously to the Caste System. The existence of Caste and Caste Consciousness has served to keep the memory of past feuds between castes green, and has prevented solidarity.[6]

Indologists like Patrizia Norelli-Bachelet argue that Hinduism in its origins was a cosmological system in which present day concerns were completely absent. To read into ancient Hinduism conclusions from today's practices would mean imbuing it with ideas that it could not have understood at that time. She cautions against doing sociology of what ultimately was a cosmology. In cosmological terms, difference need not be for exclusion or exploitation. Cosmologies are based in an order which derives itself from a cosmic understanding of the universe which sees all occurrences ultimately as being purposive. For Norelli-Bachelet, the attribution of a caste, and the subsequent role to be played in society, to an individual depended on planetary configurations at the time of birth. The positions of planets in the horoscope were therefore the determinants of ones caste.[7] Patrizia Norelli-Bachelet's argument is that ancient Indian cosmology has been sublated into social practices with the inexorable march of time and the human civilization itself.

An examination of these arguments suggests that there is no consensus regarding the origin of the caste system but there seems to be a general agreement about the transformation of the caste system into an exclusive and exploitative process. It can be argued that if there is an agreement about the nature of the caste system in the recent past and in the present, that itself should be sufficient reason to eliminate it and embark on a path of social reform. However, such a conclusion could be counter productive because time has demonstrated that the realization that caste works on the principle of exclusion has in no way contributed to its elimination. It is perhaps imperative, then, that one stops looking at caste as a tool of exclusion practiced by some at the expense of others. Otherwise, one could easily lapse into a process of mouthing homilies and platitudes which ultimately bear no significance for the transformation of society. The necessity is clearly for understanding the various levels at which the process of exclusion occurs. The first step towards this understanding would be to stop dividing people into two broad categories - of the exploiters and the exploited. What needs to be appreciated is the fact that within the ranks of the exploiters there are the exploited and that within the ranks of the exploited exist the exploiters. The cause for the emergence of this process in Indian society is the caste system and the logic it firmly embeds into the minds of all people who are a part of Indian society.

This is perhaps the most appropriate time to discuss logic of the caste system. The main attribute of the caste system comes out of its organizational structure. Gandhi was right when he said that it was the system of organization evident in armed forces. Each caste for him was seen as a unit in itself but it was part of a larger organization.[8] In this there is logic of territoriality. Each caste grouping is a domain and seeks to be its own master. But in the end Brahminism had foisted a certain kind of hierarchy. What makes the hierarchy work is the fact that at every level there is a perception that the superiority of one caste group can be challenged while the same group seeks to establish its own superiority. In *Interrogating Caste,* Dipankar Gupta claims that there was no passive submission to Brahminical hegemony from the Kshhatriyas and the Vysyas, the castes that formed the upper caste structure. While the Kshatriyas accept the priestly position of the Brahmins, they certainly claim to be the most important group in a village because the Kshatriya is the first one to receive 'prasadam' after the performance of a puja.[9] In the lower section of the Hindu caste hierarchy the touchable 'sudras' claim a superiority of position over the untouchables or the 'chandalas'. Within the untouchables there is yet again a manifestation of hierarchy where the 'Mahars' consider themselves to be above the 'Chamars'.

What makes the situation piquant is the fact that there is no uniform terminology used to designate different castes in different parts of the country. Castes like the Kammas and Reddys of Andhra Pradesh have no equivalents in the other parts of the country. Traditionally both Kammas and Reddys have been considered to be a part of the sudra grouping. However, since that would push these 'upper castes' into the lower part of the caste hierarchy both groupings have tried to establish themselves as descendents of Kshatriyas. The present political situation in Andhra Pradesh is clearly a competitive one, where the Reddys and the Kammas are actively involved in excluding the other from the power structure. This trend can be seen in the case of the lower castes as well. There are rough equivalents of the Mahars and Chamars in Andhra Pradesh as Malas and Madigas respectively. It is generally believed that in the caste hierarchy the Madigas are placed lower than the Malas. Apart from the Malas and the Madigas there are 58 other castes that are a part of the list of the Scheduled castes in Andhra Pradesh at the present time. The Malas and Madigas are the dominant in this list both because of a numerical superiority and a proximity to traditional centres of power in the society. Not only are most people unaware of the names of these caste groupings other than Malas and Madigas, they are simply unaware of their existence even. By not being an integral part of the discourse of caste groups of Andhra Pradesh, these groups have been excluded from the public sphere of discussion. The Malas and the Madigas today have taken adversarial postures where the latter accuse the former of usurping all the benefits of reservation given to the Scheduled Castes. The only solution that the Madigas have claimed is the categorization of Scheduled castes into sub-groups of A, B, C and D.[10] The Malas rejoinder to this is that this is tantamount to dissolution of Scheduled Caste solidarity by pointing at difference rather than shared common experience.

This whole process has led to controversies of a political nature and the resolution of this has been left to investigative committees and their reports. In the case of Andhra Pradesh it is the Usha Mehra Commission that has been appointed to go into the claims of either group.[11] The report submitted by the commission goes into the various opportunities that have been availed of by both the groups. What is of consequence to this paper is the fact that there are perceptions of exclusion within groups that have been considered to be cohesive. The topography of Indian society today firmly suggests that there is no one pattern of exclusion and exploitation. As in a causal chain where a cause is also an effect, those who are excluded are also a part of the process of excluding. It is this realization only that can help identify the true cause and nature of exploitation rather than the construct of the meek versus the mighty, which at best can only provide a partial picture and that too a distorted one. The way to eliminating exclusions lies in correctly understanding what it is in the first place.

NOTES AND REFERENCES

1. These developments are well known to all and need no further proof.
2. Gandhi did claim that there was a necessity to convert the social variable into a political one in order to organize people against the British.
3. http://www.trinicenter.com/WorldNews/ghandi5.htm
4. *Ibid.*
5. http://ccnmtl.columbia.edu/projects/mmt/ambedkar
6. *Ibid.*
7. Norelli-Bachelet, Patrizia, "Caste, Culture and Cosmos" in *World Affairs The Journal of International Issues,* January- March 2002, Volume Six. Number One. p. 121
8. http://www.trinicenter.com/WorldNews/ghandi5.htm
9. See Dipankar Gupta, *Interrogating caste: Understanding hierarchy and difference in Indian society,* (New Delhi: Penguin Books, 2000).
10. Justice P. Ramachandra Raju Commission was appointed by the Government of Andhra Pradesh in the year 1996 and it recommended the categorization of Scheduled Castes in Andhra Pradesh, of course at the behest of the then Chief Minister, Chandra Babu Naidu.
11. National Commission to examine the issue of sub categorization of Scheduled Castes in Andhra Pradesh. Report submitted to Ministry of Social Justice and Empowerment on the 1st May, 2008.

3

Social Inclusion and Social Justice: A Historical Perspective

SHURA DARAPURI

"Social Inclusion" can be defined as a series of positive actions to achieve equality of access to goods and services, to assist all individuals participate in their community and society, to encourage the contribution of all persons to social and cultural life and to be aware of, and to challenge all forms of discrimination. In other words, social inclusion is all about ensuring the marginalized or excluded and those living in poverty have greater participation in decision making which affects their lives as well as allowing them to improve their living standards and their overall well-being. Inclusion may also be defined in terms of circle of improved rights of access to the social and economic world, new opportunities, recovery of status and meaning and reduced impact of disability. Key issues will be availability of a range of opportunities that users can choose to pursue, with support or adjustments where necessary; for example, education, work, joining virtuous social, cultural and religious groups, friendships and relationships, raising a family and participating in civic life (jury service, voting, political office).

In nutshell, social inclusion is all about participation; it is a method for social justice. It is about increasing opportunities for people; especially the most disadvantaged and excluded people, to engage in all aspects of community life. Prior to understanding inclusion it is important to understand exclusion. It is argued that social exclusion offends against human dignity, denies people their fundamental human rights and leads, in conjunction with social and economic instability, to marginalization and deepening inequalities, which threaten the stability of democracy. Social inclusion, therefore, appears to be an unconditional good. This paper is mainly divided into two sections: one discusses the exclusion aspect and other inclusionary efforts made by the Dalits which are also recognized as expressions of protest against the ascriptive social order.

In the Indian context, Prakash Louis defines two types of excluded persons: *(i)* Social groups *(ii)* Sectoral groups.[1] Social groups include dalits, tribals/indigenous people, religious and linguistic minorities, the most backward castes, and especially women and children among these social groups. Prominent examples of sectoral groups are agricultural labourers, marginalized farmers, child labourers, domestic workers, informal/unorganized sector workers, contract workers, plantation workers, fishing communities, manual scavengers, rural and forest-based communities, vernacular speaking social groups, and people with disability.

Everyday forms of social exclusion suffered by these social groups include being termed 'untouchables'—a socially excluding reference to a group of people who contribute to the overall cleanliness of society. This form of exclusion under the caste system gets legitimacy from religious texts and beliefs. Hence, in the Indian context, institutionalized attempts to exclude, to segregate a segment of the population from the social order play a crucial role. This is not a situation where a particular individual 'ill-treats' another person; instead, the social process itself is discriminatory in its principles and practices. Thus, social segregation is an institutionalized form of social distancing expressed in physical separation.

As social exclusion is not only about attitudes but is built into the social structure; changing attitudes will not necessarily change social exclusion. The social structure of a society contributes to the formation of its attitude, and the attitude in turn contributes to the maintenance of the social structure. There is no easy way out of this horribly vicious circle. Since social exclusion is about domination, discrimination and deprivation, those who benefit from it do not want to introduce any change, while those who are discriminated against, who are supposed to be 'inferior', 'incapable', 'less meritorious' and 'lower' are not in a position to mobilise and organise to alter the existing social system. They do not want to remain in the dehumanising social order but fear that they may be subjected to repression if they resist exclusion and discrimination.

Inspired by the ideas of Dr. B.R. Ambedkar and others, Dalits have initiated transformation not only in nomenclature but also in perceptions about themselves and about the perceptions of others about them. This has resulted in a serious difference between the perceptions of Dalits and dominant castes.[2] It was found that the negative and derogatory perception of the dominant castes about Dalits is that they are dirty and filthy, thieves and robbers, lazy, gluttonous (*pethu, khau*), dishonest and ungrateful. This negates the reality. For instance, empirical data does not support the perception that Dalits are gluttons. The reality is that Dalits, like anyone else, eat to survive. Studies have shown that since Dalits are often deprived of a regular supply of food, they consume food as and when available.

Dalits, perceptions about themselves is that they are capable but get no opportunities; they are hardworking but do not get the fruits of their labour; they are often put in a situation where they are forced to rob or lie; they are culturally talented and are not immoral; on the contrary, they are sensitive and emotional. Some would argue that this perception is unrealistic, even aspirational. However, Louis argues that a community that is at the receiving end also has scope for looking at the reality of their lives in a positive light. In his paper 'Caste, Social Exclusion and Poverty Linkages—Concept, Measurement and Empirical Evidence', Sukhadeo Thorat explains how in Indian context one of the most widespread and powerful forms of exclusion—that based on caste—works.

The caste system divides people into social groups in which the civil, cultural and economic rights of each individual caste are predetermined or ascribed by birth and made hereditary. The assignment of civil, cultural and economic rights is, therefore, unequal and hierarchal. Moreover, it provides for a regulatory mechanism to enforce the social and economic organisation – social ostracism—and justifies it on religious grounds.

Caste-based exclusion and discrimination denies its victims access not only to economic rights but also to civil, cultural and political rights and opportunities. Caste-based exclusion thus prevents disadvantaged groups from interacting freely and productively with others and taking part in the full economic, social and political life of the community. Exclusion can be practised in the labour market through the denial of jobs; in the capital market through the denial of access to capital; in agriculture through the denial of sale, purchase or leasing of land; and in the consumer market through the denial of sale and purchase of commodities and consumer goods.

Definition of Caste

The word "caste" is of Spanish and Portuguese origin. Caste means lineage or race. It is derived from the Latin word Castus, which means pure. The Spaniards were the first to use it, but its Indian application is from the Portuguese, who had so applied it in the middle of the fifteenth century. The current spelling of the word 'Caste' appears in 1740 in the "academies", and is hardly found before 1800. Before that time it was spelt as 'cast.' In the sense of race or breed of man it was used as early as 1555 A.D.[3] The Spanish word "Casta" was applied to the mixed breed between Europeans, Indians (American) and Negroes.[4] But "caste" was not used in its Indian sense till the seventeenth century.[5] The Indian use is the leading one now, and it has influenced all other uses. As the Indian idea of caste was but vaguely understood, this word was loosely applied to the hereditary classes[6] of Europe resembling the castes of India, who keep themselves socially distinct. Darwin has applied this word to different classes of social insects. The Portuguese used this word to denote the Indian institution, as they thought such a system was to keep purity of blood. Caste are to be distinguished in one point from the hereditary classes, like those of Europe who marry among themselves, that the people not born in those classes could rise to that class by their ability, while nobody can go into a higher caste. In other words, inclusion is determined by birth alone, and maintained exclusively on the exclusion of others. In other words, caste system not only decides the position of Hindu-individuals but also decides the position of non-Hindus e.g. the Mohemmedans and Christians according to Hindu social theory.[7] The Hindu communal view of history follows the same line today emphasizing the distinction between the original inhabitants of the land and those who migrated later.

According to this view all those who migrated to India and their descendants are subjected to exclusion. "Thus the Muslims, Christians and Parsis, who are not indigenous to India and hence the excluded section should either 'indianize' themselves or live like 'second class citizens without any rights or privileges.' This naturally raises the question who the original inhabitants of India were? Were the Aryans to whom the upper castes Hindus trace their lineage indigenous to India? The opinion of scholars of ancient history, based on archaeological and linguistic evidence, has been that Aryans had migrated to India, in all probability in small groups, over a period of time. If this view is correct the assumption that the non-Hindu is the only 'outsider' becomes untenable and the historical rationale for the Hindu nation based on Vedic lineage also becomes suspect. The present attempt to invent the indigenous origins of Aryans, which is supported more by speculation rather than tangible evidence, is rooted in an anxiety to overcome this paradox. The distinction between the indigenous or included and the 'outsider' or excluded is also sought on the basis of the pure and the impure; the claim to purity traced to the idyllic past uncontaminated by the intrusion of the 'outsider', which is an essential ideology of religious fundamentalism. One among the various indicators of this distinction is food habit: those who ate flesh and those who did not."[8]

"Caste is due to the occupation which a man's forefathers were in; therefore, no question of inclusion arises, also tradition forbids 'raising caste in the Kali age, the age of discord'. Though no man can raise his caste, he can degrade it"[9] That is exclusion is possible and acceptable. Fear of exclusion strengthens the inclusiveness of caste. Exclusion is perpetuated by neglect of the ceremonials or by connection with the "low and barbarous." In such a case he may either degrade himself completely or hold an intermediate position. As a man may lose his position in the caste, so a caste may lose its position in the society. Taking to low trade is one of such things which may cause degradation or exclusion of a caste. There are certain occupations considered higher than the others. Among the occupations assigned to the people the occupation of a writer is superior to that of a merchant; that of a goldsmith superior to that of a coppersmith, and so on. Superiority of one defines inferiority of other; in other words, inclusion is determined by the exclusion of other. Certain animals also have certain degrees of status varying from sacred and clean to unclean and foul. And the caste which serve these animals are subjected to inclusion and exclusion, accordingly. A caste is again excluded out by giving up or not having the traditional rules of purity of the surrounding dominant castes and by irregular conduct from their standard. In western India, some castes are excluded by the use of wine and meat, and even by that of tobacco.[10] Many Brahmin castes in certain localities have lost in status by using meat, which is used in those localities only by non-Brahmins. Eating of beef and of pork and of vermin is considered most degrading, amounting to exclusion. Literary and archaeological evidences provide no evidence however, to support non-vegetarianism of Vedic Aryans[11] leading to exclusion.

After a survey of the evidence from various excavations since 1921, the doyen of Indian archaeologists, H.D. Sankalia, has opined that "the attitude towards cow slaughter shows that until the beginning of the Christian era the cow/ox were regularly slaughtered for food and for the sacrifice etc., in spite of the preaching of Ahimsa by Mahavira and the Buddha. Beef eating, however, did decrease owing to these preachings, but never died out completely". The literary evidence from the Vedic and later periods are also plenty. Panini, for instance, calls a guest a *Goghna*, which means one for whom a cow is killed. Even Vivekananda refers to instances of Rama and Krishna drinking wine and eating meat and Sita offering meat, rice and wine to the river goddess Ganga in Ramayana and Mahabharata. In fact, he considered the meat eating habits of the Aryans a virtue and attributed the decline of the Hindus in modern times to the departure from it! Yet, the slaughter of cow and eating beef are now invoked as signs of otherness or exclusion in a bid to distinguish the indigenous or included from the 'outsider'or the excluded. The change in the mode of life of the Brahmins is important, as the Brahminical model followed by the other castes is that of the Post-Vedic Brahmins.[12] The harder the rules of ceremonial purity; the more easily they are broken making additions in the ranks of excluded. The Indian method of exclusion of an individual also must be understood in order to understand the propriety of some rules regarding the treatment of the low classes. If an individual is excluded by his caste fellows, nobody in the caste will marry him or dine. Sometimes if the offense is as grave as the killings of cow whole village will outcaste him and the priest will not attend any ceremonies in his house. Intensity of exclusion varies depending on the gravity of the 'crime'. Exclusion is determined by birth and also at any juncture.The point that needs to be reiterated is that an individual may lose a caste but not gain one. In other words, any individual may be excluded on any pretext at any juncture but no provision or procedure is prescribed towards inclusion. It is for the same reason fear of exclusion has worked wonders on the caste system that it still continues even today.

Efforts at Social Inclusion From Within

The efforts for the social inclusion of the excluded groups took place at various junctures of history. One such process that deserves to be mentioned here is Sanskritisation, Sanskritisation is the process by which a 'low Hindu caste,' or tribal group, changes its customs, ritual, ideology, and way of life in the direction of a high, and frequently, ' twice –born' caste.[13] In other words, it may be regarded as an effort towards inclusion and an exhibition of resentment to their exclusion, non-acceptance of their status of exclusion entrusted by societal norms. Sanskritisation, 'efforts towards inclusion, may only result in 'positional changes' in the system and does not lead to any 'structural change'.[14] The caste system remains intact. Sanskritisation is not confined to Hindu castes but also occurs among tribal and semi tribal groups such as the Bhils of Western India, the Gonds and Oraons of Central India, the Pahadis of the Himalayas. This usually results in the tribe undergoing Sanskritisation claiming to be a caste, and therefore, Hindu. In the traditional system the only way to become a Hindu was to belong to a caste.[15]

> In India there might be some agreement in each area as to who are Brahmins and who untouchables; such consensus is absent with regard to Kshatriyas and Vaishyas. Kshatriyas and Vaishyas status seems to be claimed who have traditions of soldiering and trade respectively. Neither Kshatriyas nor Shudras in different parts of the country have a common body of ritual. Many of them do not undergo the essential sacraments (samskaras), characteristic of the twice born varnas. Any caste that achieved political power at the local level could advance a claim to be Kshatriyas.[16]

The historian K.M. Panikkar has maintained that there has been no such caste as the Kshatriyas during the last two thousand years of history. The Nandas were the last "true" Kshatriyas and they disappeared in the fifth century B.C. Since then every known royal family has come from a non-Kshatriya caste including the famous Rajput dynasties of medieval India.[17] Panikkar points out that the Shudras seem to have produced an unusually large number of royal families even in more recent times. The Palas of Bengal belonged to that caste. The great Maratha Royal House whatever their function today could hardly sustain their genealogical pretensions connecting them with Rajput descent.[18] One of the most important functions of genealogist and bardic castes was to legitimize mobility from the ranks of lower castes to the Kshatriyas by providing suitable genealogical linkage and myth. This inclusive trend was characteristic of a group, not of an individual or a family. Sanscritisation provided an established avenue to 'passing'. Thus Agra Chamars call themselves Jatav (corruption of Yadav) and it is not unknown for a Jatav to claim to be a Brahmin. Some scholars identify them with Karewara or leather worker mentioned in the tenth chapter of Manu's Dharmashastra. The father of the caste was a Nishada (the tenth offspring of a Brahmin father and a Sudra mother and the mother a Vaidcha (offspring of a Vaisya father and a Brahmin mother. It is evident that offsprings of intercaste marriages were subjected to exclusion. Since the beginning of this century, particularly in the twenties and thirties, the Jatavs have asserted a distinct identity and have even refused to be referred to as Chamars. In some places they are referred to as Jatua ,a variation of Jatav.It is felt by many scholars that they were originally Jats, the dominant caste in western Uttar Pradesh and Haryana, but for some reason they came to be called Jatua, Jatavs violently resist being referred to as Chamars. During the 1931 census, they fought for the inclusion of the Jatavs as caste distinct from the Chamars.

In Swami Atma Ram's *Gyan Samudra*, it is mentioned that according to *Lomash Ramayana* which is found in Nepal, the Jatavs trace their ancestory to a gotra of the Lord Shiva. Thus it was stated that the Jatavs are the Kshatriyas. Besides in *Jatav Jivan* (1924) and *Yaduvansh ka Itihaas* (1942), the Jatavs are mentioned as a separate jati of the Kshatriya race. Some of them consider themselves Adi Hindus (original Hindus) following Achhutananda's Adi Hindu movement which swept some areas in north India in the 1930s. Following Dr. Ambedkar's assertive hypothesis, they now consider themselves to be the descendants of the original inhabitants of their area (sons of the soil) who were once Buddhists but subsequently became Hindus under the influence of the immigrant Aryans. In Uttar Pradesh, the Jatavs are distributed in Agra and Mathura districts. A majority of the Jatavs in Agra are migrants from the rural areas who came to Agra after Independence.[19] The Jatavs living in

Rajasthan are grouped with the Chamars. It is believed that they revolted against the oppression of the upper caste and appealed to Raja Kishan Singh to identify them as Jats. Jatav and Jatia are the synonyms. They have their clans to regulate marriage alliances. They use Singh as their surname.[20] This might be regarded as expressions of self assertion and steps towards inclusion from exclusion. When a low caste became wealthy it usually followed this up by sanskritizing its style of life and claiming to be a high caste. Noniyas, Ahirs, Teli or Distillers and many others took this beaten track to high status, although similar mobility was extremely difficult for untouchables who had become wealthy by local standards. "Sanskritisation" was a step to resolve the inconsistency between newly acquired wealth and low ritual rank. In the Indian context it made only "passing inclusion" (partial inclusion) possible.

A series of medieval socio-religious movements termed as the Bhakti movement of medieval India which peaked in the fifteenth and sixteenth centuries in the north with the emergence of a remarkable line of subaltern saint poets (Kabir, Ravidas, Dadu and Nanak, among many others)[21] posed a challenge to exclusion of certain sections of society, it indirectly also defied the positions of so called "included sections" by "preaching the fundamental equality of all religions and the unity of Godhead, holding that the dignity of man depended on his actions and not on his birth, protested against excessive ritualism and formalities of religion and domination of the priests and emphasized simple devotion and faith as the means of salvation for one and all."[22] Starting in the deep south in the sixth century gradually spreading northward through Karnataka and Maharashtra and engulfing north India and Bengal from the fifteenth century onward these movements from below are a watershed in the Indian history not only in religious literary terms but also in broader socio-cultural contexts. Bhakti movement was an effort towards inclusion in the area exclusively meant for the upper castes.

> The so-called lowly origins of its popular heroes are a striking feature of the Bhakti movement which was also animated by the lively presence of many outstanding and powerful women, their egalitarian syncretism encompassed in its bosom of folk Hinduism and Islamic egalitarian thinking especially of the Sufi variety."[23] The top leaders

who shared striking similarity on this count included outcaste Brahman Basava, the leather-worker Haralayya, and the proto feminist Akka Mahadevi (Karnataka); the tailor Namdev, the village servant Chokhamela, the grocer Tukaram the vegetable grower Savata Mali (Maharashtra); the weaver Kabir, the cobbler Ravidas, the cotton comber Dadu Dayal, the rebellious princess Mira, the Khatri Nanak, the potter Gora, the barber Sena (north). Though the multi-faceted monotheistic, sometimes even agnostic, Tamil Sittars or the Siddhas like the Tirumular, Sivavakkiyar and Pambatti Sittar who sang subversive songs did not belong to the established Bhakti stream, they shared their anti caste radicalism with Kabir, Ravidas, and Tukaram.[24]

True, the long-drawn cultural movements consisted of several streams and regional variations but there was uniformity in the fundamental tenets. The leaders of the movement in all regions were close in spirit to the heterodox traditions- the Buddhist, the Jain, the Sahajyani offshoot of Buddhism, the Tantrik and the Nathpanthi. Tantrik and the Nathpanthi ideas were expounded by the non-conformist ascetics called Siddhas who were generally non-brahmans and mostly drawn from the lower orders of society. Caste was the main target of these leaders. It was to them what the Church, the symbol of organized and 'degenerated' Christianity was to the eighteenth century French philosopher Voltaire. The methods of 'inclusion' deployed by them were to compose the verses in vernaculars and interact with the masses in their own idiom.

Their contempt for Sanskritic tradition and scriptural authority was rooted in this medieval shramanic tradition, chiefly represented by the Sahajiya Buddhists and Nath-yogis who were popular in Bihar and eastern India. From the early medieval period perhaps as early as the eighth or ninth century the Siddhas and Yogis had been communicating their ideas in the common tongue, 'bhasha' in some form of western Apabhransha or old Bengali. Language has been used very effectively in the past to enforce 'exclusion'. Whatever their religious and cultural orientation, there was no question about their thoroughgoing social radicalism. Anyone, irrespective of caste, creed or sex could be initiated into the Tantrik and

Nathpanthi orders. There are instances of women from the category of 'Untouchables' being accepted as gurus.[25]

The Social reformers of the early nineteenth century, particularly the Christian missionaries, appropriated the Bhakti traditions to some extent to attack 'exclusion' ascribed by the Brahmanical Hinduism and the caste system. They were also aware of the nature of the pre-colonial protest movements like the 'Vaishnava' cults and hence some of the ideas of the Bhakti tradition were embedded in the preaching of the missionaries.[26] The educational and socio-religious efforts of the missionaries also contributed immensely to a new awakening among the 'excluded' sections especially the Dalits.

Traditional or pre-British India may be regarded, on the whole as a religious society whereas modern India experienced steadily increasing secularization since her conquest by Britain. An indication of the widespread desire for inclusion among the marginalized groups comes from an unusual source, namely, the Census operations.

> In Ghuryes words, various ambitious castes quickly perceived the chances of raising their status. They invited conferences of their members and formed councils to take steps to see that their status was recorded in the way they thought was honorable to them. Others that could not but resent this "stealthy" procedure to advance equally eagerly began to controvert their claims. Thus a campaign of mutual recrimination was set on foot. The leaders of all but the highest castes frankly looked upon the Census as an opportunity for pressing and perhaps obtaining some recognition of social claims which were denied by persons of castes higher than their own.[27]

Census authenticated their inclusion, and erased, though in imperfect manner, their remotest semblance to exclusion. It might be said that the historical role which Indian rulers had played as the final arbiters of the ranking of castes within their jurisdiction, including the ability to promote as well as demote castes was now transferred by the people to the new rulers and the ranks accorded to the castes in census reports became the equivalent of traditional copper plates grants declaring the status, rank and privileges of a particular caste or castes. O' Malley has recorded that at the time of the 1911 census operations Hundreds of petitions were received from different castes–their weight alone amounts to one and a half maunds[28] requesting that they might be known by a new name, be placed higher up in the order of precedence, be recognized as Kshatriya and Vaishya, etc. Here it needs to be pointed out that although the lower castes disputed their degrading status and reinterpreted some of the Hindu texts, they were not aspiring to become Brahmins, but were contesting/negating the Brahmanical interpretation."[29]

They were questioning their exclusion from the higher order and inclusion in the lower order, questioning the authority which ascribed such discriminating statuses that reserve certain privileges for few and excludes out the rest completely. They in no way wanted to lose a chance of giving expression to their feelings of discontent with their ascribed status and of reinterpreting their past to express their aspirations for a better future. "Their urge for ritual equality was very much rooted in their secular conception of modern society. They visualized a nation and civil society free of inequality and social oppression. They intended to emerge as free and equal citizens of the civic/political community of the emerging nation."[30]

Over the years this tendency became so pronounced that at the 1941 census the British Census Commissioner eliminated the column about caste.[31] The method of making a claim was more or less stereotyped. The occupation, the style of life, or name of the caste group would be mentioned in support of the claim. The similarity of the caste name to a historically respectable caste or tribe would be pointed out, the myth regarding the origin of the caste would be described, and its linkage with an epic hero, or divine or semi divine figure would be stressed. Thus the hunters (Bedas) of Mysore would claim kinship with Valmiki, the putative author of the epic Ramayana about whom there is a legend that he was a hunter; and similarly the Shepherds (Kurubas) link their caste history with the name of the Sanskrit poet and playwright, Kalidasa who is believed to have been a shepherd by caste; reference would also be made to the sacred literature of the Hindus and a few Sanskrit quotations thrown in to add strength to the claim. In U.P. the ambitious claimants to inclusion were able to find obliging Brahman pandits who provided 'vyavasthas' or ruling to the effect that the caste in question was indeed a high one. The ruling was usually followed by citation of 'evidence' to authenticate inclusion. In the beginning the demand for being recorded in the census as a high caste emanated from the leaders of the caste group concerned. This resulted in some cases a certain amount of confusion since different sections of a single caste claimed different places, and the same caste changed its claim from census to census. The chances of the occurrence of such discrepancies diminished, though were not entirely obviated, with the formation of caste sabhas or associations. Such sabhas were not unknown previously but the census operations of 1901 made them more popular. There were numerous caste sabhas in several areas including Madras Presidency in 1911, and by the time of the next census - which incidentally came after passing of the Government of India Act of 1919, they were an all India phenomenon.[32] The caste associations articulated as well as organized the new urge towards inclusion. They represented to the census authorities the demand of the individual castes to belong to a particular 'varna' and not to a lower one, as higher would amount to inclusion and lower would exclude. Superintendent of the 1931 United Provinces Census for example received 175 claims (13 from outside the United Provinces) of which 34 were made through the caste associations. The sabhas altered the style of life of the caste in the direction of Sanskritization. This often involved the giving up of the forbidden meat (chicken, pork and carrion beef) and liquor and the donning of the sacred thread and in Uttar Pradesh and Bihar the shortening of the moaning period to correspond with that of the twice born castes. In the case of very 'low' caste it also involved the non-performance of a traditional and degrading duty such as *corv'ee* or other free labour, or carrying palanquins or beating the tom-tom on ceremonial occasions. Heightened self awareness among the castes and the formation of caste sabhas resulted in increasing the "horizontal stretch" of castes. The attempt to use the census to freeze the rank of castes often met with reactions from the high castes, their attempts to 'inclusion' often met with indifference or resorting to the use of violence in order to enforce performance of duties and keep the parvenus in their place. Thus the Rajputs and Bhumihar Brahmins of North Bihar used violence against the Ahirs (cow-herds) who claim to be Kshatriyas and donned the sacred thread.[33] But here it is to be pointed out that the "sanskritisation" model presents only a partial view of the step towards inclusion by the lower castes; it only emphasizes the ritual dimension of articulation and vision ignoring the social protest angle.[34] Thus, Ramakrishna writes: "The 'lower castes'...were seeking to imitate the so-called higher castes and adopt their ways of life in the rituals and ceremonies ...In their quest for a superior position in the society they also wanted to 'sanskritize' some of their ways of life."[35] Recent studies by O. Hanlon, Aloysius, Bandopadhyay, etc. have contributed many insights into the study of social history of the lower castes. Demand for higher position or adoption of the so-called pure ritual symbols or 'sanskritisation' need not be taken as an expression of narrow social ambitions or mere emulation of the upper castes. For, these also meant a protest against inferior position and associated disabilities, as well as appropriation of certain symbols that had so long been the exclusive privileges of a few at the top. And the demand for a share in the economic resources and political power was indeed a challenge to the existing system of their distribution.[36] Negating the sanskritisation model Aloysius observes that the lower castes movements challenge the ritual exclusion, in order to overcome civil and religious disabilities by crossing the pollution line and doing away with differentiation and distancing religious and secular symbols. These processes are basically social protests and challenges to ascriptive hierarchy...Their attempts at sanskritisation, education, claim for employment at par with the other castes and their stake to be represented in various public forums were indications of the passing away of the old order.[37]

The sweepers employed in the cities carrying on their traditional role began to organize at cultural and political levels, utilized symbols from Hindu tradition, taking Rishi Valmiki, the author of the classical Hindu epic, the Ramayana, as their patron saint and adopted his name as their own.[38]

"In Punjab, in Bhatinda village the Chamar and Chuhra call themselves 'Hindus' and locate themselves somewhere in the middle of the caste hierarchy. Thus, they ratify the legitimacy of the caste system and the concept of untouchability by acknowledging that they are lower than many castes but not lower than all."[39] In other locations in the Punjab the members of the Chamar and Chuhra castes place less emphasis on their individual caste identities. Instead, they regard themselves collectively as 'achut', untouchables," suddenly accepting a term many resent, but accepting the word to distinguish themselves from the rest of society. The lower castes with this attitude are from the two extremes; either they are better off than their caste mates in other sections of the Punjab or they are extremely disadvantaged. In the one case, their use of a single term to designate themselves represents their collective rebellion against observing the internal caste divisions that upper caste society ascribes to them; in the other, they all feel the brunt of their common social stigma so sharply that they dare not think of themselves in terms that would dignify in comparison with any of the others. But the result is the same they think of themselves collectively as "Untouchables".[40] This is again a reflection of their perception of a society, emphasizing irrelevance of the caste disparities on the one hand, and also on the other, the urgency of the need to stand united in face of the oppression.

In another area of the Punjab, a tiny village in a semi-desert area of Ferozepur district near the Rajasthan border, where the economy is far more depressed, lower caste people also characterize themselves simply as "untouchables". Their reasons for doing so, however, are diametrically opposite. In this area members of the lower castes are united by the fact that all of them, both Chuhras and Chamars function as landless labourers. Here in this case, class has replaced caste in the social consciousness of lower caste folk. The ritual observances of purity and pollution associated with caste have been forgotten in the competition between large economic divisions. The issue of inclusion is addressed with conscious contestation and negation of the Brahmanical interpretation. The urge for ritual equality, rooted in their secular conception of modern society and nation, is clearly evident.

To conclude, it can be held that in the Indian context, caste system which enjoys the religious sanction of the 'Dharmashastras' is mainly responsible for the "Exclusion" of Dalits. But the Dalits have been relentlessly making assertions in protest against their 'Exclusions' since times immemorial, varying in dimensions and forms, much before the realization and initiation by the government of the need for 'inclusive policies' in their favour to ensure their greater participation in decision making which affects their lives as well as living standards and their overall well-being in a bid to impart social justice.

NOTES AND REFERENCES

1. Prakash Louis, "Social Exclusion: A Conceptual and Theoretical Framework", presented at the PACS Programmer's poverty conference held in New Delhi in December.
2. During discussions in the workshop on reconstruction of the Dalit identity in six northern states, by the Bihar Social Institute.
3. Their (of the Nabatheens) caste is wittye in winning of substance Fardle Faciions, II, I. p. 118.
4. Faun & Ulloa's *Voyages to South America,* (1772) I, 1, iv, p. 29.
5. Examples of use in these are The Banians kill nothing and there are thirty and odd several casts of these. "Purchas Pilgr. I, 485(Y). (1613 AD).The common Brahmins have eighty-two castes or tribes, Lord Banian, 1630 AD.
6. *Her manners had not that repose. Which stamps the caste of Vere de Vere.* [Tennyson's Lady Clara Vere de Vere.] Kessinger Publishing, 2004.
7. S.V. Ketkar, *History of caste in India, op. cit.* p. 20.
8. K.N. Panikkar, "Outsider as Enemy: Politics of rewriting history in India", *Frontline* Volume 18, Issue 01, (Jan. 06–19, 2001).
9. S.V. Ketkar, *History of Caste in India,* (Delhi: Low price publication, 1993), p. 20.
10. "The consumption of liquor, a feature of Vedic ritual as well as part of Brahmin dietary disappeared in the post Vedic India", see M.N. Srinivas, *Social Change in India* (New Delhi: Orient Longman, 1972), p. 25
11. To Whom the upper caste Hindus trace their lineage.
12. MN Srinivas, Social *Change in modern India, op. cit.* p. 25.
13. *Ibid.,* p. 6.
14. *Ibid.,* p. 7.
15. *Ibid.,* p. 8.
16. *Ibid.,* p. 9.
17. K.M. Panikkar, *Hindu Society at Crossroads,* (Bombay: Asia Publishing House, 1955), p. 8.
18. *Ibid.,* p. 9.
19. K.S. Singh ,"*The Scheduled Castes*" vol. II, (Delhi: Oxford University Press, 1995), pp. 325-326.
20. *Ibid.,* p. 33.
21. Braj Ranjan Mani, *Debrahmanising History,* (New Delhi: Manohar, 2005), p. 134.
22. R.C. Majumdar, H.C. Raychaudhuri, and K. Datta, *An Advanced History of India,* 2nd Ed., (London, MacMillan and Co., 1963), pp. 403-404.
23. Braj Ranjan Mani, *Debrahmanising History, op. cit.,* p. 135.
24. *Ibid.,* pp. 135-136.
25. *Ibid.,* p. 141
26. A. Satynarayana *Dalits and the Upper Castes,* (New Delhi: Kanishka Publishers, 2005), p. 137.

27. G.S. Ghurye, *Caste and Class in India,* (Bombay: Popular Book Depot, 1950), pp. 169-170.
28. A maund is a traditional Indian weight varying from area to area. The standard mound is equal to 100Ib.(troy)or 82 2/7lb.(avoirdupois).
29. A. Satynarayana, *Dalits and Upper castes, op.cit.,* p. 125.
30. *Ibid.,* p. 126.
31. Donald E. Smith, *India as a Secular State,* (Princeton: Princeton University Press, 1963), p.304.
32. Madras Census, 1911, p.178; Census of India report for 1921, pp. 231-232.
33. Census of India Report, 1921, pp. 231-232.
34. A. Satynarayana, *Dalits and the Upper Castes, op.cit.,* p. 123
35. V. Ramakrishna, *Social Reform in Andhra,* New Delhi: 1983 and his article "A Background to the Emergence of Caste Consciousness in Coastal Andhra Pradesh" in S. Bandopadhay and Suranjan Das (ed.) *Caste and Communal Politics in South Asia,* Calcutta, (New Delhi : K.P. Bagchi & Company, 1993), pp. 101, 110.
36. S. Bandopadhyay, "Caste, Class and Politics in Colonial Bengal: A Case Study of the Namasudra Movement of 1872-1937", in *Caste and Class in India,* edited by K.L. Sharma, (Jaipur and New Delhi: Rawat Publications, 1994), p. 44.
37. G. Aloysius, *Nationalism* without a Nation, (Delhi: Oxford University Press), 1997 pp. 79-101.
38. The name and the movement was created in 1910 to discourage the Chuhras from converting to Christianity. The same allegation-that Mulk Raj, brother of the Arya Samaj leader Lala Hans Raj, created the name and movement in 1910 to discourage the Chuhras from converting tion Christianity -was made voluntarily and separately by four persons: an upper caste former member of the Arya Samaj (interview with Lala Mohan Lal, former secretary, Harijan Sevak Sangh, in Jullundur, May 1, 1971) and by three lower caste member of the Arya Samaj (interview with Sant Ram, B.A., founder of the Jat Pat Todak Mal,at village Purani Bassi, Hoshiarpur District April 18, 1971; and interview with Sohan Lal Shastri, former Arya Samaji, in New Delhi, June 25, 1971). Other versions of this story place the dates of Arya Samaj influence at 1928 and 1932.
39. Mark Juergensmeyer, *Religious Rebels in the Punjab,* (Delhi: Ajanta Publications, 1988), p. 16.
40. *Ibid.,* pp. 16-17.

4

The Constitution of India: An Antidote to the Manusmriti– Remedies to Caste and Poverty

NETRAPAL SINGH

> On the 26th January 1950, we are going to enter into a life of contradictions. In politics we will have equality and in social and economic life we will have inequality... We must remove this contradiction at the earliest possible moment or else those who suffer from inequality will blow up the structure of political democracy which this Assembly so laboriously built up.[1]
>
> – *Babasaheb Dr. B.R. Ambedkar*

Babasaheb Dr. B.R. Ambedkar identified caste and poverty as two fundamental social and economic problems of Indian society in his historical address on 25th November 1949 in the Constituent Assembly on the completion of the Draft Constitution. Caste and poverty are not only social and economic problems but they are social and economic evils and monsters in the prosperity, progress and development of Indian society. Though the poverty prevails in the other parts of the world but the case of India is unique. In India, the caste system determines the ownership and control of the natural resources i.e. land, wealth and industry. India had become Republic on 26th January 1950 with the implementation of the Constitution of India. The essential principles of a Republic are equality, liberty and fraternity. The provisions have been made in the Constitution of India to annihilate caste and eradicate poverty to achieve the goal of equality, liberty and fraternity in the political, social and economic aspects of public life of India.

There are two strong social and political realities, one that constitutes the Scheduled Castes, Scheduled Tribes, Other Backward

Classes (SC/ST/OBC) and Religious Minorities and the other that constitutes the Brahmanical castes (Brahman-Bania-Thakurs). Despite the constitutional provisions to annihilate caste and to eradicate poverty, there has been a relentless struggle between the SC/ST/OBCs and Religious Minorities (majority) on the one hand and Brahman-Bania-Thakur castes (minority) on the other over annihilation of caste and eradication of poverty in India since the implementation of the Constitution. The SC/ST/OBCs and Religious Minorities are sufferers of caste system and the victims of poverty. Brahman-Bania-Thakur castes are beneficiaries of caste system who are enjoying the monopoly in the ownership and control of natural resources, industries and public services of the country. The SC/ST/OBCs and Religious Minorities are struggling to annihilate caste and to eradicate poverty by adopting constitutional means. Brahman-Bania-Thakurs are manipulating through their socio-political institutions to maintain caste and poverty or status quo to enjoy the privileges attributed to them by caste system and, there are two constitutions in India. First constitution is the *Manusmriti* framed by Manu to protect and maintain Jati-Dharma known as Brahmanism or Hinduism. Jati-Dharma protects and promotes the interests of Brahman-Bania-Thakurs and makes them believe and practise Manusmriti in private and public life. Second constitution is the *Constitution of India* drafted by Babasaheb Dr. Ambedkar to annihilate caste and to eradicate poverty from Indian society. Contrary to the Manusmriti, the Constitution of India protects the interests of the SC/ST/OBCs and Religious Minorities and facilitates opportunities in social, political and economic life to develop them.

The understanding of the basic features of Manusmriti and the Constitution of India leads towards the understanding of fundamental social and economic problems of India. While the essential principles of Hindu Social Order exhibit the nature of elementatary features and spirit of the Manusmriti and the Fundamental Rights and the Directive Principles of the State Policy exhibit those of Constitution of India. The Constituent Assembly Debates on the Fundamental Rights and the Directive Principles before implementation of the Constitution and the policy of reservation after implementation of the Constitution reveal the contrast of caste and poverty between the Bahujan and Brahman-Bania-Thakur castes. The policy of reservation is the best example to understand and expose the Brahmanical psyche and its implications in Indian polity, administration and judiciary.

Manusmriti: Origin and Sustenance of Caste System and Poverty

In Manusmriti, Manu set three essential principles of the Hindu Social Order which are responsible for the origin of caste system in India. The first and foremost is the principle of graded inequality. Second is the principle of fixity of occupations for each caste and continuance thereof by heredity. Third is the fixation of people within their respective castes/classes.[2]

The principle of graded inequality is a fundamental principle which regulates every aspect of life. Manu is the progenitor of the Caste System who preached the sanctity of Varna and is responsible for upholding the principle of gradation and rank.[3] Gradation and sanctity of Varna, later on, was perverted into the gradation and sanctity of caste in Hindu social order. In the scheme of Manu the Brahman is placed at the first rank. Below him is the Kshatriya. Below Kshatriya is the Vaishya. Below Vaishya is the Shudra and below Shudra is the Ati-Shudra (the Untouchable). This inequality, says Dr. Ambedkar, in status is not merely the inequality that one sees in the warrant of precedence prescribed for a ceremonial gathering at a King's Court. It is a permanent social relationship among the classes to be observed - to be enforced - at all times in all places and for all purposes.[4] This system of graded inequality is merely not made legal by Manu but spiritual and moral as well. It is best illustrated in the law of slavery, law of marriage, law of punishment, and law of Samskaras and Sanyas in Manu Smriti.

The most striking feature of Manu's Penal Code which stands out in all its nakedness is the inequality of punishment for the same offence. Inequality is designed not merely to punish the offender but also to protect the dignity or to maintain the baseness of the parties coming to the Court of Law to seek justice; in other words it is to maintain the social inequality on which his whole scheme is founded.[5] In the present time the best example of Manu's law of punishment is the case of Bhanwari Devi, a Shudra Woman, who was raped by a so-called upper caste man. In the judgment given by Rajasthan High Court in the case of Bhanwari Devi, the Brahmanical Judge says that a man of upper caste (Brahmanical caste) can't rape the woman of lower caste (Shudra). The crime of Bhanwari Devi was that she opposed the child marriage in Rajasthan.

Manu fixed the occupations for each Varna (class) and made them hereditary in Manu Smriti. Manu says about the occupations of four Varnas: "But in order to protect this universe, He, the most resplendent one, assigned separate (duties and) occupations, to those who sprang from his mouth, arms, thighs and feet.To Brahmans he assigned teaching and studying (the Veda), sacrificing for the own benefit and for others, giving and accepting (of alms). The Kshatriya he commanded to protect the people, to bestow gifts to offer sacrifices to study (the Veda) and to abstain from sensual pleasures.[6] The Vaishya to tend cattle to bestow gifts, to offer sacrifices to study (the Veda) and to abstain from sensual pleasures. One occupation only the Lord prescribed to the Shudra, to serve meekly even these (other) three classes.[7]

The fixation of occupations for four Varnas debarred the Shudras from social equality (prestige and status), economic security (wealth) and knowledge (mental strength).[8] Social equality is compulsory to use the rights of citizens in life. In its absence social actions are possessed by the privileged classes.

There are three important features of Hinduism in Manu Smriti allied with economic security.[9] Firstly, Hinduism denies the freedom of vocation. Manu has fixed the occupation with leaving no space for mobility. This rule violates the principle of natural industry, skills and capacity of an individual. Secondly, Hinduism compels people to serve ends chosen by others. A Shudra, says Manu, has to serve the upper three Varnas: Brahman, Kashatriya and Vaishya.[10] Manu assigned the duty upon the King to strictly perform the fixed tasks by all castes including the Shudra. Manu directs that "the king should order each of the mercantile class to practice trade, or money lending or agriculture and attendance to cattle; each man of the servile class to act in the service of the twice born."[11] The violation of the rule fixed to the occupational duties was made punishable by the King under Law.

Dr. Ambedkar observes the impact of these rules on the life of the Shudra in spiritual and economic sense as well. His observation leads to the conclusion that in the spiritual sense they constitute the gospel of slavery. With reference to its inner meaning a slave as defined by Plato means a person who accepts from another the purpose which controls his conduct. In this sense a slave is not an end in himself. He is only a means for fulfilling the ends desired by others and the Shudra is reduced into a slave. In their economic significance the Rules put an interdict on the economic independence of the Shudra. A Shudra, says Manu, must serve.[12]

Thirdly, Hinduism leaves no scope for the Shudra to accumulate wealth. Manu prohibits the Shudra from accumulation of wealth. In Manusmriti he says, "Indeed, an accumulation of wealth should not be made by a Shudra even if he is able to do so, for the sight of mere possession of wealth by a Shudra injures the Brahman."[13] "A Brahman may take possession of the goods of the Shudra with perfect peace of mind, for, since nothing at all belongs to this Shudra as his own, he is one whose property may be taken away by his master."[14] Thus Manusmriti leaves no alternative of profession of his own choice. These rules create the condition of economic insecurity in the mind of a Shudra. Sense of economic insecurity mentally defeats him to surrender physically to fulfill the wishes of his masters.

Formal education needs educational institutions and planned reading material to study. It is also necessary to transmit the accumulated thoughts and experiences of the society, touching various subjects and aspects of the life. Without literacy and formal education the spread of the knowledge is impossible. It is striking that in Hinduism formal education was restricted only to the study of the Vedas. It is out of the belief that there is no knowledge outside the Vedas. In Manusmriti, Manu has framed the rules related to the right to study and teach the Vedas. They are reflected in the following Rules. "To the Brahman he (the creator) assigned the *teaching and studying* the Vedas. The Kshatriya he (the creator) commanded to *study* the Vedas. The Vaishya he (the creator) commanded to study the Vedas."[15] "He (the twice born) must never read (the Veda)... in the presence of the Shudras."[16] "Women have no business with the text of the *Veda.*"[17]

These rules had many-fold impacts on life of society. They privileged few and deprived many from natural rights of education. Dr. Ambedkar emphasizes that it must be realized that reading and writing have an integral connection with the teaching and studying the Vedas. The result was that the theory of Manu regarding the rights and prohibitions in the matter of teaching and the study of the Vedas came to be extended to the arts of reading and writing. According to the law of Manu reading and writing has become the right of the high class few and illiteracy has become the destiny of the low class many.[18] What impact the education may have to the life of Shudras was observed by Mahatma Phule in these rules of Manusmriti nearly before 150 years ago. His observation goes: For want of education, intellect was lost; For want of intellect, morality was lost; For want morality, dynamism was lost; For want of dynamism, wealth was lost; For want of wealth, Shudras were degraded; For want of education has caused all these disastrous![19]

In Manusmriti people had fixed in their own Varnas and caste in which they were born. It bans free exchange of ideas and discussion among the classes. It bans joys and sorrows to share. It bans inter-dining and inter-marriage among the four Varnas and different castes. It prevents people from free interaction in social life. In this regard Manu says:

> He, who seeks to preserve an exalted rank, must constantly form connections with the highest and best families, but avoid the worst and the meanest ... Not let him tarry even under the shade of the same tree with outcaste *for the great crimes,* nor with Chandals, nor with Puccasas, nor with idiots, nor with men proud of wealth, nor with washermen or other vile persons, nor with Antyavasins.[20]

Thus Manusmriti creates the social order based on graded classes, not on individuals. Similarly, it also fixed the status of the classes according to their rank and grade in the social order.

Origin of Manusmriti: An Outcome of Brahmanical Political Revolution

How did the Manusmriti and the caste system come into existence in India? The Manusmriti and the caste system are the result of the Brahmanic political revolution and triumph of Brahmanism over Buddhism in the history of India. In 322 B.C. Chandragupta Maurya, a non-Aryan Naga, established the Naga Empire of Magadha. His grandson Ashoka became the King in 273 B.C. and enormously extended the boundaries of Magadha Empire. Later this empire under Ashoka was known as the Maurya Empire or the Empire of the Great Ashoka. It is said that after the battle of Kalinga in 261 B.C. Ashoka's heart was transformed and embraced Buddhism. He made Buddhism religion of the state. It was a great setback to the Brahmanism. Brahmans lost the privilege and all state patronage and were neglected to a secondary and subsidiary position in the

Empire of Ashoka. Ashoka prohibited the animal sacrifices which was the essence of Brahmanic Religion. The Brahmins lost their main occupation of performing sacrifices which was their key source of livelihood. The Brahmins therefore lived as "the suppressed and depressed Classes"[21] nearly for 140 years until the fall of the Maurya Empire in 185 B.C. Pushyamitra Sunga, a Samavedi Brahman, who was the chief commander of Mauryan Army killed the King Vrihadratha Maurya.

How did Pushyamitra Sunga achieve the highest rank in the army under Mauryas and why did he kill the Maurya King Vrihadratha? It is said that Brahamans after losing state patronage and their main occupation appealed to the King Ashoka to grant their villages from all kinds of taxes including land tax. Ashoka accepted their plea and freed their villages from all kinds of taxes. Later such villages were called *Brahmadeya* villages. In kindness Ashoka gave them representation in the services of administration under Mauryan State. Ashoka's kindness was an insult to the pride of Brahmans. How to come out from this insulting and subsidiary position? A rebellion, says Dr. Ambedkar, against the Buddhist state was the only way of escape left to the suffering Brahmans and there is special reason why Pushyamitra should raise the banner of revolt against the rule of the Mauryas. Pushyamitra was a Sunga by Gotra. The Sungas were Samavedi Brahmans, who believed in animal sacrifices and soma sacrifices. The Sungas were quite naturally smarting under the prohibition on animal sacrifices throughout the Mauryan Empire proclaimed in the very Rock Edict by Ashoka. No wonder if Pushyamitra who as a Samavedi Brahman was the first to conceive the passion to end the degradation of Brahmans by destroying the Buddhist state and to free them to practice the Brahmanic religion.[22]

After the killing of the King Vrihadratha Maurya, Pushyamitra Sunga issued a proclamation against the Buddhist monks in which he set a price of 100 gold pieces on the head of every Buddhist monk. It is apparent that the revolution of Pushyamitra was not purely political but religious as well. The main aim of Pushyamitra was to destroy Buddhism and establish Brahmanism in its place. It is evidenced by the promulgation of Manusmriti as code of law. Pushyamitra assigned Sumati Bhargava to compose the Manusmriti. It is known from Naradasmriti that real author of the Manusmriti was Sumati Bhargava. According to scholars Sumati Bhargava composed the Manusmriti between 170 B.C. and 150 B.C. Dr. Ambedkar reveals that the Brahmanic revolution by Pushaymitra took place in 185 B.C. There remains no doubt that code known as Manu Smriti was promulgated by Pushyamitra as embodying the principles of Brahmanic revolution against the Buddhist state of the Mauryas.[23] The promulgation of the Manusmriti was the beginning of transformation of varna into caste and structuring of the caste system. Varna was not transformed into caste overnight. It took hundreds of years following three stages. In the first stage the fixation of status and occupation of a person was for a prescribed period of time, i.e., for one *yug* (a period of four years). In the second stage the fixation of status and occupation of a person was for lifetime. In the third stage the fixation of status and occupation of a person became hereditary.[24]

Manusmriti brought seven misdeeds into practice in the social structure of India. They led India to become a nation deprived of equality, liberty and fraternity, economic prosperity and spiritual advancement. They are:

> 1. It established the right of the Brahmins to rule and commit regicide. 2. It made the Brahmins a class of privileged persons. 3. It converted the Varna into caste. 4. It brought about conflict and anti-social feeling between the different castes. 5. It degraded the Shudras and the women. 6. It forged the system of graded inequality and 7. It made legal and rigid the social system which was conventional and flexible.[25]

In conclusion Manusmriti changed the social structure of Buddhist India. It introduced the caste system by converting Varna into caste. The Caste System determined the preferences of the ownership and control of the natural resources in favour of upper three Varnas. It created the condition of economic deprivation (poverty) for the Shudras by prohibiting them from accumulation of wealth. Consequently, the Shudras became physically enslaved to Brahmans, Kshatriyas and Vaishyas without wealth. It made the Shudras mental slave by depriving them from acquiring knowledge. Strikingly it dispossessed the Shudras from power (bearing arms) by giving them low social status.

The Constitution of India: Annihilator of Caste and Poverty

The Constitution of India is an antidote to the Manusmriti. It is the upholder of social, economic and political revolution in India. It is enshrined in the very preamble of the Constitution. It says, "We, the People of India, have solemnly resolved to constitute India into a Sovereign Socialist Secular Democratic Republic and to secure to all its citizens: Justice, social, economic, political; Liberty of thought, expression, belief, faith and worship; Equality of status and opportunity; and to promote among them all Fraternity assuring the dignity of the individual and the unity and integrity of the nation; in our Constituent Assembly this twenty-sixth day of the November, 1949, do hereby Adopt, Enact and Give to ourselves this Constitution."[26] Contrary to the Manusmriti, the Constitution of India ensures the social, economic and political justice to all the citizens of India with no discrimination based on varna, caste, status, creed, colour, sex, region and religion. It establishes the essential principles of equality, liberty and fraternity of a Democratic Republic.

The Constitution of India identifies caste as a social evil and poverty as economic problem of India. The fundamental rights and Directive Principles are the best remedies to caste and poverty. But these remedies are yet to be implemented in spirit by the State. The Fundamental Rights from articles 12 to 35 and the Directive Principles of State Policy from articles from 36 to 51 have been enacted in the Constitution to destroy caste system and eradicate poverty from India. The Fundamental Rights and the Directive Principles are sources of social transformation and economic emancipation for millions of the SC/ST/OBCs and Religious Minorities who are sufferers and victims of the Codes of Manu or Brahmanical Social Order.

The articles under Fundamental Rights and the Directive Principles had been evolved in a process. Article 14, Equality before law, states that the State shall not deny to any person equality before the law or the equal protection of the laws within the territory of India. Equality before law is the fundamental blow to the inequality inherited in the caste system. Inequality is the foundation of the caste system. The caste system is foundation of Hinduism. Inequality is the soul of Hinduism. Therefore, "Hinduism? Thy name is inequality."[27] Inequality is intrinsic in law of punishment in the Codes of Manu. Manusmriti determines higher punishment to low caste and low punishment to upper caste for the same crime. In the case of offence of assault Manu propounds, "With whatever member a low born man shall assault or hurt a superior, even that member of his must be slit, or cut more or less in proportion to the injury; this is the ordinance of Manu." The Codes of Manu are not only legal but moral and spiritual. The moral and spiritual underpinning is fortified in the *Puranas* and other Hindu Religious Texts. Equality before law is an uprooting of the legal, moral and spiritual base of inequality.

Objectives of the Fundamental Rights can't be achieved until there is a suitable environment to protect the rights of SC/ST/OBCs and Religious Minorities. Equality before law is handicapped if there is discrimination on the grounds of religion, race, caste, sex or place of birth. The caste system legally permits discrimination against individuals and even social groups on these ranks. Article 15 (1) prohibits the discrimination on these grounds. It states that the State shall not discriminate any citizen on the ground of religion, race, caste, sex and place of birth or any of them.[28] Article 15 (1) is shallow without the context and opportunity in public life. The matter of public employment provides the context and opportunity for discrimination and justice both under the State. The matter of public employment is a prime contention in Indian public life. Article 16 (1) states that there shall be equality of opportunity for all citizens in matters relating to employment or appointments to any office under the State.[29] Thus it advocates equality of opportunity in matters of public employment. Equality of opportunity in public employment is social justice.

Two conditions emerged in the light of Articles 15 (1) and 16 (1) from caste ridden society. First, it is fact that discrimination prevails in the caste system. Second, injustice is the part and parcel of the caste system. Injustice is reality where discrimination prevails. Discrimination and injustice are inseparable from each other. Discrimination and injustice are fundamental features of the caste system. Article 15 (1) and 16 (1) are a blow to discrimination and injustice.

There was a difficulty on the operational part of the principle of equality under Article 16 (1). By implying the principle of equal opportunities in the matters of education and public employment the problems of the backward sections of the society were ignored who were deprived from social, economic, educational and cultural opportunities for centuries. In the first instance, the principle of equality seems appropriate, but it is full of flaws. The powers to run the State in India are discriminatory in nature which emerged from the caste system. They have monopoly over public jobs in the state administration. How can there be equality of opportunity in matters of public employment among unequals? How can the law guarantee to stop discrimination when operating powers are against the law itself? The law of equality is an attack on their monopoly. Law can ensure equality of opportunity among equals. Among unequal it is protection of the disease of inequality.

Justice V.R. Krishna Iyer observes that in a terribly unequal system, equal justice is impossible and absolutist arbitrariness inevitable without a dynamic rule of law. And where ugly social realities reveal gaping disparities, equal justice under the law is but pleasing legislative prattle unless a mighty effort at leveling up or equalizing through action oriented legal process is attempted. Where social stratification has become a fossilizing fact of economic life, the technology of justice through jural uplift may have to break new legislative ground, adopt novel legal measures, inject potent statutory control systems and audit procedures so that distributive justice is actually delivered to the lowly in the social ladder. The broad basis and constant inspiration for these big changes can be found in the constitutional mandates."[30]

Equality before law and equality of opportunities in employment is the basic principle of life. Famous scholar H.G. Gans observes that three alternative outcomes of 'Equality' are generally considered: *(i)* Equality of opportunity, *(ii)* Equality of treatment, and *(iii)* Equality of result. Equality of opportunity promised under Article 16 (1) is actually a libertarian and not egalitarian principle as it allows the same freedom to everybody in the race of life.

> Equality of opportunity is also an asocial principle, because it ignores the many invisible and cumulative hindrances in the way of disadvantaged; in fact, unless the children of the poor are taken from their parents at birth and brought up in middle-class homes, most are condemned to inequality of opportunity. The people who begin their life in difficulties, they hardly take the benefits of equal opportunities.[31]

Gans observes that equality of treatment may be interpreted in two ways:

> On the one hand, it means treating people as roughly equal in impersonal social intersections... On the other hand, it means providing people with the same resources regardless of their current resources of socio-economic position; used in this sense, equality of treatment suffers from the same drawback as equality of opportunity for to treat the disadvantaged uniformly with the advantaged will only perpetuate their disadvantage.[32]

In view of above considerations, Gans observes, "Consequently, the only truly egalitarian principle is equality of results, which may require unequal opportunity or treatment for the initially disadvantaged so that they eventually wind up equal in resources or rights."[33]

To bring equality of results Article 15 (4) and 16 (4) have been enacted in the Constitution. These articles are important to make balance between the Fundamental Rights and the Directive Principles. Article 15 (4) states that nothing in this article or in clause (2) of the Article 29 shall prevent State from making any special provision for the advancement of any socially and educationally backward classes of citizens or for the Scheduled Castes and Scheduled Tribes.[34] Article 16 (4) directs the State to make provision for the reservation of jobs in public administration under the State. It states that nothing in this article shall prevent the State from making any provision for reservation of appointments or posts in favour of any backward class of citizens which, in the opinion of the State, is not adequately represented in the services under the State.[35]

These articles are the guiding principles of formation of reservation policy for SC/ST/OBC/RMs in education and public services. Reservation has been a key issue of debate in Indian politics, judiciary, bureaucracy, academia and media for decades. The entire politics of India in last 60 years is evolved around the issue of reservation. It is a battleground between the SC/ST/OBC/RMs and the Brahman-Bania-Thakur castes. *Reservation is the Fundamental Right of the SC/ST/OBC/RMs.* It is nothing less than it. It is enacted under the articles of the Fundamental Rights in part III of the Constitution. The SC/ST/OBC/RMs are fighting for power through reservation to achieve status and prestige in social and political life. The Brahman-Bania-Thakur castes are resisting reservation tooth and nail to maintain their dominance in social and political domain by retaining political power in their hands.

Reservation embodies two main objectives. First objective of reservation is to raise the level of confidence of individuals or communities belonging to the SC/ST/OBC/RMs. The SC/ST/OBC/RMs had been deprived from social status, prestige and power. Public services in India have always been the symbol of prestige and power. The representation of the SC/ST/OBC/RMs in the administration boosts their morale and makes them feel to be part of the country's rule. If somebody become the Collector or the Superintendent of Police or Secretary to the Government or Vice-Chancellor from the SC/ST/OBC/RMs, benefit related to the post are limited to his family members but it creates a great psychological impact in the minds of whole community to which the individual belongs. The whole community feels empowered on the achievement of status and power attained by the individual through reservation. It is a psychological blow to the caste system. The caste system kills the feeling of being empowered by prohibiting the members of the SC/ST/OBC/RMs to acquire higher position in public administration.

Second objective of reservation is to annihilate the caste system. How? The annihilation of caste is a two way process followed in reservation. First, it breaks practice of traditional occupations. Reservation is an instrument to adopt and practice occupations of individual's own choice free from traditional occupations fixed by the Caste System. Like the Chamars (Leather-tanners), the Balmikis (Sweepers), the Kumhars (Pot-makers) and the Dhangars (Shepherds) have been joining the professions of teaching and studying, defense, medical, engineering etc. Traditionally teaching and studying was an occupation of the Brahmins. But these days some Brahmans have joined the profession of sweeping in the government jobs. Article 19 (1) (g) guarantees the practice of any profession or to carry any occupation, trade or buisness. Secondly, reservation has created opportunity to unite various castes into one fold. The Fundamental Principle of the Manusmriti is *dividing*. Socially, caste is the principal instrument of divide and psychologically it is a state of mind. The Manusmriti has divided the SC/ST/OBC/RMs among themselves into more than 6000[36] castes in last thousands of years. Contrary to the Manusmriti the Fundamental Principle of the Constitution is to *Unite*. Reservation kills the state of mind of being the other by creating an opportunity of social unity and feeling of brotherhood among 1600 Scheduled Castes, 1000 Scheduled Tribes and 3743 castes belonging to Other

Backward Classes including Religious Minorities. They constitute more than 85 per cent of the total population of India. This aspect of reservation in public services and education has worried Brahmanical castes to become socially a minority and loose political power. It compels them to shift the focus of reservation from social and educational backwardness to economic backwardness (poverty). Reservation in education and public administration is an intense attack on the caste system.

The origin of the economic system in India lies in the caste system. Similarly, the operation of economic system is the derivation of the caste system in India. It is based on the principle of graded inequality as embodied in the Manusmriti. It is the social order which determines the economic order. The roots of economic problems are lying in social order. The correctness of social order is the correctness of economic order to ensure justice in social, economic and political life. The philosophy of Article 38 is based on the correctness of the social order for the promotion of welfare of the people. It ensues, *"The State shall strive to promote the welfare of the people by securing and protecting as effectively as it may a social order in which justice, social, economic and political, shall inform all the institutions of the national life."*[37]

This article identifies injustice-social, economic and political and inequalities in status, facilities and opportunities and directs the State to cure them. It is still a reality in India. Securing a social order in which promotion of welfare of the people is the Policy of the State laid down by Babasaheb Dr. Ambedkar in the Constitution under Article 38. The Constitution does not leave this policy in vain from the point of view of implementation. The Constitution sets the principles of the Policy to be followed by the State in Article 39. It directs, "The State shall, in particular, directs its policy towards securing: *(a)* that the citizens, men and women equally, have the right to an adequate means of livelihood; *(b)* that the ownership and control of the material resources of the community are so distributed as best to subserve the common good; *(c)* that the operation of the economic system does not result in the concentration of wealth and the means of production to the common detriment; *(d)* that there is equal pay for equal work for both men and women...."[38] The principles of an adequate means of livelihood; common ownership and control of material resources; and distribution of wealth and the means of production are fundamental elements for distributive justice. These principles too are objectives to be achieved by the Indian state and society. Agricultural land, industry, trade, and services under the state are the forms of material resources, wealth, and means of production and livelihood. Without these resources and means life has no existence. Disparity in the ownership and control of material resources and means of production and livelihood is too wide between the Brahmanical Castes and the SC/ST/OBC/RMs in India, even after passing almost 60 years since the implementation and enactment of the Constitution of India.

Article 46 is the basic Directive Principle in the making of law for the promotion of educational and economic interests of the Scheduled Castes, Scheduled Tribes and other weaker sections of the society to protect them from social injustice and all forms of exploitation.[39]

Inspiration and explanation of the Directive Principles is found in the plan of State Socialism established by Babasaheb Dr. Ambedkar in Article 2 (4) of the *States and Minorities*. The States and Minorities was a Memorandum on the safeguards for the Scheduled Castes submitted to the Constituent Assembly on behalf of the All India Scheduled Castes Federation in 1947. The plan of State Socialism proposes State ownership in agriculture with a collectivized method of cultivation and a modified form of State Socialism in the field of industry. It places squarely on the shoulders of the State the obligation to supply capital necessary for agriculture as well as for industry. Without the supply of capital by the State neither land nor industry can be made to yield better results. It also proposes to nationalize insurance with a double objective. State Socialism is essential for the rapid industrialization of India. Private enterprise can not do it and if it did it would produce those inequalities of wealth which private capitalism has produced in Europe and which should be a warning to Indians. Consolidation of Holdings and Tenancy Legislation are worse than useless."[40] State Socialism means State ownership and control in national agriculture, industry and insurance, defines Dr. Ambedkar.

Dr. Ambedkar planned to make State Socialism an essential part of the Fundamental Rights. He advised the Constituent Assembly to make State Socialism independent from the will of the Legislature and establish it by the Law of the Constitution and thus make it unalterable by any act of the Legislature and the Executive. He says, "The purpose is to protect the liberty of the individual from invasion by other individuals which is the object of enacting Fundamental Rights. The connection between individual liberty and the shape and form of the economic structure of society may not be apparent to everyone. None the less the connection between the two is real."[41]

Babasaheb Dr. Ambedkar found actual strength of the Fundamental Rights lying in the State Socialism. The State Socialism is the guarantee of economic independence of individual. The Fundamental Rights are meaningless without economic independence or security of employment for individuals in the society. Unemployment is the guarantee of exploitation. "The unemployed are thus compelled to relinquish their Fundamental Rights for the sake of securing the privilege to work and subsist,[42] says Babasaheb Dr. Ambedkar. He suggests to protect the Fundamental Rights of individuals, employed as well unemployed that the useful remedy adopted by Democratic countries is to *limit* the power of Government to impose arbitrary restraints in political domain and to *invoke* the ordinary power of the Legislature to restrain the more powerful individuals from imposing arbitrary restraints on the less powerful in the economic field.[43] He was anxious to leave the fate of State Socialism on the mercy of ordinary law framed by simple parliamentary majority. His anxiousness reveals in that those who want the economic structure of the society to be modeled on State Socialism must realize that they can't leave the fulfillment of so fundamental a purpose to the exigencies of ordinary Law which simple majorities - whose political fortunes are never determined by rational causes-have a right to make and unmake."[44] Thus the Constitutional Law is the way to protect the Fundamental Rights of under-privileged from the invasion by privileged in the society.

In regard to transform economic structure of the Indian society Babasaheb Dr. Ambedkar cautioned the Constituent Assembly about the limitations of Democracies of the World which stopped with Adult Franchise and Fundamental Rights. He says that almost all Laws of Constitution which relate to countries which are called Democracies stop with Adult Franchise and Fundamental Rights. They have never advanced to the conception that the Constitutional Law of the Democracy must go beyond Adult Franchise and

Fundamental Rights. In other words, old time Constitutional Lawyers believed that the scope and function of Constitutional Law was to prescribe the shape and form of the political structure of the society. They never realized that it was equally essential to prescribe the shape and form of the economic structure of society, if Democracy had to live up to its principle of one man, one value. Time has come to take a bold step and define both the economic structure as well as political structure of society by the Law of the Constitution.[45] Babasaheb Dr. Ambedkar's vision and plan was to transform the political structure of Indian society by Adult Franchise, the social structure by the Fundamental Rights, and the economic structure by State Socialism. Adult Franchise and Fundamental Rights were achieved by him for the SC/ST/OBC/RMs in particular and enacted in the Constitution for all. He made his best efforts to make State Socialism or the Directive Principles part of the Fundamental Rights but failed against the resistance of the statusquoist Brahmanical Castes.

The Directive principles are fundamental in the governance of the country and making laws. The fundamental difference between the Fundamental Rights and the Directive Principles is the difference of judicial application. The Fundamental Rights are enforceable in the Court. This provision is made in Article 32. Babasaheb Dr. Ambedkar wanted the Directive Principles on equal footings of the Fundamental Rights to enforce in courts. His failure is reflected in Article 37 in which the Directive Principles were put out of the purview of court. According to Article 37 the Directive Principles are not enforceable in any court. Brahmanical intelligentsia propagated only this aspect of Article 37 among public and academia ignoring and misinterpreting other significant articles of the Directive Principles.

Judicial insignificance of the Directive Principles forced Babasaheb Dr. Ambedkar to the defense of Directive Principles. He stated that the Directive Principles should not be disposed in this way. These principles are bound to affect the decisions of courts on constitutional questions, just as the provisions of Magna Carta had affected the decisions of English Judges, and Preamble to the Declaration of Independence had affected the decisions of American Judges. The attitude towards the directive was that the directive should not only be subordinated to fundamental rights but could not be given effect to if they come in conflict with the operation of any other provision of the Constitution for the mere reason that the directives were not 'enforceable in the court of law.' He emphasized that as the directive principles were nothing else than a series of provisions containing implicitly in them the doctrine of implied powers the courts should invoke them and support legislation undertaken by Parliament or State legislatures which tended to give effect to the directive principles embodied in the Constitution.[46]

Dr. Ambedkar had experienced the attitude of Brahamanical castes in the public life and the Constituent Assembly towards the promotion of the welfare and interests of the SC/ST/OBC/RMs. The power to implement the Constitution had gone into the hands of Brahmanical Castes. He was doubtful too about the right implementation of the provision made in the Directive Principles. It compelled him to make the predictive remark, "What great value these Directive Principles possess will be realized better when the forces of right contrive to capture power."[47] Capturing power for the right implementation of the Directive Principles and the Fundamental Rights by the SC/ST/OBC/RMs was the mission and ultimate wish of his life. He expressed it with deep sense of sorrow in his last message to his followers on July 31, 1956 at his residence at 26, Alipur Road, Delhi. He said that *the first worry to my mind is that I have not been able to fulfill my life's mission. I wanted to see my people as a governing class sharing the political power in terms of equality with other communities...*[48] His mission is yet to be fulfilled. The Directive Principles are a remedy to economic diseases generated from the caste system. The spirit of the Fundamental Rights and the Directive Principles is the spirit of salvation and progress. The implementation of the Fundamental Rights and the Directive Principles enacted in the Constitution is the real salvation (Moksha or Nirvana) of the SC/ST/OBC/RMs. But! The instrument to implement the Fundamental Rights and the Directive Principles is political power. In this context Babasaheb Dr. Ambedkar made his famous statement that *political power is the master key which unlocks all the doors of Progress.*

Evolution of the Constitution: The Struggle of Phule-Shahu-Ambedkar

The Constitution of India is not merely an offshoot of the Constituent Assembly from 1947 to 1949. It is the reflection of nearly one hundred fifty years struggle of the ancestors of the SC/ST/OBC/RMs who fought against the Brahmanical social system based on Manusmriti.

In 1812 the Chandals (an ex-untouchable community), Scheduled Caste of Bengal laid down the foundation of this struggle under the leadership of Shri Harichand Thakur-Guruchand Thakur. It was followed by Mahatma Phule, Chhatrapati Shahuji Maharaj and Babasaheb Dr. Ambedkar in 19th and 20th centuries in Maharashtra. Their struggle is reflected in the various charter acts introduced by the colonial rule since 1833 Charter Act to the 1935 Charter Act. The Charter Act of 1935 is known as the Second Constitution of India.

The struggle of Shri Harichand Thakur and Guruchand Thakur was first reflected in the Charter Act of 1833. For the first time in the Charter Act of 1833, it was declared that Indian who resides in the provinces of the Company will not be discriminated on the grounds of religion, race, colour or birth of place for any post under the services of the Company. Slavery was declared illegal and the Governor General was directed to take necessary steps to remove the slavery from India. Finally, slavery was removed in 1843 by the British Government. A Law Commission was established to conduct, codify and reform the Indian Law especially Brahmanical Law. Lord MaCauley was appointed the first Law Expert in the Governor General's Council and the Chairman of the Committee of Public Instruction. MaCauley framed the Indian Penal Code and introduced English as medium of instruction[49] in India. In 1835 the colonial government declared the Universal Education System according to the directions given in 1833 Charter Act.

In western Maharashtra, Mahatma Phule, an OBC belonging to Mali (Gardner) caste, was first among the Shudras and Atishudras who educated in English education system. He realized the importance of education for the Shudras and Atishudras. He started education movement for the Shudras and Atishudras in 1848. His movement spread all over Maharashtra within years. Brahmans opposed the education for the Shudras and Atishudras. The Brahman leaders like Ram Mohan Roy, whom Brahmans call the 'father of Renaissance in India,' favoured the education of only the upper castes. Mahatma Phule challenged Brahminical opposition. Mahatma Phule's education movement and his endless struggle made a serious impact on the British Government to change the education policy in favour of the Shudras and Atishudras.

Mahatma Phule's struggle for the marginalized became the fundamental principle of the colonial education Policy in India.

Impact of his struggle is reflected in the Wood's Dispatch. Wood's Dispatch is known as the Magna Carta of education in India. In the Charles Wood's Dispatch of July 19, 1854, the Court of Directors directed that "useful and practical knowledge, suited to every station in life, may be best conveyed to the great mass of the people who are utterly incapable of obtaining any education worthy of the name by their own efforts; and we desire to see the active measures of government, more especially directed, for the future, to this object, for the attainment of which we are ready to sanction a considerable increase of expenditure."[50] In 1856 the British Government declared that the educational institutions of government are intended by us to be open to all classes."[51]

Mahatma Phule submitted a memorandum on October 19, 1882 to the Hunter Commission. In this memorandum he framed mass education policy. He demanded that primary education of the masses should be made compulsory up to the age of 12 years. He demanded the same for the religious minorities, i.e., Muslims, because in his opinion they were also deprived of education like the Shudras and Atishudras. He suggested that the schools should be regulated by the Provincial or Imperial Government through municipalities under the supervision of the Education Department. In the Constitution of India the right to education became the Fundamental Right under Article 29 (2).

Mahatma Phule launched the campaign against the untouchability. In 1862 he opened a well for the Untouchables in front of his house. In 1873 in his famous book *Slavery* he appealed to the British Raj for the reservation of the Shudras and Atishudras in public services against the virtual monopoly of the Brahmans. He commenced the movement of Shudras and Atishudras in 1873 in Poona under the banner of a socio-religious organization "Satya Shodhak Samaj" to achieve the objective of his mission. After two years in 1875, Poonite Brahmans launched " Arya Samaj" under the leadership of a Gujarati Brahman Dayanand Saraswati to counter the movement of Satya Shosdhak Movement.

Chhatrapati Shahuji Maharaj, head of a princely state Kolhapur in Maharashtra carried forward the mission of Mahatma Phule. Chhatrapati Shahuji Maharaj belongs to Kunbi caste, an OBC of Maharashtra. Shahuji Maharaj implemented 50 per cent reservation for Backward Classes in his proclamation on July 26, 1902. Shahu

Maharaj transformed Mahatma Phule's request of reservation for the Shudras and Atishudras into reality. He orders:

> From the date of this order 50 per cent of the vacancies that may occur shall be filled by recruits from among the backward classes. In all offices in which the proportion of officers of the backward classes at present is less than 50 percent, the next appointment will be given to a member of these classes. A Quarterly return of all appointments made after the issue of this order shall be submitted by all Heads of Departments. *For the purpose of these orders the backward classes shall be understood to mean all castes other than Brahmins, Prabhus, Shenavi, Parsees and other advanced classes.*[52]

This order was extraordinary to transform the social life of India and first of its kind in India's history. Articles 15 (4, 5), 16 (4) and 335 reflect the impact of reservation policy introduced by Shahuji Maharaj.

Shahuji Maharaj led a crusade against the untouchability. He legally abolished the untouchability in his State. American Missionaries greatly influenced and inspired Shahuji Maharaj to abolish the Untouchability. He passed three ordinances on August 23, 1919 calling for equal treatment to the untouchables in the State and State-aided schools, and government services to eradicate Untouchability.[53] Articles 15 (2) (a) and (b) and 17 are replica of these ordinances in the Constitution of India. The Constitution of India is inspired by the said ordinances and abolishes the untouchability under article 17.

In 1917 Shahu Maharaj raised the most important demand of communal representation for the Backward Classes and the untouchables in services and the Legislative Councils. Shahuji Maharaj cited strong reason for communal representation. He states:

> Although the British are the rulers of the country, the real power rests with the Brahmin officers who pervade every rank of the service from the meanest clerk and village accountant, the Kulkarni, to the highest offices and predominate even in the Councils.[54]

He suggests the remedy, "The best way to break down this citadel of Brahmin power is to grant communal representation, not only in Councils but also in all branches of the service, high or low.

Whenever a chance occurs, preference should be given to qualified non-Brahmins."[55] Further, in a letter written to Lord Willingdon, Governor of Bombay, on 29th December, 1917 he raised the demand, "I am strongly of the opinion that these classes (the backward classes and especially the untouchables) must all be properly represented in the reformed constitution of the Government of India that is under contemplation."[56] Communal representations was most suitable way to overcome the monopoly of Brahmins in public services and the Councils.

To prevent the demand of communal representation raised by Shahuji Maharaj, Tilak and the Congress launched the Home Rule (Swarajya) movement in 1917. What is Swarajya meant by him? The meaning of Swarajya is that political power may be in the hands of the British but bureaucratic power should be in the hands of the Brahmans. It was the Law of the Manusmriti. In his speech at Ahmadnagar on May 31, 1916, defining the meaning of Swarajya, Tilak said, "Swarajya means the British Emperor and the power of English in India intact, while the administration would come in the hands of the people (Brahmans)."[57] In his speech at Yeotmal on January 9, 1917 Tilak declared, *"Our law is Manusmriti"* and emphasized that the *law (i.e., Manusmriti) orders the king to administer with the help of learned persons and Brahmins.*[58] Real meaning of Tilak's Swarajya was the Brahman Raj based on the Brahmanic religion in which Brahman is supreme authority. He repeatedly pointed out that the concept of Swarajya was as old as the Vedas and that it had religious connotation.[59] Manusmriti makes the Brahmans a privileged caste. In his scheme of Swarajya no community other than Brahmans had representation in the public administration.

In 1918, Tilak requested the British Raj to award Swarajya. He said that Swarajya would function through election. In the scheme of Swarajya, only those were entitled to get the right of vote who are educated up to graduation (graduates); those who pay income tax (money-lenders); and those who acquire landed property (landlords). The right of vote would not be given to illiterates and those who did not pay income tax and land tax. How many of the SC/ST/OBC/RMs would have been eligible to get the right of vote to elect the governments in 1918 and even today if these criteria are applied. Only Brahmans, Banias, and Thakurs will be in the majority to elect the governments.

Shahu Maharaj established the leadership of Babasaheb Dr. Ambedkar and bestowed in him the heavy responsibility of his mission in the Mangaon Conference organized on March 21 and 22, 1920 in Maharashtra. In 1919, Shahuji Maharaj introduced Babasaheb Dr. Ambedkar to his mission to put the demands of the Untouchables for communal representation. Babasaheb Dr. Ambedkar struggled to achieve the right of Adult Franchise for all adults and communal representation for the untouchables during 1919-32. He fought the battle single handedly after the sad demise of Shahuji Maharaj in 1922.

In 1919, Babasaheb Dr. Ambedkar in his evidence before Southborough Committee, a franchise committee, demanded communal representation for the untouchables with adult franchise. Before Southborough Committee he argues, "At present when all the avenues of acquiring wealth are closed, it is unwise to require from the untouchables a high property qualification. To deny them the opportunities of acquiring wealth and then to ask from them a property qualification is to add insult to injury."[60] Dr. Ambedkar rejected the scheme of Tilak and his Congress in which criteria of the level of education, amount of landed property, and the limit of income were chosen to be eligible for the right of vote. Tilak devised these criteria to deprive the majority of Backward Classes, the untouchables, and the Religious Minorities from the right of vote.

The Montague-Chelmsford reforms which are known as the first Constitution of India gave the Depressed Classes representation by nomination instead of election. The Depressed Classes were unhappy with representation, but significantly caste divisions were recognized as the principal feature of Indian society in the Montague Chelmsford report. The report recognized fully that the existence of social differences and divisions formed "a feature of Indian Society which is out of harmony with ideas on which elsewhere in the World representative institutions rest"[61] and the authors of the report apprehended that they "have to be taken into account and they must lead us to adjust the forms of popular Government familiar elsewhere to the special conditions of Indian life."[62]

The discourse that caste is basic element of Indian Social Structure and fundamental problem of Indian society was first started and brought into Indian politics by Mahatma Phule in 19th century. The struggle for Communal representation for the Backward

Classes and the untouchables was first commenced by Shahuji Maharaj. The struggle and revolt of Mahatma Phule and Shahuji Maharaj is reflected in the first Constitution of 1919. It accepted caste as the key element of Indian society and granted Communal representation for the Untouchables in the Legislature.

In 1928 Babasaheb Dr. Ambedkar worked with the Simon Commission and submitted his independent report containing views and recommendations regarding changes in the Constitution of the Bombay presidency. In that report his key recommendation was the incorporation of the Adult Franchise in the proposed Constitution of India. In his views, the adult franchise was not merely a ballot paper but the foundation of democracy and associated life. He signifies the franchise:

> If the majority had before its minds the true concept of what franchise means they would have realized that franchise, far from being a transaction concerned with the marking of ballot paper, stands for direct and active participation in the regulation of the terms upon which associated life shall be sustained and the permit of good carried on... therefore, the franchise should be extended to all adults, male and female, above the age of 21.[63]

On behalf of Bahishkrita Hitakarani Sabha, Babasaheb Dr. Ambedkar submitted a statement concerning the safeguards for the protection of the interest of Depressed Classes as a minority to the Indian Statutory Commission on May 29, 1929. In the statement of Sabha he repeated the demand of representation by election for the Depressed Classes by highlighting the importance of election and the franchise. He recognized, "Election is not only correct in principle of election from the standpoint of responsible Government, but is also necessary from the standpoint of political education. Every community must have an opportunity for political education which can't well be secured otherwise than by the exercise of the vote."[64]

In the Round Table Conferences in 1930, 1931 and 1932, he again insisted on the adult franchise and the representation in the Central and Provincial Legislatures for the Depressed Classes by election. In the Round Table Conference Gandhi insisted upon the limited franchise based on the criteria of education and property qualification and opposed separate electorate for the Depressed

Classes. The British Government awarded the representation for the Depressed Classes by granting them not only separate electorate but special electorate[65] in the Legislature under Communal Award announced on August 17, 1932. At the same time the Government declared the adult franchise for all adults without waiting Lothian Committee's (Franchise Committee) Report. It is noticeable that the Depressed Classes were given separate electorate with *Minority Status*. Dr. Ambedkar pressed the demand of separate entity for the untouchables since 1919. The second Constitution of India came into existence in 1935. The Adult Franchise, minority status, and reservations for the Scheduled Castes were enacted in the Constitution of 1935 as results of the struggle of Babasaheb Dr. Ambedkar.

The Constitutional reforms of 1919 had recognized the Depressed Classes[66] as the statutory minorities and provisions for their safety and security were embodied in it. But in the details of the framed Constitution, the British Government of India found it difficult to devise any provisions for their protection except representation in the legislatures by nomination. Keeping these inadequacies in mind, Ambedkar formulated a scheme of political safeguards for the protection of the Depressed Classes in the Future Constitution of a self-governing India, and submitted it as memorandum to the Indian Round Table Conference on November 4, 1931 along with Rao Bahadur R. Srinivasan. The Minorities Muslims, Depressed Classes, Indian Christians, Anglo-Indians and Europeans submitted a Joint Memorandum, known as *Minorities Pact* to the British Prime Minister on November 12, 1931. In the Minority Pact, minorities claimed the rights for a settlement of the communal problem. These two documents were incorporated in the Act of 1935 as the fundamental rights. The act of 1935 became was the foundation of the Constitution of 1950. Articles 14, 15, 16, 17, 32, 330, 332, 335 are expressions of the political safeguards framed by Dr. Ambedkar. The Minorities Pact is the basis of the right to freedom of religion (Articles 25, 26, 27, 28), Cultural and Educational Rights (Articles 29, 30) and Articles 331, 333, 336 and 337 for the representation of the Anglo-Indians in legislatures, certain public services and education.

Social-political rights and safeguards of the Scheduled Castes and Scheduled Tribes were enacted in the Act of 1935. The main benefit to the Scheduled Castes and Scheduled Tribes was the provision of statutory representation in education and public services in the act of 1935. The Other Backward Classes were left unidentified and without constitutional safeguards for their representation in education and public services. Babasaheb Dr. Ambedkar's struggle was not over, yet he had to overcome the coming difficulties to secure the economic rights and safeguards for SC/ST/OBCs and social and political rights for the OBCs in 1940s.

Babasaheb Dr. Ambedkar was elected to the Constituent Assembly and became the chairman of the Drafting Committee to frame the Constitution against the wishes and desperate efforts of the Congress. In 1946 according to the Cabinet Plan elections were announced to elect the Constituent Assembly to frame the Constitution of India. By this time Congress had created an army of chamchas (stooges) through Poona Pact to block the political prospects of Babasaheb Dr. Ambedkar to enter in the Constituent Assembly. In 1945-46 Congress campaigned against Babasaheb Dr. Ambedakar to elect him in the Constituent Assembly. Congress had arranged to close not only the doors but windows of the Parliament to enter Ambedkar into the Constituent Assembly. The Chandals, a Scheduled Caste, elected Babasaheb Dr. Ambedkar to the Constituent Assembly from the constituency Khulna-Jaisur in Bengal. The population of the Chandals was 52 per cent in Khulna-Jaisur. Gandhi and Nehru's Congress, violating the agreement of partition, transferred Khulna-Jaisur to East Pakistan in 1947. Dr. Ambedkar became the member of the Constituent Assembly of Pakistan. Dr. Ambedkar went to England and convinced the British to secure his place in the Constituent Assembly of India to protect the rights of the Scheduled Castes with Scheduled Tribes, Other Backward Classes and Religious Minorities in the new Constitution. The British Government warned Gandhi, Nehru and their Congress that if Dr. Ambedkar was not elected to the Constituent Assembly the British may postpone the programme of independence. Under the pressure of the British Government Babasaheb Dr. Ambedkar was again elected to the Constituent Assembly from Poona on July 9, 1947. Next day, on July 10, 1947, the British Government declared the programme of Independence.

Conclusion

Historically, Manusmriti is the origin of many problems in India. It is the outcome of the Brahmanical political revolution in which Buddhist King Vrihadratha Maurya was killed by Samavedi

Brahman Pushyamitra Sunga in 185 B.C. Manusmriti converted Vanra into Caste. It prohibited the Shudras, the majority population (SC/ST/OBC/RMs), from acquiring education, wealth and power (arms). Caste destroyed physical strength (strength to organize). The sanctions on education destroyed the mental strength of the Shudras and want of wealth made them physically slave to Brahman-Bania-Thakurs. The prohibition on taking arms made the Shudras politically enslaved to their Brahmanical masters. To maintain these principles Manusmriti preaches inequality and injustice in social, economic and political life and promotes discrimination, hatredness and conflicts among different castes. Manusmriti protects the rights of castes rather than of individuals.

Mahatma Phule raised the banner of revolt against the caste system. He broke the monopoly of Brahmans in education. His mission opened the doors of education for the SC/ST/OBC/RMs. Chhatrapati Shahuji Maharaj broke the monopoly of the Banias (Vaishayas) by implementing 50 per cent reservation for the SC/ST/OBC/RMs in public services under the administration of Kolhapur. Following this, Babasaheb Dr. Ambedkar attacked the monopoly of the Thakurs (Kshatriyas) by snatching the right of vote from their clutches. In democracy, vote is the ultimate weapon to acquire political power. The Constitution of India is the reflection of the struggle and socio-political movement of these Bahujan ancestors. It is best reflected in the Fundamental Rights and the Directive Principles. The Fundamental Rights and the Directive Principles are the remedies to caste and poverty in India. Contrary to Manusmriti, the Constitution enacts and promotes equality and justice in social, economic and political fields and prohibits discrimination and untouchability. The Constitution of India protects the rights of the individuals rather than of the castes.

NOTES AND REFERENCES

1. *Constituent Assembly Debates*, vol. IX, pp. 969-970. Hereafter *CAD* for Constituent Assembly Debates. It was one of Babasaheb Dr. Ambedkar's the most famous speech ever which set the guiding principles for the future Governments in India.
2. B.R. Ambedkar, 'The Hindu Social Order: Its Essential Principles' in *Dr. Babasaheb Ambedkar Writings and Speeches*, vol. III, (Bombay: Government of Maharashtra, 1987), pp. 107-117. Hereafter *BAWS* for *Dr. Babasaheb Ambedkar Writings and Speeches*.

3. B.R. Ambedkar, 'Philosophy of Hinduism' in *BAWS*, vol. III, p. 25.
4. *Ibid.*, p. 25.
5. *Ibid.*, p. 31.
6. *Manusmriti*, Chapter I, Verses 87-91, cited in *BAWS*, vol. III, pp. 111-112.
7. *Ibid.*, p. 112.
8. B.R. Ambedkar, 'Philosophy of Hinduism' in *BAWS*, vol. III, pp. 38-39.
9. *Ibid.*, pp. 39-40.
10. *Ibid.*, p. 39.
11. *Ibid.*, p. 40.
12. *Ibid.*, p. 41.
13. *Manusmrit*, Chapter X, Verse 129, cited in *BAWS*, vol. VII, (Bombay: Government of Maharashtra, 1990), p. 50.
14. *Manusmriti*, Chapter VIII, Verses 417, cited in *BAWS*, vol. VII, p. 50.
15. *Manusmriti*, Chapter I, Verses 88-90, cited in *BAWS*, vol. III, p. 42.
16. *Manusmriti*, Chapter IV, Verse 99, cited in *BAWS*, vol. III, p. 42.
17. *Manusmriti*, Chapter IX, Verse 18, cited in *BAWS*, vol. III, p. 42.
18. B.R. Ambedkar, 'Philosophy of Hinduism' in *BAWS*, vol. III, p. 43.
19. Dhanajay Keer, *Mahatma Jotirao Phooley: Father of Indian Social Revolution*, (Bombay: Popular Prakashan, 1974), reprint 2002, p. 182.
20. *Manusmrit*, Chapter IV, Verse 244, cited in *BAWS*, vol. III, p. 114.
21. *BAWS*, vol. III, p. 268.
22. *Ibid.*, pp. 268-269.
23. *Ibid.*, p. 271.
24. *Ibid.*, pp. 285-288.
25. *Ibid.*, p. 275.
26. *The Constitution of India*, New Delhi: Government of India, as on the 26 January, 2005, p. 6.
27. *BAWS*, Vol. III, p. 87.
28. *The Constitution of India*, p. 7.
29. *Ibid.*
30. V.R. Krishna Iyer, *Ambedkar Memorial Lectures*, New Delhi: Jawaharlal Nehru University, 1976.
31. H.G. Gans, *More Equality*, New York: Panthon Books, 1973, cited in *Mandal Commission Report of the Backward Classes Commission*, vol. I, (New Delhi: Government of India, 1980), p. 27.
32. *Ibid.*, p. 27.
33. *Ibid.*
34. *The Constitution of India*, p. 12.
35. *Ibid.*, p. 7.
36. According to the investigation of the *Mandal Commission Report of the Backward Classes Commission*, 1980, the SC/ST/OBC & Religious Minorities are divided into 6343 castes.

37. *The Constitution of India,* p. 17.
38. *Ibid.,* p. 17.
39. *Ibid.,* p. 18.
40. B.R. Ambedkar, 'States and Minorities' in *BAWS,* vol. I, (Bombay: Government of Maharashtra, 1979), p. 408.
41. *Ibid.,* p. 409.
42. *Ibid.,* p. 410.
43. *Ibid.*
44. *Ibid.,* p. 411.
45. *Ibid.,* p. 412.
46. W.N. Kuber, *Dr. Ambedkar: A Critical Order,* (New Delhi: People's Publishing House, 1967), p. 137.
47. *Ibid.,* p. 138.
48. Nanak Chand Rattu, *Reminiscences and Rememberances of Dr. B.R. Ambedkar,* New Delhi: Falcon Books, 1995, p. 191. Nanak Chand Rattu was one the closest associates of Babasaheb Dr. Ambedkar. He had been most close to him in his last days.
49. Lord MaCauley, *Minutes on Education,* written on February 2, 1835, in this minute he set English as the medium of instruction in India. It was a milestone in the history of education in India.
50. Cited in Dhanajay Keer, *Mahatma Jotirao Phooley: Father of Indian Social Revolution, op. cit.,* p. 53.
51. *Report of the Director of Instruction for the year 1857-58,* p. 88.
52. B.D. Khane, "Shahu's Crusade against Untouchlability" in P.B. Salunkhe (ed.), *Chhatrapati Shahu Maharaj: The Pillar of Social Democracy,* (Bombay: Government of Maharashtra, 1994), p.146. Hereafter *CSM: PSD* for *Chhatrapati Shahu Maharaj: The Pillar of Social Democracy.*
53. P.B. Salunkhe, Missionary Influence on Chhatrapati Shahu in P.B. Salunkhe (ed.), *CSM: PSD,* p. 191.
54. Shahu Chhatrapati, 'A Letter to Lord Sydenhome, Ex-Governor of Bombay' in P.B. Salunkhe (ed.), *CSM: PSD,* p. 349.
55. *Ibid.,* p. 353.
56. V.S. Kadam, 'Self-Government for India and Shahu Chhatrapati of Kolhapur' in P.B. Salunkhe (ed.), *CSM: PSD,* p. 366.
57. *Ibid.,* p. 362.
58. *Ibid.,* p. 363.
59. *Ibid.*
60. B.R. Ambedkar, 'Evidence before Southborough Committee' in *BAWS,* vol. I, p. 252.
61. B.R. Ambedkar, "Statement concerning the safeguards for the protection of the interests of Depressed Classes as a minority on behalf of Bahiskrita Hitkarini Sabha to the Indian Statutory Commission (29th May, 1929)" in *BAWS,* vol. II, (Bombay: Government of Maharashtra, 1982), p. 430.

62. *Ibid.*, p. 430.
63. Dr. Ambedkar with Simon Commission (Indian Statutory Commission) prepared a report on the Constitution of the Government of Bombay Presidency which was reprinted in *BAWS*, Vol. II, pp. 337-38.
64. B.R. Ambedkar, 'Statement concerning the safeguards for the protection of the interests of Depressed Classes as a minority on behalf of Bahiskrita Hitkarini Sabha to the Indian Statutory Commission (29th May, 1929)' in *BAWS*, vol. II, p. 439.
65. In separate electorates Babasaheb Dr. Ambedkar demanded that the Depressed Classes would elect only the Depressed Classes representatives to the Legislatures in certain reserved constituencies by single vote. But under the special electorates the British Government the right of double vote to the Depressed Classes. By first vote they had to elect their own representative and by second vote they had to elect general candidate to the Legislatures. This system of election was known as 'Special Electorate'. Dr. Ambedkar said that the second vote given by the Communal Award was a priceless privilege. "Its value as political weapon was beyond reckoning". *BAWS*, vol. IX, p. 90.
66. By 1919 the term Depressed Classes commonly include the Untouchable castes, the Shudras (OBCs) and the Aboriginal and Hill Tribes (STs) but after Government of India Act, 1919 the term specifically was used for the Untouchables who after 1935 Government of India Act were termed as the Scheduled Castes.

PART–II
PERSPECTIVES ON EXCLUSION AND DISCRIMINATION

5

Caste Oppression, Economic Discrimination and Poverty among Scheduled Castes in India

SUDHAKARA KARAKOTI AND
RAGHUNATH PRASAD SAKET

A Sudra must make no collection of wealth, even though he be able; For a Sudra who has acquired wealth, gives pain to Brahmins.
– *The Laws of Manu*

Ours is a battle not for wealth or for power. It is a battle for freedom. It is a battle for the reclamation of human personality.
– *Dr. B.R. Ambedkar*

Historically, scheduled castes faced various kinds of exclusion, discrimination, denial and oppression. In the sphere of education, they were restricted from acquiring knowledge. In the economic sphere, they were restricted from gaining wealth and were exploited while working for upper castes. In the social sphere, they were restricted from participating in social and cultural activities. First part of this paper deals with the discrimination, based on official sources with the help of available macro level data. Second part presents some empirical evidence on economic discrimination, captured by few micro level studies. The paper attempts to make a link between high incidence of poverty and caste based economic discrimination with special reference to scheduled castes. The analysis is based on data from National sample survey for employment/unemployment, land ownership, occupational pattern and poverty, and Rural Labour Enquiry Report for magnitude of wage labour and wage rates of the wage labour households.

I. Discrimination

Caste based customary laws relating to education, employment and property rights have been replaced by more egalitarian constitutional rules, under which scheduled castes are supposed to have an equal access. However, despite this change, the access to the income earning assets and other capital assets to the Dalits has not improved much. There are some doubts that, despite some statutory restrictions, caste-based discrimination continues to be widespread in contemporary India also. Almost every indicator of development for contemporary India shows that scheduled castes are more deprived than the rest of the population. According to the 2001 Census, only about 54 per cent of the Scheduled Caste population as a whole was literate; about 62 per cent of rural scheduled caste women did not have even basic literacy in 2001. Estimates show that the infant mortality rate among scheduled castes is about 45 per cent higher than the non-scheduled caste/non-scheduled tribe population.

Discrimination in Land Possession and Cultivation

The NSSO data[1] for 1999-2000 shows that the proportion of landless among scheduled castes was much higher (10%) than among others (5.8%). In 2004-05 it has got reduced from 10 per cent to 2.7 per cent for Scheduled Caste while the corresponding figure for others (Non SC/ST and OBC) is 2.0 per cent. Even among the scheduled caste households that had some land, about 65 per cent had marginal holdings in 1999-2000, and this section has increased to 72.2 per cent in 2004-05. The corresponding figures for other households were about 46 per cent and 50.5 per cent in 1999-2000 and 2004-05 respectively. Only one per cent scheduled caste households owned 4 and more than 4 hectares of land in 2004-05. The corresponding figure for others is 5.7 per cent. For details see Table 1a.

If we look at households that cultivate any land, the proportion of landless among scheduled castes was found 55 per cent and 57 per cent in 1999-2000 and 2004-05 respectively whereas the corresponding figures for others were 35 per cent and 37.7 per cent. Only 0.7 per cent scheduled caste households cultivated 4 and more than 4 hectares of land in 2004-05. The corresponding figure for others is 4.9 per cent. For details see Table 1b.

The Scheduled caste households in rural India work primarily as wage labourers. As per data from the Rural Labour Enquiries, about 61.4 per cent rural households of scheduled castes primarily depended on wage labour in 1999-2000.[2] The corresponding proportion for others was 25 per cent. See Table 2.

Table–1a
Land Possession for SC and Others (Non SC/ST)

Size in (Hectare)	*SC*				*ST*				*OBC**		*Others*			
	1987-88	*1993-94*	*1999-2000*	*2004-2005*	*1987-88*	*1993-94*	*1999-2000*	*2004-2005*	*1999-2000*	*2004-2005*	*1987-88**	*1993-94**	*1999-2000*	*2004-2005*
0.0-0.00	20.4	18.1	10.0	2.7		13.3	7.2	3.6	6.5	1.6	12.5	11.2	5.8	2.0
0.1-0.40	49.7	53.6	65.0	72.2		29.9	39.1	42.8	50.0	36.4	34.4	37.9	46.3	50.5
0.41-1.00	15.4	14.9	14.6	14.7		21.4	24.3	23.9	20.2	19.5	18.4	19.5	19.1	18.5
1.01-2.00	8.6	8.0	6.5	6.7		18.7	16.5	16.3	2.0	12.8	15.5	15.1	12.8	13.4
2.01-4.00	4.0	3.9	2.8	2.7		11.9	9.9	10.6	7.5	7.6	10.8	9.9	9.3	9.9
4.01 and above	2.00	1.5	1.1	1.0		4.8	3.0	2.9	3.8	4.0	8.4	6.4	6.7	5.7

Source: Employment/Unemployment situation among social groups in India, 43rd, 50th, 55th and 61st round survey NSSO.

Note: Others for 1987-88 and 1993-94 include OBCs also.

Table–1b
Land Cultivation by SC and Others (Non SC/ST)

Size in (Hectare)	*SC*				*ST*				*OBC**		*Others*			
	1987-88	*1993-94*	*1999-2000*	*2004-2005*	*1987-88*	*1993-94*	*1999-2000*	*2004-2005*	*1999-2000*	*2004-2005*	*1987-88**	*1993-94**	*1999-2000*	*2004-2005*
0.0-0.00	20.4	18.1	10.0	2.7		13.3	7.2	3.6	6.5	1.6	12.5	11.2	5.8	2.0
0.0-0.00	73.8	52.8	55.5	57.4		30.1	32.1	33.6	39.1	40.7	50.3	35.7	35.3	37.7
0.1-0.40		22.5	23.7	20.8		18.0	20.8	17.5	22.7	19.1		17.7	21.3	19.2
0.41-1.00	13.4	12.7	12.0	13.0		20.6	22.4	22.5	17.4	18.0	17.6	17.9	17.6	16.8
1.01-2.00	7.8	7.7	5.8	5.8		17.8	16.2	15.4	11.8	12.0	15.0	14.6	12.6	13.0
2.01-4.00	3.4	3.2	2.1	2.3		9.5	6.5	8.8	6.10	6.9	9.9	8.7	8.1	8.4
4.01 and above	1.6	1.2	0.7	0.7		4.0	2.0	2.1	2.80	3.2	7.2	5.4	5.1	4.9

OBC* Separate data for OBC is not available before 1999-2000.

Source: Employment/Unemployment situation among social groups in India, 43rd, 50th, 55th and 61st round survey NSSO.

Table–2
Magnitude of Rural and Agricultural Wage Labourers for SC and Others (Non-SC/ST)

Social Group	*Rural Labour Households (Percentage)*			*Agricultural Labour Households (Percentage)*		
	1987-88	*1993-94*	*1999-2000*	*1987-88*	*1993-94*	*1999-2000*
SC	63.13	59.45	61.41	51.7	49.28	51.37
Others	31.15	30.15	25.32	23.2	23.2	19.02

Source: Rural Labour Enquiry, report of general characteristics of rural labour households, 1987-88, 1993-94 and 1999-2000, Labour Bureau, Ministry of Labour, Shimla.

Discrimination in Occupational Status

As far as occupational pattern is concerned about 20 per cent of scheduled castes in rural households were engaged in agriculture as self employed in 2004-05.[3] The corresponding proportion for others was 43 per cent. In rural India about 34 per cent of scheduled caste households were engaged in some kinds of self employed activities in 2004-05. The corresponding figure for others was 61.4 per cent. About 56 per cent of scheduled castes rural households were engaged in casual and manual kinds of work for their livelihood in 2004-05. The corresponding figure for others was 23 per cent. (Table 3a).

Table–3a
Occupational Pattern for SC and Others (Non-SC/ST)-(Rural)

		Self-employed			*Labour*			
Social Groups	*Year*	*Agri-culture*	*Non-Agri-culture*	*Total*	*Agri-culture*	*Other*	*Total*	*Others*
SC	2004-05	20.2	14.1	34.2	40.5	15.4	56.0	9.8
	1999-2000	16.4	12.0	28.4	51.4	10.0	61.4	10.2
	1993-94	20.1	10.7	30.8	49.3	10.2	59.5	9.7
	1987-88	18.9	11.0	29.9	51.7	11.4	63.1	6.9
Others	2004-05	43.3	18.1	61.4	15.6	7.7	23.3	15.3

Contd...

Social Groups	*Year*	*Self-employed*			*Labour*			
		Agri-culture	*Non-Agri-culture*	*Total*	*Agri-culture*	*Other*	*Total*	*Others*
	1999-2000	41.1	14.8	55.9	19.0	6.3	25.3	18.7
	1993-94	43.3	14.4	57.7	23.2	6.9	30.2	12.1
	1987-88	43.3	13.8	57.1	23.2	7.9	31.1	11.5

Source: Employment/Unemployment situation among social groups in India, 43rd, 50th, 55th and 61st round survey NSSO.

Thus, in rural India the proportion of scheduled castes in self employed activities (in agriculture and non-agriculture) is about half (34%) as compared to the proportion of others (61.4%). Their proportion in rural labour households is more than double (56%) as compared to the proportion of others (23%).

In urban areas, the proportion of self employed among scheduled castes households increased by 3.4 percentage points between 1987-88 and 2004-05, while the same for other households increased by 3.4 percentage points. However, data shows continued wider gap between scheduled castes (29.4%) and others (38.6%). Between 1987-88 and 2004-05 the proportion of scheduled caste workers as casual workers decreased by about 4 per cent while proportion of other workers as casual workers also declined by about similar proportion (4%). Nevertheless, continuing gap exists in the level of casual labour between scheduled castes (21.8%) and others (6.2%). For details see table 3b.

Thus, while in rural India major proportion of scheduled castes (more than 61%) engaged in manual labour, in urban India they engaged in casual labour activities for their livelihood. The lower proportion of scheduled castes as self-employed workers in agriculture (in rural) and non-agriculture (in urban areas) as compared to others revealed continuation of lack of access to scheduled castes to ownership of agricultural land and capital assets. Inadequate accesses to agricultural land and capital assets (for self-employment activities) to Scheduled Castes leave no option for them except unskilled manual work. As a result this creates an enormously high level of wage labour among scheduled castes.

Table-3b
Occupational Pattern for SC and Others (Non-SC/ST) - (Urban)

Social Groups	*Year*	*Self-employed*	*Regular Wage/ Salaried Work*	*Casual Labour*	*Others*
SC	2004-2005	29.4	41.1	21.8	7.7
	1999-2000	27.3	37.6	26.5	8.5
	1993-94	24.9	39.2	27.6	8.3
	1987-88	26.0	39.4	26.0	8.5
Others	2004-2005	38.6	44.8	6.2	10.3
	1999-2000	35.5	46.5	7.4	10.5
	1993-94	35.5	43.9	10.8	9.8
	1987-88	35.2	45.0	10.3	9.2

Source: Employment/Unemployment situation among social groups in India, 43rd, 50th, 55th and 61st round survey -NSSO.

Disparities in Employment and Wage Rates

Since about 56 per cent of the scheduled caste workers in rural areas and about 22 per cent in urban areas depend on wage employment, obviously their earnings are determined by the level of employment and wage rate. Data based on from NSS report on employment/ unemployment and Rural Labour Enquiry report on wage rates indicate discrimination for scheduled castes in employment and wages compared to others. Table 4 shows the employment rate for the scheduled castes *vis-à-vis* the others for 1977-78, 1983, 1993-94 and 1999-2000. Based on UPS and UPSS the employment for scheduled castes was 54.58, 53.09, 52.90, 46.20 per cent as against 56.28, 55.75, 53.10, and 47.60 per cent for others in 1977-78, 1983, 1993-94 and 1999-2000 respectively. In case of UPS and UPSS we do not observe significant difference in the employment rate for scheduled castes and others. In fact employment rate for scheduled caste worker is slightly higher than that of others. There should not be any surprise, in case of UPS and UPSS a person is considered to be usually employed if he or she worked more than 180 days in a year. Since scheduled caste workers have limited source of income except wage labour, their participation in work in a year is likely to be higher than others. However, the employment rate based on current daily status (CDS) indicates the pathetic scenario of SCs. The employment rate of scheduled castes turns out to be lower than that of other workers. In 1977-78, 1983, 1993-94 and 1999-2000 the employment rates based on current daily status for scheduled caste male worker were at 54.58, 53.09, 52.90 and 46.20 per cent respectively, significantly lower as compared to 56.28, 55.75, 53.10 and 47.60 per cent for other workers respectively. Data shows similar gap in the level of women employment too. For details see Table 4.

Table–4a
Employment Rate for SC and Others (Non SC/ST)–(Rural)

Status	*1977-78*				*1983*			
	SC		*Others*		*SC*		*Others*	
	M	*F*	*M*	*F*	*M*	*F*	*M*	*F*
UPS	63.8	33.28	60.98	24.98	62.24	32.65	60.21	25.09
UPSS	NA	NA	NA	NA	64.15	44.29	61.56	35.75
CWS	60.04	30.27	59.46	23.98	58.45	28.99	58.78	23.32
CDS	54.58	24.44	56.28	20.12	53.09	24.16	55.75	20.42

Source: Employment/Unemployment situation among social groups in India, 32nd, 38th, 43rd, 50th and 55th round survey-NSSO.

Table–4b
Employment Rate for SC and Others (Non SC/ST)–(Rural)

Status	*1993-94*				*1999-2000*			
	SC		*Others*		*SC*		*Others*	
	M	*F*	*M*	*F*	*M*	*F*	*M*	*F*
UPS	54.90	25.5	54.40	21.20	52.4	25.20	50.9	15.5
UPSS	56.00	35.60	55.60	30.00	53.10	32.50	52.00	22.3
CWS	54.40	29.10	54.30	25.30	50.50	27.00	50.10	19.1
CDS	52.90	24.10	53.10	21.20	46.20	21.20	47.60	14.9

Source: Employment/Unemployment situation among social groups in India, 32nd, 38th, 43rd, 50th and 55th round survey- NSSO.

The unemployment data also shows similar wider gap between scheduled castes and others. In 1977-78, 1983, 1993-94 and 1999-

2000 the unemployment rates based on current daily status for scheduled caste male workers were at 6.73, 7.16, 4.30 and 5.0 per cent respectively, significantly higher as compared to 3.90, 4.03, 2.70 and 3.50 per cent respectively for other workers. For details see Tables 5a and 5b.

Table-5a
Unemployment Rate for SC and Others (Non SC/ST)-(Rural)

Status	*Others*									
	1977-78		*1983*		*1987-88*		*1993-94*		*1999-2000*	
	M	*F*	*M*	*F*	*M*	*F*	*M*	*F*	*M*	*F*
UPS	1.10	2.20	1.10	0.40	1.30	1.40	0.90	0.30	1.20	0.30
UPSS	NA	NA	0.76	0.23	0.90	1.10	0.60	NA	1.00	0.20
CWS	2.93	1.90	3.22	2.16	NA	NA	1.90	1.00	2.50	1.00
CDS	6.73	4.00	7.16	2.23	NA	NA	4.30	2.10	5.00	2.10

Source: Employment/Unemployment situation among social groups in India, 32nd, 38th, 43rd, 50th and 55th round survey NSSO.

Table-5b
Unemployment Rate for SC and Others (Non SC/ST)-(Rural)

Status	*Others*									
	1977-78		*1983*		*1987-88*		*1993-94*		*1999-2000*	
	M	*F*	*M*	*F*	*M*	*F*	*M*	*F*	*M*	*F*
UPS	1.57	1.53	1.30	0.43	1.70	0.48	1.20	0.44	1.60	0.50
UPSS	NA	NA	1.90	0.29	1.10	0.70	0.90	NA	1.20	0.50
CWS	2.15	0.97	2.15	0.91	NA	NA	1.60	0.80	2.50	1.20
CDS	3.90	0.97	4.03	1.72	NA	NA	2.70	1.11	3.50	1.40

Source: Employment/Unemployment situation among social groups in India, 32nd, 38th, 43rd, 50th and 55th round survey- NSSO.

Thus, lower employment and higher unemployment for scheduled castes based on current Daily status shows possible discrimination against them in labour market. However, much more empirical work is required to bring clarity on the issue.

We analyzed the employment/unemployment situation between scheduled castes and others, now let us see wage rate situation. Data from Rural Labour Enquiry Report on wage rate shows discrimination against scheduled castes compared to others, (Table 6). In 1973-74 and 1993-94, the daily wage received by the scheduled caste workers was Rs.11.38 and Rs. 21.74 in rural farm sector respectively as compared to Rs. 11.26 and Rs. 21.52 for others. Contrary to this exception, in 1973-74 and 1993-94 for non-agriculture, the wage was Rs. 13.53 and Rs. 30.62 for scheduled castes, significantly lower as compared to Rs. 14.21 and Rs. 32.48 for others.

Thus, above data shows no significant difference between scheduled castes and others in the level of daily wage received by them in agricultural activities. However, as we move on to non-agricultural activities clear difference emerges between scheduled castes and others in the level of daily wage rate. This shows possible daily wage discrimination against scheduled castes in non-agricultural activities.

In case of non-agricultural activities, wage rate was lower for scheduled caste worker in almost all the states as compared to other worker. In 1974-75 wage rate was lower for scheduled caste workers in 14 of 17 major states in non-agricultural activities, which include Andhra Pradesh, Assam, Bihar, Haryana, Himachal Pradesh, Jammu & Kashmir, Karnataka, Kerala, Maharashtra, Punjab, Rajasthan, Tamil Nadu, Uttar Pradesh and West Bengal. In 1993-94 it was lower in 13 states out of 17 major states which include Andhra Pradesh, Assam, Gujarat, Haryana, Himachal Pradesh, Jammu & Kashmir, Kerala, Orissa, Punjab, Rajasthan, Tamil Nadu, Uttar Pradesh and West Bengal, (See Table 6).

Table–6
Rural Wage Rate for SC and Others (Non SC/ST)

States	*Agriculture*				*Non-Agriculture*			
	1974-75		*1993-94*		*1974-75*		*1993-94*	
	ALL	*SC*	*ALL*	*SC*	*ALL*	*SC*	*ALL*	*SC*
A.P.	7.85	7.83	19.12	18.30	9.62	8.85	25.22	22.87
Assam	14.15	13.69	26.19	23.71	12.82	12.00	34.53	30.92
Bihar	10.04	10.10	10.93	16.98	11.97	10.48	24.04	25.30
Gujarat	10.56	11.29	20.06	18.40	10.20	10.66	35.34	28.68

Contd...

States	*Agriculture*				*Non-Agriculture*			
	1974-75		*1993-94*		*1974-75*		*1993-94*	
	ALL	*SC*	*ALL*	*SC*	*ALL*	*SC*	*ALL*	*SC*
Haryana	18.70	19.21	30.56	30.21	19.44	17.23	41.05	40.38
Himachal P.	19.47	18.82	30.95	31.21	18.43	17.70	36.52	36.55
J&K	20.17	71.35	35.40	34.55	19.28	18.38	34.11	31.01
Karnataka	9.25	9.60	19.20	19.58	12.75	12.71	28.47	30.45
Kerala	20.54	21.92	43.18	41.45	19.33	16.50	52.64	47.67
M.P.	6.84	7.08	17.04	17.84	7.93	8.30	22.43	22.57
Maharashtra	8.45	7.99	19.56	19.66	11.84	8.93	33.31	34.61
Orissa	7.60	7.66	1630	38.34	7.83	7.98	20.75	16.42
Punjab	24.83	24.95	41.98	42.55	23.70	22.43	43.18	40.78
Rajasthan	12.60	13.06	27.66	29.23	13.09	12.67	34.88	34.41
Tamil Nadu	9.70	9.47	25.11	24.63	11.68	10.60	30.71	28.45
U.P.	11.14	10.76	21.59	20.07	13.70	13.01	30.26	28.14
West Bengal	11.45	11.78	24.20	23.08	15.95	15.55	29.97	29.11
India	11.26	11.38	21.52	21.74	14.21	13.53	32.48	30.62

Source: Rural Labour Enquiry Report on wage earning 1974-75 and 1993-94, Labour Bureau, Ministry of Labour, Shimla.

Magnitude of Poverty Among Scheduled Castes and Others

As we have analyzed employment rate, wage rate is found less for scheduled castes as compared to non-scheduled caste population. Their participation in self-employed and regular salaried activities is less as compared to others. They are disproportionately represented in casual and manual labour activities which have multiple impacts on the magnitude of poverty among scheduled castes when we compare it with others.

In 1993-94 about half (48%) of the scheduled caste population was below poverty line in rural areas. The poverty level among scheduled casts was high as compared to 31 per cent among the others. The incidence of poverty was 60 per cent among agriculture labour followed by 41 among non-agriculture labour. The level was relatively low for person engaged in self-employed activities in agriculture or non-agriculture sector (about 38% each). However, for each of these household types, poverty was much higher among scheduled castes when compared to non-SC/STs. For details see Table 7a.

Table–7a
Percentage of Persons Below Poverty Line in Different Occupations (Rural)

Economic Activities	*SC*			*OTHERS*		
	1987-88	*1993-94*	*1999-2000*	*1987-88*	*1993-94*	*1999-2000*
Self employed (in agriculture)	41.21	37.70		25.57	25.57	
Self employed (in non agriculture)	41.60	38.19		31.42	29.49	
Agriculture labour	59.77	60.00		53.30	52.34	
Non agriculture labour	46.49	41.44		34.45	35.59	
Other labour	29.98	29.00		19.26	20.19	
All	50.07	48.14	35.43	34.37	31.29	21.14

Source: Based on consumption expenditure survey, NSSO, 1987-88 and 1993-94 (Estimated by S.K. Thorat).

Table–7b
Percentage of Persons Below Poverty Line in Different Occupations (Urban)

Economic Activities	*SC*			*OTHERS*		
	1987-88	*1993-94*	*1999-2000*	*1987-88*	*1993-94*	*1999-2000*
Self employed	61.48	54.60		33.60	33.64	
Regular salaried work	43.69	35.28		25.26	19.04	
Casual labour	73.45	69.48		70.10	60.60	
Others	56.84	45.00		32.21	26.06	
All	56.84	49.90		37.21	29.66	

Source: Based on consumption expenditure survey, NSSO, 1987-88 and 1993-94, (Estimated by S.K. Thorat).

In urban areas about 50 per cent of the scheduled castes were below the poverty line in 1993-94. This proportion was much higher compared to others (about 30%). The incidence of poverty was higher (about 70%) among casual labour followed by self employed (about 55%). For each of these household types, however poverty was much higher among scheduled castes compared to others (non-SC/ST). For details see Table 7b.

Poverty estimates presented by Professor Thorat and Venkatesan show that the head-count ratio (HCR) for scheduled castes was about 21 percentage points more than the HCR for other households in 1999-2000.[4]

Table-8

Trends in Poverty Incidence Among Caste Groups in India

Major States	*1983*		*1987-88*		*1993-94*		*1999-2000*			
Social Groups	*SC*	*All*	*SC*	*All*	*SC*	*All*	*SC*	*OBCs*	*Others*	*All*
Andhra Pradesh	37	27	51	40	26	16	31	21	10	22
Assam	43	43	49	26	45	45	44	39	40	40
Bihar	81	64	53	50	71	58	60	43	27	44
Gujarat	39	30	48	41	32	22	18	12	5	14
Haryana	36	21	44	23	47	28	19	12	1	8
Karnataka	53	36	54	43	47	30	26	16	12	18
Kerala	62	39	62	49	36	25	15	11	5	9
Madhya Pradesh	58	49	70	55	46	41	41	32	12	37
Maharashtra	59	45	65	41	52	38	33	22	14	24
Orissa	76	68	66	51	49	50	52	40	23	48
Punjab	26	13	37	24	22	12	13	7	1	7
Rajastan	40	33	52	40	38	26	20	10	6	14
Tamil Nadu	67	54	72	49	44	32	33	15	12	21
Uttar Pradesh	57	47	57	50	59	42	44	33	18	31
West Bengal	72	63	48	32	45	41	35	20	30	32
India	**58**	**46**	**56**	**42**	**48**	**37**	**36**	**27**	**15**	**27**

Source: NSS Reports for the year 1983, 87-88, 93-94 & 1999-2000, Govt. of India, (Estimated by Thorat and Venkatesan).

Thus, the macro level data shows continuing disparities among scheduled castes and other households, and high degree of economic deprivation and poverty among scheduled castes.

II. Caste and Economic Discrimination

Now, let us capture the evidences on forms and magnitude of caste-based economic discrimination with the help of empirical studies. Very few studies have empirically examined the nature and magnitude of economic discrimination. Some of the studies conducted are referred below.

Studies Related to Discrimination in Occupation, Jobs and in Wage Payment

An Andhra Pradesh study by Venketeswarlu observed that social ostracism is being used against scheduled castes in changing of occupations.[5]

In Karnataka, Khan found that nearly 85 per cent of the scheduled castes continue engaged with their traditional occupations in rural areas. In Urban areas, however, 56 per cent had experienced a shift away from traditional occupations.[6]

Banerjee and Knight's[7] in their 1991 study of the "Delhi urban job market during 1975-76" observed that there is indeed discrimination by caste, particularly job discrimination. Discrimination appears to operate through traditional mechanism, through which untouchables are disproportionately represented in poorly paid dead-end jobs. Discrimination is much more in jobs in which contacts are more important for recruitment, compared to white-collar jobs in which recruitment involves formal method.

A study conducted by action aid[8] in 2004 in ten states covering about 550 villages observed discrimination to the scheduled castes in a significant number of sample villages both in hiring and wage payment.[9]

Studies Related to Discrimination in Land Market, Credit Market, Interest Rate and Rent

An Orissa study by Tripathi in 1994 revealed discrimination in land lease, credit and in labour markets in rural areas; 96 per cent of Scheduled Caste respondents in one village and all in the second village were discriminated in regard to wage payment; 28 per cent in one village and 20 per cent in the other faced discrimination in the share of rent; and discrimination in interest rate charged by moneylender was found in both villages.[10]

Recently, Thorat along with Mahamalik and Panth has conducted a pilot study[11] 'Caste, occupation and labour market discrimination: A study of forms, nature and consequences in rural India.' The study has found significant caste discrimination against scheduled castes in multiple spheres, besides labour market. These are:

1. Labour Market Discrimination in Rural Farm Sector

A. Employment Discrimination

(*a*) In some cases exclusion of scheduled castes has been found in processing of some crops and in cutting of some crops.

(*b*) The work related to inside the house of higher castes - complete exclusion has been found in case of scheduled caste workers.[12]

B. Wage Discrimination

(*a*) Discrimination in payment of wage rate has not been observed in a significant manner between scheduled castes and others. However, time-interval in wage payment and installment of wage payment were found much unfavorable in the case of the scheduled castes.[13]

2. Land Market Discrimination

(*b*) Price discrimination has been found in case of scheduled castes. In other words scheduled castes were required to pay higher price in the time of purchasing land than the market price. It was also found that scheduled castes sold their land to higher castes at lower price than the market price.

(*c*) Scheduled castes faced restrictions on taking the house on rent in high caste locality and in buying the land to construct the house in high caste locality.[14]

3. Input Market Discrimination

(*a*) Restrictions have been found in selling of agricultural implements (such as bullock and bullock carts) owned by the higher castes farmers to the scheduled caste farmers.

(*b*) 20 per cent scheduled caste respondents reported denial of supply of bullock labour owned by higher caste. In other words higher castes farmers denied selling their bullocks to the scheduled castes farmers.

(*c*) 13 per cent respondents reported denial in hiring out bullock to scheduled castes farmers. In other words higher castes farmers denied providing bullocks' service on rent to the scheduled caste farmers.

(*d*) 26 per cent higher caste labourers denied working in the field of scheduled caste farmer.

(*e*) It is found that scheduled castes face denial of hiring of implements and transport equipments from the higher caste farmers.

(*f*) Scheduled castes faced restrictions on hiring out their bullock to the higher castes.[15]

4. Credit Market Discrimination

(*a*) Access of scheduled caste to informal credit is very less than the rest of the farmers.

(*b*) Lack of security makes the scheduled caste farmers handicapped to suffer from less access to credit.[16]

5. Product Market Discrimination

(*a*) In product market, scheduled caste person faces discrimination in selling the vegetable, milk and fruits to the higher castes consumers.

(*b*) It is found that generally scheduled castes face denial in selling vegetable, milk and fruits, in places where their caste identity is known.[17]

Concluding Remarks

First part of this paper pointed out widespread discrimination based on official sources among scheduled castes and others with respect to possession and cultivation of land, employment/unemployment rate, wage rates, access to capital assets and the extent of economic deprivation and poverty.

Second part presented empirical studies carried out by research scholars and academicians time to time. Studies show multiple discrimination against scheduled caste, i.e. in housing, rent payment on the loan, employment, wage payment, access to agriculture land, input market, credit market, product market and so on. Though studies have discovered the possible spheres where discrimination may involve, but are lacking in the recognition of exact forms and nature of discrimination. In other words, each issue needs specific study on forms, nature and extent of discrimination, through which appropriate policy could be formulated by the policy makers to overcome multiple forms of discrimination.

For instance, Madhya Pradesh Government in 2002 has fixed quota for SC/ST in government purchases; this initiative provides at least market access to SC/ST businessmen.[18] Besides sale and purchase of goods in the market there are many economic activities (i.e., sale and purchase of land for agricultural and non agricultural purposes, labour market, input market, credit market, product market, etc.) where caste based discrimination may involve. Each of above mentioned issue needs specific study of forms, nature and extent of discrimination, which could help the policy makers in formulating and implementing appropriate policies and programmes to annihilate the multiple forms of discrimination.

*Earlier version of this paper has been presented in a National Seminar at Department of Political Science, Satna, Madhya Pradesh.

NOTES AND REFERENCES

1. National Sample Survey Report on "Employment/Unemployment situation among social groups in India" 32nd, 38th, 43rd, 50th, 55th and 61st rounds. (New Delhi, Ministry of statistics and programme implementation, Government of India).
2. For details see Rural Labour Enquiry, report of general characteristics of rural labour households, 1987-88, 1993-94 and 1999-2000, (Shimla, Labour Bureau, Ministry of Labour).
3. Persons who operated their own farm or non-farm enterprises or were engaged independently in a profession or trade on own-account or with one or a few partners were deemed to be self-employed in household enterprises. The essential feature of the self-employed is that they have autonomy, i.e., how, where, and when to produce and economic independence (i.e. market, scale of operation and money) for carrying out their operation. *Employment and unemployment situation among social groups in India, 2004-05, 61st NSSO Survey.*
4. S.K. Thorat, S. Venkatesan, "Caste Conflict, Poverty and Human Development in India," WIDER, working paper, (2004).
5. For details see S.K. Thorat, Motilal Mahamalik and S. Ananth Panth, "Caste, Occupation and labour market discrimination: A study of forms, nature and consequences in rural India", (New Delhi, International Labour Organization, 2005).
6. *Ibid.*
7. *Ibid.*

8. *Ibid.*
9. S.K. Thorat, Motilal Mahamalik and S. Ananth Panth (2005), *op. cit.*
10. S.K. Thorat, "Caste, Economic Exclusion and Poverty: Dalit deprivation in India", DFID, working paper," (2003).
11. S.K. Thorat, Motilal Mahamalik and S. Ananth Panth, *op. cit.*
12. *Ibid.*
13. *Ibid.*
14. *Ibid.*
15. *Ibid.*
16. *Ibid.*
17. This Pilot study has been conducted by Thorat along with Motilal Mahamallik and S. Ananth Panth in three states, Gujarat, Maharashtra and Orissa on "*Caste, occupation and labour market discrimination: A study of forms, nature and consequences in rural India*" Sponsored by International Labour Organization *New Delhi*, 2005.
18. For example, see Bhopal declaration (Madhya Pradesh 2002) known as dalit agenda. In order to concretize the dream mentioned in Bhopal declaration for empowerment of a cross-section of dalits, the Government of Madhya Pradesh constituted a taskforce in 2003. The taskforce formulated a 21-point action agenda to cover six broad issues.

6

Discrimination and Humiliation: The Uttar Pradesh Experience

PRAGATI BURMAN AND SUDHAKARA KARAKOTI

Untouchability means pollution by touch of certain person by reason of their birth in a particular state of family.

—Dr. Ambedkar (1948)

Untouchability is the notion of defilement, pollution, contamination and the ways and means of getting rid of that defilement. It is the case of permanent hereditary stain which nothing can clean.

—Justice N. Sreenivas Rao (1948)

Untouchability is a nationwide institution indicating three features of often observing pollution, asking to live outside of the village and not giving equal legal protection.

—M.K. Gandhi (1933)

The condition of the Scheduled Castes in many pockets of India is worse than animals; they have no place of respect and honour in the caste ridden Hindu social order. The so-called upper castes are proud of their social mores and they found nothing unusual and unbecoming in their social thinking and behavior. For them it is a divinely ordained injunction and hence to be practiced with impunity. The paper mainly deals with the socio-economic profile of Dalits in Uttar Pradesh in rural areas. There are five case studies depicting various incidents of discrimination concerning Scheduled Castes on the basis of caste. The five narratives show the vulnerable condition of the scheduled castes who are denied basic human rights where SCs are discriminated by not only the so-called upper caste Hindus but Muslims also treat the dalits with equal hatred.

The dalits have been formally excluded from religion, from education, and is a pariah in the entire sanctified universe of the 'dwijas.'

The world has moved too far, by the advance of science and technology; man has conquered space and time but the condition of the Dalits have not changed to the desired extent and they are subjected to humiliation and harassment. For centuries they have been the beasts of burden, tillers of land, hewers of wood and the carriers of water. They are looked upon as household chattels and could be met with any raw deal. The condition of Dalits begs description as daily there are some incidents and happenings where lower section of the society is at the receiving end. No doubt, there is an improvement in economic conditions of the Dalits but in social terms they had been denied the basic human rights. Untouchability is practiced in every walk of life and the Dalits had to bear its brunt silently. Especially in the rural areas the social conditions of the downtrodden people are worst. Caste for so-called upper caste is divine institution sanctioned by God and sanctified by the Hindu Shastras.

Untouchability is a distinct social institution that legitimizes and enforces practice of discrimination against people born in certain castes.[1] Some people are treated as untouchables either temporarily or otherwise for various reasons. As per the Hindu belief, certain aspect of life, in particularly those related to birth, death, and body secretions are treated as impure. Accordingly some people associated with some occupations are considered as impure. Women who have just given birth, women during their menstruating period and death in a family renders the members temporarily impure, but people carrying impure occupations like skinning of dead animals, removal of human waste, cleaning, washing cloths, delivering babies are regarded as permanently polluting. Such people are called as 'untouchables' who are not allowed to use public places. People maintain distance from them so as to avoid contact. The arrival of Aryans in India led to the division of society into castes on the basis of occupation. Individuals performing above said impure occupations were gradually treated as untouchables. The people born in these castes were regarded as untouchables on the basis of birth, with the establishment of caste system in the Indian society.

They were not allowed to use public roads, wells, temples and schools. Thus the concept of untouchability is based on purity and pollution.[2]

Caste system and untouchability, the two main pillars of Hindu social order, presents a unique case. As a system of socio economic and religious governance it is found not on the principle of liberty, equality and fraternity—the values which formed the basis of universal human rights - but on the principle of inequality in every sphere of life. In Ambedkar's view, the doctrine of inequality is the heart core of the Hindu social order. It leaves no difference between legal philosophy (law) and moral philosophy (morality).[3]

The unique features of the caste system need to be understood here. In the social sphere the caste system involves division of people into social groups (castes). The social, religious, cultural and economic rights of members of the castes are predetermined in advance by birth into that caste and are hereditary, an unequal distribution of these rights across caste groups and provision of a mechanism of social and economic exclusion calculated to ensure rigid adherence to the system and justification of the social system by the philosophy of Hinduism. In the sphere of economic rights, the Hindu social order also lays down a system of distribution, namely, it fixes the occupations for each caste by birth and its hereditary continuation; unequal distribution of these economic rights related to property, trade, employment, wages, education, etc. among the caste groups; and hierarchy of occupation based on social stigma.[4]

These features imply that the Hindu social order is based on three interrelated elements, namely predetermination of social, religious and economic rights of each caste based on birth; the unequal and hierarchical (graded) division of these rights among the castes; and provision of strong social, religious and economic barring supported by social and religious ideology to maintain the Hindu social order. In this framework the concept of "human rights" under the Hindu social system takes on a specific meaning. Unlike other human societies, the Hindu social order in its classical form does not recognize the individual and his distinctiveness as the center of the social purpose. The unit of the Hindu society is not the individual. Even the family is not regarded as a unit of society except for the purposes of marriages and inheritance. The primary unit of society is caste. There is no room for individual merit and the consideration of individual justice. Rights that an individual has are not due to him personally; it is due to him because he belongs to a particular caste. Similarly, if an individual suffers from a lack of rights, it is not because he deserves it by his conduct. The disability is imposed upon the caste and as a member of the caste that is his lot.[5]

The other implication is that the caste system also involves the principle of rank and gradation, in so far as the rights increase in ascending order from untouchable to Brahmin. It is a hierarchically interlinked system. In this framework castes are artfully interlinked with each other in a manner such that the rights and privileges of higher castes become the disabilities of the lower castes, particularly the Dalits. In this sense, in Dr. Ambedakar's view, the caste in a single number cannot exist. Caste can exist only in plural number. There cannot be such a thing as caste as a singular phenomenon. So one has to look at the castes as a system, where each is interlinked with other in unequal measures of social, religious, economic relations and rights.[6]

This hierarchically interlinked character of the caste system implies a concept of "human rights" and "human hood" which is different and unique. In this particular order of hierarchy the Brahmins are not only placed at the top but are considered to be "superior social beings" worthy of special rights and privileges. At the bottom, the untouchables are treated as "sub-human beings or lesser human beings" considered unworthy of many rights. Untouchables are considered as inferior social beings and therefore not entitled to any individual rights, i.e., civic, religious, political and economic. In fact, the disabilities are so severe that they are physically and socially isolated and excluded from the rest of the Hindu society. Isolation and exclusion of untouchables is a unique feature of the Hindu social order. Classes or social groups are common to all societies, but as long as the classes or social groups do not practice isolation and exclusiveness they are only non-social in their relations towards one another. "Isolation and exclusiveness" makes them anti-social and inimical to one another.[7]

Untouchability is an intrinsic feature of Hindu caste system that governs all aspects of life. It is a distinct Indian social instrument that legitimizes and enforces the practice of discrimination against people born in particular castes, and legitimizes practices that are humiliating, excluding and exploitative.[8] It is widely prevalent in the society, particularly in rural areas. Lower caste people are discriminated on the basis of castes; they are given subordinate position in the society. Despite being termed as 'unconstitutional', untouchability is practiced in different forms both in public and private spheres.

Everyday incidences of brutal violence against lower castes reveal that caste based oppression and discrimination is still alive and flourishing. The upper caste people often target SCs when they seek to assert their constitutional right of equality. When they demand justice they are met with violence by the upper castes in order to teach them a lesson that they should keep to their place. Dalits are often reminded of their inferior status. In some parts of the country they are not even allowed to walk through the village streets wearing clean and bright cloths, or their shirts tucked in, not allowed to draw from the wells and hand pump situated in the areas of the so-called upper caste people, and are served tea in separate glasses only meant for them, which they have to wash.[9]

A few years back, noted social scientist and civil rights activist Praful Bidwai wrote:

> The vicious oppression of 160 million Dalits is one of the most nauseating, but enduring, realities of India's countryside. To be a Dalit today means having to live in a sub-human, degraded, profoundly insecure way. Every hour, two Dalits are assaulted in India. Every day, three Dalit women are raped; two Dalits are killed. This violence has a definite function: to perpetuate the hierarchical Hindu social order, freeze inequalities, including inequality of opportunity, defend social bondage and servitude, and preserve conditions for the ruthless exploitation of the Underprivileged.[10]

Uttar Pradesh: Socio-economic Profile of Dalits in Rural Areas

Uttar Pradesh with a population of about 170 million souls is a backward state and the atrocities on the lower classes were committed with vengeance. 'Historically, Dalits have been among the most subordinate and poorest of the people in India who have been subjected to various kinds of social discrimination and economic deprivation.'[11] 'The landowning castes are mainly the Rajputs, Tyagis or Bhumihars, Jats, Gujjars, Kurmis and Lodhas mostly inhabited in rural areas. The SCs are not monolithic whole but are divided into 66 sub-castes. The Chamars top the list followed by Pasis, Dhobis, Koris, Valmikis, Khatiks and others. Among them the Chamars are the most numerous, comprising about 60 per cent of the total SC population in UP. The Chamars includes Jatav, Ravidasi, Ramdasia, Kureel, Dhore, Dhusia, Ahirwar, Jaiswar, Sankhwar and Mochi. One positive aspect about them is that by and large, they are an integrated community and inter-dining and intermarrying among them is common.[12] In the whole of north India Chamars are the strongest community and of late, they have made strides in education and economically they are well too. In services also, the Chamars are relatively in a well dominant position. As far the economic status of the SCs is concerned, they are the poorest and owns only one per cent of land.[13] The lot of Depressed Classes has remained miserable and economically poor. A large majority of the Dalit population is clustered in the ranks of landless labourers. It is against them whom the upper castes commit subtle forms of violence. The western part of UP is prosperous and progressive and the people are enterprising. The relationship between the SCs and upper castes assumed an ugly form in the eastern parts of UP where the caste system is rigid and the SCs are at the receiving end. The upper castes are not accommodating and they instigated the backward classes to keep the Dalits under their thumb. The confrontation in the villages was normally between the lower castes on one hand and the backward landowning classes on the other The Yadavs, Kurmis, Lodhas, Bhumihars and others did not show any mercy towards the lower castes. They can be as cruel as predators. No day in UP passes without incidents of beating, rape, arson against the people belonging to depressed castes. Caste Hindus have traditionally utilized public humiliation of Dalits to weaken them from challenging their oppressed status. Most of these crimes are not even reported because of police collusion with the perpetrators and fears of retaliation.[14]

Untouchability has assumed subtle and not so subtle, in fact extremely blatant, forms as well and has spread its tentacles in various segments of the body politics. The alliance between the backward castes and the SCs in UP could not endure for long and though the Samajwadi Party under the leadership of Mulayam Singh and BSP shared power, yet their partnership ultimately failed due to the differences that cropped up between them. Actually most of the atrocities on the dalits were perpetrated in the majority of the cases by the land owning upper and backward classes. The lower castes are mainly landless labourers, working on the farms of the upper castes. The immediate clash of the lower castes is with landed backward classes who seldom hesitate to use force against them. In majority of the cases, the backward classes like Kurmis and forward castes like Bhumihars were more aggressive and cruel than the other upper castes.[15] Here a few instances of blatant caste discriminations and humiliations are mentioned, where the scenario is rampant in the state of Uttar Pradesh till date.

Case 1: Dalits are Denied the Use of Spare Village Land

Bhaupur, a village 3 kilometers west of Saharanpur district, of Uttar Pradesh is a Rajput (Thakur) dominated village where the old social customs and practices easily dampens the enthusiasm of the Dalits who had to face social disabilities at the hands of the Thakurs who were too conscious of their upper caste social status and looked upon the Chamars with disdain and discrimination. 'The Thakurs were the land owning people, men of wealth, means and status. Though the Thakurs were not more in number than the Chamars, but the Pradhan of the village, Sher Singh was a Thakur.'[16] He was a man of narrow minded outlook, and was caste conscious. In his eyes lower castes carried no weight and they should meekly obey the Thakurs. The Chamars in the village were all landless labourers. They live in congested locality where there was hardly any place to sit outside. No land was left for them. Neither any ground for holding functions nor play-grounds for Dalit children. All the Gram Samaj land was under the illegal possession of the upper castes. The only open place left in that village for Chamars was the ground in front of the village primary school. Whenever any marriage party of the dalits used to come to the village, they were accommodated as guest on the premises of the village primary school. Children also used to play there, as the Thakurs did not let them play in their empty fields. The upper caste Thakurs were jealous of the fact that Chamars are making use of the land even if it was of Gram Samaj land that means government land. It was hard for them to see that the Dalits were getting any benefits from the government property. Though many of the times they warned the Chamars not to use the land but they had no alternative left as there was no land for them.[17]

Pala, a Chamar by caste fixed his daughter's marriage. He worked as a landless labourer on the fields of Thakurs. He was a poor man and had a large family to support. The *barat* was to come from a nearby village from a Chamar community. As usual the school ground was the only place to accommodate the marriage procession. The *barat* came on the date fixed. When the *barat* procession entered the village the Thakur Pradhan came with other Thakurs of the village to obstruct its way. The Thakurs asked the groom to get down from the horse. They could not bear a Chamar sitting on a horse in front of them. They decided to teach a lesson to them so that in future they don't dare to disobey. One of them shouted at the poor Chamars:

> You Chamars have forgotten your status.
> We will teach you how to behave.
> You should never forget your low caste.[18]

The lower caste bridegroom was dragged down from the horse. The Pradhan and other Thakurs started beating the groom and his relatives and who came in the *barat*. They were not allowed to go towards the place where arrangements for them were made. The Chamars wept and wailed helplessly but nobody came to help and rescue them. Even the Chamar community remained silent spectator to the hideous drama. People moved about unconcerned as if nothing unusual happened. What can they do as they were no match to the Thakurs? Moreover, most of them work on the lands of Thakurs. They can't afford to displease their masters. Their children will die of hunger if they dared to oppose. The upper castes were so accustomed to the unequal social structure that they saw nothing unusual and unbecoming of it. They could not tolerate any Dalit raising voice against them. They gave a go to human values, for them the unequal and discriminatory social ethos were the real culture which they adored in art, literature, dance and drama; and their scriptures and Shastras were always singing praises of the diabolic caste system. The untouchables being too weak socially, economically and politically were not able to fight against the onslaught of caste. The only lesson they have learnt is that if they want to survive they had to suffer. The lower castes have been tormented for centuries. For them the coming day only brings sorrow and sufferings. In a hierarchical and compartmentalized social pattern it becomes impossible for a poor man to cross social barriers.

His position is worst than an animal and he could be given a raw deal any time by the upper castes.

After sometime the Pradhan, Sher Singh got a boundary wall constructed round the school ground and a gate was built with iron doors and locked. So that in future no Dalit dared to use the place in front of the school. Even the Dalit children were forbidden to play there.[19]

Case 2: Dalit Houses are Demolished

In Indian villages, the rural economy was mainly agro based, as land is the means of livelihood and employment to many and it also led to conflicts and confrontation. Most of the land in the villages was under the possession of the upper caste whereas the people from the lower classes had to work as labourers and they were paid inadequately. They were reduced to the status of serfs and slaves. The landlords dictated their terms to them. The dalits everywhere in India suffered because they did not have land. The upper caste farmers were a clever lot and always tried to deprive the lower castes people even of 'Gram Samaj Land'.[20] They wanted to have all land in their possession. Moreover, the dalits were paid meagerly, i.e., in kind and rarely in cash. Land gives respect and esteem in rural society; so dalits also want to have some land to have the feeling of independence. But the upper castes kept them in perpetual social bondage and even a *bigha*[21] or two of land owned by the dalits was intolerable to them. They knew it well that possession of land by the lower classes would lessen their dependency and give stability and respect to them. This has been so for centuries and even in independent India the lot of the untouchables in the villages remained static and unchanged.[22]

Tajopur was a Thakur dominated village as they were in an overwhelming majority; there were 300 families of the Rajputs, all well to do and were called as Babu Sahibs, whereas the Chamars had only fifty families. No chamar had land for cultivation; they were mostly landless labourers, earned living by working on the land of Rajputs as farm labourers. All the 'Gram Samaj Land' in the village was under the illegal possession of the Thakurs. The Chamars as labourers were paid only 2.5 kg of food grains of inferior quality and little money. They also depended on the land of Thakurs for collecting fodder for the cattle.[23] The Thakurdom prevailed in the village. The poor chamars could not question the superiorty of the upper castes. The Rajputs were thus the undisputable lords of the village and any opposition to them was intolerable. The Chamars lived in segerated bastis and untouchability was observed strictly. They were forced to do *bigar* along with it they removed the skin of the dead animals. There was no question of inter-mixing and inter-dining. This condition prevailed in most of the villages of Eastern Uttar Pradesh. Some awakening had also come among the lower castes and their children went to school to learn the three RS. There were five Chamar graduates (B.A.) in the village. Among them, one Mukhram, son of Jaggu, was running a pan shop and with difficulty he was carrying on his existence whereas the other Chamar graduates were unemployed.

The cause of conflict between the Thakurs and the Chamars in Tajopur village was land. It was only 2.5 bighas of banjar land of Khasra no. 1333. This land has been in occupation of the Chamars for years, as it was used by them to skin the dead animals and some of them had also their houses there for convenience. Doodhnath Chamar was one of them. The Rajput Thakurs did not want them to keep a piece of land even if it is banjar. It was recorded as a banjar land and Chamars had acquired prescriptive rights over it because of long usage. This did not go well with the Thakurs who wanted to dispossess the Chamars of this plot.

Therefore, on 17 July 1996, Thakurs of the village came with four tractors, to occupy and plough the land. The Chamar women at first came to stop them but failed. They pleaded the Thakurs not to destroy their houses. People from dalits locality gathered and tried to restrain them from demolishing the house of poor Dalits in the field. Doodhnath's wife pleaded but of no use. The upper caste landlords were haughty and overbearing. The Chamars helplessly saw the thakurs destroying the house of Doodhnath. His wife Champa was screaming and crying for help but no one came forward to help. Her husband was not at home at that time. Kangar Ram a middle aged person, who was a tailor by profession, shouted from the crowd:[24] "We have no land and to have fodder for our cattle will become problematic for us if we oppose the Babu Sahibs."[25]

Within ten minutes the houses of Doodhnath and others were brought down to land. The wives and children kept weeping but there was no effect on the Babu Sahibs' people. They ploughed the land with the tractor. The utensils, cloths and other household articles of Doodhnath and others were destroyed by the Thakurs with their tractor. There was panic among the Chamars. Jai Nath Thakur roared from the tractor, "You Chamars are beasts of burden, fit only to serve and work like animals. How dare you posses land."[26]

Peace for the lower class meant slavery. Sixty two years of independence failed to bring any desirable change in the social condition of the lower castes. There lacked a social cohesion and awakening and majority of them were satisfied with some economic gains, which were paltry and only suffice to meet their day-to-day needs.

Case 3: Harassment of Dalit Family Residing in Upper Caste Basti

No doubt the Dalits led a life of disgrace and humiliation. Everywhere in India, the plight of the depressed classes was similar and the atrocities over them were a matter of routine. They were only to obey and carry out the commands of these so-called upper castes who should be served. Same was the condition of Berla, situated about 10 kms away from Saharanpur city, in the western Uttar Pradesh, across the polluted river Hindon. It was predominantly a Muslim majority village where the population of the lower caste, mainly the 'Khatik caste'[27], was about 15 per cent. The condition of the Khatik in the village was far from satisfactory. They were landless labourers who earned their living either by working as unskilled labourers in municipal area of Saharanpur, as rickshaw pullers and mason workers or went to work on the farms of the village Muslims as agricultural labourers. Their economy largely depends on land, and their women folks also worked as daily wage earners. No Khatik family except one owned some land for cultivation. There is no education among SCs, and in the population of 500 Khatiks there were only two boys with some education but both of them were unemployed. The government-sponsored schemes were yet to reach them, as all the benefits were enjoyed by the high caste people who owned and cultivated land.[28]

Majority of the Muslims were prosperous with good income and status. Some had milch cattle and the earning by selling milk was considerable. This had made them arrogant towards lower caste Khatiks. The condition of the scheduled castes living in the Muslim dominated village was no better than those in the Hindu majority villages. The upper caste Muslims are bigots and tended to be overbearing in their day to day behaviour; the seven hundred year old rules of Muslims have made them self-conscious and communal. The upper caste Muslims, '*Ashrafs*',[29] practiced untouchabitiy like the upper caste Hindus. Almost in all Muslim villages untouchability was observed and practiced. Even after independence, there had been not much change in the psyche of the upper castes irrespective of them being Hindu or Muslim. Muslims in India are not free from caste biases, and among them were also Jat, Gujjar, Rajput and Tyagi Muslims. Though all these upper castes swore by Quran, yet they had their distinct customs and social practices. The Pathans, Sayyeds and Mughals considered themselves superior and are called as Ashrifs whereas the lower castes among them were called as 'Ajlis'.[30]

The village of Berla was in no way different from other Muslim majority villages. The Khatiks lived on the south of the village and suffered from social indignities. All lived in one contiguous area whereas the Muslims had their own separate locality. As farmers and influential persons they had space and education. The Pradhan of the village was a lady, Rehana, wife of Chhotan Teli. The relationship of Khatiks and Muslims was based on unequal social ethos and it has assumed a semblance of slavish cordiality because there was no friction and the lower castes meekly accepted their second class status. They lacked the capacity for resistance. In Muslim dominated area they had the mentality of a ruling race. They look back at their past with a feeling of pride. The harassment and humiliations of the Dalits by the Muslims were frequent. Though they lived in separate areas, yet they could not escape occasional misdemeanor at their hands. The Muslims could not tolerate Dalits living near them. The SC localities in the village are congested and dirty and lack sufficient living space. Muslims here tended to be fanatics and could do anything in the name of religion. Such was the fate of a Khatik family of Jagdish whose house was among the Muslims. The poor dalit family was tortured and victimized for this.[31]

Jagdish a rickshaw puller in the city had a large family of five sons and four daughters. None of his children went to school; all of them remained at home helping their parents. Wife Kamla worked as labourer. The Muslim Tyagis hated them and didn't like a Dalit family to reside among them. Feeling piqued and chagrined they took resort to various ways to pester the family. They found ways to trouble them. Four years back the daughter of Jagdish, Rajbala who was only nine years was chased and beaten by four Muslim Tyagi boys without any reason, while she was cutting grass. When the girl cried, some people working in the nearby fields came at her rescue.[32] The children of Tyagis would tease them by calling them "Chuhre" "Chamar". Zahroo, a Tyagi Muslim was their neighbour who always found ways to annoy and disturb them. He was a prosperous farmer and had a tractor. He also had good income through supplying milk to the city. The behaviour of Tyagi Muslim was just as that of Hindu Tyagi. He was a vicious man and so was his family. Other Muslims instigated him against Jagdish's family. Even if ever Jagdish's children went out wearing clean cloths they had to hear taunts of Zahroos' family . If Jadish's children wore neat and clean cloths they were teased like:

abey, Khatik ke, why are you dressed in new cloths.

If one went wearing old and shabby clothes, then they used to say,

abey Khatik ke get away from us, you stink.[33]

This was their no-win situation. They were humiliated whichever way they lived. Once Zahroo's two sons forcefully entered Jagdish's house while elders were not at home. They started swearing about mothers and sisters. Jadish's youngest son was playing. There was no one else home at that time. Methab, Zahroo's elder son, grabed Kalu by his neck as a wolf; he dragged him out of his house and threw him on the ground and screamed, 'abey Khatik ke, motherfucker, where are you hiding.... Your mother....' The other son of Zahroo, Rukhsan, also went for Kalu who was on the ground. He began to slap and kick him mercilessly. It seemed like a ruffian was roughing up an innocent victim. 'Abey brother-in-law, progeny of a Khatik, let me know when you die. Today will draw oil from your tresses.' Meanwhile Methab was beating Kalu whereever he found place, the village crowd started gathering. But no one protested or retaliated. Every follicle of his body was trembling with fear. The Tyagi boys were shouting, 'If you Khatiks continue to live in our area see then what we will do with you. Leave this place as soon as possible or we will burn you and your house.'[34]

Case 4: Disallowing Dalits to Cast their Votes

Bahadurpur village, in Bijnor in Saharanpur district, of Uttar Pradesh is an upper caste dominated village where the old social values, practices and traditions were in force. Untouchability was practiced in meticulous details and the lower class people had to observe and follow the social norms obediently as if divinely ordained. It was considered all right to touch dogs and cats or cows and buffaloes, but if one happened to touch a 'Bhangi',[35] one gets contaminated or polluted.[36] Bhadurpur had mixed population but the domination of the upper caste was unquestioned; there were 250 families of Jats, 60 of Bhangi and 6 Barber caste families. Though both Bhangis and Barbers are SC castes but there is no inter-dinning and inter-marrying among them. The Valmikis were mainly concerned with cleaning of the village and removing and skinning dead animals. They clean the households of the Jats. Every person of the Valmiki caste had to clean the baithak and the ghers of 8 to 10 Jats, had to pick up dung and bring to the place where uplas or cow dung cakes were made. They usually got five seers of grain per two animals. They led a life of misery and destitution. They did not have land; it was in possession of the Jats, some of them also went to brick kilns to earn their living.[37]

The dominant Jats never let the poor Bhangis to cast their votes. The lower castes were not aware of their rights. The Bhangis and the Barber castes never thought of casting their votes nor were they acquainted with the fact that it is their fundamental right. The Jats used to stand in front of the polling booths with spears, lathis and country made pistols. No Dalit was allowed to come near the building. It was announced in the village before elections that no one from Bhangi and Barber castes would come out of their houses; if any one dared to oppose them he was beaten. This was the scene of the village in every election whether it was of Panchayat or for MP or MLA. The Jats themselves used to cast their votes to the candidates of the upper caste. Even the polling officers sent by the government present on the polling booths were threatened by them. If any lower caste person ever tried to complain, they were tortured and beaten. The police of the area was also under the influence of the high caste Jats, as they were benefited from them in many ways. The helpless dalits had no alternative but to obey and to carry out their commands.[38]

A BSP worker Nakli Ram, who was in Chandpur village to undertake cader camp, listened about Bahadurpur village where the Bhangis were not allowed to caste their vote. He asked some of the individuals from Chandpur to come with him to this village. The election for Lok Sabha was about to take place in which Mayawati was one of the candidates fielded by BSP. It was decided that Nakli Ram and some of the BSP workers of the village will go to Bahadurpur one day before the election. On the fixed day Nakli Ram with other local BSP workers entered the village. There were only people from Jat community present at the polling booth. Nakli Ram and his associates inquired about the absence of the other caste people but they got no straight answer. The moment the Jats knew that they were BSP workers and belongs to lower caste they got alarmed. Nakli Ram and his people started getting life threats from the Jats.

Kallu, a young man from Bhangi caste came to Nakli Ram's help. He used to sell bangles on his bicycle from village to village. Kallu brought them to his house and explained him the condition of the village and of the lower castes. Nakli Ram with the help of Kallu called for a meeting of the Bhangi and Barber caste people. In the meeting it was asked:

> Who wants to come with us tomorrow?
> I want people who are ready to fight for their community
> I have come here because I have no fear of death and I believe that my people wherever they live should live with dignity and freedom
> So brothers come with us.[39]

Next day, on the day of the election Nakli Ram went to the election booth with the people collected from the village and the local BSP workers of the area. The Jats were never challenged by the lower castes in that village. When they went to the polling booth the upper caste people present there tried to stop them but when the Jats saw that they can no more stop them they left after some fight. The Bhangis and Barber caste people voted for the first time in their lives.[40]

Case 5: Fining Dalits for Using Public Water Tank

Budhakheda village in Roorkee district in Uttar Pradesh had mixed population of Gujjars, Chamars, Bhangis and few houses of Gadariya caste. Among them the Gujjars were in majority and were dominant and influential caste. They were well off.

Outside on the east of the village was a public tank where separate ghats for the upper and lower caste for bathing were reserved. The lower castes including Chamars, Bhangis and Gadariyas were not allowed to use the ghats meant for the upper castes. The Sarpanch of the village was a lady from Gujjar community who was, though progressive, but under the impact of the upper castes bigots. The workers of VHP and Bajrang Dal were active in the village and preached the doctrine of Hinduism. Many of the Gujjar caste people were active members of these groups. During the summers the water of the ghats meant for Dalits used to recede, but ghats meant for the upper castes were built in such a way that even during the dry season water was available to them. The poor dalits had to face hardships during the summers as they face difficulties in bathing their cattle and washing cloths and other household articles. Yet they were restricted from the use of upper caste ghats.[41]

One day two of the sons of Hari Singh, who was Chamar by caste, Babu and Chotu, took bath in the village tank at the Gujjar ghat. The news of the Dalit polluting the water source spread like a wild fire in the village. Wave of anger and resentment took the entire village. The Gujjars took it as an insult and were not ready to tolerate this unprecedented audacity of the Chamar untouchables who had defiled the well established social norm. It created uproar among the arrogant Gujjars. After a week's confabulation and consultation panchayat was held in the village, in which the overwhelming majority was of the upper castes. The thousand years old hatred was once again visible in its original form. Ghansham, one of the elderly people of the panchayat, shouted on Hari Singh. Obscenities begin to rain from the mouth of the elder's mouth. His eyes were fierce and his body harboured devil. Lifting a heavy stick from underneath the *charpai*, the elderly hit Hari Singh on his back.

> Abey Chamar your sons have forgotton who they are
> Just because they have learnt few words.
> Don't forget who you are....[42]

The Panchayat asked Hari Singh to pay rupees fifty one thousand (Rs. 51000) as a fine to the village or leave the village. Poor Hari Singh who earned his living by working in a nearby factory on daily wages had a big family to support. It was obvious that it was impossible to pay such a big amount of money for him. No one among the SCs protested or retaliated. Every follicle of Hari Singh's body trembled with fear.[43]

Conclusions

The above-mentioned incidences of atrocities on lower castes are not a new phenomenon. These techniques are used by the upper castes to enforce their power and to maintain their superior status. These narratives show how the civil rights which all citizens should be entitled to are not only denied to the SCs, but whenever they made attempts to exercise they had to face upper caste atrocities. Since the upper castes control the rural economy, the lower castes are in no way to assert their rights as they depend on them. Their access to work, land, credit, merchandise and public facilities is cut off. All the means of living are under the control of the few privileged people from upper castes.[44]

In the end the question is: why do the higher castes continue to practice untouchability, and discrimination in social, cultural, religious, political and economic spheres? And why do they resort to physical and other violence when the untouchables try to gain lawful access to human rights and equal participation in social, political, cultural, religious and economic sphere of community life? The reasons for widespread practice of untouchability, discrimination and atrocities as well as violent reaction by the higher castes are to be found in their continuing belief and faith in the sanctity of the institution of caste and untouchability. The traditional Hindu social order continues to govern the thought process and behavior of the large majority of Hindus in rural areas. The provisions in the Constitution and law are secular and equal, but the customary rules of the caste system and the institution of untouchability are based on the principle of inequality in social, economic, cultural and religious sphere. This obviously brings a conflict between what is contained in the constitution and law, and what is contained in the traditional customary rules, norm, and values of the caste system and untouchability. People continued to follow the latter because it provides immense privilege and serves their social, political and economic interests. And when the dalits try to get equal access and assert their rights, it often invites the wrath of higher caste persons in the form of atrocities and physical violence. About the reasons for the atrocities on the SC/ST, the Report of the Commission of the SC/ST in 1998 observed:

> Some of the major causes of atrocities and other offences against Scheduled Castes and Scheduled Tribes are related

to issues of land and property, access to water, wage payments, indebtedness and bonded or forced labour. Issues of human dignity, including compulsion to perform distasteful tasks traditionally forced on Scheduled Castes, and molestation and exploitation of dalit women are also involved. Caste related tension is exacerbated by economic factors, which contribute to violence. It is the assertion of their rights, be they economic, social or political, by the Scheduled Castes and Scheduled Tribes and their development, which often invite the wrath of the vested interests. Disputes during elections, animosity due to reservation, jealousy due to increasing economic prosperity, violence related to the process of taking possession and retaining Government allotted land, tension due to refusal of SCs to perform tasks such as disposal of dead cattle or cutting umbilical cord, are manifestations of the resentment of the high caste against increasing awareness among Scheduled Castes, assertion and prosperity among the SCs. Like land, water is another sensitive issue. Accessibility of drinking water and water for irrigation and disposal of water removed from water logged areas become issues that can trigger off atrocities on SCs. Castiest favour during religious and social ceremonies, disputes arising during sowing and harvesting operations, and removal of crops from the granary after harvesting, have also been known to cause tension. Increasing awareness and empowerment of SCs, manifested in resistance to suppression, also result in clashes. [45]

The official evidence and the regional studies based on primary data revealed that in rural India in several spheres, if not in all spheres, the social behaviour of caste Hindus is still governed by the norms and codes of the traditional caste system, although there are changes in some spheres of social relations.[46] The settlements of the Dalits in rural areas are away from the caste Hindu locality, endogamy (which is the backbone of the caste system) continues, entries for the untouchables in private houses and temples in rural areas are limited, and common sharing of tea and food is also extremely limited. Pressures and restrictions on voting and political participation also prevail. The restriction on the change of occupation and discrimination in employment, wage rate, share of rent, and rate of interest charged and in sale of items from shops owned by the Dalits is still observed in some degree in the rural areas, where three-fourths of the Dalits live.

This goes on to show that the enforcement and practice of universal human rights in society is not conditioned by the formal supportive legal framework (such as the Constitution and other laws) alone. Often, cultural, social, religious and economic notions make the enforcement and practice of human rights difficult. Non-formal institutions, social, religious as well as economic, involve a framework of social behavior of their own, which may not be in consonance with the principles enunciated by the United Nations, or the Constitution of a nation in which case different sets of values may result in conflicts. It implies that unless inequalities imbedded in the social, economic and cultural structure of the Hindu society are addressed, the legal measures will make little difference in providing access to human rights to the dalits in India.

Despite the abolition of untouchability under the law it is being practiced with impunity more in breach. Caste system among the Hindus has been structured on graded hierarchy of chaturvarna and the Dalits occupy the last rung in the social ladder. Impregnable walls of separation with graded inequalities have thus been erected between different sections among Hindus. Dalits are made to serve the society and are denied even access to water sources, education, cultural life and economic pursuits. They are made to live as beasts of burden on the outskirts of the village. The abominal practice of untouchability deprives them of social intercourse, and they are beaten by the caste Hindus for the simple reason of wearing clean cloths, or drawing water from a public well, or to take marriage procession with the groom on the horse back. Their houses are burnt because they bought land under cultivation, or because of refusing to carry dead animals, or for not bowing before the caste Hindu. Any change in the situation cannot be expected without the improvement in the socio-economic conditions of the Scheduled castes. As we can make out from the case studies the dalits are the victims of discrimination as their socio-economic condition is weak in comparison to the so-called upper castes. In the rural areas, all resources are under the control of the influential castes on which the dalits had to depend. The venerable situation of the dalits can improve if they get equal opportunity in every walk of life. Political power should be grabed by these marginalized castes; then only any change can be expected in their condition. According to Dr. Ambedkar, "Untouchability is an indirect form of slavery and only an extension of caste system. Caste system and untouchability stands together and will fall together. The idea of hoping to eradicate untouchability without destroying caste system is an utter futility."[47]

NOTES AND REFERENCES

1. Ghanshyam Shah, *et. al., Untouchability in Rural India,* (New Delhi, Sage Publications, 2006), p. 19.
2. Yagati Chinna Rao, *Dalits' Struggle For Identity,* (New Delhi, Kanishka publishers, 2003) p. 21.
3. B.R. Ambedkar, "Philosophy of Hinduism" Vasant Moon (Ed.) *"Dr. Babasaheb Ambedkar Writing and Speeches"* (1987 first published), vol. 3, pp. 1-94.
4. Ghanshyam Shah, *et. al., Untouchability in Rural India, op. cit.,* p. 19.
5. *Ibid.*
6. B.R. Ambedkar, "philosophy of Hinduism, *op. cit.,* pp. 1-94.
7. B.R. Ambedkar, "Annihilation of Caste", *op. cit.,* pp. 20-35.
8. Ghanshyam Shah, *et.al., Untouchability in Rural India, op. cit.,* pp. 19-30
9. *Ibid.*
10. *The Hindu,* New Delhi, 22 October 2002.
11. *Ibid.*
12. Balwant Singh, *The Suffering People,* Saharanpur, (Ambedkar Mission Publications, 2002), p. 299.
13. For details see Kanshi Ram's views in *Bahujan Sanghatak,* New Delhi, Various Issues.
14. Balwant Singh, *Sorrows of the Suppresed,* Saharanpur, (Ambedkar Mission Publications, 2004), p. 112.
15. *Ibid.*
16. Interview with Phool Singh on 28 August, 2008.
17. Interview with Phool Singh, Kallu, Dulari on 28 August, 2008.
18. *Ibid.*
19. Interview with Phool Singh, Kallu and Dulari on 28 August, 2008.
20. Land given to landless and poor farmers in villages by the government.
21. Unit used for land measurement.
22. Balwant Singh, *Sorrows of the Suppressed, op. cit.,* p. 167.
23. Interview with Mukhram on 8 September, 2007.
24. Interview with Rajesh, resident of Tajopur, a BSP worker on 8 September 2007.
25. Interview with Kangar Ram, resident of Tajopur, a tailor by profession on 9 September 2007.
26. Interview with Doodnath, resident of Tajopur, on 8 September 2007.

27. A caste among Schulded castes, which skinned dead animals and did other unclean jobs.
28. Interview with Nakli Ram on 14 September 2007.
29. Ashrafs are considered as high class among Muslims.
30. Ajlis are considerd as dalits among Muslims.
31. Interview with Sumer, a BSP worker, on 28 September 2007.
32. Interview with Kamla on 14 September 2007.
33. Interview with Jadish, Kamla, Somti, Ramlal and others on 15 September 2007.
34. *Ibid.*
35. A Scheduled Caste, performing unclean job of cleaning toilets and houses of the upper castes.
36. Balwant Singh, *Sorrows of the Suppressed, op. cit.*, p. 26.
37. Interview with Chotan on 24 September 2007.
38. Interview with Nakli Ram on February 2008.
39. Interview with Nakli Ram, Mehar Singh and other BSP workers on 28 October 2007.
40. Interview with Kallu on 29 October 2007.
41. Interview with Hari Singh on 3 October 2007.
42. *Amar Ujala*, a local Newpaper.
43. Interview with Brahm Singh on 4 October, 2007.
44. Balwant Singh, *Sorrows of the Suppressed, op. cit.*, pp. 80-110.
45. Report of SC/ST Commission of 1998.
46. Ghanshyam Shah, *et. al.*, *Untouchabiliy in Rural India, op. cit.*, pp. 12-16.
47. Balwant Singh, *The suffering People*, (Saharanpur, Ambedkar Mission Publications, 2004), p. 94.

7

Democracy, Dalits and Exclusive Policies: A Case of Scheduled Castes in Arunachal Pradesh

CHUNNU PRASAD

International encyclopaedia of the social sciences finds the term 'Democracy' a set of ideas and political system, a feature it shares with the terms communism and socialism. Democracy is harder to pin down, however then either 'socialism' or 'communism' have found in Marxism an ideological matrix or at least a pint of reference, democracy has never identified with a specific doctrine source, it is rather a by-product of the entire development of western civilization. Democracy is beginning with a principle of legitimacy. So conceived it is both the minimal and the sole common denominator of any and all democratic doctrine.[1]

Greek democracy, as practice in Athens during the fourth century B.C., was the closest approximation to the literal meaning of the term. One could argue in effect that, the Athenian *demos* had more *kratos* (power) than any other people since. At the same time Greek democracy represents the maximum conceivable enlargement of a micro democracy. When the *demos* gathered, the Athenian system actually operates as a town meeting democracy in which some thousands of citizens expressed their ayes and nays.[2]

During the nineteenth century, the term democracy was mainly used in progressive circles as an oppositional idea. As Louis Hartz points out, the image of democracy depicted by its early advocates was basically the negation of what they wanted to destroy. Democracy so conceived is simply the reverse of absolutism, a polemical notion whose function is to oppose, not to propose. The utterance of 'democracy' is a way of saying no to inequality, injustice and coercion. But once the enemy is defeated, the problem becomes to specify what ought to be, that is, to identify equality, justice and freedom in a positive fashion.[3] Democracy, Bottmore observes, "implies that there should be substantial degree of equality among men in the sense that inequality of wealth of social rank or of education and accesses to knowledge should not be so considerable as to result in permanent subordination of some groups of men to others in any of the various spheres of social life or to create great inequalities in the actual exercises of political rights."[4]

Rousseau was one of the earliest thinkers to uphold this point of view, he said that, "there are two kind, of inequality among the human beings, one which I can call natural or physical, because it is established by nature and consists in a difference of age, health, bodily strength and the qualities of the mind or of the soul and another which may be called moral or political inequality, because it depends upon a kind of convention and established or at least authorized by the consent of men. This latter consist, of the different privileges which some men enjoy to the prejudice of others; such as that of being more rich, more honoured, more powerful or even in a position to exact obedience."[5] So here the basic understanding is that the first type of inequality is designed by the nature and the second type of inequality is man made.

Democracy in India is one of the wonders of the modern world with more than 600 million registered voters. Elected representatives form the lower house of parliament called the Lok Sabha while nominated members form the upper house called the Rajya Sabha. The elected government appoints the prime minister. In a federal structure, the states have considerable powers not least in delivery of poverty alleviation programmes. Members of state assemblies together with members of parliament elect a president for a five year term, the office being largely ceremonial.

Coming to the meaning of exclusion and discrimination, Oxford English dictionary define exclusion as the act of preventing from entering a place or taking part in daily life which could be anything related to the dignity of basic human beings and discrimination generally defined as the practice of treating particular group in society less fairly than other. Discrimination can be based on gender, race, disability or religion and belief. Religion and belief is a broad issue and difficult to classify. Factors of such discrimination and contentious issues for ethnic minority communities include dress restriction, ignorance of religious customs, working on religious days/holidays, recruitment, application and promotional practices. Social exclusion is not necessarily a sudden product of the project or emergency situation, but has its roots in pre-existing discrimination and exclusion patterns in communities. In the Indian context, the caste system excludes Dalits and Adivasis in a routine fashion from participation in decision-making and access to resources and social mobility. Patriarchy excludes all women from resources and decision-making. The term social exclusion was originally coined in France in 1974 and has gained wide currency in recent years. Today there is a common feeling and understanding among social scientists on the definite features of social exclusion and the means by which it perpetuate poverty and inequality of marginalized and socially disadvantaged groups. But the term "Social exclusion" has been examined mainly in Western Europe and USA and other developed countries and appropriate policies have been working to fight social exclusion in these countries. Although developing countries including India have initiated some strategies to fight social exclusion and discrimination there is a clear absence of comprehensive policy framework.

Inequality in society is to be eliminated, according to liberal philosophy by abolishing discrimination and upholding the principles of 'equality of opportunity'. The universal declaration of Human Rights under Article 2 proclaims that:

> every one is entitled to all rights and freedom set forth in the declaration without distinction of any kind such as race, colour, sex, language, religion, political or other opinion, birth or other social origin, property, birth or other status.[6]

Constitutionally the provision of reservation was provided to the Scheduled Castes, Scheduled Tribes and Other Backward Castes in the government jobs due to the untiring efforts of Babasaheb Dr. Bhimrao Ambedkar. But because of the anti-reservation as well as various level of opposition to these provisions the full benefits of reservation policies are not reaching to the people belonging to excluded groups of the society. Not only this, the government departments and institutions are being handed over to the private sector for the last several years on the pretext of poor economic condition of the government without providing the facility of reservation in the privatised sectors at any level.

The constitution of India makes a specific provision for reservation of seats in the legislative bodies and in the appointments to services at the union and the state levels for certain classes/castes. Article 15 (1) which states that 'the state shall not discriminate against any citizen on ground only of religion, race, caste, sex, place of birth or any of them' also provides in clause (4) of the same article that, nothing in this article or in clause (2) of the Article 29 shall prevent the state from making any special provision for the advancement of any socially and educationally backward classes of citizens or for the Scheduled Castes (SC) and Scheduled Tribes (ST).[7] Accordingly, constitution makes necessary provisions in Articles 14 to 17, 23, 25 to 30, 38, 46 and 330 to 342. This policy of reservation has come in for severe criticism by foreign observers like Sir Ivor Jennings and others for various reasons.[8] It is however to be noted that Dr. B.R. Ambedkar, the principal architect of the constitution had an important role to play in determining and incorporating the reservation policy in the constitution of India.[9] On the day when Indian constitution was adopted Dr. Babasaheb Ambedkar said on the 26th January 1950:

> We are going to enter into a life of contradiction. In politics we will have equality and in social and economic life we will have inequality. In politics we will be recognizing the principle of one-man one vote and one vote one value. In our social and economic life we shall, by reason of our social and economic structure, continue to deny the principle of one-man one value. How long shall we continue to live this life of contradiction? How long shall we continue to deny equality in our social and economic life? If we continue to deny it for long, we will do so only putting our political democracy in peril. We must remove this contradiction at the earliest possible or else those who suffer from inequality will blow up the structure of political democracy which the constituent assembly so laboriously built up.[10]

As we know the Hindu society and individuals are segregated into compartmental units on the basis of their birth and parental vocation. Each compartmental unit is a caste.[11] The caste system is the steel frame of Hinduism. It was more ancient than the Vedas.[12] The system is undemocratic and authoritarian. It is a rare setup in which economic imperialism; political tyranny and social fascism are inseparably fused together.[13] In the words of J.H. Hutton, "no comparable institution to be seen elsewhere has anything like the complexity elaboration of the rigidity of caste in India."[14]

Considering the general disabilities experienced by the underprivileged communities, the chief architect of the Indian Constitution Babasahab Dr. Ambedkar wrote specific provisions in the constitution to enable them to achieve accelerated development. Articles 15, 16, 17, 19, 23, 29, 35, 38A, 46, 164, 244, 244A, 275, 320 (4), 330, 331, 332, 333, 334, 335, 338, 339, 340, 342, 371A, 371B and 371C of the Indian constitution are aiming at promoting and safeguarding the interests of the SCs, STs and Backward Castess.[15] Reservation is the operational form of the special constitutional provisions. Reservation is of threefold in the legislatures, in the education and in the jobs. The rationale for granting special privileges was that the founding fathers of the constitution felt that mere granting of equal rights would not be sufficient for Depressed Classes.[16] As these people had remained deprived of education, political power, economic and social benefits for centuries, they were in no way competent to compete with the members of the higher castes and privileged classes.[17]

An Indian history book says that the history of this country begins with the coming of the alien 'Aryan' into this subcontinent. So, if this is the case the very general question arises: was this country of a no-peoples land prior to Aryans? If there were people where did they go now? The Dalits of India have been called as Adi-Karnataka, Adi-Dravida, Adi-Andhra, Adi-Hindu, etc. The word 'Adi' means 'First-original' or 'Aboriginal-earliest'; the term 'Madiga' is said to have derived from the word 'Maha Adi' (first and the foremost). It has been believed that 'Maharashtra' is named after Mahar Dalits. Similarly, almost all the Scheduled Castes and Scheduled Tribes have been considered as indigenous people. Why have they been leading a wretched life in their own land? Instead of ruling this country why are they toiling as sweepers, scavengers and landless bonded labourers? How did they become slaves in their own country? What has gone wrong? What is their history? Why their history has not been recorded anywhere?

Before going to discuss this issue it is very necessary to know who are these untouchables are whose history one knows to write. These untouchables are Mahars, Mangs, Madigas, Balmikis,

Paraiahs, Pulayas, Jatavs, Pasis, Doms, Lalbegis, Dusadhs, Bhangis, Namosudras, Mauryas, etc. People generally in this country say that, Dalits are slaves, bonded labourers. Some says, 'outcaste' people are living outside the villages[18] because they are in the outside of the chaturvarna scheme of social stratification, and hence became untouchables. Yet others say that they are 'alienated' Depressed Class of people engaged in the filthy works such as sweeping, scavenging, carrying the dead animals, etc since time immemorial. Long years ago, the continents of Asia, Africa and many parts of the world were ruled by the brilliant brave, beautiful, most talented and industrious black people. These blacks built the Egyptian Civilization, Mesopotamian Civilization, Indus Valley Civilization and such other world's oldest civilizations.

Long history recognized that the Nagas (Scheduled Castes) of India were the indigenous people belonging to great civilization, who latter became the untouchables. Nagas were one such people who built Indus Valley Civilization. They were a cluster of thousands of tribes originally inhabited in Indian subcontinent, variously known as the Nagadweepa, Nagamandala, Nagaloka, Nagabhumi, Cheranadu, Cheramandala, Jamboodweepa, Pathala, etc. The Asuras, Rakshas (Rakshakas), Pishachas, Nishadas, Bhootas, Dhanavas, Dhaityas, Kalas, etc. were the different Naga tribes who had their own tribal kingdom in Nagamandala. The townships of Nagas were called as 'Nagaras' and the well-disciplined prosperous lifestyle of the Nagas was described as 'Nagarikathe' (civilization). Citizens of those Nagas were called as 'Nagarikas' (civilians). The language of the Nagas was 'Dravida (in Southern part of India)', which was in a highly developed than today's popular languages such as Kanada, Tamil, Telugu, Malayalam, Tulu, Malta, Oron, Godba, Kuruk, Brahmi etc. All these languages are derived and developed from the ancient 'Dravida' language.[19]

Around 2,000 BC, Aryans came to India (earlier called Nagaland) in search of food and shelter, because generally they were nomadic people who always use to move from one place to another. The Asuras, Dhanavas and Rakshasa king of Naga race who were well known for their generosity and benevolence had not only provided them food and shelter, but also allowed them to settle in their kingdoms and permitted land for their livelihood. It was this indiscriminate move that brought untold miseries to the Nagamandala. Aryans started creating rifts among the different Naga tribes to make their position safe and secure. The land of harmony and peace become the field of enmity and vengeance.[20] The great Naga Civilization started crumbling. Their Nagaras were destroyed one after another. The Aryans became the advisers to the Naga kings and saw that all the kings were always engaged in mutual distraction. Aryans themselves took force and conducted the raids that destroyed the famous cities of Harappa and Mohenjodaro. By the time the Nagarajas realized the mischief of Aryans and their own ignorance, it was too late. Things had gone out of their control.[21]

Most of the Naga kingdoms were brought under the indirect control of Aryans. The ungrateful ruthless Aryans had slowly introduced caste system a socio political order among the different Naga tribes in which one tribe was kept over the other tribes in a graded manner. The Aryan sat tight on top of all claiming superiority over the subordinate Naga tribes, the indigenous people who got fitted into the caste system with four 'varnas' or 'classes', called as Chaturvarna scheme or varnashrama dharma where they called themselves as Savarniyas or Savarnas. This heinous social system was manufactured by religion and codified into scriptures.[22]

As against the glorious civilization of Nagas the most disgraceful Aryan Civilization came into existence. Free sex, drinking soma and sura, gambling and such other civil indulgences were popularized as the religious rites to please the Aryan gods. Infect these were actually the official functions to have open sex, boozing, gambling, animal sacrifice and merry-making. The immoral way of living introduced by the Aryan rulers started infecting even others too. Consequently, the common mass of people was pushed into poverty, ignorance, hunger and unemployment.[23]

The Nagas were so much frustrated and depressed by the ruthless rule of the Aryans that they were unable to do anything on their own. They were eagerly waiting for someone who raises them up. Finally they met Gautama Buddha, an enlightened master from Sakya clan of Naga race, in 600 BC, who preached the great principles of equality, liberty and fraternity (morality). These principle's came into French revolution, very recently also Mahatma Gandhi learned these principles from Buddha's Dhamma. Buddha introduced

'Meditation' in place of Aryan rituals. In place of hatred and violence he brought universal love, brotherhood and non-violence. He placed the concept of morality in place of exploitative 'god' concept, and against all types of animal sacrifice. The Buddha Dhamma became the way of life of the badly needed tribes. They took special interest in spreading the Buddha Dhamma through the Nagamandala. They had also sent Buddhist Bhikkus to British Isles and Afghanistan to spread the message of Buddha. The Naga Buddhist civilization gave birth to several great emperors and empires, which flourished for over one thousand years.[24]

In the year 642 BC, Magadha kingdom was in today's Bihar. Bimbisara, the fifth ruler of this dynasty who developed the Magadha kingdom into an empire, became follower of Buddha, the world-honoured master. In 413 BC, King Mahananda of Sisunag dynasty was killed by an adventurer called Nanda and established Nanda dynasty. Latter Nanda too become the Buddhist and had spread the Dhamma. In 322 BC, Chandragupta Maurya of Sisunag dynasty deposed the last Nanda king and set up Maurya dynasty. And once again the Naga Empire of Magadha continued to flourish with great fame.

After the Kalinga war, emperor Ashoka of Maurya dynasty, became a Buddhist and opened a new chapter in the world history. He was the first emperor to extend his rule over the entire Asian conquests. He sent his own children as Bhikkus to spread the Dhamma all over the world. When emperor Ashoka made Buddhism the state religion and entire Nagamandala was abundant with peace, prosperity and progress, naturally the Aryans were thoroughly disgusted. They were smarting under the prohibition on animal sacrifice throughout the Maurya Empire proclaimed in the very rock edict by Ashoka.

Today the Naga Buddhist is called as 'Dalit' who belong to the greatest tradition of ferocious but benevolent race Nagarace. It was Dr. Ambedkar who struggled against all types of injustice, which he called the Annihilation of caste, in his book. He also helped Nagas to identify their enemies. That is why it is said that the history of India is a mortal conflict between Buddhism and Brahmanism. Dr. Ambedkar wanted Dalits to be the governing class, because only after getting power it will be possible to remove all the evils of caste system.

A new study has revealed that Indians belonging to higher castes are genetically closer to Europeans than the individuals from lower castes, whose genetic profiles are closer to those of Asians. The study compared genetic markers located on the Y chromosome and the mitochondrial DNA between 265 Indian men of various castes and 750 African, Asian, European and other Indian men. To broaden the study, 40 markers from chromosomes 1 to 22 were analyzed from more than 600 individuals from different castes and continents. The comparison of the markers among these groups confirmed that genetic similarities to Europeans increased as caste rank increased. The study, led by Michael Bamshad of the University of Utah, in Salt Lake City, and his colleagues, is reported to be the most comprehensive genetic analysis to date of the impact of European migrations on the structure and origin of the current Indian population. The article appears in the May 2001 issue of *Genome Research*.[25] The caste system, defined in ancient Sanskrit texts, determines a person's rank in society. The Brahmins, who are traditionally priests and scholars, held the highest rank in Hindu society. Warriors and rulers made up the Kshatriya who was the next in line to the Brahmin. Merchants, traders, farmers, and artisans were the third caste called the Vysya. The Shudras were the fourth rank and consisted of laborers. Because of strict rules forbidding marriage between men and women of different castes, these four classes remained distinct for thousands of years. Bamshad's team found that Y chromosomes from the Brahmin and Kshatriya closely resembled European Y chromosomes rather than Asian Y chromosomes. The Y chromosomes from the lower castes bore more similarities to the Asian Y chromosome. The mitochondrial DNA showed the same pattern. The authors believe that their results support the notion that Europeans who migrated into India between 3,000 and 8,000 years ago may have merged with or imposed their social structure on the native northern Indians and placed themselves into the highest castes.[26] Analysis of the paternally transmitted Y chromosome among Indians in general indicated that the Y chromosome had a more European flavour. Maternally inherited mitochondrial DNA among Indians is more Asian than European. This suggests that the Europeans who entered India were predominantly male.[27]

The unending struggle that has been going on for the past 4000 years and more is only the game of power and nothing else. To understand the whole politics of power one should know the real history of India. The researchers should go deeply to explore all the hidden facts which never have been discovered by any historian; the reason is that they are in a very professional mind, always looking name and fame and not looking to find the fact and reality.

The northeast Indian states are generally called as the eight sisters, viz. Assam, Arunachal Pradesh, Meghalaya, Mizoram, Manipur, Nagaland, Tripura and Sikkim. They have their own problems and their problems cannot be clubbed together; their issues are very much similar but solutions are different, because demands and situations are different. This is the reason why one has to see the problems of these states differently. As it is well known, the state of Arunachal Pradesh, the land of rising sun, is one of the most peaceful states in the entire north eastern region of India. But after 1964, bitterness came into the peaceful nature of the state; the reason is the refugee problem in the state. Whatever the case may be if we compare with the other states of northeast it is more peaceful of all the north eastern states.

Arunachal Pradesh is the biggest state (83,743 sq. km) area wise, and population wise, it has very small population of 1,091,117 out of which 573,951are males and 517,166 are females. The concern here is to focus on the conditions of Scheduled Caste population in the state. If we analyze the politics of reservation in the state we come to know that the state is having 80 per cent reservation for Scheduled Tribes and 20 per cent for General (general includes all the people other than Arunachalees viz. SC/ST/OBC/Women/ Others of other states). Before 1964 the reservation in the state was in the ratio of 50:50 i.e., 50 per cent reserved for Scheduled Tribes and 50 per cent for the General (Non-Arunachalees). Over a period of time strong movements, protests took place on the question of reservation with the refugee problem in the state and developmental issues. All Arunachal Pradesh Students Union (AAPSU), one of the most popular and powerful student organizations with popular village support, started demanding the 100 per cent reservation for Scheduled Tribes in the state. Many months have been engaged to discuss to the reservations, and lastly Government of India, Government of Arunachal Pradesh, and other student organizations had come to the conclusion that 80 per cent will reserved for the Arunachalees (Scheduled Tribes) and 20 per cent for General public.

According to 2001 census, of the total population in Arunachal Pradesh, 60 per cent belongs to tribes and 40 per cent belongs to non tribes. What is striking is the Scheduled Caste population in the state. According to the 2001 census Arunachal Pradesh, which is included in the 6th Schedule of the Indian constitution, has a total of 6,188 Scheduled Caste population out of which 3590 are males and 2598 are females, and these populations are denied their rights of representation in the state, the rights like right to get trading license in their own name to do business, right to job in the government sectors and other basic rights. According to the primary abstract, Census of India (Arunachal Pradesh) 2001, the Scheduled Caste populations are in the regions of Bansphors, Bhummalis or Malis, Brittials, Dhupis or Dhobis, Duglas or Dholis, Hiras, Jalkeots, Jhalos, Malos or Jhalo-Malos, Kaibarttas or Jaliyas, Lalbegis, Macharas, Mehtars or Bhangis, Muchis or Rishis, Namasudras, Patni, Sutradhars.[28]

Before going to focus the problem in Arunachal Pradesh, a brief ethnographic information about the state is useful here. When one talks about the history of Arunachal Pradesh, it goes back to hundreds of years into tradition and myth. Local tradition regards the country around Sadiya as the ancient Vidarbha. Ancient puranas have many references to the region. History of Arunachal Pradesh can be traced only when Ahom Kings began to rule Assam in the 16th century. The British took possession of Assam in 1838. British government had brought Arunachal Pradesh also under their administrative control.[29]

Though the history of the growth of political process in Arunachal Pradesh dates back to 1875 when the British Government started to define the administrative jurisdiction by drawing an Inner-Line in relation to the Frontier Tribes inhabiting the North Frontier Tracts (NFT), the area was kept outside the purview of regular laws of the country. There after the British followed the policy of gradual penetration to bring more areas under normal administration. By the year 1946, the North East Frontier Tracts (NEFT) were recognized into four frontiers tracts namely, Sadiya, Lakhimpur, Tirap and Sela Sub-Agency and Subansiri area and administrated by the Governor of Assam in his discretion. By virtue of the Indian Independence Act 1947 the Government of Assam assumed administrative jurisdiction over North East Frontier Tracts and the Governor of Assam was divested of his discretionary powers.[30]

The Government of Assam administered the NEFT during the period from 15th August 1947 to 26th January 1950. After India's independence, a sub committee headed by Gopinath Bordoloi was appointed by the Constituent Assembly of India to recommend the future pattern of administration of the North Eastern Frontier Tracts. The Bordoloi Committee recommended that since the administration has been satisfactorily established over sufficiently wide areas, the Government of Assam should take over that area by the strength of a notification. But for various considerations, particularly problem of communication and defence, Government of India decided to administer North East Frontier Tracts as "Exclusive Area" through Governor of India. In the year 1950, the plain portions of these tracts namely Balipara Frontier Tract (BFT), Tirap Frontier Tract (TFT), Abor Hill District and Mishimi Hill Districts were transferred to the Government of Assam.[31] In 1951 the units of the tracts were reconstituted again and Tuensang Frontier Division (TFD) was created which latter merged with Nagaland. The remaining portion of the tracts after the introduction of the North East Frontier (Administration) Regulation 1954 was designated as the North East Frontier Agency (NEFA). Thereafter the administration was brought under Ministry of External Affairs (MEA) and in August 1965, it was brought under the supervision and control of the Ministry of Home Affairs (MHA). It remained so, till the attainment of Union Territory status by Arunachal Pradesh in 1972, under the 27th Constitutional Amendment Act of 1971.[32]

It was only in 1975 that, by virtue of the enactment of 37th Constitutional Amendment Act 1975, the Pradesh Council was constituted as a separate Legislative Assembly and Lt. Governor were appointed as the head of the Union Territory of Arunachal Pradesh. The Pradesh Council became provisional Legislative Assembly having 23 members during 1975 to 1978. The first elected Legislative Assembly constituting of 33 members (30 elected members and 3 nominated) was formed on 4th March 1978, which lasted only for about 20 months. In November 1979, the Assembly was dissolved and president's rule was imposed which continued till January 1980. The second General Election was held in January 1980, the third General Election for Legislative Assembly was held simultaneously with the General Election for the eighth Lok Sabha in December 1984 and the Assembly was continued till January 1986.[33]

On 20th February 1987 Statehood was conferred on Arunachal Pradesh under the 55th Constitutional Amendment Act of 1986, and it became the 25th state of the Union of India. In fact the evolution and formation of Arunachal Pradesh is a tribute to the farsighted tribal policy formulated by 'Verrier Elwin' in its initial stages. Arunachal Pradesh in area wise, it is the largest state in the North Eastern Region of India (NERI) with around 83,743 sq. km, having not more than eleven lakh population. It forms a complex hill system of Shivalik and Himalayan origin and is criss-crossed by numerous rivers and streams. The state shares a total of 1630 kms of international boundary with neighbouring countries: 1030 km with China, 160 km with Bhutan and 440 km with Myanmar. The Mc-Mahon line defines the International boundary between India and China. Administratively the state is divided into sixteen districts. Capital of the state is Itanagar in Papumpare District. Itanagar is named after Ita Fort, meaning Fort of bricks, which was built by

District Wise Population in Arunachal Pradesh

S. No.	*Districts*	*Town*	*Total*	*Male*	*Female*
1.	Tawang	Tawang	34705	17676	17029
2.	West Kameng	Bomdila	74595	42638	31957
3.	East Kameng	Seepa	57065	28743	28322
4.	Papumpare	Itanagar	121750	64122	57628
5.	Lower Subansiri	Zero	97614	49184	48430
6.	Upper Subansiri	Daporizo	54995	27873	27122
7.	West Siang	Along	103575	54139	49436
8.	East Siang	Pasighat	87430	45139	42299
9.	Upper Siang	Along	33146	17844	15302
10.	Dibang Valley	Anini	57543	31280	26263
11.	Lohit	Tezu	143478	77252	66226
12.	Changlang	Changlang	124994	65608	59368
13.	Tirap	Khonsa	100227	52461	47766
14.	Lower-Dibang Valley	Roing	N.A	N.A	N.A
15.	Kurung Kumey	Laying-Yangte	N.A	N.A	N.A
16.	Anjaw	Hawai	N.A	N.A	N.A

Ahom Kings in 14th century AD. The Hindu influence penetrated along the Brahmaputra up to the Dibang valley. Sacred centres sprung up between 11th and 13th centuries. The ruins of the Bhishmark site have reportedly been located in the Dibang Valley and those of Parsuram Kund in Lohit district.[34]

Arunachal Pradesh has 26 major tribes with many of sub-tribes. The major tribes are Adi, Apatani, Bugun, Galo, Hrusso, Jingpho, Khamba, Koro, Memba, Mcyor, Mishmi (including Idu, Taroon and Kaman), Monpa, Nyishi (incliding Bangru and Puroik), Sajolang, Sartang, Sherdukpen, Tagin, Tai Khamti (including Khamyang), Yobin, Tangshang (including Muklam), Lonchang, Tutsa, Tikhak, Howoi, Longri, Mungrey, Mushung, Lungphi, Joglai Ngaimong, Ponthai, Khalak, Lungkhai Iiallry, Chellim, Sheehu, Shiangwal, Rcra, Shiangte, Lowchang, Dohe, Moitai, Hatseng Gajee, Gaja, Kochong, Laki, Gallon, Chamehang, Ringkhu, Shohra, Bowngtai, Rourong of Changlang district and Nocte, Wanchoo and Tutsa of Tirap district. Chakmas and Hajongs are also included in the census as the population of Arunachal Pradesh.[35] The All India Anthropometrical Survey (AIAS) extended to Arunachal Pradesh under the people of India project suggests that the people of Arunachal Pradesh are short, below medium in stature, have a round head, a medium broad nose and a broad face.

Most of the communities of the state believe in traditional tribal religion. Important aspects of tribal religion are the observance of various festivals, ancestral worship and taboos. The beliefs in malevolent and benevolent spirits and deities and rituals performed by the concept of the supreme beings or gods (called variously as Ske, Matai, Rang, Rangkuwa by different communities) constitute the animistic tribal religions. Donyi-Poloism is the major tribal religion of Arunachal Pradesh. It has a vast mythology with all its mundane and supernatural elements. Donyi-Polo is a combination of two terms Donyi means 'Sun' and Polo means 'Moon'. Donyi is the source of power and energy for living beings, which cannot be disputed scientifically and philosophically. Thus, Donyi-Polo, the spiritual source and symbol is believed to be the supreme power governing the universe.

A festival is the day or a period of celebration and an essential part of the socio-cultural life of the people. Festivals reflect the customs, traditions and lifestyle of the people. Like other parts of the

Percentage of Various Religious Groups in Arunachal Pradesh

S. No.	Religion	Total Percentage
1.	Hindus	34.6
2.	Muslims	1.9
3.	Christians	18.7
4.	Sikhs	0.2
5.	Buddhists	13.0
6.	Janis	0.0
7.	Others/Animism	30.0

India, in Arunachal Pradesh also festivals are celebrated with great joy, enthusiasm and most importantly, with a feeling of togetherness. The festivals of Arunachal Pradesh serve a two fold purpose a thanks giving ceremony in homage to God and for his gifts of good crops and freedom. Animal sacrifice is a common ritual in most of the festivals of Arunachal Pradesh.[36]

The political system of Arunachal Pradesh may be defined as a part of the total process, which engaged in the maintenance or establishment of social order or social equilibrium among the Arunachalees. It essentially consists of the activities connected with the political institutions of the area in its broadest sense, a political system of institutionalized customs by which law, order and peace are maintained in a society. The traditional forms of government govern almost all the communities of Arunachal Pradesh. The Diying Ering Committee introduced modern democratic norms in Arunachal Pradesh by providing the people an opportunity to exercise their rights for franchise. Till 1967 Arunachal Pradesh was represented in the Lok Sabha by a member nominated by the President of India. The first general election was held on January 3, 1980 for the formation of a Legislative Assembly during its tenure as a Union Territory. At that time there was only two political parties, namely the Congress (I) and People's Party of Arunachal Pradesh (PPAP). So far two Assembly and Parliamentary elections have taken place and the people have taken part without any fear or compulsion.[37]

The total population of Arunachal Pradesh in 2001 Census has been 1,097,968. Of these 6,188 persons are Scheduled Castes (SCs), constituting 0.6 per cent of the total population of the state. The list of SCs of Assam is applicable to Arunachal Pradesh, Meghalaya and Mizoram. As such, sixteen communities are notified as SCs in the state. In 1971 Census, total SC population was 339. The number has steadily increased in subsequent years. In 1981 Census, the total SC population was 2,919. This became 4,052 in 1991 Census. In 2001 Census, the SC population in Arunachal Pradesh increased further to 6,188 persons. The state has registered 52.7 per cent decadal growth of its SC population in 1991-2001 Census.[38] Namasudra (21.6%), Kaibartta (21.4%), and Dhupi (11.1%) are the major SCs in the state of Arunachal Pradesh. They together constitute about 55 per cent of the total SC population of the state. Six SCs namely Mahara, Patni, Jhalo, Hira, Dugla, and Lalbegi are small in numbers and have less than hundred populations each.[39]

Scheduled Caste Population, 2001

S. No.	*Name of the Scheduled Caste*	*Total Population*	*Proportion to the Total SC Population*
	All Scheduled Castes	**6,188**	**100%**
1.	Namasudra	1,334 21.6	21.6
2.	Kaibartta	1,327 21.4	21.1
3.	Dhupi	688 11.1	11.1
4.	Brittial-Bania	496 8.0	8.0
5.	Mehtar	409 6.6	6.6
6.	Jalkeot	331 5.3	5.3
7.	Muchi	275 4.4	4.1
8.	Sutradhar	247 4.0	4.0
9.	Bansphor	193 3.1	3.1
10.	Bhuinmali	137 2	2.2

As per 2001 Census, more than half of the SC population has been reported to be living in urban areas. Of the three main SCs, Dhupi (Dhobi) has recorded the highest (61%) urban population, followed by Namasudra (57.4%) and Kaibartta (29.2%). The sex ratio of total SC population in the state is 724, which is quite low. Of the three main SCs, the Dhupi has recorded the lowest sex ratio of 658. The state has recorded child sex ratio (0-6 age group) of 938, which is exactly at par with the national average for SCs (938). Namasudras have recorded more female children in their population of 0-6 with child sex ratio of 1049. The child sex ratio is, however, low among Kaibartta (813) and Dhupi (820). In 2001 Census, 67.6 per cent of the SC population of the state has been recorded as literate, with male and female literacy being 76.3 per cent and 55 per cent respectively. Kaibartta has recorded the highest literacy rate of 77.5 per cent. Dhupi and Namasudra are at par each having above 69 per cent literacy rate. The percentage of workers to total population (WPR) among the SCs is low at 38.4 per cent. More than half (56.6%) of the male population have been returned as workers, while the female WPR is low at 13.2 per cent. Out of the total workers, an overwhelming 90.2 per cent are main workers, with 93.3 per cent males and 71.6 per cent females as main workers.[40]

Distribution of Workforce Among SCs

Percentage of Workers

	Total Workers	*Main Workers*	*Marginal Workers*
Total	2,375 (38.4 %)	2,142 (90.2%)	233 (9.8%)
Male	2,033 (56.6%)	1,897 (93.3%)	136 (6.7%)
Female	342 (13.2%)	245 (71.6%)	97 (28.4%)

The SCs in Arunachal Pradesh are not primarily dependent on agricultural pursuits. Merely 13.4 per cent of the total SC main workers have been recorded as cultivators, 1.2 per cent agricultural labourers, and 2 per cent in household industry. Thus, a high of 83.4 per cent of the total main workers among SCs have been recorded under industrial category of "other works". Dhupi has recorded the lowest percentage (2.4%) of their main workers in agriculture (i.e. cultivators and agricultural labourers), followed by Namasudra (15.9 %). However, it is a high of 41.8 per cent among Kaibartta. As regarding marital status, 52.8 per cent of the SCs are never married, 45.2 per cent married, 1.7 per cent widowed, and the remaining 0.2 per cent divorced/separated. Kaibartta has recorded a high of 3.3 per cent widowed in their population. The overwhelming majority of the SCs in Arunachal Pradesh are Hindus.[41]

The Scheduled Tribes of Arunachal Pradesh are protected by the constitution under different provisions. The northeast states are included in the 6th Schedule of the constitution and have been given special status and rights to protect the tribal groups. In case of

Arunachal Pradesh, the Bengal Regulation Act 1873 (the inner-line regulation) check outsiders to enter in the state freely without proper inner line pass.[42] But we also know that the Scheduled Castes population of this country have also been protected by the constitution whose conditions are worse then any other community of the world. There are different safeguards, laws, articles which protects the Scheduled Castes population from all types of exploitation, exclusion, discrimination and injustice physically or physiologically. The very basic question which arises in the mind of all those scholars who believed in humanity is that if the state of Arunachal Pradesh has reservation policy on the 80:20 proportion, i.e., eighty per cent for the tribe and twenty per cent for others non-Arunachalees (non-tribes), which is not at all a problem, but the very basic question is about that twenty per cent which has to be specified.

The problem lies with the rest of the twenty per cent. The Scheduled Castes, who are born or migrated fifty years before, who adopted state's culture and identity, should be given justice. As the Scheduled Castes population in Arunachal Pradesh is coming under the general category, it is an important issue to deal with. The Scheduled Castes population in the state are no doubt are the migrants, but they migrated before fifty years, settled and mixed with the soil of Arunachal, and adopted Arunachal's culture and identity. The issue correctly to be related with the theory propounded by a well known physiologist Nimmi Hutnic who opines that A+B=C, in which A=Different identity, B=Different identity, C=Adopted one identity. In this A belongs to the different identity, B belongs to the different culture which gives result C. It means A belongs to different culture and identity, B belongs to different culture and identity, and over a period of time they developed or adjust with new identity i.e., C.[43] The point here is that the Scheduled Castes possess the same position in the Indian states of Arunachal Pradesh. The people behave more like Arunachalese, and food habits, language, and identity have been changed, and they share more commonality with the tribes of the region. However they are more sufferers as they are suffering in other states in the other parts of India; they are the landless, jobless, homeless, cloth-less people.

If we go deep into these issues, the exact problem here is that the problem here is the people who migrated before fifty years back, settled in the environment, spent their whole life, cannot be treated in the general category, or to be more specific, cannot be included in the 20 per cent. Because if you open 20 per cent for general and include Scheduled Caste population in that 20 per cent. It is nevertheless doing injustice to them and snatching their rights to get their representation in the all sectors one as regional backwardness and another as the most marginalized. When Government open 20 per cent of reservation for general population those who belong to high caste who never visited or spent any time in the state, getting good education, having good financial background are benefiting more, or all the twenty per cent is being captured by these populations who never have been the part of the state. As a Scheduled Castes of Arunachal Pradesh who are born and grown up in Arunachal Pradesh, they should be given reservation in the state in that twenty per cent. At least five per cent should be reserved to these marginalized groups who are one of the most backward landless groups in the state. The demand is not in that 80 per cent but the demand is in that twenty per cent where five per cent seats are to be reserved for the Scheduled Caste population. In any case this population cannot be treated as general because these populations are landless, doing the entire menial works in the state since from fifty years. Their children are continuing as usual and have to be protected. This population in any case should be given some percentage of reservation in the government jobs, and representation in the Assemblies and other sector for their upliftment, to minimise the injustice which has been done over a period of time. Government of Arunachal Pradesh have all information about the Scheduled Caste population, about their condition. But even knowing everything, and not trying to understand their problems, is really to be criticized strongly for the inhuman act. Even after knowing that the Scheduled Castes population's condition is worse than that of the Scheduled Tribes, the government is not taking any step to implement any policies and programmes for their upliftment. Instead of doing any welfare activities, the Government of Arunachal Pradesh is cancelling trading licenses of these populations, charging heavy taxes on different occupations, which is creating problem to get two time meal a day easily. The Government of Arunachal Pradesh, Government of India and all the Student organizations who are considering themselves as the social workers should think and work out for the Scheduled Castes population's problem in state and support to implement at least 5 per cent reservation for them in the state in different sectors, to fill the gap of injustice.[44]

The Central as well as State Governments initiated many developmental activities to strengthen the political economy of the state but none of the policies and programmes has any inclusive provisions for Scheduled Castes of Arunachal Pradesh listed in the census of 2001. The initiatives like the encouragement of the establishment of industrial undertakings in the private and cooperative sectors for the sustainable development of the state, employment opportunities and gainful self-employment in industrial and allied sectors for the local population of Arunachal Pradesh are given. Investors from outside the state will be encouraged to invest in the state. Hundred per cent equity ownership of an industrial unit by entrepreneurs will be allowed for a maximum period of thirty years, and by the end such equity holding will be reduced to forty nine percent, the remaining fifty one per cent being held by a local Arunachal Tribal entrepreneur or a group of local tribal entrepreneurs or the State Government, if it considers necessary to do so. Outside entrepreneurs may be allowed to hold land on lease for a period of thirty years, after which the lease may be renewed for a further period of thirty years. The consideration for the lease may be in the form of annual or lump sum payments or as equity. (The lease may be used as security for loans from financial institutions.) Development of all industries will be encouraged. To begin with, industries based on locally available raw materials, Textiles (handlooms and power looms) and handicrafts, electronics and knowledge based industries and industries based on nontimber forest produce will be given preority.

Tourism, medical services, educational services and a package of incentives for all eligible industrial units have been devised. A programme for the development of infrastructure facilities, inter-alia including the establishment of industrial estates, industrial growth centers, Integrated Infrastructure Development Centers, strengthening of existing industrial estates, export promotion, industrial parks, export promotion zones, Border trade, will be taken up in a phased manner. Reserves of minerals will be explored and exploited commercially through appropriate agencies. Government will make special efforts for development of local entrepreneurial, managerial and technical skills. For this purpose, special training and educational programmes, including women, will be put on a sound economic and commercial footing and the state will ensure smooth flow of credit for new industrial projects, village industries and rural artisans. The District Industries Centers (DIC) and financial institutions will work in close cooperation. There will be no licensing requirements for industry save as may be provided by any law or Central Government policy.[45]

State Level Industrial Empowered Committee comprising of the concerned Secretaries and representatives from banking and financial Institutions will be formed to grant the requisite clearances and facilitate the establishment of industries from a single window. This Empowered Committee will be headed by the Minister of Industries and will meet as often as necessary. The Government will strengthen the DICs with adequate and basic facilities. Each DIC will have an Udyog Sahayak Cell to guide entrepreneurs in the setting up of project report and arrangement of finance for the projects. There will also be a women's cell in each DIC to give special attention to the women entrepreneurs. A data bank will also be created in each DIC for the benefit of the entrepreneurs. The District Level Industrial Advisory Boards will be reconstituted for monitoring the working of the District Industries Centers.

NABARD has identified 10 sectors for development, which include sectors like agriculture, fish rearing and processing, rural retail trade, sericulture and silk textile fiber products, construction, small plantation products, handloom, handicrafts products in cane and bamboo and wood. These activities are to be developed for creation of additional employment in the rural areas. All relevant Departments will be associated in the implementation of these schemes. A package for the revival of sick industries in the SSI and Tiny sector will be devised by the Industries Department. The State Government will gradually vacate economic space for the private and cooperative sectors and the public and state sectors will be economic players only if absolutely necessary. To generate employment among women and to encourage women entrepreneurs, the Government will reserve 33 per cent of industrial sheds, development plots in Industrial Area/Estate/Growth Centre etc. for women. In order to speed up the SSI Registration process, the JDI/DDI/ADI will be empowered to register the SSI units. A single window service cell will be set up for assisting entrepreneurs to get all required technical project or activity in the district. Units fulfilling all formalities of registration will be given provisional or permanent registration by the District Industries Centres/Directorate of Industries immediately.[46]

However, only sweeping and other dirty jobs have been given by the Government to the Scheduled Castes in the state for which they are recognized for centuries. One has to know that it was only by the efforts of Babasaheb Dr. Bhimrao Ambedkar[47] tribes of Arunachal Pradesh in particular and India in general are availing opportunities.

Is this India we are proud of and talk about for her rich culture, belief of humanity? Ask this question simply: who is responsible for I myself, our fore-fathers or someone else who are to be superior among humans over others. Is this motherland of ours that we are proud of? We need to be focused on the issue of caste more than any other issues, because it is destroying the basic understanding of humanity. It is destroying our identity for whom India is known as the country of peace, non-violence, brotherhood, equality among all. We have to think once again to find out the solution of this type of dirty mentality of those people, particularly educated, who can bring equality and brotherhood among all. We always talk about equality, justice, fraternity, peace but we never talk about the basic requirements of the 21st century through which we could achieve the said concepts.

Lastly, I conclude by saying that a legal solution to the problem has to be sought out within a time bound period and fulfil the legal requirements of the Scheduled Castes who are the most backwards in the Indian state of Arunachal Pradesh. Their historical injustice should be removed by giving their due share so that they live a dignified life as human beings in their own land. They should be included in the education, employment, assemblies, etc. of Arunachal Pradesh so that they should avail all those opportunities which other scheduled castes of India so far are availing.

Note:

Part of this paper presented at a *National Seminar on* Social Exclusion, Poverty and Livelihood of Marginalized Groups in India-need for effective Inclusive Strategies, on 24th and 25th September, 2008, *Mangalore University*, Karnataka.

NOTES AND REFERENCES

1. *International Encyclopaedia of the Social Sciences*, SILLS, (D.V.), p. 112.
2. *Ibid.*, p. 115.
3. *Ibid.*, p. 116.
4. T.B. Botomore, *Elites and society* (London, C.A.Watta and Co., Ltd., 1994), p. 122.
5. J.J. Rousseau, *A Dissertation on the origin and foundation of the inequality of mankind*, (everyman's edition) quoted in T.B. Botomore, p. 122.
6. B.A.V. Sharma and K. Madhusudan Reddy (ed.), *Reservation Policy in India* (New Delhi, Light and Life Publishers, 1982), p. 62.
7. See the provision related to Tribes of India in general and North East in Particular for detail understanding about the rights of the Scheduled Tribals.
8. See constitution of India related to the rights of backward Castes.
9. *Ibid.*, p. 122.
10. B.R. Ambedkar's address to the constituent assembly, November 25, 1949. Cited in B.A.V. Sharma, and K. Madusudha Reddy, *op. cit.*, p. 227.
11. A.R. Desai, *Social Background of Indian Nationalism* (Bombay, Popular Prakashan, 1990), p. 243.
12. *Ibid.*
13. J.J. Hutson, *Caste in India: Its Nature, Function and Organization* (Oxford, Oxford University Press, 1951), p. 56.
14. *The Constitution of India*, Government of India, Ministry of Law and Justice (Article related to reservation and welfare for weaker section of the society).
15. P. Satyanarayana, "Reservation and Attitudes of Political Parties" in B.A.V. Sharma and K. Madhusudan Reddy (ed.), *Reservation Policy in India* (New Delhi, Light and Life Publishers, 1982), p. 122.
16. S.S. Anant, *The changing concept of caste in India,* (Vikas Publication, 1972), p. 23.
17. B.A.V. Sharma, and, K. Madhusudan Reddy (ed.), Reservation *Policy in India* (New Delhi, Light and Life Publishers, 1982), p. 62.
18. See writings of Dr. B.R. Ambedkar, on the origin of Untouchables.
19. *Ibid.*
20. See the small booklet *Nagaloka* published by Gopinath on the origin of untouchables.
21. *Ibid.*
22. *Ibid.*
23. *Ibid.*
24. *Ibid.*
25. M. Bamshad *et al.*, "Genetic evidence on the origins of Indian caste populations", *Genome Research* 11, (May 2001), pp. 994-1004.

26. P.P. Majumder, "Indian caste origins: genomic insights and future outlook", *Genome Research* 11.
27. Bijal P. Trivedi, "Genetic evidence suggests European migrants may have influenced the origins of India's caste system", May 14, 2001.
28. See SC/ST Modification order 1956 and inserted by Act 69 of 1986. Also see the Scheduled Caste Report on Population, 2001.
29. Chunnu Prasad, "Natural Resource Management and Sustainable Development: A Study in Arunachal Pradesh", *Social Action*, Vol. 58, April-June 2007, pp. 200-207.
30. Chunnu Prasad, "Arunachal Pradesh and the Inner-Outer Line Regulation of 1873-1874 of North East Frontier Agency", *Third World Impact*, Vol. XVIII, No173, January-March, 2007, pp. 15-19.
31. N. Osik, *Modern history of Arunachal Pradesh 1825 to 1997* (Itanagar, Himalayan Publication, 1999), pp. 57-62.
32. *Ibid.*
33. *Ibid.*
34. Chunnu Prasad, "Natural Resource Management and Sustainable Development: A Study in Arunachal Pradesh", *Social Action*, Vol. 58, April-June 2007, pp. 200-207.
35. See S.K. Singh, *People of India: Arunachal Pradesh*, and also articles by S. Dutta, Deepak K. Singh and Chunnu Prasad on the issue related to the Chakmas and Hajongs of Arunachal Pradesh in detail.
36. Chunnu Prasad, "Natural Resource Management and Sustainable Development: A Study in Arunachal Pradesh", *op. cit.*, 200-207.
37. *Ibid.*
38. See detail information of the Office of the Registrar General, India about the Scheduled Caste Population of Arunachal Pradesh (2001).
39. *Ibid.*
40. *Ibid.*
41. *Ibid.*
42. Chunnu Prasad, "Arunachal Pradesh and the Inner-Outer Line Regulation of 1873-1874 of North East Frontier Agency", *Third World Impact*, Vol. XVIII, No. 173, January-March 2007, pp. 15-19.
43. Nimmi Hutnic, *Ethnic Minority Identity* (Oxford, Clarendon Press, 1991), on melting pot theory.
44. Chunnu Prasad, Arunachal Pradesh Denies the Rights to Scheduled Castes in the State, *Radical Humanist*, Vol. 433, May 2006, pp. 33-34.
45. Information published by the State Information department, Government of Arunachal Pradesh on the political economy of the state.
46. *Ibid.*
47. Baba Sahab Dr. Bhimrao Ramaji Ambedkar who was an untouchable fought, sacrificed and worked for both the Scheduled Castes and

Scheduled tribes of India and made various constitutional provisions to protect the rights of these populations to minimize the gap of injustice, discrimination, exclusion which has been done centuries over centuries. Being Scheduled tribes dominated state; Arunachal Pradesh is discriminating and excluding Scheduled Castes from getting all opportunities.

8

Chinki: Is it a Racial Category or a Vilification Tag?

N. WILLIAM SINGH

Thematizing Social Exclusion and Social Discrimination

When people talk about social exclusion and social discrimination, the first thing that comes to people's mind is about forms of inequality. Inequality may be in terms of economic inequality, gender disparity, gulf between majority and minority races and so forth. In a sense, inequality is also a term, which is very much related with the existing forms of social exclusion and social discrimination. Sociologists used to conceptualize forms of social exclusion on topics like racism, caste and class. Later the concept was extended into the discourse on gender relations and ethnic relations. At those earlier times, social exclusion etymologically means new sources of inequality. Social exclusion in those times meant to be the ways in which individuals or certain group of individuals remained cut off from full involvement in the aspects of wider society. For example, people in poor infrastructure areas couldn't fully be exposed or couldn't participate in the mainstream social activities. Social exclusion as a concept refers to a broad range of factors that prevents groups and individuals from having equal opportunities as enjoyed by the majority of the population.

Another aspect that is related to the discourse on social exclusion is the notion of social integration. Themes on social exclusion also sometimes relate to level of social integration. Social exclusion asks a basic question at the level of social integration, whether they have equal access to essential goods and services such as transportation, insurance, etc and equal accessibility to common institutions such as schools and healthcare facilities. It asks whether different individuals or groups have been integrated properly or improperly in the public domain. That's why Sociologists like Anthony Giddens are of the view that social exclusion can also be understood through the level of inclusion.

To the same extent, we can also argue—social exclusion is also related with the notion of relative deprivation. Feeling of relative deprivation was experienced by those individuals, families, and groups of certain races who cannot participate in certain social activities, in representation and in certain social activities that are considered to be normal. Lack of participation is not just due to natural or physical causes. Rather, there is always a social or a policy mechanism, which simply negates some groups of individuals from participation. Sociologist T.K. Oommen once wrote that if an individual or a group of individuals is being located at the periphery and some being placed at the core, that creates an imbalance, i.e., those at the periphery will obviously feel deprived and those at the core or the center will feel privileged. Somehow or the other, the concept of relative deprivations also echoes the forms of social exclusion to some extent. Social exclusion refers to a situation in which multiple deprivations prevent individuals from participating in important areas of societal activities. Literally socially excluded means absence of upliftment mechanisms to find work, inability to participate in societal public sphere in a more comprehensive manner.

One of the interesting approaches in explaining social exclusion was advocated by Pete Townsend, P. Corrigan and U. Kowarzik.[1] They conceptualized social exclusion along the lines of relative deprivation. They put forward two types of relative deprivation, i.e., material deprivation and social deprivation. Material deprivation is the type of deprivation, which occurs due to the lack of basic needs of human beings. For example, deprivation in terms of food, clothing, housing, medical facilities at work and deprivation in terms of educational institutions. Such deprivations lead to serious social deprivations. Social deprivations highlight deprivation in terms of employment opportunities, deprivations in terms of family activities, lack of integration with other communities, lack of participation in social institutions, recreational deprivations and educational deprivations. The point to be noted is that material deprivation or social deprivation, are like twins or sides of the same coin. Those who are relatively deprived experienced both forms of deprivation.

A. Walker and C. Walker[2] explained social exclusion as the dynamic process of being shut out fully or partially from any of the social, economic, political and cultural systems, which determine the social integration of a person in society. The main proposition of A. Walker and C. Walker is supposed to be—social exclusion simply acts as a mechanism to consider the role of those who run the show on excluding other groups and the level of certain privileged groups. In general it is those who are not relatively deprived that practically run the show of excluding the under-privileged groups. Brian Nolan and Christopher T. Whelan made the meaning of social exclusion more acceptable. Nolan and Christopher mentioned–social exclusion should highlight the gap between those who are active members of society and those who are forced to the fringes, increasing risks of social disintegration.[3] Further Nolan and Christopher explained that social exclusion is a fact for the person concerned and for the society that is a process of change and is not a fixed or a static situation.

The argument, which is put forward, is that social exclusion and the levels of social exclusion can be seen in a relational approach. Relational approach here means the level of differences in terms of power between the privileged and the under-privileged groups, between the fortunate and the unfortunate groups, the level of participation between those powerful and the non-powerful in public sphere and the level of benefits which one group experiences than other. Relational approach also responds to the question of social integration by classifying the level of disintegration and the forms of social exclusion, which groups or individuals experienced. Relational approach can also consider the role of individuals or groups who are relatively deprived as compared to others. It is the level of deprivation in relation to the level of privileges, and the forms of social exclusion that occur. In a discourse on social exclusion, one should not simply look at forms of social exclusion. Level of social discrimination in terms of social integration, rate of excluding minority from mainstream participation or the existing forms of relative deprivation should not be seen as a single entity. The above-mentioned social conditions should be seen as related to another. One societal existence ignites other forms of social conditions. Social existence and social conditions should be seen towards a more relational way.

Social discrimination in its simplest term means treating someone unfairly. Every type of society practices some forms of discrimination whether in race relations or in ethnic relations. In contemporary times, modern societies are all diverse in its ethno-racial composition. Factors like migration, rapid industrialization, urbanization, and modernization in every sense also led to mixing up of various groups of people. It is hard to find any non-diversified society particularly in this era of Globalism. As a result, issues of social discrimination are a matter of serious concern to nation building and in the discourse of several academic disciplines. In every type of society social discrimination or unfair treatment usually happens in the sphere of inter-race relations, between ethnic relations, inter-caste relations, and inter-class relations and in gender relations. From the sociological point of view sociologists like W.G. Sumner and Franklin H. Giddings[4] explained social discrimination as cultural ethnocentrism expressed as a phenomenon of dislike of the others. Ethnocentrism simply leads to stereotyping about socially derived beliefs of each ethno-racial group about other ethno-racial groups. Such stereotyping leads to serious sociological significance. Social discrimination sometimes concentrates also on patterns of dominance and oppression. For example, in the Indian society, caste as a form of social discrimination is not just about purity and pollution. Caste system is also many times seen as a form of social discrimination by practicing forms of dominance and oppression.

Another aspect that lends a better understanding to the concept of social discrimination is the degree of social integration. Social integration refers to the set of factors like central institutional context, constitutional measures by reference to which different kinds of individual and collective actions acquire significance as measures for greater or lesser degree of social cohesion. For any type of society, primary reference point for the analysis of social integration has to be the complex unity of democratic, market or welfare state relations whose claim to legitimacy is based on their embodiment of different kinds of rights enjoyed by the different ethno-racial groups. The degree of social integration being enjoyed by different communities and individuals can be understood only when forms of social discrimination exist. For example, the level of social integration enjoyed by the minority groups in split labor market, certain ethnic groups as fit for the particular job like the Mexicans as domestic helpers in Unites States signifies the level of poor social integration. In such cases, forms of social exclusion occur.

David Lockwood introduced the notion of civic stratification. According to Lockwood, civic stratification is the way in which the structures of life-chances and social identities are the direct or the indirect result of the institutionalization of citizenship under conditions of social and economic inequality.[5] To Lockwood, civic stratification leads to serious unintended consequences on social integration. Further, Lockwood highlighted – civic stratification can be seen from two views, and first, to the extent in which state's interlocking institutions function effectively to maintain the level of social integration. Effectiveness of state's interlocking institutions can be observed in delivering the goods to the citizens irrespective of their cultural differences. Secondly, forms of civic stratification can be seen at the level of social integration through the structuring and legitimizing of inequalities. The main flaw in Lockwood's approach on civic stratification is too much emphasis on state's institutional approach. Civic stratification can also be viewed from the structures of the society. State guarantees equal rights to every civic individuals and civic groups. The point to be mentioned here is that the social inequalities, forms of social exclusion, social discrimination and disruptions on social integration happen not just due to the state's institutional factors. Forms of social discrimination like gender inequality, caste based discrimination, and ethno-racial based split labor market opportunities have been due to dominant modes of thought influencing in every social structure not by state; state doesn't promote discrimination.

Glen G. Cain explained social discrimination as the label attached to the valuation of some personal characteristics, which is related to job performances and existing performances.[6] In fact it is true that social discrimination takes place in every type of society when certain valuations exist above actual conditions. The point needs to be added here on Cain's explanations is that, in every type of society valuations differ. For example, certain valuations like tribes are backward in some societies may not be true in some other societies, simply because of the reason like modernization had indeed changed social conditions of tribes from backwardness towards development or the conditions of gender discrimination and gender disparity may vary from one society to another. But in general, forms of social discrimination take place usually when inferences are measured and evaluated based on personal attachments. The point which is to be added here is that some personal characteristics especially ascribed to another groups by some groups is a disease which has no remedy. Such factors lead to several social consequences and life chances.

Social discrimination also involves study of conflicts witnessing in the society. When certain social groups try to discriminate other groups, protest or conflict usually takes place. As groups or individuals struggle over forms of differential treatment, society will witness conflict as an outcome of it. While explaining social discrimination one should also take into account forms of conflict as an outcome. Social discrimination refers also to the differential treatment on the basis of some personal attributes. Differential treatment based on personal attributes leads to certain social consequences in the form of social discrimination and sometimes in the form of protest or conflicts. That's the reason why sociologists and economists often fall into the trap of forms of conflict as the base while explaining social discrimination. Marxist oriented sociologists and economists, while explaining forms of social discrimination, usually regard the nature of conflict determined by measures of production as their focal point for analyzing social discrimination. For example, certain measures of production are better rewarded for one group than another as in the case of split labor market. In such situations, conflicts usually happen between the labor groups due to the fact that whites are better rewarded than blacks for educational attainment.

Some of the theoretical advancements on social discrimination had been advanced based on the relative differences of power enjoyed by the different groups of people.[7] Lester Thurow,[8] Hubert M. Blalock,[9] and Stanley Lieberson[10] have used differential power approach, which gave the argument that social discrimination occurs as long as there are differences of power between the groups of individuals. Those who are privileged always strive to maintain their privileged status by discriminating others. Another interesting theoretical advancement on social discrimination is the institutional approach taken by Gameson and Modigliani,[11] Glazer,[12] and Jencks.[13] Institutional approach on social discrimination gave the opinion that social discriminations can be explained and debated in terms of social policy such as affirmative action, reverse discrimination and equality of opportunity. One of the interesting features of institutional approach on social discrimination highlights the fact that it is the public institutions like the court and judicial magistrate, which define social discrimination. Public institutions like the court engages itself in defining social discrimination and their explanations vary from time to time. That's why Barbara Bergman claimed that the meaning of social discrimination has been left itself to the courts to define what behaviors are discriminatory and what are not.[14] It seems that courts always respond to definitions of social discrimination by involving in judgments on and sensitivity to what is socially disapproved. The point mentioned here is that the understanding those forms of social discrimination vary in accordance with the types of public institutions and the existing social structures. A relational approach based on the relation between forms of existing public institutions and existing social structures should also be taken into account if someone wants to explain social discrimination in a more meaningful manner. It is quite amazing that any type of public institution is always ready to blame any forms of social discrimination, while the existing social structures like the cultural belief systems, dominant modes of thought, ethnocentrism, attributions and tags of some groups promote forms of social discrimination. Should we blame the state's institutions or the dark veil covering group's mind?

Racism into Another Dimension

Seeing another ethnic group as inferior is indeed a natural gift to the humans. Also considering an inferior group as derogatory or ignorant poor souls happens to be the consequence of human modes of thought. History is witnes to several evidences that tried to abolish slavery. The World Conference on Racism, Durban 2001 also came to the conclusion that racism has indeed come to an end. The question still remains with no absolute answer: 'has racism died or has it reincarnated into some new forms?'

In 1884, twenty-four years after the abolition of slavery, the Encyclopedia Britannica continued to express racism in same length and breadth. The description on racism which they found in Encyclopedia Britannica of 1884 according to sociologists, Harlambos and Heald, was that the African Negroes occupied the lowest social position in the evolutionary scale and this was supposedly demonstrated by their abnormally long arms and lightweight brains.[15] The argument, which I put forward here, is that racism has been a fact, which always tries to persist even if enlightened citizens tried level best to put to an end. As long as the earth revolves around the sun, racism is going to spin in a new fashion sharing its orbit with the earth. The ideology of racism seems very difficult to erase. According to racial theorist Michael Banton, it was assumed that racial differences had existed from early period of pre-history when different stocks had been created either by god or by some natural catastrophe. Banton also gave the opinion that the idea of race *'as a type'* gained its popularity as people of European origin came into closer contact with other groups.[16] Another racial theorist Howard Winant also expresses origin of racism along the same line. Racial categorization of human beings was a European invention.[17]

Ruth F. Benedict defined racism as the dogma that one ethnic group is condemned by nature to congenial inferiority and another group is destined to congenial superiority.[18] Pierre Van Der Berghe defined racism as any set of beliefs that organic, genetically transmitted differences, whether real or imagined, between human groups are intrinsically associated with the presence or the absence of certain socially relevant abilities or characteristics, hence that such differences are a legitimate basis of invidious distinction between groups socially defined as race.[19] Richard T. Scaheffer also predicted that firstly, racism is defined as a set of beliefs or ideas. Secondly, those beliefs are regarded as having the potential to lead individuals to develop prejudice defined as negative attitudes towards an entire group of people.[20] Descriptions on racism should not be seen only in terms of their phenotypical and biological elements. If we considered racism only in the phenotypical and biological category, we simply couldn't express the societal elements of every racial category. The most wonderful element is those social appendages on racial categories which depict the nature of social stratification existing in every type of society based on racism. Racism no longer becomes just an ideology to be analyzed. Racism also becomes an important factor on determining life chances i.e. on themes of social exclusion and other forms of social prejudice, social discrimination, etc. The point to be mentioned here is that racism is not just an ideology, but it has elements of social attaches, which directly or indirectly affect life chances in the forms of social exclusion and social discrimination.

It is widely agreed that the theoretical contribution on racism began with the growth of Chicago school. W.E. Dubois' *The Philadelphia Negro* also formed an important component on the growth of Chicago School of Sociology, despite of the fact that Chicago school is famous for its contributions on urban sociology. With the growth of theoretical perspectives on racism, the primordial thought on racism also shifted towards a new direction. At the very beginning, racism was understood generally in terms of their phenotypes and biological components. Biological conception tries to explain racism in terms of human traits to designate a racial group for negative reasons. Later on by middle of the twentieth century, racial theorists tried to keep aside the popular conception on racism and attempted to formulate racial theories based on the foundations of social structure. Chicago sociologists broke purposefully the doctrine of racial biology that had characterized earlier conceptions on race. Chicago school emphasized on the social construct with the increasing clarity of the position that race is a product of the social relations rather than naturally given phenomenon.[21] Racial theorists debunked the popular conception of race based on biological determinism. Fredrik Barth noted that races, as most social scientists acknowledge, are not biologically understood but socially determined categories of identity and group associations.[22] Harold Winant was also of the view that race can be defined as a concept that signifies and symbolizes socio-political conflicts and interests in reference to different types of human bodies.[23]

Approaches on Racial Theories as a form of Social Exclusion and Discrimination

In the very beginning of the growth of racial theories, racial theorists relied on Marxist approach. Race was seen as a form of class along Marxist lines. Marxist theorists on racism adopted ideology of class exclusion, class segregation, class struggles and class discrimination in theorizing racial forms of social exclusion and social discrimination. Since class struggles and class discrimination have been regarded as the central explanatory tool for every form of society and social life, theorists like Oliver C. Cox[24] and Victor Perlo[25] regard racism to a legitimizing ideology used by the bourgeoisie to divide the working class. To Cox racism is not an abstract, natural, immemorial feeling of mutual antipathy between groups, but rather a practical exploitative relationship with its socio-attitudinal facilitation. In other words, Cox explained that racism is a set of beliefs used to justify and therefore to sustain the exploitation of one group by another racial group. Some new generation Marxists attempted to theorize racism as an ideology. This group of new generation Marxists equates the idea of class dynamics as the driving force which ignites the tendencies for racial dynamics.[26] Such Marxists viewed race as an existing form of resistance between the different races. For example, Bonacich's work on racism explains an interesting approach by regarding race relations and racism as products of a split labor market.[27] Theoretical perspective as forwarded by Bonacich on race is within the primacy of distribution within the working class. But to all Marxist theorists on racism, racial antagonism is still a byproduct of class dynamics and class differentiation within the existing form of social system and relations of production. The point sufficed here is that the major flaws in the Marxist approach are not explained because the theorists couldn't elaborate the significance of racial prejudice over ethno-cultural belongings. Marxist theorists on racism simply advance their position by viewing racism as a pure phenomenon of political economy. Belongings over ethnic groups, cultural groups and minority groups were simply not taken into account. Ethnic belongings and cultural belongings are the base for any societal foundations. If any race or a group of races needs to be analyzed properly, one cannot negate the importance of ethno-cultural belongings. Marxist theorists on racism don't even regard such ethno-cultural belongings as secondary factors for racial discrimination and racial exclusion. The argument to be forwarded here will be elaborated in the later part of this paper.

Institutionalist approach on racism defined racism as a combination of prejudice and power that allows the dominant race to institutionalize its dominance at all levels in society.[28] Theorists of Institutionalism approach on racism opine that racism as a form of social exclusion and social discrimination flourishes due to the existing systems of institutions. Institutions in every social system have their own set of rules, beliefs, values that tolerate the majority to exercise its influences and doctrine of selectivity. In the same perimeter, theorists like Marie Barrera, Robert Blauner and Joan W. Moore viewed racism as an institutional matter based on a system in which the white majority raises its social position by exploiting, controlling and keeping down others who are categorized in racial or ethnic terms.[29] However, Institutionalist approach faces certain limitations in the wider objectives of the modern nation states. Modern nation states don't promote racism or racial exclusion through its various institutions. Blue-print of several institutions of modern nation states have its arms wide open to welcome every racial category. The main fallacy is in the functioning of those institutions itself. It is at the level of functioning and at the level of praxis that the institutions don't escape the wrath of criticism. It is the question of how those who manage several institutions try to maintain certain standards. It is this question of efficacy and maintaining certain standards that leads to discrimination and exclusion of certain minority races. Who did operationalize and functionalize the institutions? The answer will always be the same; it is the dominant and the majority races that run the whole show.

According to racial theorist Harold Winant, races were created for some function. Winant formulated a socio-historical understanding on racism. Socio-historical understanding on racism opined that racial categories are created, inhabited, transformed and destroyed.[30] In this sense, race should be regarded as an organizing principle of social relationships that shapes the identity of individual actors at the micro level and shapes all spheres of social life at the macro level. Winant is one of the very few racial theorists who advance the understanding on racism and racial ideology that directly serves the purpose of various forms of social discrimination and social exclusion. The perspectives on racism by racial theorists like Michael Omi and Harold Winant were based on socio-historical analysis. Omi and Winant define racial as the socio-historical process by which racial categories are created, inhabited, transformed and destroyed.[31]

Theoretical approach on racism based on the existing social system was put forwarded by E. Bonilla Silva. Silva explains that racialized social system refers to the societies in which economic, political, social and all ideological levels are partially structured by the placement of individuals in racial categories or races.[32] By structure, Silva signifies the network of interactional relationship among actors as well as the distribution of socially meaningful characters of actors and group of actors. On general understanding, races can be typically identified by their phenotypes and biological features. But, forms of social exclusion, social prejudice and social discrimination exist due to such understanding on biologics. Silva is one of the racial theorists who attempt to explain the questions on the forms of racial discrimination and exclusion of various races by some superior races based on social factors rather than biology.

Citizens of Northeast India as a Variety

Northeast part of India still remains one of the most excluded and unexplored portion in India. Northeast India is one of South Asian land frontiers which through much of the twentieth century have attracted large scale *illegal* migration from the rest of the subcontinent.[33] These sparsely populated areas are also famous for tribal groups inhibiting the hills and plains. Sometimes, northeast part of India is also labeled as the anthropological laboratory. Several tribal groups which have inhabited in northeast part of India since time immemorial reveal some similar features. All these tribal groups are racially different from other racial groups residing in India. Tribes of northeast India belong to the Mongoloid racial groups and Tibeto-Burmese races. Tribes in northeast India have been experiencing social changes to a great extent. Modernization, urbanization, western education, changes in terms of socio-economic aspects, socio-religious changes have been witnessing in different aspects at all the tribal societies of northeast India. Indeed, the rate of change since the beginning of the early twentieth century is so formidable. The role played by colonial administrators and Christian missionaries had a huge impact on the patterns of social changes being witnessed in the Northeast India. Till today, often-recommended colleges and schools in Northeast India were due to the efforts of Christian Missionaries.

Students, working people, professionals, lawyers, bureaucrats, ministers, and officials, whenever they moved out of northeast India, often face forms of exclusion and discrimination. Indeed, there was a mockery incident or you can call it a comic story, which the former speaker of the Parliament Purno A. Sangma told in an NDTV interview. Purno mentioned that the former Chief Minister of Nagaland and the present Governor of Goa S.C. Jamir were asked to produce his Republic of India 'Passport' at the Taj Palace hotel in New Delhi, that too at the presence of the chief secretary and official staff of Nagaland. I am sure a layman would think that incident in a naive manner. Events like this such as on the question of misjudged identity and citizens of northeast as otherness usually ensue within the mainland Indian nation. Not at anywhere else in the world. Failure to recognize even a fellow citizen's identity and belongings indeed shows how 'de-multicultural' the citizens of India are, despite its diverse nature. Will Kymlicka strongly believe that the faith of the nation can be revealed not only on the justice of its basic institutions of the state, but also on the qualities and attitudes of its citizens e.g. their sense of identity on the regional, ethnic or religious identities, their ability to tolerance and questions of working together?[34] Charles Taylor also reiterates that recognition of identities easily suffice who they are and the fundamental characteristics of a human being.[35] Failure to recognize the citizens of northeast India in a more appropriate manner leads to the formation of northeast India as a variety in itself. The point to be added here is that it is on the question of racial minority and on the question of tribes which predominantly inhabit in northeast part of India that this region remained excluded and discriminated socially, economically and culturally not just topographically.

On what grounds citizens of northeast India were excluded and discriminated by the mainland India? It is on the question of misjudged identity, racialized presumption, and citizens of northeast as a minority racial category. Such questions if un-answered properly lead to politics of exclusion. The issue is even more disturbing if the masses of citizens from northeast India who are living outside the region for certain reasons are considered. There are masses of students who have been pursuing their higher studies due to the unavailability of center for excellence in various academic disciplines. Not just students, but many professionals and lawyers have been pursuing their livings outside of northeast India. Incidents on question of 'north-east as racial otherness', and northeast as 'minority category' have been occurring in other destinations. The question of otherness i.e. northeast India as a rather different item from the Indian mainland crops up easily to a non-northeasterners. The more disturbing element seems to be the fact that northeast India is racially and culturally different from the majority of Indian population. Difference from the majority or the so-called mainland Indians paves the way to misjudge identity and its cultural belongings. When a minority group's identity is misjudged and un-recognized it often leads to obnoxious and derogatory statements about the particular minority groups especially in a country like India.

Genesis of Chinki

In fact the term 'Chinki' won't be there in any encyclopedia and dictionaries. It is generally believed that the term Chinki originates from 'Chin' and 'ki'. Chin is a racial term, which is often, used to connote the Mongoloid races and the Tibeto-Burmese races. And, 'ki' is a suffix, which is usually used, in Hindi words and Hindi literature. In fact majority of the ethnic groups in northeast part of India belong to the mongoloid and Tibeto-Burmese racial group. People from northeast India resemble biologics different from the mainstream races of India with different phenotypical and genotypical features. Mainstream races in India are either Dravidians or the Aryan races. Even in institutions where the author of this paper studied, i.e. University of Delhi and Jawaharlal Nehru University, New Delhi, students and visitors from northeast India are often being labeled as 'oh! that Chinki'. Even in places where I visited outside of Delhi and outside of northeast part of India, I was being told by many of my friends and colleagues that citizens from northeast part of India were being treated inferiorly and being labeled with the derogatory term Chinki. Whether to literate or illiterate citizens outside of northeast India, they have at least some idea and social connotations of the term Chinki. In modern day, usage of Chinki can be found in newspaper and media too. Chinki has become a new identity, which is not yet recognized by the Indian state. But, unofficial recognition of the terminology is indeed huge and it ignites a large negative social space that can be usually labeled as forms of social discrimination and social exclusion.

Issues of Exclusion and Social Discrimination

When a normal child or any ordinary person grows up in a normal family as a normal person, there is no disproportion between the life chances of the person and the person's identity. When those ordinary persons move out of the native place for better opportunities in life, persons from northeast face a myth of a vilified identification tag. Such vilification tag is labeled as 'Chinki'. This tag is not a socially affable tag, because it leads to several socio-political, socio-economic and socio-cultural underestimations. Simply because of the reason—normal or ordinary person faces the wrath of vilification tag and underestimations due to their racial differences, which is difference of biologics. It is very clear from the explanations of the racial theorists that difference in races leads to several social attributes, which directly affects the life chances of any normal persons of the minority races. Racial theorist Harold Winant explained that races were created for some function. Winant formulated a socio-historical understanding on racism. Socio-historical understanding on racism opined that racial categories are created, inhabited, transformed and destroyed.[36] Affecting any life chances due to any social estimation is a sign of social discrimination and social exclusion. The question which keeps on echoing to peoples mind—is it because of being racial difference or into the category of minority racial groups any ordinary person from northeast India faces underestimation? Social underestimation by labeling a minority racial group with any vilifying tag like 'Chinki' is nevertheless a sign of social discrimination and social exclusion. Racism based on the existing social system as submitted by E. Bonilla Silva is also valid in the case of such forms of social discrimination being faced by people from northeast India. Silva explained that racialized social system refers to the societies in which economic, political, social and all ideological levels are partially structured by the placement of individuals in racial categories or races.[37] Ordinary persons from northeast India face forms of social exclusion and social discrimination outside of northeast India at several times. Even in matters of job appointments and selection procedures, people from northeast India are being considered as *secondary* options. The secondary factor comes from nowhere but simply because of racial difference, being a racial minority and due to pre-conceived social attributions. Underestimations, secondary options are because of the fact that racial minorities usually face social attributions in terms of negative attaches only. Negative attaches being labeled to any racial minority is also a form of oppression being experienced by the racial minorities.

Chinki becomes a new identity that is being used in the socio-political and economic relations within India. This new identity itself becomes an identification tag to segregate and practice the politics of exclusion in the Indian institutional setup, informally. To suffice, citizens from northeast India cannot participate fully in the decision making bodies of higher authorities. Who gives a heavy thought on any voices from people from northeast India? Any outsider will see these laggings on representation in public sphere and decision-making authorities. Chinki as a new identity also faces the wrath of the split labor markets. In the sweat shops and in the labour markets, people from northeast India face social discrimination and social exclusion. Eligible candidates and eligible people from northeast India are being treated inferiorly in job applications too. The main reason behind is due to their derogatory social attributes on their identity and social expectations generally believed by the institutional setup, as racial theorists like Oliver C. Cox[38] and Victor Perlo have argued.[39] As mentioned earlier, racism is not an abstract, natural, immemorial feeling of mutual antipathy between groups, but rather a practical exploitative relationship with its socio-attitudinal facilitation. In other words, Cox explained that racism is a set of beliefs used to justify and therefore to sustain the exploitation of one group by another racial group. What Stuart Hall had mentioned in his essay 'Who needs Identity?'[40] is also true in the case of racial minorities of northeast India. To Stuart Hall, new identities are constructed within, not outside for some reasons, at least for some socio-political and socio-economic reasons. Let's reconsider the fact and remind the readers that has there been any top ranking official from northeast India in the Indian bureaucracy, Indian judicial services, Indian defense services or any Indian institutional set up. The answer is not at all. Is it because of their incompetency or is it because of being in a racial minority? The construction and usage of new identity terminology should also be understood in specific historical and institutional sites. Stuart Hall submits the opinion that the issue of identity emerges within the play of specific modalities of power and there is more the product of making the difference and exclusion than they are the sign of an identical naturally constituted unity.[41] One must understand the process of creating new identities very lucidly.

Any normal person from northeast India faces forms of social discrimination and social underestimations especially in the split labor market. Ordinary citizens from northeast India are also being employed and used for certain profit motives. The September issue of *Outlook* magazine in 2007 reported some disturbing social practices in Bangalore city of India. People from northeast India are being employed as salesmen and sales women in up market retail sectors. Also, some of the students who were studying there are being employed as bar attendants because of their different facial features. Certain ethnic groups suitable for certain jobs mainly in the informal sector are examples of the highest degree of social discrimination and social exclusion being approved by profit motive principles. For example in North America, Hispanics are treated as more suitable for domestic helps. Indians, Pakistanis and Bangladeshis are more suitable as cabbies on the streets. The point to be submitted here is that the profit motive principles also lead to forms of racial discrimination and social discrimination. Marxists also viewed race as an existing form of resistance between the different races. For example, works on racism by Marxist-influenced scholars regard race relations and racism as products of a split labor market.[42] Forms of social discrimination as forwarded by Marxist theorists still hold valid for minority races inhabiting in India. Forms of racial exclusion and social discrimination are within the primacy of distribution within the working class. The most disturbing element is that some under-privileged and minority racial groups in India are being exploited for profit motive principles. Some racial minority groups like the people from northeast India are also socially attributed as suitable for certain types of derogatory jobs in the labor market.

Minority racial groups from northeast India confront forms of social discrimination and social exclusion even in the formal sector. A combination of prejudice and power that allows the dominant races to institutionalize its dominance at all levels is also witnessed in the case of northeast India. Institutionalist approach on racism opines that racism as a form of social exclusion and social discrimination flourishes due to the existing systems of institutions. If someone looks at the level of functioning of several institutions operating in northeast India any outsider will be surely amazed. There is a separate ministry widely known as DONER (Directorate of North Eastern Region) just for northeast India. Is it for good or for worse? Is it necessary to have such a ministry? What is the reason for establishing such ministry? The plans outlaid by such ministry don't finish up at all or are delivered in time. In blueprints and reports it sounds nice, but something is really wrong. Why unequal treatment? The higher authorities have been implementing special policy just for northeast India. I think it will be useful to reiterate the former vice-chancellor of NEHU (North Eastern Hills University) Mrinal Miri's reprimand that the idea of a nation having a policy towards a part of itself is odd.[43] Institutions in every social system have their own set of rules, beliefs, values that tolerate the majority to exercise its influence and doctrine of selectivity.[44] At the same length and breadth theorists like Marie Barrera, Robert Blauner and Joan W. Moore also viewed racism as an institutional matter based on a system in which the white majority raises its social position by exploiting, controlling and keeping down others who are categorized in racial or ethnic terms.[45] The point to remind here is that the northeast India remained underdeveloped and remained untouched due to the institutional setup since independence. Several institutions operating in northeast India receive so many complaints. It is only at the amount of complaints that the people of northeast India used to realize social discrimination due to racial differences. For namesake, these institutions have its arms wide open to welcome every human irrespective of differences; but when it comes to real situations, people of northeast India are being treated as hyphenated citizenship. By hyphenated citizenship, the issue which I would like to reiterate goes analogous to explanations given by Michael Walzer. Due to in-equations in the institutional set up within India, minority groups like minority races and underprivileged groups like the weaker sections have not been able to fully participate in the public sphere. This leads us to a realization whether the institutional set up within India is fair enough or does it poise its notion of justice. Institutional set up in India blindly asks itself the question of efficacy and maintaining certain standards. Forms of discrimination and exclusion of minority races and minority groups become vivid when institutions attempt to answer it. The fact remains that the whole show for operationalizing institutions in the Indian social context is run by the dominant and the majority races.

Labeling the citizens of northeast India as Chinki has serious consequences in the relationship between the subjects and the discursive patterns on growth of identity. If a vilification tag like Chinki is being ascribed to the whole northeast India informally, it leads to serious unintended consequences on their life chances, which is in fact happening right now. Social Status of the identity is itself beleaguered and the real process of identification is scrapped in such a way for social under-estimations and negative social attributions only. As a matter of fact, negative social attributions on northeast India for being a tribal dominated area had resulted in several social consequences. The ascription of vilification tag like Chinki itself gives more wounds on their social identity. The paper reiterates here what Michel Foucault opined that the process of identification itself should be a reconceptualization or should think in its new displaced or decentered position. But that is not enough in the process of identification. Process of identification should always be in the relationship between subjects and discursive patterns on growth of identity. Process of identification should also re-articulate the relationship between politics of exclusion and forms of social discrimination.

NOTES AND REFERENCES

1. For details see Pete Townsend, P. Corrigan and U. Kowarzik, '*Poverty and Labour in London*' (London, The Low Pay Publications, 1987), (Reprint 2007).
2. See A. Walker and C. Walker, '*Britain Divided: the growth of social exclusion in the 1980s and 1990s*' (London, Child Poverty Action Group, 1997).
3. As quoted from Eduardo Bonilla Silva (1997), 'Rethinking Racism: Towards a Structural Interpretation' in *American Sociological Review*, Vol. 62, No. 3 (June 1997), pp. 465-480.
4. Michael Harlambos and David Heald, *Sociology: Themes and Perspectives*, 5th edition (London, Collins, 2000), pp. 189-289.
5. David Lockwood (1996), 'Civic Integration and Class Formation', *The British Journal of Sociology*, Vol. 47, No. 3, September 1996, pp. 531-500.
6. Glen G. Cain (1986), 'The Economic Analysis of Labour Market Discrimination', in Orley A. Shenfeller and Richard Layard (eds.), *The Handbook of Labour Economics*, Vol. 1 (Amsterdam, Elsevier Publications, 1986), p. 694.
7. Garry Becker, *The Economics of Discrimination*, 2nd edition (Chicago, University of Chicago Press, 1971).
8. Lester Thurow, *Generating Inequality* (New York, Basic Books, 1975).
9. Hubert M. Blalock Jr., *Towards a Theory of Minority Group Relations* (New York, Wiley Publication, 1967).
10. Stanley Lieberson, *Making it Count* (Berkeley, University of California Press, 1985).
11. A. Gamson William and Andre Modigliani, 'The Changing Culture of Affirmative Action' in *Research in Political Sociology*, Vol. 3, 1987, pp. 137-177.
12. Nathan Glazer, *Ethnic Dilemmas: 1964-1982* (Cambridge, University of Harvard Press, 1983).
13. Christopher Jencks, 'What must be equal for opportunity to be equal?' in Norman E. Bowie (ed.), *Equal Opportunity* (Bouldet, West View Press, 1988), pp. 47-74.
14. Barbara Bergman, *The Economic Emergence of Women* (New York, Basic Books, 1986).

15. Michael Harlambos and David Heald, *Sociology: Themes and Perspectives*, 5th edition (London, Collins, 2000).
16. Michael Banton, *Racial Theories* (Cambridge, Cambridge University Press, 1987).
17. Howard Winant, *Racial Conditions: Politics, Theory, Comparison* (Minneapolis, University of Minnesota Press, 1994), p. 172.
18. Ruth F. Benedict, *Race and Racism* (London, Routledge and Kegan Paul, 1945), p. 87.
19. Van Der Berghe Pierre, *Race and Racism: A Comparative Perspective* (New York, John Wiley and Sons, 1967), p. 11.
20. Richard T. Schaeffer, *Racial and Ethnic Groups*, 4th edition (Illinois, Scott Foresmann, 1990), p. 53.
21. Immanuel Wallerstein, 'The Construction of Peoplehood: racism, nationalism, ethnicity' in E. Balibar and Immanuel Wallerstein (eds.), *'Race', Nation, Class* (London, Verso, 1991); Robert E. Park, *Race and Culture* (Glencoe, The Free Press, 1950).
22. Fredrik Barth, 'Introduction', in F. Barth (ed.), *Ethnic Groups and Boundaries: the Social Organization of Cultural differences* (Bergen, Universitets Forleget, 1969), pp. 9-38.
23. Howard Winant, *Racial Conditions: Politics, Theory, Comparison* (Minneapolis, University of Minnesota Press, 1994).
24. Oliver C. Cox, *Caste, Class and Race* (New York, Doubleday, 1945).
25. Victor Perlo, *Economics of Racism in U.S.A.: Roots of Black Inequality* (New York, International Publishers, 1975).
26. Edna Bonacich, 'Advanced Capitalism and Black/White Relation in the united states: A Split Labor Market interpretations' in T. Pettigrew (ed.), *The Sociology of Race Relations: Reflections and Reform* (Free Press, New York, 1980), pp. 341-362; Stuart Hall, 'Who needs Identity?' in Paul du Gay, Jessica Evans and Peter Redman (eds.), *Identity: A Reader* (London, Sage Publication, 2000), pp. 15-31; Gerry Cohen, 'Reconsidering Historical Materialism' in A. Gallinicos (ed.), *Marxist Theory* (Oxford, Oxford University Press, 1989), pp. 88-104; John Solomos, 'Varieties of Marxist Conception of 'Race', Class and the State: A Critical Analysis' in J. Rex and D. Mason (ed.), *Theories of Race and Ethnic Relation* (Cambridge, Cambridge University Press, 1986), pp. 84-109; John Solomos, *Race and Racism in Contemporary Britain* (London, MacMillan, 1989).
27. Edna Bonacich, 'Advanced Capitalism and Black/White Relation in the United States: A Split Labor Market interpretations' in T. Pettigrew (ed.), *The Sociology of Race Relations: Reflections and Reform* (New York, Free Press, 1980), pp. 341-362.
28. Rodolfo Alvarez, Kenneth G. Lutterman and Associates, *Discrimination in Organizations: Using Social Indicators to Manage Social Change* (San

Francisco, Jossey-Bass, 1979); Stokley Carmichael, *Stokely Speaks: Black Power to Pan Africanism* (New York, Vintage Books, 1971); David Wellman, *Portraits of White Racism* (Cambridge, Cambridge University Press, 1977).

29. Maria Barrera, *Race and Class in the South West: A Theory of Racial Inequality* (Notre Dame, University of Notre Dame Press, 1945); Robert Blaunner, *Racial Oppression in America* (New York, Harper and Row, 1972); Joan W. Moore, 'Colonialism: The Case of the Mexican—Americans', in *Social Problems,* Vol. 17, 1970, pp. 463-472.
30. Howard Winant, *Racial Conditions: Politics, Theory, Comparison* (Minneapolis, University of Minnesota Press, 1994), p. 55.
31. Michael Omi, Howard Winant, *Racial Formation in the Unites States: From 1960s to the 1980s,* 2nd edition (New York: Routledge, 1994), p. 55.
32. Eduardo Bonilla Silva, 'Rethinking Racism: Towards a Structural Interpretation' in *American Sociological Review,* Vol. 62, No. 3, June 1997, pp. 465-480.
33. Sanjib Baruah (2005), *Durable Disorder: Understanding the politics of Northeast India* (New Delhi, Oxford University Press, 2005), p. 185.
34. Will Kymlicka, *Contemporary Political Philosophy: An Introduction* (London, Oxford University Press, 2002).
35. Charles Taylor, *Multiculturalism and the Politics of Recognition,* (Princeton, Princeton University Press.1992).
36. Howard Winant, *Racial Conditions: Politics, Theory, Comparison* (Minneapolis, University of Minnesota Press, 1994), p. 55.
37. Eduardo Bonilla Silva, 'Rethinking Racism: Towards a Structural Interpretation' in *American Sociological Review,* Vol. 62, No. 3, June 1997, pp. 465-480.
38. Oliver C. Cox, *Caste, Class and Race* (New York, Doubleday Publications, 1945).
39. Victor Perlo, *Economics of Racism U.S.A.: Roots of Black Inequality* (New York, International Publishers, 1975).
40. Stuart Hall, 'Who needs Identity?' in Paul du Gay, Jessica Evans and Peter Redman (eds.), *Identity: A Reader* (London, Sage Publication), pp. 15-31.
41. *Ibid.,* pp. 16-31.
42. Bonacich, 'Advanced Capitalism and Black/White Relation in the United States: A Split Labor Market interpretations', *op. cit.;* Hall, 'Who needs Identity?' *op. cit.;* Cohen, 'Reconsidering Historical Materialism.', *op. cit.;* Solomos, 'Varieties of Marxist Conception of 'Race', Class and the State: A Critical Analysis', *op. cit.*; and also see his *Race and Racism in Contemporary Britain, op. cit.*

43. Mrinal Miri, 'Northeast: A point of View' (A public Lecture), Available online: http://www.manipuronline.com/features/May 2002/north-east 14.2htm.
44. Alvarez, *Discrimination in Organizations: Using Social Indicators to Manage Social Change, op. cit.*, Wellman, *Portraits of White Racism, op. cit.*
45. Blaunner, *Racial Oppression in America, op. cit;* Moore, 'Colonialism: The Case of the Mexican—Americans', *op. cit.*

9

From Untouchables to Dalit Christians: Conversion and Social Exclusion

L. DAVID LAL

Conversion carries the connotations of abrupt behaviour whereby people are supposed to give up their old ways in a bound and embracing an entire new pattern of belief and behaviour. Conversion implies accepting a set of beliefs and practices which is quiet different from the system and religious commitment previously experienced. In Indian context conversion is related not only to spiritual aspect but also to material aspect. Conversion is not a new phenomena in Indian society, the exodus of people converting (particularly the Dalits) to Christianity generated lot of debate over time and again. The plight of Dalits in Christianity even after the conversion for more than a century continues. They are forced to live a life of exclusion. The various kinds of discrimination practiced in the society, church and by the state are unique in nature for the Dalit Christians. This paper attempts to address the practices and complexities of the Dalit Christians.

Discussion of the conversion problem in India has been a subject of great debate for many years now. Conversion is a term commonly used for the process of people changing their faith from one religion to another. In India conversion is not only a series of action to achieve a religious migration but it also has a significant role in social[1] and political[2] arena. Conversion to Buddhism, Bahaism, Jainism, and Islam in the past has been a challenge to the traditional religion and the inequalities existed there within. Among these conversions occurred in different periods, this paper closely studies conversion to Christianity.

The character and extent of Christian conversion not only provide material of some interest for the students of the sociology of religion, but also throw important light on the conceptual framework on conversion. This paper is divided into two sections: Section I will map the existing theories and concepts and investigate the reasons behind set of beliefs, system of truth and religious commitment. It discusses various meanings of conversion in Indian context and the different opinions. Section II enquires about the conversion of Dalits into Christianity in a historical perspective. Furthermore, the Christian conversion is not possible without referring to the caste issue. The significant part of Christian converts belongs to the ex-untouchable communities across India. It will also throw light on the condition of Dalit Christians in the post-conversion phase. The practice of discrimination and social exclusion against the Dalit Christians will be the special focus of this paper.

I

This section of the paper will address the different conversion theories and concepts. Conversion predominantly falls under the field of religious studies. A combination of disciplines including psychology, sociology, theology and ethnology allows for an interesting study into so-called 'conversion' phenomena and takes it to new horizons. In the earlier period there was no proper study to understand the various dimensions of conversion; however, from the beginning of twentieth century the social scientists felt the need to conceptualize conversion. In the wake of the worldwide wave of new religious movements like Esoteric, Hare Krishna, Japanese Buddhist movement, the resurgence of traditional religions and the conversions by the people have led to a quest for understanding the various phenomena behind conversion. This section of the paper will do an interpretative and a critical analysis on the existing theories on conversion.

Theoretical Pluralism

Most of the investigation on conversion has been concerned primarily with an attempt to identify the causes of conversion. The existing literature on conversion can be put into two main phases of research. The first phase with the early 20th century was dominated by theological, psychological and the 'Coercive persuasion' or 'Brainwashing' model of conversion.[3] The next phase began in the

1960s; this phase gave the study of conversion a new dimension with sociological and theoretical observations. The publication of the 'Lofland-Stark conversion model' in 1965 signaled the arrival of the period of explanatory attempts that rely heavily on sociological thinking and empirical methods.[4] Researchers of the later phase have investigated number of reasons and causes for conversion. These investigations were theoretical and empirical. They may be grouped into the following categories: first, psycho physiological responses to conversion and induced stress; second, predisposing personality traits and cognitive orientations; third, situational factors that induced stress; fourth, predisposing social attributes; fifth, a variety of social influences; lastly, casual process explanations involving the confluence of a range of elements.[5]

In defining the phenomena of conversion two distinctive approaches are followed: the normative approaches and descriptive approaches. The normative approaches in defining conversion are viewed according to the 'theological' convictions of a particular tradition; on the reverse the descriptive approaches seek the practical experiences in conversion process.[6] The later approach of conversion is largely a product of the last two decades as new religious movements like Jesus Army, Jehovah Witness, Japanese Buddhist Movement, etc. focused upon the individual transformation. This approach investigates the changes and intention behind conversion.

Richardson points out that old or traditional conversion paradigm, with its deprivation and strain assumptions about the passivity of human beings, is giving way partially to a new paradigm. The new or alternative conversion paradigm stresses human as volitional entities who assign meaning to their actions and to the action of others with a social context.[7] Apart from these few theories of conversion, the process is also described in terms of Social Behavior: where individuals considered as nuclear subjects learn and adopt the normative behavioral patterns of the movement with which they affiliate. Other theories define conversion in cultural terms, as a change in the symbolic presentations, rituals, etc. This perspective draws conversion as a change in the universe of discourses. With the growing investigators in the field of sociology of conversion, they interpreted it as a change in social context. The effective Lofland and Stark Theory depicts conversion in terms of diminishing interpersonal ties in one social network and intensifying them in another network. This conversion model has been recognized as an important step towards a new conversion paradigm by focusing on the process of conversion.

Describing conversion, Bainbridge gives two alternative sociological theories to explain religious conversion: Strain Theory and Social theory. As per the former theory, people join a religion in order to satisfy conventional desires that unusual personal or collective deprivations have frustrated. In joining a religion, the person or group adopts an ideology that transforms deprivation into virtue. According to Social Influence Theory, people join a religion because they have formed social attachments with persons who are already members and because their attachments to their non-members are week.[8] As Bainbridge has remarked, a contribution of both of these theories is probably the best explanation and the Lofland/Stark (1965) conversion model encompasses both the theories. Although in 1977, Lofland employed the activist analysis to note that the model embodies a thoroughly passive actor, it seems most useful for elucidating the conversion process, because the model incorporates all the possible stages of this process and an activist view of human being to some extent as well as perspectives within a social context.[9]

Conceptualization of Conversion

The study of conversion from one religion to another has been a traditional subject of interest for anthropologists and members of other disciplines. Conversion is not only linked with spiritual basis but also with psychological, sociological and other aspects of human being. George Jackson in 1908 delivered a lecture on the psychology of conversion and he attacked against attempts to conceptualize and operationalize conversion by saying,

> It matters ... little what principle of classification we adopt or we adopt any at all. What does matter is that we steadfastly resist all attempts to 'standardize' conversion.[10]

The researchers today are familiar with the words and they devote the research in pinpointing the causes of conversion without conceptualizing clearly. There are, however, a few works that address this conceptual issue. We will see the traditional and the few existing conceptions of conversion. However, conceptual clarity here is very important, since understanding the causes presupposes the ability to identify the causes.

Conversion as abrupt Shift of Behaviour

The main topic in the literature of conversion is that the experience involves a personal change. This understanding dates back to the biblical usage of the term and the cluster of words to refer to it: Hebrew words 'Shub' and the Greek word 'ephistrephein', 'strephein' and 'metanoia'. These words indicate dramatic change, turning from one viewpoint to another.[11] In spiritual psychological sense it is a process, gradual or sudden, by which a self hitherto divided and consciously wrong, inferior and unhappy becomes unified and consciously right, superior and happy, in consequence of its firmer hold upon religious realities.[12] In earlier times scholars debated whether conversion involves sudden, gradual or multiple and serial changes.[13]

W.H. Clarke characterizes conversion as 'that type of spiritual growth or development which involved an appreciable change of direction concerning religious ideas and behavior. Most clearly and typically it refers an emotional episode of illuminating suddenness, which may be deep or superficial, though it may also come about by the gradual process.'[14] Under the radical personal change we can put four kinds of distinguishable change: the commonplace kind of a role change called 'Alternation' that occur without disrupting an individual's worldview;[15] the 'consolidative' variety illustrated by 'a person raised in a Southern Baptist Church, who rejects these beliefs for drugs and perhaps eastern religion and then becomes a Jesus person;[16] the 'regenerative' type associated with St. Augustine, whose mother's deep religious conviction influenced his early years. 'Adhesion' refers the possibility of participating in religious groups and rituals without assuring a new way of life.[17] These conceptual distinctions are useful in so far as they suggest that personal change is not one-dimensional and that conversion is but one type of personal change.

Conversion as Paradigm Shift

Many works have pointed out that it is indeed something more fundamental than beliefs and identities that change when one undergoes conversion. Speaking of shift in 'sense of ultimate grounding' or 'root reality,[18] is also a paradigm shift of behaviour from one to another.[19] As Travisano puts it as a 'radical reorganization of identity, meaning, life', it is also certainly a 'universe of discourses'.[20] Viewed in these lights, conversion is not only change in values, belief and identities, but significantly it entails the displacement of one's universe of discourse by another or the ascendance of a formally peripheral universe of discourse to the status of a primary authority. Here nominal belief thus becomes 'real' belief, and what was previously general to the consciousness becomes particular. These universes of discourse can take place once both in radical and gradual experience of conversion. These are the theoretical and conceptual frameworks across the discipline evolved over many years.

Conversion – An Indian Meaning

Conversion in India has been largely studied from the historical point of view which maps the dates and various events of conversion. The fundamental queries on the nature and characteristic of conversion, whether it is 'conversion' or 'adhesion' or 'alternation' as discussed above, are still to be investigated in Indian context clearly. Since 1930s conversion has taken a deep root in Indian political, social, religious and cultural system. The quest for locating a proper definition has began amid the freedom struggle and the large scale conversions to Christianity. Two prominent leaders, Father of Nation Mahatma Gandhi and Messiah of Dalits (self-chosen and largely accepted term to refer ex-untouchables) Ambedkar, have inquired the concept of conversion.

Historically conversion in India has been viewed differently in different periods but conversion to Christianity takes us back to medieval period when people converted en masse to Islam; 'collective conversion'21 to Christianity came during the 19th and 20th centuries in India, and the conversion to Sikhism took place at the end of 19th century in Punjab. These are not restricted to the colonial era, there were conversion of the Mahars of Maharastra to Buddhism, which is still an ongoing phenomenon; people converted to Bahai faith, and also several groups to Jainism and Islam.[22] Unlike western model of conversion where lot of investigations took place for understanding the conversion between the religious sects and new religious movements, in India the phenomenon is very unique as largely there has been conversion among different religions from traditional religion. It is also unique because the converts since the medieval period belong to only one section of the society.[23] Why they went for religious change? What are the causes behind it? As

Copley calls, the 19th and 20th century conversion from Hinduism (the traditional religion) was a cultural migration towards Christianity; it was psychological, political, cultural, and in many cases spiritual in nature.[24] Many people argue dalits are not fully aware of the religious change; moreover, they are not volatile. Certainly the minds of the dalits are no *tabula rasa* awaiting impressions from other religious hands which seek to write upon it. It is rather the result of centuries of oppression and religious, social bondage which has given expression through conversion. In the face of these points, the conversion of dalits was with religious consciousness, abrupt and facing away from the traditional and towards the new, that too in the face of fearful odds. Conversion in India was not a radical personal change, rather it can be called a paradigm shift of fellowship and an abrupt shift of behavior whereby people gave up their old beliefs.[25] Dalits actively planned, made choices, and generated many of their life experiences before renouncing their traditional religion. They are active seekers and are characterized by 'autonomy' and 'search for meaning' in other faith.

The theory and the model for conversion in India can be best in the words of Ambedkar who himself planned and analyzed the benefits of conversion to the Dalits for twenty one years before announcing his conversion. The following lines are from his speeches published later under the meaningful title 'Muktikonpath' (which is the liberation path?) and by the Buddha Dhamma Education Society of India.[26]

> According to me, this conversion of religion will bring happiness to the Dalits and to the Hindus. So long as you remain Hindu, you will have to struggle for social intercourse, for food and water and for inter-caste marriages... by conversion, the roots of the quarrel will vanish... This path of conversion is the only right path of freedom which ultimately leads to equality.

Ambedkar was of the opinion that the untouchables would be strengthened by conversion and would thus be able to gain equality, liberty and happier existence.[27] Ambedkar, rather than relying on the goodwill of caste Hindus (upper castes), preferred to fight for separation and autonomy from caste ridden Hindu society. 'Conversion', he argued, ' as important to the ex-untouchables as self government is to India... this is not the slightest different in this ultimate goal.'[28]

The Dalits for ages were living in a graded society with the feeling of inferiority. When they came in collision with other religions (Islam and Christianity) saw egalitarianism and freedom which resulted in conversion. Ambedkar also viewed that conversion in India should be viewed from two aspects: 'Social as well as Religious' and 'Material as well as Spiritual'. There are factors required for the upliftment of an individual; they are Sympathy, Equality and Liberty. Does the traditional religion Hinduism offer these to the untouchables? Does Hinduism stand for change? Hinduism does not provide any scope for change. But 'Conversion is sort of a change' and a movement from the age old stagnant place. Change in name and with change in religion, creates an overall shift in the identity.[29] In order to explain the reasons as to why he had decided to change his religion, Ambedkar convened another conference in Bombay on May 30-31, 1936. Concluding his forceful speech at the conference he said: [30]

> The Hindu religion doesn't appeal to my conscience. It doesn't appeal to my self respect. I tell you very specifically; Religion is for Man, and not man for Religion. To get human treatments convert you. Convert for getting organized. Convert for becoming strong, Convert for securing equality, Convert for getting liberty, and Convert so that your domestic life may be happy.

On the contrary, Gandhi from 1931 to 1937 in his campaign began to speak about conversion. Unlike Ambedkar, Gandhi saw conversion as something not good for the society. He distinguished falsely 'material' from genuinely 'spiritual' motives for conversion and he gave a corresponding critique of the actual motives for conversion among Dalits (ex-untouchables). Gandhi has also described that the vast majority of Dalits who had converted to Christian religion had done only for 'convenience' through false material inducements. He not only questioned the conversion of dalits but also questioned the operationalization of missionaries in India. For him conversion is purely a spiritual process as he laid emphasis on *atmaparivartan* rather than *dharmparivartan*. Gandhi calls the conversion in India, a step taken without knowing the true meaning and the depth of spiritual consequences. As Chandra

Mallampalli[31] describes, in Gandhi's words, the Harijans (Gandhi's term for the ex-untouchables), ignorant 'children' who are incapable of grasping the content of Christianity were converting merely for material reasons: [32]

> I do maintain that the vast mass of Harijans, and for the matter Indian humanity, cannot understand the presentation of Christianity, and that generally speaking their conversion wherever it has taken place has not been a spiritual act in any sense of the term. They are conversions for convenience. And I have had overwhelming corroboration of the truth during my frequent and extensive wandering.

Gandhi in addition to the spiritual angle also implies his concept of *swadeshi* in the issue of conversion. While addressing Madras Christian College in 1916, Gandhi outlined his philosophy of *swadeshi*, which stressed idea of economic, political and cultural self-reliance.[33] Moreover, he also understands conversion as 'anti-national'; he argued, conversion was legitimated when it inspired moral growth within the framework of one's own tradition and led to greater dedication to one's country. Conversion to Christianity, moreover, breached the principle of *swadeshi* and amounted to 'de-nationalization'.[34] Gandhi gave a diverse perspective on conversion which is mostly status quoist. He viewed conversion purely from the spiritual not material aspect.

To conclude this section, over the years there has been exceptional work done by the sociologists and psychologists in the sphere of religious conversion. In India we always use conversion as merely as a shift in religious allegiance. And also, it looked as a struggle against the status quo and a liberating force for the oppressed. In moral terms to label an incident as conversion is to assert a change from less desirable to more desirable conduct, and that the convert is now more capable of appropriate self-regulation as a result of coincidence of individual and positive transcendent purpose. It is a quest for autonomy, a protest against a social order and an exodus of Dalits moving towards Liberation. However, about the conversion motives, causes and methods have not been properly studied in India like in the west. Much emphasis is given to the historical and political aspect not the social and psychological aspect.

II

Conversion of Dalits to Christianity: A Historical Inquiry

Historical inquiry into the conversion of untouchables to Christianity will help us to know the genesis of the problem within the Christian fold and a formation of a new social group known as 'Dalit Christians'. Christian community existed in India from the first century of the Christian era with the traditional claim that the St. Thomas, one among the disciples of Jesus Christ who came to Kerala.[35] But very little material is available in favor of this argument. There is enough historical material to prove the existence of Christianity in Kerala from the 4th century, with the arrival of emigrants from Syria, they established the history of Syrian Christians (a 'group movement' because they preserved caste like social form). From there onwards, existed a social distinction among the Syrian Christians, as 'Southist' Syrian Christians, who claim direct descent from Thoma of Canae, and will not inter marry with 'Northist' Syrian Christian.[36] This was the beginning of a new religious establishment and social group in India.

Vasco De Gama's arrival in Calicut in 1498 for the second time (first visit in 1497) marked the beginning of missionary activities in India. But this initial period is described as painful and a terrible chapter in the history of Christianity; as they were the most unchristian of men.[37] Kaye also remarks: 'Maffeus candidly acknowledges that the unholy lives of the Portuguese formed one of the main obstacles to the conversion of the natives.'[38] The first western missionary was a Roman Catholic Jesuit Francis Xavier, who arrived in October 1542. He soon translated the Apostles' Creed, The Lords Prayer and Ten Commandments into Tamil. It is believed through this method he baptized 700,000 people belonging to different caste groups, but the majority of the converts were from 'Paraiah' community (outcastes), and he also reached to other places as well.[39] Next Missionary Roberto De Nobili arrived in Madurai, Southern India in 1606. He saw that Christianity is only being practiced by the low caste people earning the name 'Pharangis' for Portuguese. He rejected the example of Xavier and went to convert the dominant class and sought their converts among the Brahmans. Nobili declared himself as the high priest, not a Parangi (low caste) but a royal priest from Rome. He followed the Brahmin way, practiced untouchability, ate vegetarian food; it worked as many upper caste

Hindus become Christians,[40] and that also helped establishing a caste ridden church. The high and low caste Christians were forced to worship at different places in the same church. Kaye makes the observation that the Jesuits went among the people with great parade of caste and declared that they were born from the head of Brahma (creator God) himself.[41]

In 1706, the first protestant missionary group visited India from Europe. They had a different method of converting the people unlike the former; they began translating the scriptures, preaching moral oral teaching and baptizing large number of untouchables from different communities. Most of their converts were from the lower poor castes. They considered this kind of work as subordinate to spiritual work. In the eastern part of India, the first protestant missionary of English reached in 1758. C.F. Andrews says: 'Jews, Chinese, Armenians, Portuguese and small groups of Hindu converts has visited his congregation.'[42] Later, the Baptist Missionaries began to work in Calcutta and laid down the future of the Christian community in North India and had direct bearing upon the Church future. The protestant 'Mass conversion' began in 1818 when over 3000 Nadar (Shannars) were Baptized in Thirunelveli and South Travancore.[43] Madras presidency witnessed the steady growth in the Christian converts. The caste oppression by the caste Hindus were high in Tamil Nadu that forced untouchables to find a solution. The solution for the undignified life was to convert. By 1900 there were 63,152 adherents to Christianity in that area. Parayars (Sambavars) also became Christian in large number.

The United Presbyterian Mission in Punjab began its work in Sialkot in 1855 and within 60 years all but few hundred members of Chura caste (an outcaste) had converted to become Christian. The Lutheran Missionaries in Central India worked mainly among the tribes; some untouchables were also converted and the number increased to 3,95,695 which is quite an eye raising number. The American Baptist Church and Church Missionary Society (CMS) worked in Andhra Pradesh and thousands were converted, especially from the Paraiya caste and in 1928 CMS members in Krishna District increased to 1,22,500. Mass Movement (Mass Conversion) by Malas and Madigas (untouchable castes) were very huge. Even today they have a good population in Andhra region.[11]

In the United Province, the Methodist Episcopal Church, American Presbyterian Mission and CMS worked and converted large numbers of untouchables from Mazhabi Sikhs between 1858 and 1871. In Assam 59,000 Christians were reported in 1931 census. Mass movements took place also in tribal districts of Bihar and Bengal; the outcastes of Gujarat, the Dhuriya Chamars of Bihar, Doms of Banares, Kumaons and Garwal Hills were converted. In Kannada District the Panchama Caste largely participated in Conversion Movement. Since the arrival of Missionaries in India, they traveled different parts of the country and converted different castes and tribal groups. The hope was held out that within half a century the conversion of the outcastes would create a Church of 30-40 hill peoples.[45] The success of the missionaries in large part accounted for the fact that by 1931 the Indian Christian population touched 6.2 million giving the distinction of 3rd largest religion of the Country. Among the Christian converts the maximum numbers of the people were from the so called ex-untouchables.

Conceptualizing Dalit Christians: Who are they? Are they Dalits or Christians?

During the mass conversions of untouchables to Christianity in the early decades of 20th century, attempts of Christian community to bring the Christian federation of India under a single umbrella of Indian Christian community had been strained by the divisions and diversity of Indian Christian population. Though caste system does not exist in Christian religion but Christian population in India is divided among caste Christians (the converts from the high caste Hindu) and the Dalit Christians. This section of the paper attempts to problematize the Dalit question among Christians and its relation with the caste system and then discuss the social exclusion of Dalit Christians by the caste Hindus, by the caste Christians and by the State.

Before going any further let us first know the meaning of 'Dalit'. The term Dalit was coined by a Marathi social reformer and revolutionary Mahatma Jyotirao Phule in 19th century to describe the 'Outcaste', 'Panchamas', 'Avarnas' and 'untouchables' as the oppressed and broken victims of the Indian caste ridden society.[46] The term 'Dalit' in Sanskrit is both a noun and an adjective. It has been derived from the root 'dal' meaning to 'crack', 'split'. Using it as a noun or adjective, it means 'burst', 'split', 'broken' or 'torn as under', downtrodden, scattered, crushed, destroyed.[47] The right definition of dalit in its contemporary usage have come from a letter written to Elianor Zelliot by Gangadhar Pantavane, a Professor of Marathi at Milind College in Aurangabad and founder editor of Asmitadash (Mirror of Identity), the chief organ of Dalit Literature.

> 'To me, Dalit is not a caste. He is a man exploited by the social and economic traditions of this country. He does not believe in God, Rebirth, Soul, Holy Books, teaching separatism, Fate and Heaven because they have made him a slave. He does not believe in Hinduism. Dalit is a symbol of change and revolution."

Dalits include 'those menial castes, which have born with the stigma of untouchability because of the extreme impurity and pollution connected with their traditional occupations'.[48] Dalit is a name which the people belonging to those castes at the very bottom of caste hierarchy have adopted. Dalit is an untouchable who cannot be touched because his touch automatically pollutes the one who touches him or whom he touches and the things which he touches. Such 'touch' is not limited to direct physical contact. It is also transmitted through food and drink. Moreover, it also gets transmitted through the shadow or even a glance of an untouchable fall on the touchable person or possession, '*asprishya darshanam doorikaranam*'. Even worse form of untouchability is also carried by the lower caste, they are known as unseeble, unapproachable. Dalits are not permitted to approach within a certain distance of high caste (say 30 feet in the case of a Brahmin) or even to be seen by them. Thus, the connotation of the term untouchable included 'unapproachable' and 'unseeable'. Dalits face all the inhumane atrocities because they fall outside the traditional four fold caste hierarchy (*chatur varna/ varnashrma dharma*).[49]

In the 1970s, with the emergence of Dalit Panthers inspired by the Black Panthers of American Blacks, used the word "Dalit" for solidarity and the unity of all untouchables in India. Later on in the academic and the social sphere it was widely put into practice. Dalits have used this term for themselves for three important reasons. First, the label indicates that the condition of the Dalits has not been of their own making or choosing. Secondly, there is an element of military built into it the label. Dalits seek to overcome the injustices and indignities forced upon them so as to gain the equality and respect hitherto derived them. 'Dalits' also indicates that all these castes (Paraiahs, Chamars, Mahars, Bhangis, Valmikis, Churas, Solankis, Mahars, etc.) have a common struggle for dignity, equality, justice and respect under a common name.[50] In order to get rid of the age old suppression and oppression the Dalits marched their journey to the leave Hinduism and embrace other religions. Dalits across India found solace in Christianity and they converted in large numbers from different castes and different regions.

Dalit Christians

The Christian religion does not prescribe any kind of discrimination on the basis of race or sex or otherwise; it is supposed to be the propagator of equality for all. The concept of equality can be traced in one of the scriptures written by St. Paul:[51]

> There is no longer Jew or Greek, there is no longer slave or free, there is no longer male or female; for all of you are one in Jesus Christ.

Christianity places the highest value in each person's human dignity, which Christians believe in God's gift to humanity when God created each and every human being in his own image. In Christian belief human beings become sons and daughter of God when they accept Jesus as lord and receive the Divine life. Hence all Christians are a single family. So, there cannot and should not be discrimination among them. Hence the lower castes in India became Christians. But, in the social, economic, political and even in religious sphere, like Hindus, they are also stratified; this stratification will draw a clear picture of the reasons behind the social exclusion as well.

Christian community in India is not a homogeneous community, they have major denominational difference among them, such as Catholics, Protestants, Baptists, etc. and each denomination has further division into several sects. They vary in theologies, traditions and also liturgical patterns. But, this not the concern of this paper, here it aims to study the discrimination of Christians on caste lines in Indian society in general and particularly within the church. There are no authoritative estimates available regarding the population of Dalit Christians due to the absence of any caste-religious census. But a recent study on Dalit Muslims and Christian Communities[52] has made some rough estimates with the National

Sample Survey Organization (NSSO). The general procedure followed by the report is to ascertain the NSSO shares or proportions and to apply these proportions to the population totals obtained from the Census. These Census figures are obtained from the actual population counts of 2001, while the NSSO figures are estimates based on the sample for the 61st Round survey done in 2004-05. The estimated population of Dalits in Christianity in Rural India, Census 2001 count of population is 1,58.9 lakh and Urban India is 81.9 lakh. Estimated Caste composition of religions in Rural India in 2004-05 is: SC- 9.4 per cent, OBC- 20.9 per cent, Upper Castes- 30.8 per cent, ST- 38.9 per cent; and in the Urban India is: SC- 17.5 per cent, OBC- 31.8 per cent, UC- 40.3 per cent, ST- 17.5 per cent.[53] A large majority of almost 90 per cent of Indian Christians share status as Dalits and Tribal.[54] Another estimate shows that as a result of continuing mass conversion among the dalits in India, the population of Christians continued to grow from 2,284,300 in 1891 census to 4,754,000 in 1921 and by 1931 it increased to 6,296,763.[55] Thus it is estimated that among the Christians almost 75 per cent belong to backward and untouchable castes.[56]

Discrimination and Exclusion of Dalit Christians in Indian Society

The Dalit Christians, like their counterpart Dalit Hindus, face different kinds of social and economic exclusion. A study conducted by Kananaikal and team[57] on the SC converts to Christianity in Tamil Nadu shows that in the social and economic sphere the situation of ex-untouchable (SC) converts as a whole continues to be same as that of the non-converts from the same caste. Dalit Christians as it is mentioned already are a subject of subjugation even after conversion. In order to break the shackles of the continuing dehumanization, Dalits renounced the traditional Hindu religion. Historically 'outcastes' were kept outside the fold of *chaturvarna* (Brahmin, Kshatriya, Vaishya and Shudra). Dalits were '*Avarna*'. They were the lowest of low. The caste Hindus still treat converted Hindus with the same degree of discrimination like the Dalit Hindus. The change of religion did not change the mind of the oppressors. Dalit Christians are still treated as untouchables in many parts of the country. They are forced to be dependent on the caste Hindus for their livelihood. According to Nirad C. Choudhary:[58]

> All the Christian groups of India retain the mark of caste system. They continue their caste status and pride of caste

even in the generation born to Christianity and merely converted to the new religion.

Dalit Christians lag behind in every field of development; the caste Hindus living in the society still do not allow them to move up. Many of the atrocities against the Dalit Christians by the caste Hindus are merely reported as atrocities on Christians. Dalit Christians are grouped under single umbrella, Christians. Several discriminations against Dalit Christians are in common day to day practice, but are reported as discrimination against Christians. For instance, in 1993, in a non descriptive village, Chundru of Andhra Pradesh, 12 Dalit Christians were massacred by the Reddys allegedly because a Dalit Youth sat with his feet up in local cinema hall and accidentally touched an upper caste youth sitting in the seat in front of him. This massacre happened because the youth was a Dalit Christian and not a Kamma Christian or a Reddy Christian.[59] Incidents like these are very common across India.

Dalit Christians are still forced to live in outskirts of the village, '*thathi*' (out of caste colony) in rural Punjab or '*cheri*' (paraiah colony), '*Basti*' (sweeper colony), even so many years after independence from the traditional religion and the British Rule. People belonging to these vulnerable groups are not allowed to use the public places. Excluded in every way, the basic right to freedom is not enjoyed by these sections of the society. Moreover, the caste Hindus also look the converted low castes as 'Anti-Nationalists' as the Hindu Fundamentalist organizations and their outfits such as RSS, Bajrang Dal, Bharatiya Janata Party call conversion as 'de-nationalization'. Christians in general and Dalit Christians in particular are tortured for leaving the traditional religion, by which the majority of the Hindus identify themselves. In response to these kinds of calls, Ambedkar said that he would be called communal by the nationalists and patriots for converting and getting away from Hinduism and also for supporting the human rights of Dalits.[60] In an identical way the loyalty of Dalit Christians to the State is questioned again and again.

Rigid graded system operates specially designed to suit particular sections of the society, socially, culturally, politically, educationally. Dalit Christians are overall victims in all the above spheres. Recently, with the emergence of Hindutva Politics, the Dalit Christians are the worst targeted, as the caste Hindu fanatics are reconverting them forcefully in many areas in India. The recent attacks in Orissa where the Dalits and the Tribal families are forced to reconvert ended in a communal clash in September 2008.[61] Incidents like these are a growing phenomenon against Dalit and Tribal people belonging to Christianity. They are not only excluded but rather forcefully included into the same oppressive traditional religion from where they converted. The Dalits Christians are still living on the margins of the society. The report by Satish Deshpande where the poverty profile, average consumption levels, occupational structure and educational status comparatively analyzed clearly shows the variation among the Dalits of different religions as well as different castes. Dalits are located nearly same in all religions.[62] Conversion has hardly been fruitful to the Dalit Christians; the experience of the discrimination is same.

Discrimination and Exclusion of Dalit Christians within Christianity

The early Christians affirmed equality to all men in relation to God. Whenever and wherever inequality perpetuated, numerous egalitarian protests movements for equality within the Christian church had risen from the very beginning. It is an interesting fact that Christianity does not support discrimination and exclusion, but the church and the authorities historically exclude the Dalits from all the aspects of Christian sphere. From the conversion date till today the Dalit Christians are bearing the brunt of caste practices by caste Christians. Since the birth of Christianity in India, with the establishment of Syrian Christians have been able to survive for centuries largely because they have been encapsulated within the caste society, regarded by Hindus as occupying recognized place within the caste hierarchy.[63] Practices of Hindu culture can be viewed from their customs even today. Moreover, as mentioned earlier in the section that deals with the history of conversion, Indian converts could not detach themselves from the social context.

Within Christianity, the shape and form of discrimination and social exclusion of Dalit Christians and related issues varied at different periods. In opposition to that they have challenged the caste practices within and outside the church. With the communal award in 1932 the Dalits had grown more vocal in their demand for fair treatment for all, for the first time within Christian Institutions. They either strove to become more integrated into the life of respective Christian communities or assertive from the caste Christians.[64] The purpose of conversion was carried on these two points, as conversion stood for autonomy from one social system and integration in another social system. Discrimination and Exclusion within the church forced them to stand for the integration process and that resulted in conflict between the Dalit Christians and caste Christians.

During the years of Mass conversions and later on as well Dalit Christians had to challenge the marginalization of their community within the church. In 1916, group of caste (vellalars) went to the court against the Bishop of Trichiropoly and several Nadar Christians demanding caste privileges in Holy Family Church at Vadankakulam demanded the court for differential practices. The caste Christians demanded re-erection of walls separating the Dalit Christians and caste Christians, exclusive ownership of Holy Family to Vellalar community, and separate entries for both the groups as they cannot be together. Incidents like these were visible in the vicinity of church compound regularly. In another incident at National Arcot District of Madras presidency, in 1936, at the celebration of annual festival of 'Our lady of seven Dollars of catholic church' an issue emerged for dragging a car of 'Our Lady' which was traditionally dragged by the caste Christians. The priest offered Dalit Christians to drag, and this proposal triggered volatile reaction by the other group.[65] At Trichiropoly, caste Christians defamed a pariah priest for removing the railing that divided caste Christians and Dalit Christians; this incident instigated huge problem within the Church. The caste Christians broke away from the Our Lady of seven dollars Catholic Church and organized separate church and communion services. In a similar incidence in 1936, Dalit Christians demanded the right to be seated with Caste Christians during the prayer at St. Mary's Cathedral at Kumbakonam. The T-Shaped hall with two wings had one for Dalit Christians and other for Caste Christians. Contemporary discriminatory practices include separate cemeteries, separate seating arrangements in the place of worship for the high and low caste Christians even today. As the Dalits converted to come into the fold of Christianity, they were culturally alienated and discriminated within and outside the Christian Institutions. Recently in Tamil Nadu following the discrimination in the church of Our Lady of Rosary, located in the center of Eraiyur, the Dalit Christians of the village have been on the fast demanding that the Archbishop recognize the Sagaya Matha Chapel they had built for new Dalit parish. Against this caste Christian Vanniars attacked the Dalits badly resulting in huge clash.[66]

In the Christian organization also they are badly excluded. Dalit Christians constitute nearly 65 per cent of Catholic population in Tamil Nadu and only 3.8 per cent among the priests and nuns are Dalits. There is only less than eight Dalit Bishops in India among the nearly 155 catholic bishops in India. It is quite clearly visible the degree of exclusion by the caste Christians done to the marginalized sections of the society.

Discrimination and Exclusion of Dalit Christians by Indian State

The exclusion of Dalit Christians by the Indian State can be studied from the pre-independence and post-independence perspectives. During the colonial period the Englishmen failed to understand the exploitative nature of caste that is deeply embedded in Indian society. The Dalits within Christianity were viewed under the large umbrella of 'Indian Christian Community' comprised of caste Christians as well. In the system of communal representation which led to the formation of representative bodies for the articulation of viewpoints of Indian Christians, the Dalits were not treated as separate entity. This made these representative bodies speak for only the highly educated caste Christians leaving behind the voices of so-called Dalit community. In the pre-independence period the scenario got worse as the Government of India too failed to understand the plight of Dalit converts to Christianity.

The Dalit converts from the Christian background are excluded in the affirmative actions of Central Government. The reservation of Dalit Christians have been shaped by number of considerations and in these several years it failed to give reservation to the Dalit Christians. On the other hand, the Presidential Order of 1950 and its subsequent amendments have included Dalit Sikhs and Dalit Buddhists who are also converts from Hinduism. The Indian constitution empowers President of India to specify the castes and groups, which can be considered as Schedule Castes. By Presidential Order 1950, only Hindu Dalits were considered as SCs and could be provided with rights bestowed by the Constitution to the SCs. By an amendment in Constitutional Order 1950, in 1956 Dalit Sikhs were included in SC category. Later in 1990, the constitution was yet amended and the Buddhists were also included in SC category.

This depriving of Dalit Christians from SC status has much deeper implications. They are denied not only the opportunities to come up in economic and educational ladder but also from the protection to Dalits that has been provided by acts such as Scheduled Castes and Scheduled Tribes (Prevention of Atrocities) Act 1989, Protection of Civil Rights Act 1955 and Protection of Civil Rights Rule 1977. Thus, Dalit Christians are not only denied of reservation but also from redress in case of caste atrocities. Despite recognition by Mandal Commission that caste among Christians exists in India; Dalits are not included in SC category. Both Mandal Commission and Backward Class Commission of Andhra Pradesh recommended extension of SC status to Dalit Christians. Apart from this, attempt was there to introduce the Constitution (Scheduled Caste) Order (Amendment) Bill in 1986 by P.J. Kurien. Another Private Member Bill was introduced by Narayan Swami to raise the same issue. In 1996, Welfare Ministry proposed to include Dalit Christians into SC category; a bill was listed to be introduced regarding same issue but could not be forwarded. Time and again the question of discriminatory attitude of state towards Dalit Christians has been raised. There are strong arguments for inclusion of Dalit Christians in SC category based on arguments of justice and fairness.[67]

Concluding Remarks

The critical examination of this paper on definitions and meaning of conversion and the condition and plight of Dalit converts to Christianity has suggested the importance of three factors in particular in this paper. First, among the various existing theories and concepts, careful research on the conceptualization of conversion is still needed. Still most of the conceptualization remain ambiguous and are not explicitly presented especially in Indian context. Moreover, understanding the indicators of conversion or other models close to conversion such as adhesion is very important for the study about Indian conversion. Another important aspect of conversion is to the question whether knowledge about religious conversion can be generalized to explain the political transformation and practices in India. These important points are very significant to develop a better view about the conversion process. Second, Dalit conversion to Christianity in a large scale in expectation to break the shackles from the age old caste discrimination and social marginalization resulted in establishing another kind of social group known as Dalit Christians. They also suffer a similar pattern of social exclusion even after their conversion. Third, Dalits converted to Christianity in order to escape from the age old machinery of subjugation and oppression fell into another kind of discrimination and exclusion by Indian society and Church. With the emergence of democratic political order, the Dalits converted to Christianity lost the benefits of affirmative action provided to other Dalits belong to Hindus, Sikhs and Buddhists through the President's Order.

The conversions of Dalit Christians have not reduced the pain of caste oppression. The system continues to exist even after coming out of it. Narrating the story of post conversion and the experiences of discrimination and exclusion, *My Story*, a poem by Gurram Joshua (1885-1971) says how he had been misled by 'religion' and the 'caste practices' thereafter.

We believe that angels bathe
In the pit where Sita sacrificed herself
Inculcating such stories in the young minds
We ensured their total acceptance.

Many a time did I read the Bible in the Church
Sincerely did I pray for the removal of untouchability
Took baptism like all others
Loved even my enemy as my own brother
Always kept my word of honor
But the all-pervading false faith breaks my heart.[68]

This pain suggests all; Joshua and other Dalit Christians showed a drift into a separate, autonomous space removed from constraints of the church authorities. He walked out from the Christian fold and established humanistic approach all through his life. Conversion on the ground and reality are distinctly different which was tasted by Joshua. Conversion in India still continues to undoubtedly give the hope of equal status but in practice, from the state to the society, Dalit Christians remain discriminated and voiceless.

NOTES AND REFFERENCES

1. Conversion is not only a religious process but also viewed as social emancipation.
2. Politically conversion used to show as a numerical strength of any community. In 1931 census with the increase of Christian population there started a movements against conversion.

3. W. James, *The Variety of Religious Experience* (New York: Longman Publication, 1902); E.D. Star Buck, *The Psychology of Religion* (New York: Scribers, 1915); G.A. Coe, *Psychology of Religion*, (Chicago: University of Chicago Press, 1917); E.T. Clark, *The Psychology of Religious Awakening*, (New York: McMillan, 1929). Also refer for detailed discussion, J.C Moloney, 'Psychic Self-Abandon and Extortion of Confession', *International Journal of Psycho-Analysis*, vol. 36 (1955), pp. 53-60; J.G. Miller, 'Brain washing: Present and Future,' *Journal of Social Issues*, vol. 13 (1952), pp. 5-20; R.J. Lifton, *Thought Reform and the Psychology of Totalism: A Study of Brainwashing in China* (New York: Nortan, 1961); E.H. Schein, *Coercive Persuasion: A Socio-Psychological Analysis of the 'Brainwashing' of American Civilian Prisoners by the Communist China* (New York: Norton, 1961).
4. J. Lofland, *Doomsday Cult: A Study of Conversion, Proselytization, and Maintenance of Faith*, (New Jersey: Englewood Cliffs-Prentice Hall, 1966); M. Hierich, 'Change of Heart: A Test of some widely held theories about conversion', *Australian Journal of Sociology*, vol. 83 (1977), pp. 653-80; J.T. Richardson, 'Conversion Careers: In and Out of the Religions, *Sage and American Behavioural Sciences*, vol. 20 (1978), pp. 805-918; D.G. Bromley and A.D. Shupe, 'Just a few years seems like a lifetime: A Role theory approach to Participate in religious movements. In Research in Social Movements, Conflict and Change, (ed.) L. Kriesberg, (Greenwich, Conn: JAI, 1979).
5. D.A. Snow, and R. Machalek, 'The Sociology of Conversion', *Annual review of Sociology*, Vol. 10 (1984), pp. 167-190.
6. L. Rambo, *Understanding Religious Conversion* (New Haven: Yale University Press, 1993), p. 6.
7. B. Kilbourne, and J.T. Richardson, 'Paradigm conflict, Types of conversion and conversion theories', *Sociological Analysis*, Vol. 50 (1) (1988).
8. *W.S. Brainbridge*, 'The sociology of conversion', in H. Newton M., and S. Samuel (ed.), *Handbook of Religious Conversion* (Birmingham, Ala: Religious Education Press, 1992).
9. J.T. Richardson., 'Conversion and Careers', *Society*, Vol. 17 (1985), pp. 47-50.
10. George Jackson, *The fact of Conversion: The Cole Lecturers for 1908* (New York: Revell, 1908), p. 97.
11. V.B. Gillespie., *Religious Conversion and Personal Identity: How and Why People Change* (Birmingham, Ala: Religious Education, 1979), pp. 12-17.
12. James William, *The Varieties of Religious Experience: A Study of Human Nature* (London: Longman Green, 1903), p. 189.
13. See J.B. Pratt, *The Religious Conversion* (New York, McMillan, 1926); W.H. Clarke, *The Psychology of Religion: An Introduction to Religious*

Experience and Behaviour (New York, McMillian, 1958); J.T. Richardson, 'Conversion and careers', *Society*, vol. 17 (1980), pp. 47-50; D.J. Parucci, 'Religious Conversion: A Theory of Deviant Behaviour', *Sociological Analysis*, vol. 29 (1968); F.R. Lynch, 'Towards a theory of Conversion and Commitment to the Occult,' ____. American Behaviour Scientist, vol. 20 (1977), pp. 887-908.

14. W.H. Clarke, *The Psychology of Religion: An Introduction to Religious Experience and Behaviour*, (New York, McMillan, 1958), p. 191.
15. D.F. Gordon, 'The Jesus People: An Identity Synthesis', *Urban Life Culture*, vol. 3 (1974), p. 166.
16. R.V. Travisano, 'Alternation and Conversion as Qualitatively Different Transformations' in G.P. Stone and H.A. Faberman (ed.), *Social Psychology Through Symbolic Interaction* (Waltham, Mass: Ginn-Blaisdell, 1970), pp. 594-606.
17. A.D. Nock, *Conversion* (New York: Oxford University Press, 1933), pp. 6-7.
18. M. Heirich, 'Change of Heart: A Test of Some widely held theories about Religion', *Australian Journal of Sociology* (1977), pp. 673-675.
19. T. Kuhn, *The Structure of Scientific Revolution* (Chicago: University of California Press, 1962).
20. G.H. Mead, *Mind, Self and Society* (Chicago: University of California Press, 1962), pp. 88-90.
21. J.W. Picket, *Christian Mass Conversion Movements* (New York: 1933), p. 23.
22. For historical understanding of conversions into different religions in India, M. Mujeeb, *The Indian Muslims* (London: Georgen Allen and Unwin Ltd. 1967); Lionel Caplan, 'Caste and Castelessness Among South Indian Christians', *Contribution to Indian Sociology (NS)*, vol. 14, No. 2 (1980); Imtiaz Ahmad (ed.), *Caste and Social Stratification among the Muslims* (New Delhi: Manohar Book Service, 1984); Susan Bayly, Saints, Goddesses and Kings: Muslims and Christians in South Indian Society, 1700-1900, (New Delhi: Cambridge University Press, 2004); and Rowena Robinson and Sathianathan Carke (ed.), *Religious Conversion in India: Modes, Motivation and Meanings* (New Delhi: Oxford University Press, 2003); William Garlington, 'The Bhai Faith in Malwa,' in *Religion in South Asia*, ed. by G.A. Oddie (New Delhi: Manohar Publishers, 1977).
23. Initial phase of Mass Conversions from 17th to early 20th century to Christianity were largely from the Dalit community. Dalits wanted to integrate to a new socio-religious system which also provided equality and liberty.
24. Anton Copley, *Religion in conflict: Ideology, Cultural contact and Conversion in late colonial India* (New Delhi: Oxford University Publication, 1997).
25. Mario Fasero, 'A Theory of Conversion to Exclusive Religion and

Political Faith', Paper presented at the annual meeting of the European Public Choice Society, Durham, U.K., (March 31st-April 3rd, 2005).

26. Speech published in 'Mukti kona patha' (which is the liberation path?) (Extracts of Marathi text were edited by Khairamode (caritra, vii: 87-89) and by the Buddha Dhamma Education Society of India (1992).
27. Johanness Beltz, *Mahar Buddhists and Dalit: Religion, Conversion and socio-political emancipation* (New Delhi: Manohar Publication, 2005).
28. B.R. Ambedkar, 'Why go for conversion'? *Writings and Speeches of B.R. Ambedkar*, vol. 5 (Bombay, Government of Maharashtra, 1989).
29. B.R Ambedkar, *Conversion as Emancipation* (New Delhi: Critical Quest, 2004).
30. B.R Ambedkar's written speech in Marathi at the conference held in Bombay on May 30-31, 1936. This speech was first published in the Maharashtra Government's special Issue, 'Lok Rajya' brought out on April 16, 1981. It had been translated into English by Vasant Moon and was first published with 'Oppressed Indian', the organ of BAMCEF. Also published in the Jantak Lehar, Jalandhar (Punjab), Vol. 3, No. 4, April 1986.
31. Chandra Mallampalli, *Christians and Public life in Colonial South India, 1863-1937: Contending with Marginality* (London: Routledge Curzon, 2004), p. 180.
32. 'Conversion for Convenience', *Harijan* (June 12, 1937), CMPI, 61.
33. Swadeshi was a philosophy of self-reliance which primarily represents the economic term.
34. 'For Christian Indians', *Young India*, August 20, 1925, CMPI, 69.
35. Cyril Bruce Firth, *An Introduction to Indian Church History* (Madras, 1981), p. 2.
36. C.P. Mathew and M.M. Thomas, *The Indian Churches of Saint Thomas* (New Delhi: ISPCK, 1967), p. 19.
37. *John William Kaye, Christianity in India: An Historical Narrative* (London: 1859), p. 15.
38. *Ibid.*, 15.
39. *Ibid.*, 21.
40. David G. Mandelbaum, *Society in India* (Bombay, 1990 reprint), p. 267.
41. John William Kaye, *op. cit.*, p. 34.
42. C.F. Andrews, *North India* (A.R. Mowbray Publishers, 1908), p. 3.
43. Robert L. Hardgrave Jr., *The Nadars of Tamil Nadu: The Political Culture of a Community in Change* (Berkley: University of California Press, 1969), pp. 43-70.
44. G.A. Oddie, 'Christian Conversion Among Non-Brahmins in Andra-Pradesh with special reference to Anglican Missions and the Dornakal Diocese, 1900-1936' in G.A. Oddie (ed.), *Religion in South Asia* (London: Curzon Press, 1977).

45. J.H. Beaglehole, 'The Indian Christians: A Study of a Minority', *Modern Asian Studies*, vol. 1, No. 1 (1967), p. 60.
46. Eleanor Zelliot, *From Untouchable to Dalit: Essays on Ambedkar Movement* (New Delhi: Manohar Publishers, 1992), p. 271.
47. James Massey, *Dalits in India: Religion as a source of bondage or liberation with special reference to Christians* (New Delhi: Manohar publishers, 1999).
48. John Webster, *Religion and Dalit Liberation: An examination of Perspectives* (New Delhi: Manohar publications, 1999), p. 11. Also see Webster's 'Who is a Dalit?' in S.M. Michael (ed.), *Dalits in Modern India: Vision and Values* (New Delhi, Vistar Publications, 1999), pp. 68-79.
49. Sangharikshita, *Ambedkar and Buddhism* (Glasgow: Windhorse Publication, 1986).
50. John Webster, 'The Dalit situation in India Today', *International Journal of Frontier Missions*, (Spring 2001).
51. St. Paul, 'Galatians', Chapter 3:28, New Kings James Version, *Holy Bible*.
52. Satish Deshpande and Geetika Bapna, *Dalits in Muslim and Christian Communities: A Status Report on Current Social Scientific Knowledge;* prepared for National Commission For Minorities, Government of India, 2008.
53. For details see NSSO 61st Round Unit level Data.
54. Pradeep Madhan, *Communalism in India: A Paradigm shift to Indian Politics* (Delhi: Author Press, 2001), pp. 184-185.
55. Bhagwan Das, 'Social Exclusion Problem of Dalits', in B. Das and J. Massey (ed.), *Dalit Identity*, (Delhi: ISCPK, 1995), p. 51.
56. J. Massey, *India 50 years of independence: 1947-1997, Dalits: Issues and Concerns* (Delhi: B.R. Publication Corp., 1998), p. 70.
57. Jose Kananaikil, *Scheduled Caste Converts in Search of Justice, Constitution (Scheduled Castes), Orders (Amendment) Bill, 1990.*
58. *Nirad C. Chaudhari, The Continuum of Circe (An Essay on the people of India)* (Bombay, 1983 reprint), p. 310.
59. Prakash Louis, 'Caste-based Discrimination and Atrocities' on Dalit Christians and the need for Reservations', *Working Paper Series*, IIDS, Vol. II, No. 04 (2007).
60. Bhagwan Das (ed.) *Thus spoke Ambedkar*, Vol. 1 (Jullundar: Bheem Patrika Publications, 1963), p. 19.
61. 'Communal Fire: Sangh Parivar's violent campaign against Christians in Orissa as a part of political project', *Frontline* (September 26, 2008).
62. See Report prepared by Satish Deshpande and Geetika Bapna, titled *'Dalits in the Muslim and Christian Communities: A status Report on Current Social Scientific Knowledge'* prepared for National Commission for Minorities, Government of India, 2008.

63. Duncan B. Forrester, *Caste and Christianity* (London: Curzon, 1980).
64. Dalits having left with two options of integration and autonomy within Christian institutions. Refer Gail Omvedt, *Dalits and the Democratic Revolution: Dr. Ambedkar and the Dalit Movement in Colonial India* (New Delhi: Sage Publications, 1994), p. 114.
65. Chandra Mallampalli, *Christians and Public Life in Colonial South India, 1863-1937: Contending with Marginality* (London: Routledge Curzon, 2004), p. 180.
66. *'A house divided'*, *Frontline*, April 25, 2008.
67. For detailed discussion, see Prakash Louis, 'Caste-based Discrimination and Atrocities' on Dalit Christians and the need for Reservations', *Working Paper Series*, IIDS, Vol. II, No. 04 (2007); Satish Deshpande and Geetika Bapna, *Dalits in Muslim and Christian Communities: A Status Report on Current Social Scientific Knowledge*; prepared for National Commission For Minorities, Government of India, 2008.
68. Quoted by Chandra Mallampalli, in *Christians and Public Life in Colonial South India, 1863-1937: Contending with Marginality, op. cit.*, 2004 from Gurram Joshua, *My Story*, Unpublished copy provided by Joshua Foundation, Hyderabad.

10

Systematic Exclusion of Dalits in Indian Society

RABINDRA KUMAR

The policy makers, political parties, academicians, Non-Governmental Organizations and Human Rights Organizations are under comfortable illusion that 'untouchability is a thing of past which we got rid off by planned development and social reforms. Therefore this matter has been put out of the agenda of all. Although the Indian constitution officially outlaws untouchability, the practice of untouchability continues to operate in many parts of India even after five decades of independence. The illegal abuse of basic human rights is the everyday experience of Dalits who endure discrimination, violence, insults and humiliation. In countless villages, Dalit communities are excluded from the society and continued to be prohibited from taking water from the village wells, and entering village temples. Segregation of drinking vessels in public restaurants, forcing dalits to render the services like manual scavenging, cremation and removal of carcasses, preventing them to exercise their voting rights, and segregation of seating in village Panchayats continue even now.

Imposed Identity

The Hindu social order does not recognize the individual as a centre of social purposes. It is based primarily on varna and not on individuals. There are four varnas: (1) Brahmins, (2) Kshatriyas, (3) Vaishyas and (4) Sudras. There is another social category beyond the Varna that is Panchama or outcastes or Dalits. Thus, the Hindu society is not the same thing as individual Brahmin or the Kshyatriya or the Vaishya or the Shudra. It includes all of them.

Hindu dharma is based on the theory of karma, three gunas and the transmigration of the soul. All these three theories are applied to justify the social order. By *karma* (action) are caused the various conditions of men: the highest, the middle and the lowest. In consequence of many sinful acts committed by one's body, voice or mind that individual in the next birth will become a bird, or a beast, or a low caste person respectively. Three *gunas* (qualities) dominate the body, distinguished by quality. The study of Vedas, austerity, knowledge, purity, etc. are marks of the quality of activity whereas cruelty, covetousness, evil of life, etc. are marks of dark quality. Each of these qualities man obtains various through transmigration. It is the preponderance of various qualities that determines the birth of a man as a Brahmin or a Shudra or an untouchable. Those who commit sins go into inferior existence or wombs; and those who lead an ideal life obtain cessation of birth and death.

The doctrine that the different varnas were created from different parts of the divine body has generated the belief that it must be divine will that they should remain separate and distinct. It is this belief which has created among individual Hindus an instinct to be different from each other. The varna is often claimed not only to be of the nature of castes but up to point to be castes. Brahmin and Kshatriya at any point of time represent a particular caste, while the term Vaishya, in recent years, is being associated with some qualifying adjectives. As a matter of fact none of the four terms for varna now represent anything but groups of caste.[1] The Hindu social order is a ladder of castes placed one above the other, together representing an ascending scale of respect and descending scale of contempt. As opposed to the principles of liberty, equality and fraternity, according to Dr. Ambedkar,[2] the Hindu social order is based on the principle of graded inequality, fixity of occupation and fixation of people with their respective castes.

In this social order, the lowest social group has been labeled by various names starting from 'Asprishya' (untouchable) to present day legalized label as Scheduled Castes and more recently identified as the Dalits. In the annals of Indian history they were addressed by different imposed identittes like *Chandals, Avarna, Antyavasin, Bahya, Atchhut, Asprisya, Parihas,* Scheduled Castes, etc. Untouchability with its manifold manifestation is rooted in the notions of purity and pollution, which is believed to have developed in the later Vedic period, when the Brahmanic literature emerged in the form of *Smritis*, *Samhitas* and the *Upanishads*. These terms used in different Brahminic literatures are significant. Segregation was the natural corollary to the ardently preached and widely shared belief in pollution, and several terms such as *Ashprasya* (not touch), *Antya* (the last or at the end), *Bahya* (outside pale of *Chaturvarna* and hence outcaste), *Antyaja* (born at the end), *Antavasin* (those who live in the end) testify to the current practices.[3] Perhaps, all this meant a conscious perpetuation of an old state of affairs and created a definite barrier to free mixing

PRATILOMA SONS

Authority	*Parentage*		
	Father	*Mother*	*Sons*
1. Baudhayana dharmasutra	Sudra	Brahmana	Chandala
	Sudra	Ksatriya	Ksatta
	Sudra	Vaisya	Magadha
	Ksatriya	Brahmana	Suta
2. Gautama dharmasutra	Sudra	Brahmana	-
	Sudra	Ksatriya	Vaidehaka/Pulkasa
	Sudra	Vaisya	Valdahaka/Ayogava
	Vaisya	Brahmana	Magadh/Ksattri
	Vaisya	Ksatriya	Magadh/Dhariva
	Ksatriya	Brahmana	Suta
3. Vaikhanasa Smarta Sutra	Sudra	Brahmana	Chandala
	Sudra	Ksatriya	Pulkasa
	Vaisya	Brahmana	Magadha
	Ksatriya	Brahmana	Suta
4. Arthasastra of Kautilya	Sudra	Brahmana	Candala
	Sudra	Ksatriya	Ksatta
	Sudra	Vaisya	Ayogava
	Vaisya	Brahmana	Vaidehaka
	Ksatriya	Brahmana	Suta
5. Manusmriti	Sudra	Brahmana	Candala
	Sudra	Ksatriya	Ksatta
	Sudra	Vaisya	Ayogava
	Vaisya	Brahmana	Vaideha
	Vaisya	Ksatriya	Magadha
	Ksatriya	Brahmana	Suta

Source: Prabhati Mukherjee, *Beyond The Four Varnas*, Delhi: Motilal Banarsidass, (1988), pp. 47-49.

in future. This term also shows that they were living in separate quarters and they were pushed to the corner by the victorious invaders. Other terms were used in Brahmanic literatures to humiliate and morally demoralize them. The following are the terms used in different Hindu scriptures.

A question that arises from the Brahmanic literature is whether varna intermixing, inter-dining and inter-varna marriages were prevalent at that time. Certainly not, because that time society was too closed. The above mentioned table shows that these generic terms developed into a specific caste name in the later Vedic period. The progenies of inter-varna marriage were used to demoralize and also exclude the original inhabitants of this country (untouchables) from mainstream of the society. Such kind of hatredness can be found and observed till today against the untouchables by Savarnas.

Forms of Untouchability Practices

Untouchability can be observed in actual behavior, ideas, beliefs, and in the feelings of individuals. It is observed that in contemporary times; the practice of untouchability has modified itself to become subtle. The various forms of untouchability practices in the various parts of the country including Orissa are tabled below.

Prevailing Forms of Untouchability Practices[4]

Sl. No.	*Untouchability Practice*	*Forms of Practice*
1.	Denial of Drinking Water	1. In case of common water source for scheduled castes and Savarna the following forms are observed in the Villages. (*a*) Scheduled castes are not allowed to fetch water but Savarnas draw the water for the scheduled castes and pour into their pots. They have to wait until caste Hindu people come and are pleased to fetch the water for them. (*b*) Scheduled Castes are not supposed to touch the pots of Savarna. (*c*) Scheduled castes have to fetch only after Savarnas draw water.

Contd...

Sl. No.	*Untouchability Practice*	*Forms of Practice*
		(*d*) In most of the villages separate wells and bore-wells persist for SCs and Savarnas. In case of acute shortage of water Savarna can fetch water from SC water sources. But on the contrary, if similar situation arise for SCs, they are denied. In case Savarna castes want to fetch water from Scheduled Castes' bore-well they primarily are supposed to clean the bore-well and its surroundings.
		(*e*) In case of natural lakes, ponds and tanks scheduled castes are supposed to fetch from the downstream where savarnas do not approach.
2.	Pouring Drinking Water into their Hands	1. Mostly confined to workplace.
3.	Prohibit Entering into Savarna Houses	(*a*) Scheduled castes are not allowed to enter into their houses and they are compelled to stand far away from the houses of Savarnas.
		(*b*) Scheduled castes can only go to certain parts of their houses i.e. the outer extension of the house, outside the threshold but not the interior parts of their houses. SCs are sometimes allowed to enter to store their agricultural products at the time of harvest.
4.	Segregation at Feasts	(*a*) On the occasion of marriage or a function in Savarna families, SCs are not invited; in case invited they are supposed to dine after the Savarnas finish their turn.
		(*b*) In certain cases SCs are supposed to get their plates and in certain instances they are told to wash their plates after the dinner.
		(*c*) In most of the cases SCs are served at a distant place from the hosted premises.

Contd...

Sl. No.	*Untouchability Practice*	*Forms of Practice*
		(*d*) Sometimes they are served in towels or they hold their upper garment.
5.	Discrimination in Schools	(*a*) Segregation in sitting – SC students have to sit separately that too at backside. (*b*) Abusing by caste name. (*c*) Not allowed to eat together with Savarnas. (*d*) Segregation of water facilities. (*e*) Discrimination between SC and Savarna teachers. (*f*) Not admitting children in schools at Dalitwadas.
6.	Prohibition of Sitting in Public Places	(*a*) SCs are not allowed to sit on public places. (*b*) SCs have to sit separately at some distance from other caste people. (*c*) SCs have to stand at these places with folded hands. (*d*) SCs are allowed to sit at down level.
7.	Prohibit Walking in Savarna Localities	(*a*) SCs are not allowed to walk with sandals in vicinity of Savarnas. (*b*) Not allowed to use umbrella in Savarna localities. (*c*) Not allowed to ride cycles, rickshaws; in certain cases not allowed going even on bullock carts.
8.	Forced Services	(*a*) Drum beating for funerals and festivals/ Jataras. (*b*) Grave digging. (*c*) Cremation. (*d*) Chappal making. (*e*) Removal of carcasses. (*f*) Scavenging. (*g*) SCs are supposed to sweep the whole village at the time of festivals and Jataras.
9.	Denial of Services	A. *Laundry Services* (*i*) Denial of laundry service. (*ii*) Even laundry shop owners deny ironing clothes of SCs.

Contd...

Sl. No.	*Untouchability Practice*	*Forms of Practice*
		B. ***Barber Services*** *(i)* SCs are denied to provide hair cutting services. *(ii)* In some cases if a family member is providing hair cutting services to SCs, the same person is not supposed to provide service to Savarnas. *(iii)* In certain cases they render service to SCs in SC locality, but they purify themselves immediately after coming back to their house. C. ***Denial of Entry into Shop*** *(i)* Prohibited entry into the shops. *(ii)* Allowed but should not touch anything. *(iii)* Should stand in separate line not touching SCs.
10.	Untouchability in Giving and Receiving Things in the Shop	❖ Not allowing touching items and having to show with a small stick while purchasing. ❖ SCs should stand outside the shop and exchange takes place by throwing money and item. ❖ Keeping separate tray for SCs by which exchange takes place.
11.	Discrimination in Health Services	❖ Separate line for SCs. ❖ Avoiding physical touch in checkup and prescribing medicines. ❖ Health workers do not visit SC wada/ sahi/Basti at all. ❖ Asking SCs to come to main village for treatment.

Perceptions on Untouchability

It is observed that untouchability is not only touch-me-not-ism it is much more complex. It is a prejudice much stronger than the racial prejudice and more dangerous because it is invisible. In the course of time the avoidance of physical contact has disappeared in most of the villages and urban areas—but behavioral attitudes and the untouchability forms have changed accordingly. Untouchability can be observed in actual behavior in the ideas and beliefs, and feelings of individuals. These might differ according to the demographic or social characteristics of individuals or they may be uniform. It also happens that the same group might not observe it in another situation. Individuals of different groups might not always observe untouchability in the same situation.

It is argued that untouchability is but virulent form of poverty and illiteracy; as such once these problems are solved, the problem of untouchability will automatically come to an abrupt end. Of course, the economic and educational development may help in minimizing the gravity of the problem, but could not root it out. In the caste society, it is social inequalities, which are predominant but not economic equalities.

Hindu society is based on the caste system; as such caste and its relative status occupy importance and not their economic condition. So far as the accesses to socio-religious, economic and political activities are concerned, literacy has no relevance since there is a very high percentage of discrimination towards the literate. Even who are rich, educated and bestowed with some status are being subjected to the same humiliation as poor, illiterate and ordinary persons, only on account of untouchability.

Therefore, it can be said that even through untouchability is linked with poverty and illiteracy; it would not go with eradication of them. Untouchability is an independent institution, coupled with prejudice and hatred in respect to a section of people. Had it originated out of poverty and illiteracy, it would have been equally observed in the case of poor and illiterate Caste Hindus. But they are not discriminated on the ground of untouchability. So far untouchables are concerned, untouchability is the cause and the poverty and illiteracy are its effects. Even though poverty and illiteracy made the problem of untouchability more severe and complicated and are intermixed to greater extent, they are by no means one and identical.

J.H. Hutton[5] opines that untouchability is the consequence of ritual impurity. He says: 'The origin of the position of the exterior castes is partly racial, partly religious and partly a matter of social custom. There can be little doubt but the idea of untouchability originates in taboo.' Von Fuere-Haimendorf[6] believes that untouchability is an urban development and is the result of an unclean and ritually impure occupation. Once untouchability had developed in urban or semi-urban settlements, its gradual spread to the villages was inevitable for it is everywhere in the towns which set the standard.

Stephen Fuchs[7] proposes a new theory regarding the origin of untouchability. He said that there is sufficient evidence to prove that the Aryans as well as the Dravidians on their arrival in India still belonged to such an animal breeding culture. They must have brought along also their aversion to manual work and to foreign people. The Aryans on their slow advance throughout northern India and the Dravidians wandering down along the west coast into South India encountered on their way a multitude of earlier settlers who either submitted passively to their conquest or were defeated in fierce battles. As conquerors they managed to impose many of their cultural values and prejudices on the subject peoples of India. Adding to their inherited attitude to manual work and racial purity, they gradually developed a new dimension, namely that of ritual purity, a unique Hindu caste system which is intimately connected ideologically with the concept of untouchability.

F.G. Bailey[8] says 'caste is a system of ranks which is related to differential control over the productive resources.' Each person in the caste system performs economic, political and ritual roles and except for certain anomalies, there is a high degree of coincidence between politico-economic rank and the ritual ranking of caste. The anomalies are mainly apparent at the uppermost and lowermost ranks of the ritual system. A Brahmin of scant economic means does not fall to a low ritual rank nor can a wealthy untouchable attain high ritual rank. For caste groups between these two extremes, their ritual rank tends to follow their economic rank in the village community.

Dumont has criticized Bailey's interpretation of the caste system. According to him ritual purity is the code of the caste system. According to Dumont, the ritual purity is the code of the caste hierarchy. It has no differential control over productive resources[9] and caste represents the institutionalization of hierarchical values. In his holistic conception of caste, hierarchy is expressed in an Indian cultural code of relative purity and impurity in a continuously graded status order whose extremes are the Brahmins at the top – the most pure men and Untouchables at the bottom – the least pure of men. Brahmins and Untouchables are conceptually opposed in number of ways that contribute to their archetypal purity and impurity. The Brahmin lives at the centre of the village and is a 'god on earth', while the Untouchable lives outside the village and is apparently excluded from religious life.

For Dumont, however, this opposition of Brahmin and untouchable is also a complementarily – the completion of a 'whole' by two equally necessary but unequally ranked parts. The impurity of the untouchable is conceptually inseparable from the purity of the Brahmin. Since the execution of impure tasks by some is necessary to the maintenance of purity for others. Society is a totality made up of two unequal but complementary parts. Separation pervades the entire caste system. The most notorious separation is that of Untouchability. The members of the four main varnas, which constitute the mouth, arms, thighs and feet of Brahma do not accept water which has been handled by those castes which are outside Brahma's auspicious body. Untouchable castes are not admitted because the bodies and minds of such persons are considered to be impure, dull or otherwise unfit for initiation. Dumont's position has been severely criticized by several anthropologists and sociologists like Gerald Berreman, Khathleen Gough and Joan Mencher.[10] It is a common criticism of Dumont that his use of Brahmanical sources in understanding Hindu society commits him to a Brahminical view of society and that Untouchables may conceive of society differently.[11]

Many anthropological writings have been devoted to the cultural traditions of low-caste groups. They have emphasized the differences between the socio-religious ideology of upper castes and lower castes especially Untouchables, who have been traditionally been kept outside the Varna.[12] They have analyzed Hindu society from below – the bottom up view. Kathleen Gough points out that cultural differences between the high and low castes are due to political and economic variables generated by the upper Castes. Untouchables have a distinctive social and cultural subsystem. Similar views are found in the writings of Joan Mencher, Bernard Cohn, Robert Miller and Gerald Berrreman. According to their approach, Untouchables are seen to have demystified caste and its accompanying ideology, seeing the caste system in an objective and culture free way for what it really is – a system of oppression. Joan Mencher feels that Caste system is a system of exploitation of lower caste people.

Bernard Cohn[13] also regards the untouchables as the bearer of an alternate social and cultural system, different from the upper-caste culture. In his analysis of the untouchables, *Chamars of the North India,* he finds the untouchables as differing from the high castes i.e. the social and spatial separation between untouchable and high castes. Because untouchables cannot hear the Vedas, or be served by Brahmins, or enter high caste temples, they suffer from a kind of communication block. The result of this block, however, is not a form of culturelessness, but the retention of a historically prior pre-Aryan little tradition. Unlike the great tradition of the higher castes and of the Brahmin in particular, the little tradition of the untouchable contains a 'pre-Aryan and non-Brahmanic religion, which emphasizes the propitiation of goddesses of disease and the use of mediums and exorcists.

Robert Miller[14] has studied the untouchable Mahars of central India. He writes that the Mahars have been building a tradition which can hardly be called a distinctive variant of the great tradition cognate to those of the four major varnas of 'Hindu society'. In fact, the untouchables (Mahar) are building on a counter great tradition which has always existed in India, as an antithesis to the Brahmanic tradition. In this counter tradition, 'equality is opposed to inequality', individual ability is opposed to ritualism and escape from the system is opposed to movement within the system.

B.R. Ambedkar[15] also propounded a thesis on the origin of untouchability. This distinction between the Hindus and untouchables in its original form, before the advent of Untouchability, was the distinction between Tribesmen and broken men from alien tribes. It is the broken men who subsequently came to be treated as untouchables. There are two root forms in which the untouchability has sprung.

(*a*) Contempt and hatred for the broken men as for Buddhism by the Brahmins.

(*b*) Continuation of beef-eating by the broken men, as it had been given up by the others.

Ambedkar tries to explain what he means by broken men. He proposed an inventive hypothesis. The primitive society remained nomadic and warlike in the beginning. They began to attack the settled tribes as the latter were wealthier. In addition, they had grain which the nomads wanted but did not possess. The settled men needed defenders as they had lost their warlike spirit. They employed broken men – defeated nomads and stray individuals who needed protection and shelter. These became mercenaries of the settlers, but were not wallowed to stay within the settlement. They were kept at a distance, as they belonged to different tribe. They were treated with disrespect, as broken men and as mercenaries.

The practice of untouchability in India made Ambedkar suffer at the hands of *Savarnas*. Elsewhere slavery, serfdom and villainy have all vanished but the practice of untouchability had existed in India from times immemorial and it is still continued. The root cause for this caste system owes its origin to the Vedic ideals of varnashrama dharma. 'The root of untouchability is the caste system, the root of caste system is religion attached to varna and the root of varnashrama is Brahmanical religion and the root of Brahmanical religion is authoritarianism and political power'[16]

The Hindu religion divided the society into four varnas which included an occupational hierarchy as each caste was allotted a particular work. In other words, there was no division of labour but actually it is division of laborers. Ambedkar said, 'Caste system is not merely division of labour it is division of labourers. It is a hierarchy in which the division of labourers is graded one above the other.'[17] The concept of God and the related Hindu religious customs tend to preserve the caste system intact. Religious doctrines made the untouchables believe that they are born to suffer and fit only to do menial jobs. 'Besides caste hierarchy and economic backwardness, psychologically also people of lower caste were brainwashed through religious propaganda.'[18] He added, 'Caste does not result in economic efficiency, caste cannot and it has not improved the race. Caste has however, done one thing. It has completely disorganised and demoralized the Hindus.'[19]

Ambedkar wanted that everyone should be treated at par with others and there cannot be discriminations just because one happens to be born as untouchable. Ambedkar said that 'the religion which teaches man to behave with another man in an inhuman manner is not religion but infamy. The religion which does not recognize a human being as a human being is a curse. The religion in which the touch of animals is permitted but the touch of a human being pollutes is not a religion but the mockery of religion.'[20]

Hindu religion is based on the principle of caste hierarchy and graded inequality. If the concept of caste is removed there is no Hindu religion. For a Hindu, the caste is more important than anything else. Ambedkar opined, 'a Hindu public life is caste. Virtue has become caste ridden and morality has become caste bound.'[21]

The religious doctrines have been accepted as the code of conduct for all. If that is so how to make the untouchables understand that it is the religion which made them to lead a miserable life in the garb of caste. So Ambedkar said, 'it is not possible to break the caste without annihilating the religious notions on which the caste system is founded.'[22] He added, 'the socio-religious disabilities have dehumanized the untouchables and their interests at stake are therefore the interests of humanity.'

The caste Hindu have a code, which the Dalits are required to follow; this code lays down the acts of omissions and commissions which the caste Hindus treat as offences.[23]

1. The Dalit must live in separate quarters away from the habitation of the Hindus. It is an offence for the Dalits to break or evade the rule of segregation.
2. The quarters of the Dalits must be located towards the south, to the main settlement of caste Hindus since the south is the most inauspicious of the four directions. A break of this rule shall be deemed to be an offence.
3. The Dalits must observe the rule of distance, pollution or shadow of pollution as the case may be. It is an offence to break the rule.
4. It is an offence for the member of the Dalit community to acquire wealth.
5. It is an offence for one of the Dalit community to build a *pucca* house.
6. It is an offence for a member of a Dalit community to put on a clean dress, wear shoes, put on a watch or gold ornaments.
7. It is an offence for a member of the Dalit community to ride on a horse or a palanquin through the village.
8. It is an offence for a member of the Dalit community to sit on chair in the presence of a caste Hindu.
9. It is an offence for a member of the Dalit community to take a procession of Dalits through the Hindu caste area.

10. It is an offence for a member of the Dalit community to speak a cultural language.
11. The Dalit must do *begari* (serve without payment) of the caste Hindu. It is an offence for the Dalits to deny it and to demand minimum wages.

The members of caste Hindu internalized these codes through the socialization process. These codes are visible in the rural areas and invisible in the urban areas. It has become the state of mind in each and every member of the caste Hindu. Due to this code the caste Hindu have never shown any fellow-feeling for the Dalits and they have also excluded them from the mainstream of the society. Although the Dalits are dependent on the caste Hindus, they have only been ill treated and humiliated. If the Hindu society plays its part in maintaining the established order, so does the Hindu officials of the state. They have made established order impregnable.

Although the untouchability has been abolished by the constitution, a report issued by the National commission for Scheduled Castes and Scheduled Tribes underscored that 'untouchability', the imposition of social disabilities on persons by reason of their birth in certain castes, is still practiced in many forms throughout the country. Untouchability is not only in physical form but is dwelling deep in the minds of the people. The main causes for the continuance of untouchability even after 60 years of Independence are the result of deep rooted caste system.[24]

The deep rooted caste system manifests as follows:

(a) Carrying on of unclean occupation by the Scheduled Castes,
(b) Illiteracy,
(c) Lack of awareness among the Scheduled Castes, and
(d) Rigidity and bias created by religious literature.

We find the following basic facts as far as the Dalits are concerned:

(i) Dalits find themselves at the bottom of most human development indicators.
(ii) Their social and economic backwardness is clearly related to their religion-sanctioned exclusions from all walks of public life.
(iii) Discrimination is not a thing of the past but an every day reality.

We may summarize the types of exclusion faced by Dalits as follows:

Types of Exclusion Faced by Dalits

Sources of Deprivation/Exclusion	*Types of Identities*	*Nature of Oppression*	*Needs*
1. Lowest status in Caste hierarchy	Untouchables	Social repression	Social equality
2. Powerlessness	Subject	Political disenfranchisement	Political participation
3. Poverty	Slave	Economic exploitation	Bargaining for the betterment of economic condition
4. Culturelessness	Not a human being	Cultural repression	Cultural Revolution & Negation of Brahmanism
5. Educationlessness	Ignorant/ illiterate	Repression at various level	Equal education Facilities

Ambedkar did not stop with mere speeches and writings. He entered into direct action. All agitations spearheaded by Ambedkar took place when the freedom struggle was on. He believed that India's freedom struggle was 'a struggle for power' as distinguished from freedom, so long as the cause of the freedom was not the cause of the untouchables, and refused to join the freedom movement.

In 1927 a conference was convened at Mahad. All arrangements were made and it was announced that the untouchables would take water from the common tank at Mahad. On the appointed day, Ambedkar took water from the Chowdar Tank and drank it. Immediately all the downtrodden who were assembled there also followed their leader and took water from the tank. He said, 'at the outset let me tell those who oppose us that we did not perish because we could not drink water from the Chowdar Tank. We now want to go to the tank only to prove that we are also human beings.'[25]

In the same place in 1927 a temple entry conference was also arranged. The untouchables were not traditionally allowed to enter the temple. The savarnas wanted to build a separate temple for the untouchables. Ambedkar said, 'the most important point we want to emphasise is not the satisfaction you get from the worship of the image of God, but the plain fact is that a temple is not defiled neither by the presence of an untouchable nor the purity of the image affected by it. That is why we oppose the idea of separate temples for us and insist on entering the ones'. Ambedkar addressed the conference and said that the untouchables are determined to enter the temple. He wanted that the 'Hindu society should be organized on two main principles – equality and absence of casteism.'

The struggle was not over. Mahad witnessed another scene. Ambedkar was against Manusmriti since it is only a charter of rights for the caste Hindus and keeps the untouchables as slaves for ever. He considered this teaching of Manu as detrimental to the welfare of the downtrodden. He was a rationalist and did not believe in the principles of Manusmriti. The bonfire of Manusmriti took place. This was a great blow to the orthodox Hindus.

Ambedkar represented the untouchables at Round Table Conference (1930-32) and succeeded in getting separate electorate. But it was thwarted, and he was forced to sign the Poona Pact to save life of Gandhi which provides for joint electorate with reservation. Ambedkar did not have any faith in the joint electorate because he thought that untouchable persons elected through reservation with the help of other castes will not be able to work for downtrodden. The untouchable representatives identify themselves with the party and forget their own community. In a joint electorate the Scheduled Caste representatives are only silent spectators and not active participants to protect the interests of the Scheduled Castes. It is because 'they have to depend on the mainstream political parties to attract caste Hindus and other voters. This dependence in reality meant subservience to the caste Hindu leaders who dominate the mainstream political parties.

Ambedkar's only aim in his life was to elevate the untouchables from the deteriorating conditions in which they were living. He never h d any other ambition. When he cooperated with the British or Congress it was only to get social justice for the downtrodden. He said, 'ours is a battle not for wealth or for power. It is a battle for freedom. It is a battle for the reclamation of human personality.'

Conclusion

We may conclude that untouchability, the imposition of social disabilities or exclusion of persons by reason of their birth in certain castes is still practiced in many forms throughout the country. It is not only in physical form but is dwelling deep in the minds of the people. The main causes for the continuance of untouchability even after 60 years of independence are the deep rooted caste system and rigidity and bias created by religious scriptures or Brahmanic literature. Therefore, Ambedkar calls upon the Hindus to annihilate the caste which is a great hindrance to social solidarity and to set up a new social order based on the ideals of liberty, equality and fraternity—in consonance with the principles of Democracy. He advocates inter-caste marriage as one of the solution to this problem. But he stresses that the belief in the shastras is the root cause of maintaining castes. He, therefore, suggests that make every man and woman free from the thralldom of the shastras, cleanse their minds of the pernicious notions found on the shastras and he or she will inter-dine and intermarry. He advocated that the society must be based on reason and not on atrocious traditions of caste system.

NOTES AND REFERENCES

1. Rabindra Kumar, 'Atrocities on Dalits: Structural Dysfunction', *Fourth World Journal*, No. 16, (Bhubaneswar, NISWASS, 2002).
2. B.R. Ambedkar, *Writing and Speeches*, vol. 3, (Bombay, Government of Maharashtra, 1989).
3. *Ibid.*
4. The data on forms of untouchabitlity had been collected by students of NISWASS during the studies of scheduled castes (Gokha, Ganda, Ghasi and Kandara) in 2003-04.
5. J.H. Hutton, *Caste in India* (Oxford, Oxford University Press, 1963).
6. Von Fuerer-Haimendor, 1950 'foreword' in Stephen Fuches, 'The children of Hari: A study of the Nimar Balahis in the central Provinces of India', 1950. Vienna Verlog Herald quoted for S.M. Michael (ed.), *Dalits in Modern India: Vision and Values*, 1999.
7. Stephen Fuchs, At *the Bottom of Indian Society: The Harijan and other Low Castes* (Delhi, Munshiram Manoharlal, 1981).
8. F.G. Bailey, *Caste and Economic Frontie*, (Manchester, Manchestor University Press, 1957).
9. Louis Dumont, *Homo Hierarchicus: Religion, Politics and History in India* (Paris, Mouton, 1970).
10. Gerald Berreman, 1971, 'The Brahmanical view of caste' Dipankar Gupta (ed.), *Social Stratification* Delhi Oxford University Press (1992), pp. 80-92; Kathleen Gough, 'Harijan in Thanjavur' in K. Gough and H.P. Sharma (eds.), *Imperialism and Revolution in South Asia*, New York, Monthly Review Press (1973); P. Mencher Joan ,'The Caste System Upside Down,' in Dipankar Gupta, ed., *op. cit.*

11. J. Freeman, *Untouchable: An Indian Life History*, London, Allen and Unmin, 1979; Richard Burghart, 'Sociology of Indias: An India cultural Approach to the study of 'Hindu Society'', *Contribution to Indian Sociology* 17 (1983); Owen M. Lunch, 'Method and Theory in the Sociology of Laws, Dumont: A Reply', in Kenneth David (ed.), *The New wind changing identities in South Asia*, Paris, 1977.
12. Mark Juergensmeyer, *Religion as Social Vision: The Movement Against Untouchability in Twentieth Century Punjab*, Berkeley University of California Press, 1982; R.S. Khare, *The Untouchable as Himself Ideology: Identity and Pragmatism Among the Lucknow Chamars*, (Cambridge: Cambridge University Press, 1984).
13. Bernard Cohn, 'The Chamar of Senapur: A study of the changing status of a Depressed Castes' quoted from S.M. Michael (ed.), *Dalits in Modern India: Vision and Values* (New Delhi, Vistar Publications, 1954).
14. Robert Miller, 1966, 'Button, Button—'Great Tradition, Little Tradition, Whose Tradition?' *Anthropological Quarterly* 39, 26-42; Quoted from S.M. Michael (ed.), *op. cit.*
15. B.R. Ambedkar. 'Who were Untouchables?' *Writing and Speeches*, Vol.?, *Bombay*, Government of Maharashtra, 1979.
16. Oneil Biswas, *A Phenomena Named Ambedkar* (New Delhi, Blumoon Books, 1988), p. 28.
17. B.R. Ambedkar, *Writings and Speeches*, vol. 3 (Bombay, Government of Maharashtra. 1979), p. 67.
18. *Ibid.*
19. *Ibid.*, p. 50.
20. *Ibid.*
21. *Ibid.*
22. *Ibid.*
23. B.R. Ambedkar, *Writings and Speeches*, Vol. 5 (Bombay, Government of Maharashtra, 1979).
24. Government of India, Fourth Report 1996-97 and 1997-98 Vol. 1, National Commission for Scheduled Castes and Scheduled Tribes, Government of India.
25. Dhananjay Keer, *Dr. Ambedkar: Life and Mission*, *op. cit.*

PART–III
EXCLUSION AND DISCRIMINATION IN EDUCATION

11

Emerging Challenges of Equality: Private Educational Sector in Kerala

G.S. SURESH BABU

It has been a widely accepted fact that education is a vital component for economic development, and social capital for developing society. Among other things, the highly celebrated Kerala model has proved this by achieving total literacy. However, the question of sustainability of the very model is criticized nowadays as the present developmental indicators show deeper inequality among the marginalized sections of society.[1] The experimental bit of this paper would slowdown its empirical investigation into the question of how equality is compromised by the educational institutions operated by both the private, aided and unaided managements over the years in the backdrop of a paradoxical situation of decentralization of governance conjoining with the process globalization in Kerala. Needless to say certain critical areas were left outside the ambit of the decentralized governing process in the aided and unaided educational sectors. It has been born out from two contentious issues, notwithstanding the recent report of the Kerala Education Act and Rule (KEAR) 2008, which unfolded several issues in this regard. Firstly, although a huge burden for the state in terms of paying salary to the aided educational institutions, it could not control over certain crucial decisions like appointing teaching and non-teaching staff in these institutions. Secondly, as Local Self Governance has already been a key factor in the affairs of lower primary schools in the backdrop of 73rd and 74th amendment of the constitution, till date no direct involvement, in the governance of the private educational institutions by the local bodies, has been made. Instituting a statutory agency to look after the affairs of these private institutions and bringing into the purview of local self governance, perhaps, as it assumes, the state wanted to ensure both justice and democratization of these educational institutions.

Admittedly, the entire discourse on privatization in India today, in the backdrop of globalization, revoked again the question of equality on the road to democratization. It underscores an urgent need for democratization based on the principles of equality in the private education sectors in Kerala. Since the large share of financial and other kind of resources is flowing towards these private institutions in different forms, should we consider them as private? In fact, these institutions were established as philanthropic based on certain egalitarian values like justice and equality. It was possible by the great visionary leaders of the 19th century with the support of the local people and Christian missionary aid. Now, it is assumed that the state has not only financial liability, but also no control over most of its crucial policies with regard to ensuring justice. The KEAR report clearly delineates this fact. According to the report, 'whenever a person is appointed in an aided school by a manager, it becomes a life long financial liability to Government in terms of salary gratuity, pension, etc. At present the benefit of 60 per cent of the Government expenditure goes to aided schools. However, the Government has no role in ensuring the selection of candidates based on social justice and constitutional provision. In fact on the basis of huge amount expended so far all the properties of the aided school ought to have become the assets of Government.'[2]

It is in this context, it is a welcome step by the government, as the report underlines, that affirmative action is to be implemented to ensure equal opportunity and to make sure of transparency and democratization, linking with local level governance institutions. Although these issues are very familiar to the Kerala society, now it brought about central debate turned around again on the very fundamental issues of equality. It is shocking to notice that the non-operationalization of affirmative action policies particularly for recruiting teaching and non-teaching staff in the private aided educational institutions, for the last 50 years in Kerala, although it has been very successful in other states like Delhi. This perhaps proved a fact that why backwardness, both in social and economic terms, has still been perpetuating among the marginalized communities in the state. Had it been operationalized way back in 1957, these marginalized communities would have mobilized not only in sharing resources of the state but, very crucially, would have produced an intellectual capital by themselves for their respective groups and society at large as well. In all probability, they would have developed cultural and intellectual energy to cope with the new situation in the era of knowledge society. Curiously, one is yet to see any instance to show that these policies were implemented effectively. As a result, a dependency syndrome,[3] has been created by the conscious effort of the state at one side and the cultural stigma based on caste preferences tear apart these marginalized communities to make dialogue with modern institutions on the other. Further, no effort has been made by the state, to enhance their capital assets for institution building as they have traditionally been lacking it, unlike other dominant caste groups.

Crisis of the Model

Instead of conceptualizing what we have discussed earlier, politicians, governmental agencies and academics projected data by comparing the enrolment rate of SC/ST students in the educational institutions in Kerala with other states. As it went on high, this indicator became a showcasing piece in the new paradigm called 'Kerala model'. Regrettably, the real issues of representation and quest for equality were sidelined. The communities of Kerala were also not exceptional in this regard. Whenever the state wanted equal space, for every community to be represented, in the entire affairs of the educational system, the dominant communities protested in their rhetorical styles of liberation struggle, pastoral letters, etc. In other words, ethics of the Protestant in the west has been reproduced by the Catholics in Kerala in order to breathe a new spirit of capitalism by controlling centers of education as a vast reservoir of knowledge capital. In this unholy journey, the dominant caste-Hindus like Nair community, was also well tuned with the process of capital accumulation. If the Protestants in the west challenged the supremacy of religious orthodoxy in the public sphere, in Kerala they experimented by challenging the very public sphere to make their supremacy over the state. It clearly indicates the post-colonial trajectories of the state versus society dichotomy. Precisely, it shows, how rapid, that a model is replacing its past, nonetheless the fact that the very past has been a selective consciousness for certain privileged and pushing out others as marginalized. In this context, the present should not be seen as an ultra-modern; instead, tradition has been perpetuated time and again into the modern. The state of affairs of the educational system in Kerala in general and the private sector in particular is becoming a new epistemological site to see how it operated into the cultural fragments of this society.

Certainly this historical failure has to succumb very urgently, if one wanted to see the sustainability of the very model. However, the history sometimes does not give any plausible answer to this question. Firstly, the political will of the state has been debunked by the strong entrepreneurial educational groups in Kerala. Precisely, the state apparatus proved its inability to control it, over the years, although the same issues were brought, at first time, onto the Legislative Assembly way back in 1957 by the then Minister of Education Prof. Joseph Mundassery. Secondly, the dominant groups, with a larger share of social capital in terms of educational infrastructure, have never understood the need for sharing these scarce resources with the subaltern fellow citizens. Added to this, passive attitude of the academic community had never brought these pertinent issues into the academic discourses. It perhaps shows the intellectual bankruptcy of the state as it has been passive or uncritical to the latest development discourses as far as the question of equity is concerned. Yet, there is another reason behind it as well. The existing paradigm of development model with its state patronage might not have allowed this scientific community to slow down their experimental bits from the rapid process of making one-sided positive image of the very model. Such a serious issue, handled carelessly by these different apparatuses of the state and society, later on resulted into reproducing the age old inequality even in the highly celebrated Kerala Model of development as well.[4] It also indicates the fact that, in the wake of globalization and its operationalization through privatization, as widely been discussed among the academics, it would crystallize inequality based on caste/class preferences.[5]

At a time when the nation is seriously discussing the issues of inclusive policy, Kerala certainly is found in different atmosphere. Because of the overarching ideological state apparatus, with the backbone of proletariat, Left party in Kerala have consciously undermined the cultural formations of subaltern groups. Hence, slowly and steadily capital formation was consolidated in the hands of few dominant religious and caste groups with the state patronage, in the form of building-up educational institutions. If these primordial communities once used their cultural capital as a symbolic weapon to mobilize them to make their presence felt in the public sphere, later on the same culture started controlling the public good by managing educational institutions. It was not merely politicization of ideology, but was a clear politicization of interests. In this conscious un-thought social engineering, certain communities were sidelined, with new forms of stigma attached, in the margins of these discourses. This sheer negligence in the political and ideological arena is being provoked, while one looks at the upsurge of the subaltern masses in the political landscape of Kerala in the last two decades. For instance, the militant struggle waged by the Kerala Dalit panther movement against all kinds of discrimination, exploitation and violence, Adivasi struggles for their right over land and mobilization among Dalit Christians brought about a new challenge before the state. Certainly, the latter is the symbolic victims of these whole processes. In the wake of privatization,[6] these struggles become sharpened, as it is assumed that, they will be the worst suffers of the neo-liberal policies. Therefore, one cannot rule out the emergence of these new social movements, as the protest has always been a weapon of the weakest to assert their felt needs and articulate their deprivations.

A historical detour to the growth and development of educational institutions in the private sector would not give certain sociological insights. It is because, to begin with, culture has triumphed over the state politics, or cultural reproduction consciously or unconsciously was developed into the modern institutional structures, particularly, when one looks into the governing principles of aided educational institutions in Kerala. It doesn't mean that it is pathology; instead, it is the very failure of imbibing the core values of modernity. What needs to be understood from it, however, is that the same culture is becoming a yardstick to the less privileged. That is why these communities were under-represented in teaching positions. As the latest report shows, out of total 1,06,936 teachers only 353 (0.33%) among the Dalits and 87 (0.08%) among Adivasis were found in the aided educational institutions.[7] No plausible explanation is available on the question why these aberrations are seen in extending affirmative action in the aided educational institutions, other than caste based discrimination. In fact, there is no logic in saying that no qualified candidates are available, as these very institutions nurtured large number of qualified educated youth from these communities. This unnatural tendency reproduced intellectual hierarchies based on caste and religious lines and the affluent got more than what the deprived got.

Aided Institutions and their Legitimate Claims

It is true that the state could not exercise control over these so called aided managements as they tried to assert by themselves with the patronage of the same state apparatuses time and again. Getting interim court verdicts, for instance, in favor of them, perhaps, crystallized their legitimate claims. In fact, conflict between the state and the management is not new. It basically began from 1930s onwards, after noticing that several private institutions were found to be corrupted. However, despite acknowledging these facts, the Education Reform Committee of 1933 could not take any action to manage these institutions properly. This resulted in perpetuating corruption. The second incident was in 1945, when the Government of Travancore tried to take over the control of all the private primary schools. Because of the organizational protest by the private management, this could not succeed. The third incident was in the post-independent period, with the introduction of the Education Bill of 1957, after communist government assumed power in the state. The state had no intention in nationalizing these institutions; however, it was very keen in appointing teachers based on certain accepted criteria in order to ensure fair representation of different communities. The government could not do anything except accepting the responsibility of paying salary to the teaching and non-teaching staff of aided institutions.[8] Virtually, the government failed to set up a selection committee for appointing teachers. This very cultural superiority went on to that extent, as we know, to overthrow the first communist led ministry from the power. As a matter of fact, nobody dares question this cultural hegemony crystallized in the form of private management as it becomes stronger and stronger because of the passive attitude of the government since independence. Most importantly, the academic community, as most of them drawn from the same private institutions, had hardly brought about any dialogue of these unintended consequences of it.

A moot question needs to be asked here, however, is that whether these very private institutions are to be called private. A historical detour to the establishment of these colleges would not signal any private claims. Instead it was a result of collective effort of the State Government and the individuals along with different communities of Kerala society. In fact, the role of the government was very crucial in the beginning particularly donating land for the establishment of educational institutions. Way back in 1813, for example, government had donated land to build Syrian College, CMS College (Kottayam), Mahatma Gandhi College, (Thiruvananthapuram), Sree Narayana College (Kollam), Union Christian College (Alwaye) and recently a huge grant was given to purchase land for starting Devaswom Board College in Sasthamcotta.[9] In addition to this, University Grants Commission starts assisting from the 6th five-year plan onwards in the key areas such as infrastructure development and faculty improvement. Further, crores of rupees are paid per year out of the government coffers to these institutions to meet the expenditures. There are free accessibility of infrastructure of the state and different type of concessions and exceptions starting from land recurrence to tax relaxation extended to these institutions as well. Then, how come one can claim that it is private. Even if they are constituent on minority groups they cannot move away from social responsibilities. It is in this context that the claims for private management, to begin with, are not plausible. There is an urgent need to record, if it is not yet, what kind of concessions and privileges are being given to these aided institutions to make them into the present condition.

What we are witnessing today is that the private argues as if it has no social responsibility to address its own cultural problems, although this question alarmed the moral and ethical side of our value system. The radical approaches taken by the social movements in Kerala slowed down these value systems into pragmatic questions. If one sees the Kerala context, although the educational infrastructure was created by the Christian Missionaries in the pre-independent period, the vibrant socio-cultural movements of the 19th century in Kerala tried to make these scarce resources available to the masses. Apart from Christian missionaries, local level movements like SNDP, SJP and MES along with the dominant caste like Nairs started asserting themselves to democratize educational institutions and establish their own institutions. The logic behind starting these institutions, although it had different interpretations, was basically based on philanthropy. Later on the state itself appreciated the role of missionaries along with other social groups in this regard. When the demand for education went up, severe competition was found among these communities based on caste and religious cleavages and they were interested to start more and more educational institutions. And very importantly their growth rate over the years was remarkable. While comparing the data of 1962 with 1993, rate of governmental schools came down from 40 per cent to 36.6 per cent of the total. Among the private institutions, the highest number (25.5%) was found among the Hindus followed by Christians (23.4%). Among the Hindus, if Nairs hold larger share, among the Christians it was with Catholics. However, Muslims had roughly four per cent (see Table 1). The higher educational sector, in fact, was predominantly controlled by the aided managements (see Table 2). Unlike schools, Christian institutions were controlling 40.4 per cent of the total private colleges followed by the Hindus (24.7%) and Muslims (8.1%). Their presence was more found in technical education like training and engineering than arts and sciences. Certainly the magnificent role played by the private agencies, which were born out from different social segments in the field of education, needs to be appreciated. However, the quest for certain structural changes in tune with the need of society somehow was compromised. Particularly, it was on the question of recruiting teaching and non-teaching staff, as it created a reservoir of employment opportunity.

Table-1
Schools Managed by Different Agencies

Agency	*1962*		*1974*		*1993*	
	No.	*Per cent*	*No.*	*Per cent*	*No.*	*Per cent*
Hindus	*2728*	*27.5*	*3194*	*28.8*	*3076*	*25.5*
Christians	*2339*	*23.6*	*2338*	*21.1*	*2816*	*23.4*
Muslims	*472*	*4.8*	*919*	*8.3*	*1301*	*10.8*
others	*382*	*3.8*	*313*	*2.8*	*454*	*3.8*
Private total	5921	59.6	6764	61.0	7647	63.4
Government	4008	40.4	4320	39.0	4406	36.6
Total	9929	100	11084	100	12053	100

Source: Administrative Report 1962, Education Department, Directorate of Public Instructions, 1974, 1993.

As the report shows, in the Higher Secondary sector there were 24550 teachers including principal and lab assistants out whom

Table-2
Colleges Managed by Different Agencies 1993

Agency	*Arts & Sciences*		*Training*		*Engineering*		*Total*	
	No.	*Per cent*	*No.*	*Per cent*	*No.*	*Per cent*	*No.*	*Per cent*
Hindus	43	25.3	5	26.3	1	11.1	49	24.7
Christians	69	40.6	9	47.4	2	22.2	80	40.4
Muslims	15	8.8	1	5.3	0	0.0	16	8.1
Others	3	1.8	0	0.0	0	0.0	3	1.5
Private Aided	130	76.5	15	78.9	3	33.3	148	74.7
Government	40	23.5	4	21.1	6	66.7	50	25.3
Total	170	100	19	100	9	100	198	100

Source: Administrative Report of the Education Department, 1993.

Table-3
Teaching Staff in Higher Secondary Schools

Post	*Govt.*		*Aided*		
	No.	*Per cent*	*No.*	*Per cent*	*Total*
Principal	699	57.2	523	42.8	1222
Teacher (Sr)	6131	50.2	6073	49.8	12204
Teacher (Jr)	4291	49.4	4397	50.6	8688
Lab Assistant	1378	56.6	1058	43.4	2436
Total	12499	50.9	12051	49.1	24550

Source: Directorate of Higher Education, 2005.

those from aided schools constituted 49.1 per cent (see Table 3). Similarly, in the colleges, out of 10619 total teachers, 8745 (82.4 %) were drawn from the private aided sector (see Table 4) and larger number of them were found in Kottayam and Ernakulam districts. Further, out of 7580 non-teaching staffs in the colleges, 85.9 per cent were in the private. With regard to engineering colleges, out of 3079, 2026 (65.8%) teachers were in the government colleges. However, in colleges under MG University, 50 per cent of the teachers were from aided colleges, followed by Kerala (34.5%) and Kannur (34.4%) Universities (see Table 5). Sadly to be noticed, hardly any information is available about the social background

Table-4
Teaching Staff in the Arts and Science Colleges

Year	*Govt.*		*Private Aided*		
	No.	*Per cent*	*No.*	*Per cent*	*Total*
1995	1738	14.9	9937	85.1	11675
2000	1981	17.0	9668	83.0	11649
2004	1874	17.6	8745	82.4	10619

Source: Economic Review, 1995, 2000, 2004.

Table 5
Teaching Staff in Engineering Colleges

University	*Govt.*		*Aided*		
	No.	*Per cent*	*No.*	*Per cent*	*Total*
Kerala	642	64.5	353	35.5	995
MG	350	50.0	350	50.0	700
Calicut	640	64.6	350	35.4	990
Kannur	394	100.0	0	0.0	394
Total	2026	65.8	1053	34.1	3079

Source: Director of Technical Education, 2005-06.

of the teachers in the aided institutions till today. The legitimacy of recruiting teaching and non-teaching staff is also widely questioned, as it was found that selections were made only after making compulsory donations to these institutions.[10] While the amount of donations went up in tune with the great demand for jobs, the private aided management not only habituated this compulsory donation as lucrative business, but also produced a byproduct in society as consumerist culture of buying these jobs. It was also well known fact that management quota was auctioned on payment basis. How rapidly we forget the historical location of how the educational system has been evolved and how to demystify the value of pedagogy as critical idiom to nurture the future citizen assertive and responsible. In the wake of globalization, the new trend among mostly the aided institutions to shift their attention to self-financing colleges has proved that education is increasingly becoming a marketable commodity in the booming private sector.

Self-financing Sector: A Mask for Marketization of Knowledge

Today in fact, the higher educational sector in Kerala is facing a new challenge, certainly one of mushrooming self-financing institutions. The new shift in the educational sector, as it is visible today, has made the social responsibility redundant while treating education as profitable commodity to be marketed, since its demands are high in Kerala. In a rhetoric style, while launching self-financing colleges in Kerala, the government conceptualized a new formula as two self-financing colleges equal to one government college.[11] The rationale behind by the government was to maximize the intake so that it can cater wider demands of this scarce resource. On the other hand, from a management perspective, it was basically site for maximizing their profit. It is in this changing scenario, the entire critical pedagogic system was appropriated by money market.[12] Perhaps, the booming self-financing sector and their protest against the Kerala Professional College Act (KPC Act) 2006 to protect their autonomy should be born in mind in this context. As K.N. Panikkar[13] rightly pointed out, since the private management controlled major chunk of the available opportunities, the capitation fee charged was lucrative while they kept holding relative autonomy.[14] Such a market oriented attitude not only restricted to a segment of society but also perpetuated their interest in it. To begin with, although the presence of self-financing schools were almost very negligible, as the latest report shows there were 856 schools in 2006 (see Graph 1). However, in Higher Secondary sector, their presence was visible and the growth rate over the years was phenomenal. It is reported that 26.5 per cent of increment was found in unaided sector. Contrary to it, growth rate of aided educational institutions had come down from 40.4 per cent in 2003 to 31.5 per cent in 2006. In other words, aided managements perhaps turned their attention more into self financing than aided as the data show (see Graph 2). Similarly, the growth rate among the unaided colleges had gone up from 11.8 per cent in 1995 to 46.9 per cent in 2006. As against the unaided growing trend, the involvement of aided sector had been slashed down from 70 per cent in 1995 to 42 per cent followed by the state funded colleges from 18 to 11 respectively (see Graph 3). Quite surprisingly, a remarkable growth rate is observed in engineering colleges in Kerala. Out of total 69 colleges, 57 (82.6%) were in unaided sector followed by 13 per cent in government sector in 2002. Declining trend of both the

GRAPH 1

Growth of Schools

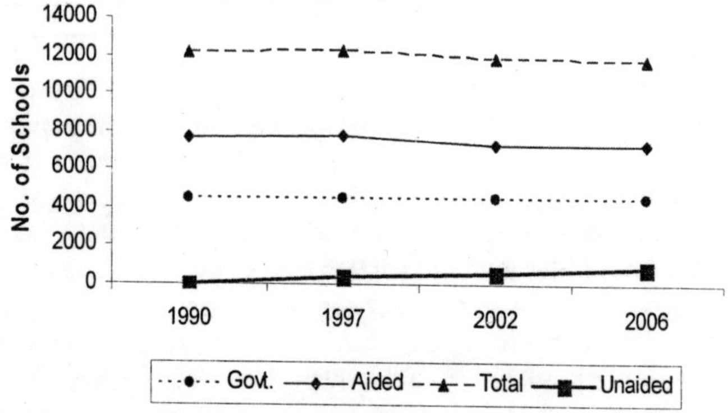

Source: Economic Review, 1998, 2004 and 2006.

GRAPH 2

Growth of Higher Seconday Schools

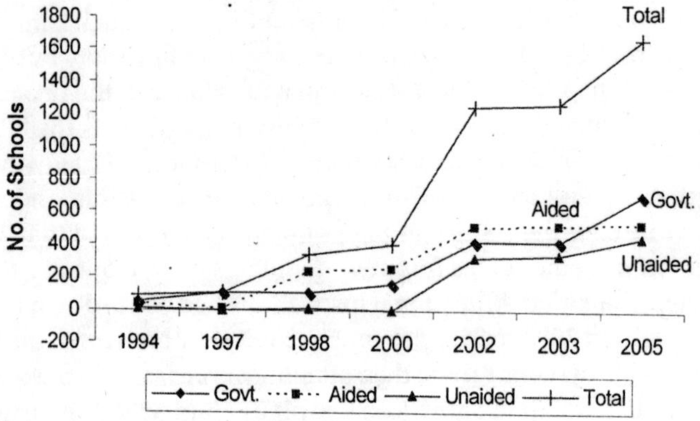

Source: Economic Review, 2002, 2003 and 2005 State Planning Board, Thiruvananthapuram.

arts and sciences and engineering colleges over the years in the government sector indicates that the state is retreating from higher education (see Graph 3). In nutshell, it can be said that the state is no more a crucial player in the higher education sector. As a result, new players, in the form of self-financing, assume their inevitable presence today in the educational market with lucrative attitude.

GRAPH 3

Growthrate of Colleges 1995-06

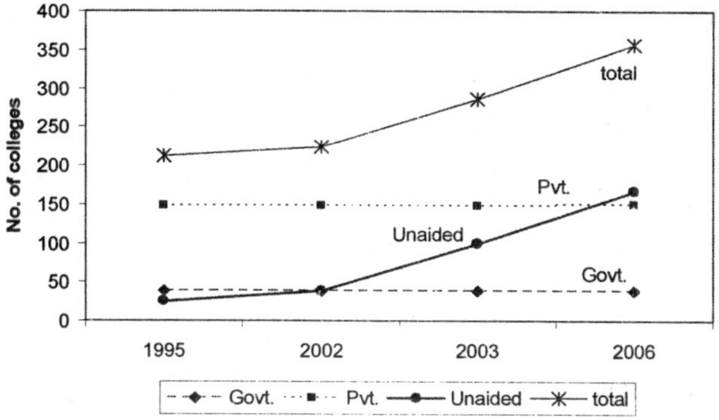

Source: Economic Review, 1997, 2002, 2003, 2005.

Concluding Remarks

Since the state cannot make huge investment in the education sector, only way to ensure equity and justice is through appropriate policies and their pragmatism, particularly looking into the marginalized communities. In this regard, the state has to take stock of the cognizance of the new social movements, as it is the children of enlightenment in our times to understand the implicit marginalization of the world today and articulate possible means to overcome from it. It is equally important to move beyond the narrow domains of legal and political measures. A movement towards equality in social terms can be charted as manifest in the growth of specific 'sameness' or similarities institutionalized in the social structure of the community.

Educational institutions in modern society can be seen as the experiential laboratories in making sense of these cherished values for cognitive structural formation. There are possibilities in the educational institutions to operationalize these value systems by enhancing different terrains of interaction such as peer group formation, teacher-student dialogue and above all curricula revisions, created by the very structure. Through social interaction with diverse specific cultural communities, a new hybrid identity can be evolved by ensuing equal representation of all communities. In this sense, a systematic pedagogic vista for knowledge production and reproduction are to be improved by diversifying its stake holders. It is in this context that educational institutions in Kerala have potential than any other state to become a role model by cherishing these values. It completely appeals for an enduring form of modern outlook with great inter-subjectivity regardless of primordial pre-occupations like caste, gender, religion, etc. Needless to say, this society needs to be celebrated while accepting its plural tradition in a real sense. What is lacking in the very laboratory of experimental vision of the Kerala model is that it reduced everything into statistical extrapolation in which the qualitative structural undercurrents were not taken up seriously. Perhaps, it could be a blind sociological mapping about our critical understanding of a society. Yet, it has to travel a long journey, not be made out of institutions of learning as stereotypical teaching machines, instead to enhance reflexivity and criticality.

NOTES AND REFERENCES

1. For example, a detailed study shows that the disparities in income were highly been reflected based different caste groups. The sharp differences were found between high caste Brahmins with salaried white collar jobs, on the one hand and communities such as Muslims and the Scheduled Castes and Scheduled Tribes with low income from their wage labour. And these differences in income based on caste were perpetuated in attaining education and job as well (UN Development and Economic and Social Welfare, 2000), p. 131.
2. *Kerala Education Act and Rule*, Revision Committee Report, (Thiruvananthapuram, Government of Kerala, 2008), p. 58.
3. M. Kunhaman, *Globalisation: A Subaltern Perspective* (Thiruvananthapuram, Centre for Subaltern Studies, 2002).
4. M.A. Oommen, 'Reforms and the Kerala Model', *Economic and Political Weekly*, Vol. 43 (2), January, 12, 2008, pp. 22-25.
5. In a series of articles, exclusionary practices based caste and religious cleavages and priorities are found in the private institutions through empirical studies. See Surinder S. Jodhka, and Katherine Newman (2008), 'In the Name of Globalisation: Meritocracy, Productivity and the Hidden Language of Caste'; Aswini Deshpande, and Newman Katherine, 'Where the Path Leads: The Role of Caste in Post-University Employment Expectations'; and Sukhadeo Thorat, and Paul Attewell, 'The Legacy of Social Exclusion: A Correspondence Study of Job Discrimination in India', *Economic and Political Weekly*, Vol. 42 (41), pp. 4125-4140 (2007).
6. The suicidal attempt by Rajani, an engineering student of an unaided

college had sensitized the entire Kerala society almost a month during the incident.

7. *Kerala Education Act and Rule, op. cit.*
8. Abdul Salim, P.R. Nair, *Educational Development in India: The Kerala Experience since 1800* (New Delhi, Anmol Publications, 2002), pp. 17-219.
9. E.T. Mathew, *Financing Higher Education: Sources and Uses of Funds of Private Colleges in Kerala* (New Delhi, Concept Publishing Company, 1991), pp. 34-35.
10. From a sample study conducted among the 25 colleges, it was found that except eight colleges, all insist on compulsory donations as a legitimate condition for getting appointed. And the range of donation varies from place to place and college to college, see E.T. Mathew, *Financing Higher Education, op. cit.*, p. 96.
11. Binoy Viswam, 'Self-financing Colleges', *Mathrubumi*, 12-18 October (2003), (In Malayalam).
12. G.S. Suresh Babu *Privatization of Higher Education and Its Impact on Dalits in India* (New Delhi, unpublished M.Phil Dissertation of SSS/ JNU, 2006).
13. K.N. Panikkar, 'Kerala Education Act: A Model for the Nation', See Editorial, *The Hindu* Daily (August, 7th 2006).
14. It was reported that in order to get a seat for MBBS, the managements auctioned the quota in range of Rs. 20 to 25 lakhs per student. See *Mathrubhoomi*, the Daily Malayalam Newspaper, July 2004, 5.

12

The Politics of Tribal Education and Governance: The Orissa Experience[1]

PANKAJ DEEP

Education plays an important role in human development. Education helps directly in increasing economic productivity and enhances earning power; it improves the power of understanding, enables a person for better socialization. It enhances the cultural level of the human values in society. Education is an inseparable link to the progress in every aspect of human life and is a major contributing factor in enhancing quality of life. Education is one of the principal means available to foster a deeper and more harmonious form of human development and thereby to reduce poverty, exploitation, ignorance, etc. Illiteracy is invariably associated with deprivation, socio economic under-development and exclusion. This expression is found in the resolution at the world conference on education held in March 1990 at Jomtien, Thailand.

Education enriches life and helps an individual to develop his personality. It is of special significance for tribal people who are facing a critical and transitional situation in the development process to adjust themselves to the changing world. One detrimental effect of an illiterate begins in pre-school years; the formative stage of life, when attitudes are shaped and that would tend to persist. The educational programs help to place responsibility before rights. Education determines the rate at which economic progress is achieved and benefits, which can be derived from it.

We have a democratic political set up in India which is the largest democracy in the world. The Democratic governments are to be elected in every five years as per the constitution of India that will be responsible for the governance of the country. In part IV of the constitution the Directive Principles of State Policy directs the government to implement such welfare policies so as to establish a welfare state in India. Government must be committed to remove imbalances and inequalities in society so that every one will get an equal share in the country's growth. It is the duty and responsibility of the democratically elected government to eradicate imbalances and inequalities in the society to have an inclusive development[2] in the country. The constitution of India calls upon the state (Article 46) to 'promote with special care, the education and economic interests of the weaker sections of the people, and, in particular, of Scheduled Tribes and Scheduled Castes and shall protect them from social injustice and all forms of exploitation.'[3]

Since independence we have been actively thinking and planning for the development of tribal people in order to alleviate their suffering and to remove obstacles to their development. To realize the idea of equality and social justice the Indian constitution lays special emphasis on the education of the children of backward classes such as the Scheduled Castes and Scheduled Tribes through affirmative action by incorporating special provisions. Though a lot has been done for the socio economic and educational development through the schemes launched in various successive five year plans since 1951, they do not seem to have benefited them up to the mark.[4] Even after sixty years of constitutional and legal support from state intervention, the tribal communities are still among the most underprivileged people of India. They are severely affected by poverty and its manifestations, such as low levels of literacy, healthcare, hunger and malnutrition. They suffer social and political marginalization and remain vulnerable to exploitation by the more powerful and are being excluded by both the process and outcomes of development. The main cause of tribal backwardness is exploitation, poverty, ill health and illiteracy. They live on the outskirts of forest and the modern technology is beyond their reach. The man causes is illiteracy and because of illiteracy they are facing other problems such as hunger, ill health, malnutrition, indebtedness, etc. Here the paper examines the efficacy of State's educational development strategy and its delivery to its people. The ability of the state to provide basic education (as per the constitutional commitment) to its toiling masses has been explored. Here the main thrust of argument is: Has the state achieved the goals it proclaimed from time to tome? Has the state achieved the goals of universalization of primary education proclaimed in the constitution (DPSP)? If yes, then to what extent and what degree? What are the measures of accountability evolved if at all? These are the questions, which have been explored and examined in the case of tribal educational administration.

II

In India, the Scheduled Castes, Scheduled Tribes (STs 8.2%, SCs 16.20%),[5] and backward classes constitute together the majority of the population. But the assets and resources possessed by the majority is proportionately less than the minority. Among them the tribes are the most neglected and in a vulnerable position in terms of broader development indicators such as literacy, poverty ranking, etc. Keeping in mind the above mentioned problems special provisions have been made in the constitution for the development of the backward classes such as Scheduled Castes and Scheduled Tribes through positive discrimination to achieve the greater equality and social justice.

For promotion of education among the Scheduled Tribes many schemes are in operation such as educational complexes in low literacy pockets for the development of ST girls' education in tribal areas; girls' and boys' hostels for Scheduled Tribes; establishment of Ashram Schools in tribal sub-plan area; post-metric scholarship; national overseas scholarship scheme for higher studies in abroad; book bank scheme; scheme for upgradation of merit; coaching for competitive examinations, etc. The National Policy on Education (NPE 1986) considered human being as a positive asset. It states that human beings are one of the precious national resources, which need to be cherished, nurtured and developed with care. The policy further articulated the intent to lay special emphasis on the removal of disparities and to equalize educational opportunities by attending to the specific needs of those who have been denied equality so far.[6]

The role of education in human resources development is that of a catalyst. The catalytic action of education in this complex and dynamic growth process needs to be planned meticulously and executed with great sensitivity. To realize the aims of Article 45, the directive principles of state policy (DPSP) in Indian constitution guarantees provision of free and compulsory education to all children up to 14 years old, which has been incorporated in fundamental rights, Article 21-A in 2003. This target was to be achieved within 10 years of its declaration. But due to ineffective policy implementation, defective education system and socio-economic problems, even after 60 years of independence the target of universalization of elementary education has not been achieved. This shows that only making good policy will not automatically translate it into action and realize its objectives. The core issue is the implementation. How it is being implemented to realize the goals is an important issue.

It is unfortunate that despite constitutional provisions and efforts made by Union and State Governments for the tribal communities, who are at a very critical stage of their history, they are facing a new situation to adjust themselves to the changes. Education is of special significance here. Due to lack of access to education from very beginning, tribes are in a position of handicap in dealing with the modern administrative system. Although theoretically, governmental efforts in the field of tribal education have been towards removal of disparity between tribals and non-tribals, in practice however desired result have not been achieved so far. These policies have failed to bring out expected improvement in their situation. Though it has brought forth a perceptible improvement in the literacy and socio-economic condition of tribes, yet the schemes which are applied to tribal areas are not able to cater to the needs and aspirations of the people and have failed to solve the problems of imbalances in tribal areas in terms of literacy rates and access to education. Tribes are at the lowest level of education pyramid. No doubt there has been a substantial increase in the literacy rates of tribes since 1981, the gap between the literacy rate of Scheduled Tribes and those of non-tribal population is not only persisting but also found to be widening, as shown in Table 1.

Table–1
Literacy Rates of STs and Total Population (7 Years and above), India 1931-2001 (In Per cent)

Sl. No.	*Census Years*	*Total Literacy Rate*	*Tribal Literacy Rate*	*Gap between Total and Tribal Literacy Rates*
1.	1931	7.50	0.75	06.75
2.	1961	29.29	08.54	20.75
3.	1971	34.05	11.29	23.21

Contd...

Sl. No.	Census Years	Total Literacy Rate	Tribal Literacy Rate	Gap between Total and Tribal Literacy Rates
4.	1981	36.20	16.35	19.85
5.	1991	52.20	29.60	22.60
6.	2001	65.38	47.01	18.28

Sources: *(i)* Compilations based on census of India 2001; *(ii)* Educational profile of States/UTs, Department of Education, Ministry of HRD.

The picture of tribal education becomes murkier if we look at the figure for women. Although the female literacy rate, which is an important indicator in the field of education among STs has increased substantially from 4.85 per cent in 1971 to 34.36 per cent in 2001, the gap between ST female and the general population (female) has also been widening as shown in Table 2.

Table–2
Female Literacy Rates of STs and Total Population (7 Years and above) India, 1971-2001 (in Per cent)

Sl. No.	Census Years	Total Literacy Rate	Tribal Literacy Rate	Gap between Total and Tribal Literacy Rates
1.	1971	18.69	4.85	13.84
2.	1981	29.85	8.04	21.81
3.	1991	39.29	18.19	21.10
4.	2001	53.67	34.76	18.91

Note: Includes SCs, STs and general female population.
Sources: (1) Author's estimation based on census of India 2001; (2) Abstract of Selected Educational Statistics 2002-03, Planning, Monitoring and Statistics Division, Department of Secondary and Higher Educations, Ministry of HRD.

The rates of drop-outs/push outs are another crucial indicator in the field of educational development. Though there has been a steady decline in respect of both general and ST students, the problems of dropouts happen to be a common feature and are more serious for ST students. While both the categories have been showing a decreasing trend from 1990-91 to 2002-03 the problems still appear to be the worst with regards to ST students which is shown in table 3. They hold very high dropout rates of 51.37 per cent in class I to V, 68.67 per cent in class I to VIII, 80.29 per cent in class I to X during

Figure 1: Literacy Rates of Total Population and Tribal Population (1971-2001)

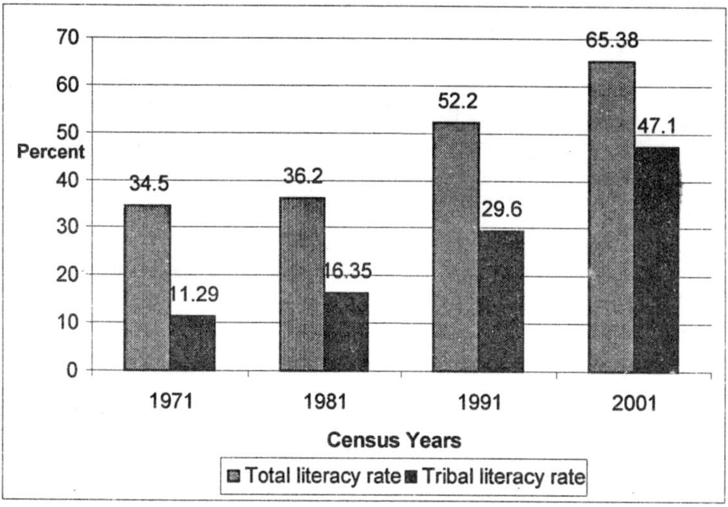

Note: Total Literacy includes SCs, STs Population. *Source:* based on Table 1.

Figure 2: Female Literacy Rates of STs and Total Population (7 Years and above), India 1971-2001

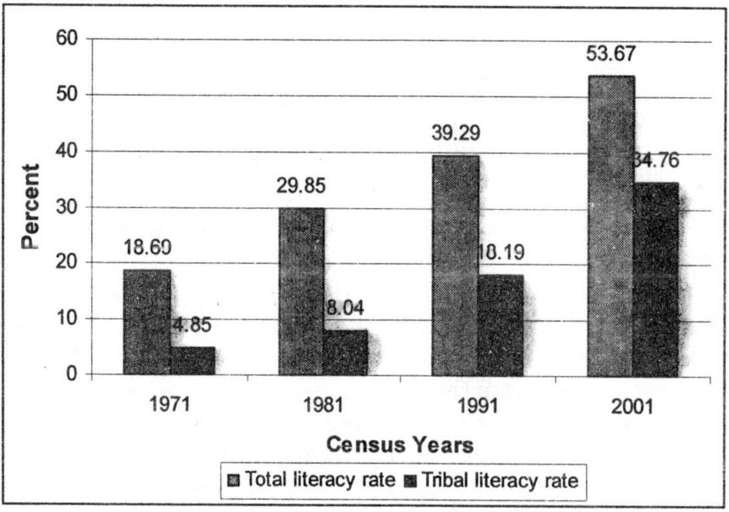

Note: T.F.–Total Female, includes SCs, STs and General. *Source:* Based on Table 2.

2002-03. Also the gap between the general population and the STs is found to be widening from 13.67 per cent in 1990-91 to 17.71 in 2002-03, at the secondary level, which is a curse of much concern.

Table-3
Drops Out Rates Among STs and Total Population 1990-91, 1998-99, 2002-03 (In Per cent)

Category	*Classes (I –V)*			*Class (I-VIII)*			*Class (I-X)*		
Years	*1990-91*	*1998-99*	*2002-03*	*1990-91*	*1998-99*	*2002-03*	*1990-91*	*1998-99*	*2002-03*
Total Students	42.60	39.74	34.89	60.90	56.82	52.79	71.34	67.44	62.58
ST Students	62.52	57.36	51.37	78.57	72.80	68.67	85.01	82.96	80.29
Gap Among STs and Total	19.92	17.62	16.52	17.67	15.98	16.12	13.67	15.52	17.71

Source: Author's estimation based on Abstract of Selected Educational Statistics 2002-03, Planning, Monitoring and Statistics Division, Department of Secondary and Higher Educations, Ministry of HRD, GOI, New Delhi-2004.

The rate of drop outs/push outs is very high among the school going children of tribal communities as the siblings start helping their parents' subsistence from the formative stage itself. Besides, there is no conducive atmosphere at home. The other problems in the promotion of education in tribal areas are sparseness of population, small size of habitation and difficulties of communication although some residential schools know as 'Ashram schools' have been established in the tribal areas, in addition to providing stipends to the tribal day scholars. The available educational infrastructure in tribal areas is inadequate to meet the requirement of elementary education. The problem of infrastructural weakness in respect of the educational administration in the tribal regions has been admitted by the state education department of Orissa in the discussion paper prepared for the UNDP sponsored workshop to consider the project 'universal outreach of literacy by 2000 A.D.' The situation is similar in other states with the exception of the North Eastern tribal majority states.

III

Orissa is one of the poorest states in India, with 47 per cent of the population living below the poverty line. About 87 per cent of the population lives in rural areas. The Adivasis constitutionally known as the Scheduled Tribes constitute 23.20 per cent[7] of the total population belonging to 62 ethnic communities. The tribals are the most marginalized and poorest among the poor and depend on their labour. They are concentrated mostly in the districts of Malkangiri, Rayagada, Koraput, Nabaragpur, Sundargarh, Keonjhar, Mayurbhanj and Kalahandi.

Education is the most important thrust area for the socio economic development of any educationally backward communities like Schedule Tribes. Both the Central Government and State Governments have undertaken various measures to improve the educational status of this community, through various steps like provision of pre-metric and post-metric scholarships, hostel facilities, free distribution of nationalized text books, and garments. For encouraging enrollment and reducing dropout rates, Mid-Day-Meal (MDM) scheme has been introduced in all primary schools in the state. Sevashram (40 seated) and residential Sevashram (100 seated) co-education schools are introduced in tribal sub-plan areas, imparting education up to class V. Similarly, Ashram Schools (for boys) and Kanya Ashram (for girls) are residential schools imparting education up to class VII, which is functioning under the department of SC and ST Welfare. In order to make education popular among the SCs and STs State Government is providing hostel facilities at primary level known as primary school hostel (PSH) which is 40 seated for both boys and girls, attached to mass education.

Many programmes related to primary education have been implemented since long back. They include Early Childhood Care Education (ECCE), District Primary Education Programme (DPEP), Elementary Education (EE), Mid-Day-Meal Programme (MDM), Sarva Shiksha Abhiyan (SSA), Education Guarantee Scheme (EGS), etc.

Early Childhood Care Education (ECCE)

In Orissa, this programme is being implemented since 1982, with the assistance of UNICEF. The main objective of this programme is to motivate children in the age group of 3-5 years towards primary education with a view to achieve the aim of Universalization of Elementary Education (UEE).

District Primary Education Programme (DPEP)

The District Primary Education Programme (DPEP) was launched in Orissa in the year 1996-97 with a view to achieve the long cherished goal of universalization of Primary education in the state through district specific planning. DPEP is a centrally sponsored program. The objectives of the DPEP are to provide access to primary education for all children, to reduce the drop-out rate to less than 10 per cent, to increase learning achievement of primary school children by 25 per cent, reduce the gap among gender and disadvantaged social groups to les than 5 per cent.[8]

Elementary Education (EE)

Universalization of Elementary Education (UEE) has been adopted as one of the components of basic minimum services. The objectives of universal elementary education covers three aspects of elementary education: *(i)* Universal access and enrollment, *(ii)* Universal retention of children up to 14 years of age, *(iii)* substantial improvement in the quality of education to enable all children to achieve essential level of learning. Keeping the need for universalization of primary education, elementary education has been expanded in the state.[9]

Operation Blackboard

The scheme addresses the problem of physical infrastructure in the schools. A number of primary schools are functioning in the state without proper building and other essential infrastructure. Under the scheme, governments have taken steps for providing basic infrastructure including school buildings in rural areas since 1990-91.

Sarva Shiksha Abhiyan (SSA)

The aim of the programme is to achieve the constitutional goal of universalization of elementary education and provide useful and quality education to all children in the age group of 6-14 years by 2010. It ensures transparency and accountability of the school system to the community.[10] The objectives of the programme include:

(i) All children of 6-14 age groups should be in school by 2003.

(ii) All children should complete 5 years of schooling by 2007.

(*iii*) All children should complete 8 years of schooling by 2010.
(*iv*) Universal retention by 2010.
(*v*) Bridge all gender and social category gaps at primary level by 2007 and at upper primary level by 2010.
(*vi*) Infrastructure improvement in schools.
(*vii*) Focus on elementary education of satisfactory quality and on education for life.

A profile of the tribal literacy in Orissa is presented in Table 4. The overall ST literacy rate in the state is 37.4 per cent. It is 51.5 per cent among males and 23.4 per cent among females. According to 2001 census, out of all districts, Sundergarh has achieved the highest literacy rate (64.22%) whereas Malkangiri has recorded the lowest literacy rate. Social group wise literacy rate in Orissa is the lowest in the case of ST population and is the highest among general castes. The gap between them is 26.78 per cent in 1991 and 25.7 per cent in 2001. Literacy rate among the ST population has been increased, but the gap between the general population and STs is still not only found persisting but also increasing. Further, if we look into the female literacy, the gap between general population and ST female population is also found increasing. It was 24.47 per cent in 1991 and it increased to 26.65 per cent in 2001 (Table 4). Though the literacy rate of ST population increased from 22.31 per cent in 1991 to 37.4 per cent in 2001, the gap between general population and ST population is still high in the state, more than at the national level. In all India level, it is 18.28 per cent whereas in state level it is 25.7 per cent (Table 4); it is still high and remains a matter of concern.

Table–4
Literacy Rates of Total Population and ST Population (Orissa)(In Per cent)

Category/Year	*1991*			*2001*		
	Person	*Male*	*Female*	*Person*	*Male*	*Female*
Total population	49.09	63.09	34.68	63.1	75.3	50.5
STs population	22.31	34.44	10.21	37.4	51.5	23.4
Gap between total population and STs population	26.78	28.65	24.47	25.7	23.8	26.65

Source: Author's estimations based on census India 1991-2001, *op. cit.*

Thus, there are two thrust areas for human development in the state, a broadbased and rejoining balanced growth strategy, led by the agricultural sector and the promotion of literacy, with special emphasis on female literacy. Region specific strategies are required to achieve positive results in both areas. These two basic requirements, taken together, will increase the demand for human capital, primary education, and primary healthcare.

The rate of dropout is one of the important indicators of internal efficiency of the education system. In Orissa, the rate of dropouts is found to be very high, i.e., 34.7 per cent at primary level and 59.0 per cent at upper primary level in the year 2002-03.

If we look at dropout rates social group wise, it is the ST students who rank highest in dropout rates from class I to X. It is 84.97 per cent whereas the general population has only 71.74 per cent (as shown in Table 5) in 2002-03.

Table–5
Drop Out Rates Among STs and Total Students (Orissa) in 2002-03 (In Per cent)

Category	*Class(I-V)*	*Class (I-VIII)*	*Class (I-X)*
Total students	46.13	61.73	71.74
ST students	56.28	78.12	84.97
Gap among STs and total students	10.15	16.39	13.23

Note: Total students include ST students.
Source: Author's estimation based on Abstract of Selected Educational Statistics 2002-03.

Issues and Concern

Universalization of elementary education (UEE) has been a national goal since independence. The recent amendment to the constitution (Art. 21-A) which has made elementary education a fundamental right of the citizen, guides the formulation of policies and programs in this area. To universalize the elementary education many programs and policies have been implemented both in center and in the state of Orissa, such as Operation Blackboard and various (EFA) Education for All projects (1987-88), District Primary Education Programme (DPEP), Sarva Shiksha Abhiyan (SSA), etc. Concerted efforts towards the goal of UEE during the last five decades have resulted in a manifold increase in the number of institutions, teachers and students. But the fruits have not reached to certain sections of population such as scheduled tribes when compared to the non tribal population.

Despite the programme of universalization of primary education (UPE), which has been in effective operation since 1986, the literacy rate of STs remained as low as 47.1 per cent (2001), while the general literacy rate reached 65.38 per cent. Similarly, the female literacy rate of STs stood at 34.1 per cent which is also much lower in comparison with 54.16 per cent in respect of general category. As the 2001 census data reveals that there are tribal districts like Malkangiri in Orissa where the literacy rate of STs is as low as 31.28 per cent while there are districts like Aizawal in Mizoram with as high as 88.49 per cent. Further, the gap between the general population and that of the STs is also found to have widened from 19.9 per cent to 22.6 per cent between 1981 and 1991, as discussed earlier. Adding to this is the problems of intra-and inter-state/district and inter-community variations in the literacy rates of STs. Although the drop-out rates have been showing a declining trend among STs in class I to X from 85.01 per cent in 1990-91 to 80.29 per cent in 2002-03, yet the same is still very high, when compared to 71.34 per cent and 62.58 per cent of general students respectively for the same years indicating a gap of 13.67 per cent and 17.71 per cent.

The growth of tribal education has not been as satisfactory as expected. The reasons which are responsible for the problems of high dropouts and poor performance of the tribal children could be categorized under two heads:

1. Factor related to socio-cultural background of the tribes – It includes poverty, ignorance, lack of awareness, illiteracy of parents, unfavorable study environment of pupil in the home, psychological constraints, geographical isolation, linguistic constraints, etc.
2. Systematic factors – It includes:[11]
   - *(a)* Problem of school building (shortage of classrooms).
   - *(b)* Lacking infrastructure facilities.
   - *(c)* Shortage of teachers.
   - *(d)* Lack of teaching aids.
   - *(e)* Teacher absenteeism.

(*f*) No regular mid-day-meals, which lack a monitoring system.
(*g*) Books to the students are not given from the very beginning of the academic year. It is given in the middle of the year and also not full set of books.
(*h*) Stipends to the students of classes VI-VII are not given in time, and because being late, money is spent in non-academic purpose.
(*i*) School timing.
(*j*) School curriculum, etc.

The problems of teacher absenteeism, lack of commitment and motivation of the teachers are creating hurdles in achieving the policy goals in primary education. Lack of infrastructure and teaching aids in the schools are adding to the problem. Almost all the teachers try to avoid postings in remote areas, because of lack of infrastructure facilities and transportation problems in the remote areas. Either they prefer transfer to urban areas or to areas well connected with roads and having modern infrastructure or to the nearby areas of their villages. This is projected as an artificial shortage of teachers in the areas. It contributes as the main reason of poor performance of primary education in tribal areas. This anomaly could be checked by regular inspections and supervisions with strict punishments such as stopping of increments, salary, suspension, etc. There should be a provision of incentives to teacher's serving in remote tribal areas such as Kashipur Block in Rayagada District, various parts of Malkangiri District, Kotagarh Block in Kandhamal District, etc. No doubt, there is shortage of teachers in rural schools in many cases but adequate teachers are not the sole factor for the efficiency and effectiveness of delivery of primary education at the school level. Rather, what holds the key is the commitment on the part of the teachers. But it is lacking among the teachers. VEC is supposed to supervise and monitor the village school education. But it is not happening in almost all the villages of the tribal areas. Though VEC enjoys institutional support, they are yet to be strengthened. The Head Master usually bypasses the authority of the VEC. He sometimes takes advantage of illiteracy of the member of VECs.

Coming to the next issue regarding tribal culture and the schools, it is observed in the tribal areas that the overall study environment in the schools, school timing, school curriculum, textbooks, etc. are quite difficult to adopt for a tribal students. As most of them are the first generation learners, they speak their own dialect at their home and they have a distinct culture which does not match with the urban and middle class based culture of the school. Interface between home language and school language is major challenge in ensuring retention and quality improvement; it discourages students to continue in the school and it is one of the factors which push students out of the school. As a result, this leads to high rate of dropout of tribal students. It is found from the various studies that curriculum and culture play a greater role and impact in the children's education both in terms of access, retention and performance. Inequalities of cultural background of pupils have a direct correlation with inequalities in attainment and performance of pupils' education.[12] Hence this has to be kept in mind when we are planning and implementing the educational policies. And bilingual approach should be preferred up to a minimum standard (i.e. 3rd or 4th) in teaching, so that children would not feel alienation in terms of language and he/she can interact more with his peer groups and teachers which will directly create curiosity in the mind of the children to be in school and concentrate in study. The most important and crucial reason for high rate of school drop out and poor performance of tribal children is the chronic poverty among the tribal community. It is not the case that the parents are not interested in their children's education. Rather they do not have any other option than to engage their children in household earning for their survival. The choice is between food and education and poor parents go for the former in terms of priority. It is a matter of priority for parents as to whether they will send their children to school or not. This priority becomes a compelling task to poor tribal parents who are living in abject poverty. To check the above-mentioned problems certain steps must be taken by the government on priority basis such as:

- Establishment of residential schools (Ashram Schools) in all the tribal villages with availability of full infrastructural and modern facilities.
- To solve the language problem of the tribal students the teachers should know the concerned tribal language and teaching should be in tribal dialect in schools for the students up to class III. Slowly, the students should be taught in other medium.

- Government should encourage and organize training programmes for teachers to learn the concerned tribal language and it should be compulsory for every teacher to take the training and know the language of the area/tribe where one is posted (in tribal areas).

The most important issue behind the tribal education and its performance is to be addressed; the issues of poverty and livelihood are found the most crucial causes of tribal student drop outs and exclusion from schooling. Poverty has a spiral impact on tribal life. So, it needs to be addressed properly. Thus, the administrative mechanism should meticulously handle tribal administration keeping in mind the above mentioned problems. Then only the administration would be helpful for the progress of the tribes and their socio economic life enhancing progress in literacy and education. Education directly enables them to participate in public action and take share of development.

Thus, the problems need to be approached with a different emphasis. The areas that require attention are the following: improvement in the quality of teaching and other infrastructural facilities in schools, changes in curriculum and working hours, and consideration of other socio-economic factors which influence their enrolment and dropout.

Concluding Remarks

Education is the first step towards any development in human life. Education gives the sprit, ability and thought for future vision in life. It is like blood in life; without education life becomes ineffective and it is equivalent to eyes with no power of vision. Education has long been identified as one of the most important determinants of economic growth. It is both an indicator as well as an instrument for any kind of development. Education helps directly in the life of human being in various ways. Education helps know and pursue community living. Knowledge and social life are the main pillars of day to day life. The importance of education in human lives has been realized by the policy makers. And for this purpose, many policies and programmes have been implemented both by the Central Government and State Government to convert the vision into action and to improve the education of the people in general and the underprivileged class such as Scheduled Tribes in particular.

Since the inception of the first Five-year plan various programmes have been implemented to improve the educational level of the Scheduled Tribes and to reduce the gap between the literacy level of general population and the Scheduled Tribes. The programmes included Educational Complexes in Low Literacy Pockets for the Development of ST Girls Education in Tribal Areas, Girls' and Boys' Hostels for Scheduled Tribes, Establishment of Ashram Schools in Tribal Sub-Plan Area, Post-metric scholarship, National overseas scholarship scheme for higher studies abroad, Book bank scheme, Scheme for upgradation of merit, Coaching for competitive examinations, etc. along with the other general educational programmes like Early Childhood Care Education (ECCE), District Primary Education Programme (DPEP), Elementary Education (EE), Mid-Day-Meal Programme (MDM), Sarva Shiksha Abhiyan (SSA), Education Guarantee Scheme (EGS), etc. In spite of these special education programmes for tribes, the condition of tribal education is in very critical stage and the tribes are in the lowest stratum of the educational parameter. The literacy gap between the tribal and the general is not only persisting but also widening. The subject of inequality in terms of access, enrolment, retention and performance has come to the forefront of the debate. Inadequate access of education has been reduced to some extent with the increase of schools, but there are still acute problems of schools and performance. It is because of the defective planning in educational administration and ineffective implementation which ignored the culture of the tribal people and their social life on the one hand and the lack of political will not to address their economic life on the other.

NOTES AND REFERENCES

1. Earlier version of this paper has been presented at National Symposium on Tribes, *Rethinking Paradigms in Anthropology: Connecting Research and People*, Organised by Department of Anthropology, University of Delhi (26th-28th December 2008).
2. The politics of development includes all groups and all peoples of the state. There must not be any practice of discrimination and social exclusion both in the process of development and its outcomes. The fruits of development of the nation must be shared equally by its entire people. No section of the society should be left out from the process of development. See Robert Jenkins and Elima Barr, *Social Exclusion of Scheduled Caste Children from Primary Education in India, Draft Paper* (New Delhi, UNICEF, October, 2006).

3. P.M. Bakshi, *The Constitution of India with Selected Comments* (New Delhi, Universal Law Publishing Company, 1997), p. 73. See also P.L. Mehta, 1991, *Constitutional Protection to Scheduled Tribes in India: Retrospect and Prospects* (New Delhi, H.K. Publication, 1991).
4. S. Chanana and Vinay K. Srivastava, 'Tribal Welfare: Problems and Prospects' *Mainstream*, May 19 (1990), p. 15.
5. Government of India, *Census Report 2001: Population (Provisional) Totals*, Registrar General and Census Commission of India, GOI, New Delhi.
6. Quoted in Government of India, 2003, *Education for All: National Plan of Action India*, Department of Elementary Education and Literacy, Ministry of Human Resource Development, GOI, New Delhi, p. 27.
7. Government of India, 2001, Census Report, *op. cit.*
8. Government of Orissa, *Economic Survey 2004-05*, Directorate of Economics and Statistics, Planning and Co-ordination Department, GoO, Bhubaneswar, p. 14/2.
9. *Ibid.*, p. 14/2. See also Government of India.2003, *Education for All: National Plan of Action India*, Department of Elementary Education and Literacy, Ministry of Human Resources Development, GOI, New Delhi, pp. 24-25.
10. Government of Orissa, *Economic Survey 2004-05*, *op. cit.* See also Government of India, *Annual Report 2003-04*, Ministry of Human Resources Development, Department of Secondary and Higher Education, GOI, New Delhi; Arun C. Mehta, 2004, *Elementary Education In Rural India: Where Do We Stand?* NIEPA, New Delhi, Government of India, 2007; *India 2007 Reference Annual*, Publication Division, Ministry of Information and Broadcasting, GOI, New Delhi; Government of India, Annual Report 2003-04, Ministry of Human Resources Development, Department of Secondary and Higher Education, GOI, New Delhi; Government of India, 1986, *National Policy on Education*, GOI, New Delhi
11. Government of India, *Census Report 2001*, *op. cit.*
12. See P. Bourdieu and J.C. Passeron, *La reproduction. Elements pour une theorie du systeme d' enseignement*, (Paris: Les Edition de Minuit, 1970); (English language edition: *Reproduction in education, society and culture* (2nd edition), (London: Sage Publication, 1990). For more details refer R. Nash, 2001, 'Class, ability and attainment: a problem for the Sociology of Education', in *British Journal of Sociology of Education*, 22 (2), pp. 189-202.

13

Social Exclusion and Elementary Education: A Case Study of STs in India

SUJIT KUMAR CHOUDHARY

The 83rd constitutional amendment recognized the education as a fundamental right of all Indian citizens; disparities continue to be pronounced between the various castes and tribes. People from marginalized sections, especially Scheduled Castes, Scheduled Tribes, minorities and women, have still been excluded from many walks of life, whether social, political, economic and educational, whatever may be the reason for this exclusion. Among these marginalized groups, the Scheduled Tribes make up 8.2 per cent of the population and consistently fare poorer across various indicators related to elementary education. Furthermore, the structural causes of social exclusion, such as continued high level of poverty present among Scheduled Tribes, also remain as significant constraints. This paper analyzes the extent of social exclusion of Scheduled Tribe children in elementary education in India and argues for a comprehensive policy response which addresses the various barriers to accessing education of this disadvantaged group. For this, the paper will review the underlying causes of the disadvantaged status related to elementary education of children from Scheduled Tribes (STs) which are largely unaddressed and therefore remain as significant barriers to attending school. The paper concludes by proposing for an appropriate social policy to adequately respond to social exclusion in elementary education in India. In this regard, a holistic approach should be adopted including addressing the structural and basic causes of the problem in a context-specific, comprehensive manner.

Conceptual Framework of Social Exclusion

What precisely does exclusion mean? Who is excluded and why? How does this concept differ from that of poverty? Does exclusion refer to a problem in the distribution of wealth or a loosening in the ties that bind society together? These are some questions that will be addressed before we take on the issue of social exclusion of scheduled tribe children from elementary education. Social exclusion is a term used widely in the UK and the rest of Europe and was first found used in France. It is used across disciplines including education, sociology, psychology, politics and economics. Social exclusion means being unable to access the things in life that most of the society takes for granted. The term, however, is not systematically analyzed, though it is about the character of the social system and about the dynamic development of social structures. 'Exclusion' is something that is done by some people to other people. Political theorists of social exclusion allow that they can be consequences of economic transformation; it is the fault of 'society' as a whole.[1] Buvinic[2] summarizes the meaning of social exclusion as follows: 'The inability of an individual to participate in the basic political, economic and social functioning of society and it involves, 'the denial of equal access to opportunities imposed by certain groups in society upon others.'

Another definition is offered by Madnipour *et al:*

> Social exclusion is defined as a multi-dimensional process, in which various forms of exclusion are combined: participation in decision making and political processes, access to employment and material resources, and integration into common cultural processes. When combined, they create acute forms of exclusion that find a spatial manifestation in particular neighbourhoods.[3]

Social exclusion can also be explained in terms of group interactions aimed at maximizing values and minimizing costs. According to Jordon, 'Individuals are most vulnerable when they have fewest personal capacities and material resources... but none of these threatens their survival so long as they enjoy the protection afforded by membership of an inclusive group that co-operates productively and redistributes its product.'[4] Jordon goes on to say that 'all interactions take place in the context of norms, practices and institutions that steer, stabilize and regulate them.'[5]

Members regulate each other's actions by reinforcing norms of social obligation, and offer mutual support and assistance on a reciprocal basis. 'All social formations have rules about rights as well as obligations, which determine when, where and how the goods for final consumption will be distributed. These rules are laid down collectively, but result in individual entitlements.'[6]

It is important to distinguish the idea of 'social exclusion' from the somewhat simpler notion of 'poverty'. According to Walker and Walker:

> We have retained the distinction regarding *poverty* as a lack of the material resources, specially income, necessary to participate in British society and *social exclusion* as a more comprehensive formulation which refers to the dynamic process of being shut out, fully or partially, from any of the social, economic, political or cultural systems which determines the social integration of a person in society. Social exclusion may, therefore, be seen as the denial (or non-realization) of the civil, political and social rights of citizenship.[7]

For Walker and Walker, the opposite of exclusion is integration, with integration understood in relation to the idea of citizenship as it was formulated by Marshall.[8] John Veit-Wilson has made a very important distinction between 'weak' and 'strong' versions of the idea of social exclusion. He puts it as follows:

> In the 'weak' version of this discourse, the solutions lie in altering these excluded people handicapping characteristics and enhancing their integration into dominant society. 'Stronger' forms of this discourse also emphasis the role of those who are doing the excluding and therefore aim for solutions which reduce the powers of exclusion.[9]

UNESCO (United Nations Educational, Scientific and Cultural Organization) established the MOST (Management of Social Transformation) programme in 1992. The MOST made policy paper (numbered 2) which deals with social exclusion on a world scale.

The concept of exclusion has come into ever greater use with the deepening of the social crisis. Contrary to what occurred in the Industrial Revolution of the last century, the rich now have less and less need for the labour power of the poor. Exclusion seems to have replaced exploitation as the primary cause of poverty.[10]

However, they immediately qualify this position, as outlined by Bessis:

> The two phenomena of exploitation and exclusion are not, however, totally independent of one another. Can one say, as does Philippe Van Parijs that the successes obtained by European welfare states and trade unions in the struggle against exploitation rendered exclusion the predominant form of social injustice? ... These questions regarding the respective importance of the two phenomena are not a matter of simple quarrel among specialists. The response one gives to them generates policies that assign priority either to the struggle against exploitation or the battle against exclusion.[11]

The argument being presented here is that exclusion is a crucial contemporary form of exploitation, and that indeed there is nothing new about it. The battle against exclusion must be a battle against exploitation. But on the other, Byrne argues that exploitation is also a statement about what exclusion is not. In his words,

> Exclusion is not dominion. It is not to do with identity considered either as something either intrinsic or self-chosen. It is to do with economic relations. This is a highly contentious point. Let me say straight away that I actually do think that a neo-Durkheimian treatment of exclusion in relation to identity is worthwhile and that exclusion can really be thought to have a lot to do with excluded identities, but that is not what the current debate on social exclusion is essentially concerned with. In other words 'identity exclusion' although always subject to modification by the economic relations of phases of capitalism, has an intrinsic content of its own and may exist under all forms of economic relation.[12]

The problem of social exclusion, in fact, is usually raised due to the problem of equal opportunity, as some people are more subject to such exclusion than others. Marginalization of certain groups is a problem even in many economically more developed countries, including the United Kingdom (UK) and the United States (US), where the majority of the population enjoys considerable economic and social opportunities. It is, however, critical to take note of the particular form of exclusion in the Indian context, where ascriptive rather than achieved characteristics are the basis of exclusion.

Overview of Scheduled Tribes in India

The Indian Constitution assigns special status to the Scheduled Tribes (STs). The Government of India's approach to historically marginalized groups draws on provisions made in the Indian Constitution, which contains explicit state obligation towards protecting and promoting social, economic, political and cultural rights. 'The State shall promote with special care the educational and economic interests of the weaker sections of the people and, in particular, of the Scheduled Castes and the Scheduled Tribes, and shall protect them from social injustice and all forms of exploitation' (Directive Principle of State Policy, Article 46). The Constitution mandates positive discrimination in government services, state-run, and sponsored educational institutions. Amendments to the Constitution also enabled representation of SCs, STs and women in local governance structures.[13]

Traditionally referred to as adivasis, vanbasis, tribes or tribals, STs constitute about 8.2 per cent of the Indian population.[14] There are 573 Scheduled Tribes living in different parts of the country, having their own languages and dialects with more than 270 such languages in India.[15]

According to the 2001 census,[16] the tribal population in India is 84.32 million. The largest number of tribal people is in Madhya Pradesh (12.23 million), followed by Orissa (8.14 million) and Jharkhand (7.08 million). However, the largest proportion of tribes in total population is in Lakshadweep (94.51%), followed by Mizoram (94.46%), Nagaland (89.15%), Meghalaya (85.94%) and Arunachal Pradesh (64.22%). Nine States–Madhya Pradesh, Chattisgarh, Orissa, Jharkhand, Maharashtra, Gujarat, Rajasthan, Andhra Pradesh and West Bengal—together account for more than four-fifth of the tribal population in India.

There are 16 million ST children (10.87 million in 6-11 years and 5.12 million in 11-14 years) as on March 2001, out of the total child population of about 193 million in the age group of 6 to 14 years in the country.[17] Realizing that Scheduled Tribes are one of the most deprived and marginalized groups with respect to education, a host of programmes and measures were initiated since Independence. Elementary education has been a priority area in the *Tribal sub-plans* since the 5th Five Year Plan. Education of ST children is considered important, not only because of the Constitutional obligation but also as a crucial input for total development of tribal communities.

Scheduled tribes children remain disadvantaged, even more than SCs, across many social indicators. Table 1 shows that, on an average, in India, 27.09 per cent of the population live below the poverty line in rural areas, compared to 45.86 per cent of the ST population and 23.62 per cent in urban areas compared to 34.75 per cent of the ST population.

Table–1
Population Below Poverty Line in India, SC and ST (NSSO, 1999/2000) (In Percentage)

Population Below Poverty Line (%)	*India*	*SCs*	*STs*
Rural Areas	27.09	36.25	45.86
Urban areas	23.62	38.47	34.75

Source: National Sample Survey Organisation.

Social Exclusion of Scheduled Tribe Children

There has been a significant increase in overall literacy rate and school participation rates across the country since the early 1990s. Gender and social disparities have also declined with an overall increase in school attendance. This is confirmed by the data from various sources including the National Family Health Survey II (1998/99), Reproductive and Child Health Survey 2002-04, the 2001 Census and routine monitoring information from the Department of Education. The country is approaching near universalization of enrolment at the primary stage. The Gross Enrollment Rate has increased from 90 per cent in 2003-04 to 98 per cent in 2004-05. Similarly, the net enrollment rate has risen from 72 per cent to 82 per cent during the same period.[18] A number of factors have contributed to the rising enrollment rate including the introduction of mid-days meals, opening of alternate schools, promoting the participation of Parent-Teacher Associations (PTAs) and massive enrolment drives. A Constitutional amendment was passed in 2002 making free and compulsory education a fundamental right for children aged 6-14 years. The national and State Governments continue to deliver the programme *Sarva Shiksha Abhiyan* (SSA), which aims to achieve universal elementary education by 2010.

While enrolment and attendance in primary school has increased, the quality of education remains a major concern. Little emphasis has been placed on making education more relevant or in encouraging learning by doing and learning by observation. Activity-based and child-centered learning arrangements are still very weak. There are many situations where children mechanically go through five years of primary education and emerge barely literate, leading to community apathy towards schooling. The poor quality of education is reflected in the continuing low level of completion rates of primary school. The National Sample Survey Organisation (NSSO) and National Family Health Survey (NFHS) collected data on the 'level of education completed', whereas the Reproductive Child Health Survey (RCHS) provided data on the years of education completed. Using completion rates of five years of schooling as a key indicator of education status, Table 2, based on the RCHS-II (2002-04) shows that ST population is even more disadvantaged than SCs in terms of education status. Regarding the accessibility of the education system for this disadvantaged group of ST children, issues such as the language of instruction, remoteness of their habitations, poverty and other factors are working as barriers.

Table–2
Completion Rate of 10-12 Years by Caste
(RCHS II, 2002-04)

Social Group	*SCs*	*STs*	*Others*
Male	36.3	32.6	44.8
Female	32.3	26.6	44.1

Source: Reproductive Child Health Survey.

Based on the National Family Health Survey of 1998/99, Table 3 shows that only 56.3 per cent of ST children of age 7-17 are currently attending school compared to 81.3 per cent of higher caste groups. Furthermore, 29.7 per cent of ST children never attended school compared to 7.6 per cent of children from so-called upper castes.

Table–3
Per cent of Children Aged 7-17 by Schooling Outcomes (NFHS, 1998-99)

Caste/Religion of the Household Head	*Never Attended*	*Ever Attended*	
		Dropped Out	*Currently Attending*
Hindu SC	20.8	13.0	65.7
Hindu ST	29.7	13.9	56.3
Hindu other	7.6	10.6	81.3
Other	7.8	10.7	81.1

Source: National Family Health Survey.

Table 4 indicates the disparities in rural areas between children from STs and also between the poorest 20 per cent compared to the richest 20 per cent of households using data from RCHS-II for boys and girls. This survey defined economic status based on household's ownership of assets such as electric fan, radio/transistor, pressure cooker, telephone, bicycle, car, tractor and water pump among others. The table indicates that ST children are disadvantaged compared to children from other castes in each of the economic groups, but also that the economic status of the household is a very important discriminating factor in accessing education. The table also indicates that girls are disadvantaged compared to boys in the lower economic group, but less so in the higher economic group.

Table–4
Percentage Children in 10-12 Years Age Group Who Have Completed at Least 5 Years of Schooling Across Economic Groups and Gender in Rural Areas (RCHS, 2002-04)

Rural	*Male*			
	SC	*ST*	*Other*	*Total*
Poorest 20%	23.5	22.9	22.2	22.5
Richest 20%	50.0	56.9	54.2	52.9
	Female			
Poorest 20%	17.4	15.5	18.5	16.5
Richest 20%	52.5	45.4	55.1	53.0

Source: Reproductive Child Health Survey.

According to a UNICEF supported Baseline Survey which was undertaken in 2005 by the National Sample Survey Organization in 43 districts in different states of India, there are significant disparities in attendance rates and also learning achievements between children from scheduled tribes and others. Graph 1 indicates the percentage of children (6-14 years) attending school, which is 66.4 per cent for STs, even lower than SCs, compared to 83.6 per cent for children from other castes. As mentioned previously, this is an indication of the multiple disadvantages which tribal children face including poverty, remoteness and learning in another language. Graph 2 indicates the percentage of children who can read and write, where a difference is found between ST children and children from other castes with 52.4 per cent for the former compared to 72.0 per cent for the latter.

Graph 1: Percentage of Children Attending School (NSSO, 2005)

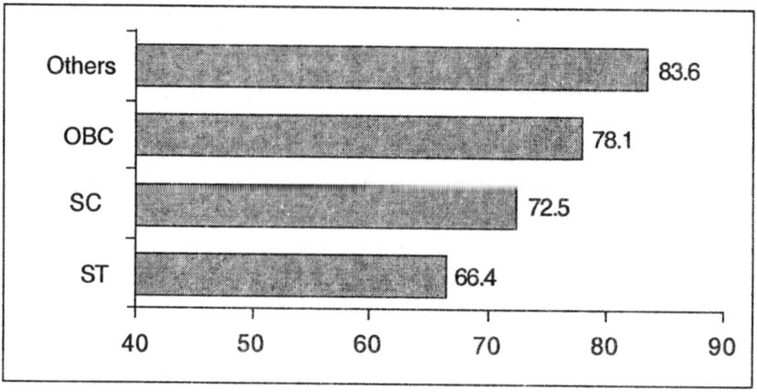

Graph 2: Percentage of Children 6-14yrs Who can Read and Write (NSSO, 2005)

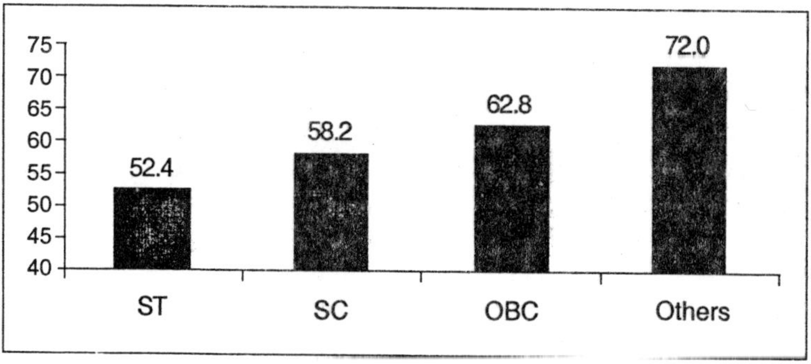

Reasons for the Disadvantaged Status of Scheduled Tribe Children

In fact, more data and research are needed to know the disparities in education present among tribes in India. Each region in India has specific characteristics related to this issue; the following section will summarize the key issues which are common throughout the country.

The physical distance to school is often cited as a barrier for children in India particularly at the higher levels of middle and secondary school. However, in addition to the physical distance, the 'social distance' to the school also needs to be considered. According to a study conducted by MODE in 1995, 'SC/ST families tend to live in colonies segregated by a kilometer or more from the main village. A school in the village within walking distance for the families in the main village would still be at a distance to these children.'[19] The 'All India Education Survey' of 1998 shows that 78 per cent of tribal population and 56 per cnet of tribal habitations have been provided primary schools within the habitation. Although 11 per cent of tribal population and 20 per cent of tribal habitations have schools within less than one kilometer radius,[20] and 10 per cent of the tribal habitations have schools beyond a distance of two kilometer, which is problematic when there is no public transportation and families do not own transportation. In addition, Murray and Russalie Wax (1964) in their study of formal Education in Indian community have shown that isolation, lack of communication and social distance are the important factors in the problems of education in primitive communities. They pointed out that isolation affects, in many contexts, the community as a whole, the school within the community, the people within the classroom and the teacher within the educational system.[21]

Another element of social exclusion of SC and ST children from elementary education in India is the extent to which discrimination is practiced by teachers and also teacher absenteeism in such schools. 'Teachers in India are predominantly upper caste and bring their own understandings of the legitimacy of caste relations into the classroom. Dalit children are expected to run errands and are assigned menial tasks such as sweeping and cleaning the classrooms. Higher rates of teacher absenteeism were reported when children were mainly from Dalit and tribal communities.'[22]

However, Toppo[23] has pointed out that one of the reasons of social exclusion of ST children in education has been the distance from the traditional system of education, called Dhumkuria, which has been losing significance, in the wake of modern educational system. Sachchidananda,[24] tried to unravel educational problems of the scheduled tribes in Bihar that are responsible for the exclusion of these communities. Among the problems enumerated include lack of facilities, apathetic attitude of teachers, discrimination in matters of peer-group formation, low educational aspiration, etc.

Heredia[25] undertakes a study mainly on twofold investigation: the impact of the school on the students and how it can be adopted to their culture; and the influence of the school on the community and how it can be adjusted to its needs. The participatory method used, involves a three-way comparison between mission, government and other private schools, made at three levels: the individual (students, parents, teachers), the school and the community. Sharma,[26] on the basis of a study of educational backwardness of tribal students, has analyzed that factors of exclusion of tribal children in education are due to their backwardness. He outlined the basic problems of tribal backwardness as large families, scarcity of funds and meager means of living. At the same time, he also argues that other factors of backwardness are illiterate families, neglected behavior of teachers towards tribal students, poverty, sickness of tribal children and problem of language and low level of intelligence (?). Different reports have analyzed the problems of tribal people that lead to exclusion from education. According to Government of India reports,

> The Indian Council of Social Science Research (ICSSR) and the National Council of Educational Research and Training (NCERT) have initiated survey on tribal education. But it needs no emphasis that the national surveys should be implemented by intensive studies on individual tribal groups, so as to gain a clear and comprehensive understanding of the problems and perspectives on tribal education in different regions. The education Commission (1964-66) also stated that different tribal people are at varying stages of economic development. A uniform approach between different tribal areas as applied in mechanical manner will not serve the purpose in view.

> Aspects of tribal education, which might call for special attention, will vary from area to area and no plans should be prepared in understanding the problems, which arise in different contexts.'[27]

Moreover, the Backward Classes Commission,[28] the Scheduled Areas and the Scheduled Tribes Commission,[29] L.R.N. Srivastava,[30] and others have pointed out that the slow progress of education among the tribes in India is due to inadequate provision of schools for these communities. The tribes generally live in inaccessible areas in small and scattered villages and therefore, schools are not available for all of them. Almost all the studies on tribal education in India pointed out that 'poverty' and 'neglect' happened to be the root cause for the slow progress of their education.[31]

Revellow[32] in her article, 'The School Drop Outs,' contended that one of the principal reasons for high dropout rate in the tribal areas at the primary stage is the curriculum. She suggested that the curricula should be built around local situations. A different study conducted on tribal sub-plan area of Gujarat[33] shows that there is a considerable social class and inter-tribe difference in their educational attainment. This study shows that the educational development of tribes living with caste Hindus is impressive while on the other hand, a large number of tribal people are still unaware of the facilities and programmes for their education. Thomson[34] has shown that educational gaps in various communities in a country arise owing to differentials in the provision of educational facilities, socio-economic status of parents and lack of motivation for education. The effects of these factors are inter-connected. The inequalities of educational reward acts as a negative feedback on educational attainments.

Verrier Elwin Committee Report[35] contains information and findings about the fundamental problems of education in tribal areas. The committee was of the view that a great deal of caution was necessary for starting compulsory education for tribes. The committee suggested the making of orchards of fruit trees in the compounds of all schools. Besides, the Dhebar Commission[36] made some observations on education. Education provided in a mechanical manner without much planned efforts, according to the commission, resulted in high wastage, stagnation and non-participation. The sectoral approach could not allow education to accelerate progress.

This is more so in case of those tribal areas which were not covered by Tribal Development Block Schemes. The Dhebar Commission has also suggested comprehensive educational model for tribes whose problems are unique.

Several other studies have highlighted socio-economic problems as the major cause of social exclusion of tribal children in education. Isolation from the mainstream of Indian life and culture, their technological, economic, social, political and educational backwardness in comparison to the non-tribals, superstitions and rigidity among tribal parents are some of the major problems for the slow growth of tribal education. Sujatha[37] found that the instability of family life due to the frequent changes of spouses did not help better enrollment of Yanadi children. She has further reported that in tribal welfare hostels, the children were feeling lonely and in schools they were feeling inferior to the higher caste children and teachers. Similarly, Abbasayalu[38] found that 3.75 per cent of tribal parents have admitted to their general inferiority complex vis-à-vis non-tribals. Extreme poverty, inability to afford to the necessities of education, inadequacy of financial assistance for meeting the cost of boarding, lodging, books, etc. were some of the economic problems found to be hindrance in their way of education as reported by Dasgupta,[39] Sachchidananda,[40] Kaul,[41] Sujatha,[42] Medhi,[43] and Sharma.[44] Dasgupta[45] in the case of Santhal education, found that a large number of children were remaining absent in the schools because they had to spend long hours on domestic or outdoor work that brought some economic relief to the family. In this context the study of Ambasht[46] reported that girls give every kind of assistance to their mothers at home, while boys are busy in collecting minor forest products and fire-wood, cattle grazing, hunting, and helping their parents in the field. The tribal parents look for immediate economic benefit rather than to invest in education. Similar findings have been reported by Mishra.[47] Naik,[48] however, stated that children of upper caste Bhil society have been able to go to school and could take advantage of the scholarships and hostel facilities made available to the tribals. Further, he provided that more children from large size families were in schools than from small size families.

Recent years in India have seen a proliferation of private schools, both aided and unaided, and alternative and education guarantee schemes. Data is limited on the actual number of private schools and also the numbers of children attending these schools. At the primary level, 6 per cent of rural children and 19 per cent of urban children are studying in private unaided schools; this proportion goes up when we include the 31 per cent of children who are studying in private aided schools.[49] Among the reasons for the growth of private schools is the reported decline in government-school quality (poor infrastructure, shortage of teachers, lack of accountability of government schools leading to teacher absenteeism and negligence). This gives way to a positive preference for private schools, even though they may have a relatively poor infrastructure, less qualified teachers and are definitely more expensive.[50] The proliferation of private schools in rural and urban areas has the potential of further widening the divide between different sections, as children from Scheduled Tribes cannot afford private schools. From the information which is available, one can conclude that the ST children predominantly attend the poorly functioning government schools or alternative schools.[51] This situation has, however, resulted in one district education official commenting that the public school system is slowly turning into a system for SC and ST children only (i.e. children of other castes attend private schools).[52]

Policy Implications for the Inclusion of Tribal Children

India is a welfare state, committed to the welfare and development of its people in general and of vulnerable sections in particular. The Constitution of India is said to be a Magna Carta for the SCs, STs, OBCs and women in respect of the special provisions made for them, e.g., reservations in jobs and educational institutions and the provisions against discrimination.[53] The preamble, directive principles of state policy, fundamental rights and specific sections, namely, Article 38, 39 and 46 in the Constitution of India stand testimony to the commitment of the state to its people. Article 46, a Directive Principle of the Constitution, suggests that the State shall take special care of the educational interests of the weaker sections particularly SCs and STs. Even Article 15 (4) in the section of Fundamental Rights states that nothing shall prevent the State from making special provisions for the socially and educationally backward classes particularly the SCs and STs.[54]

The Ministry of Tribal Affairs was constituted in October 1999 to provide more focused attention towards development of Scheduled Tribes. There are various educational schemes/programmes made by the state for promoting education of the SCs and STs. The general policy guidelines under the National Policy on Education (NPE), 1986 aims at the 'removal of disparities' and 'equalization of educational opportunities' among the SCs and STs.[55]

By a general and extensive welfare policy, the government's resolutions favored cuts in costs of education and abolishing school fees. Besides, the schemes of mid-day meals have been introduced, textbooks have been highly subsidized, study loans and financial assistance have been made available to college going students, etc. In addition, several educational reforms aimed at equalizing opportunities for educational attainment have been introduced (e.g. ten years school education, and 10+2+3 university education), which are enumerated in the policy resolutions.[56]

During the 1990s, the focus of the large-scale District Primary Education Programme and more recently the Sarva Shiksha Abhiyan (SSA) (Universal Primary Education Campaign) addressed the inadequate budgetary resources and the poor quality of teaching, which were regarded as two key constraints to achieving universal participation. However, while it is obvious that universal elementary education demands a significant increase in financial allocation, it is also evident both from the experience in India and global experience that finances alone will not ensure attendance of disadvantaged populations. One of the development objectives of the SSA is 'enrolment of children of SC and ST will be near parity with that of other groups', which in itself is a relatively modest objective as it focuses on enrollment, rather than completion of learning achievements, and also mentions 'near parity' rather than parity. However, the approach the program has adopted is not sufficiently comprehensive in addressing the above mentioned constraints and will therefore fail to influence the relevant decision-making processes which relate to a child's education status, particularly related to the issues faced by SC and ST children.

In addition to this large-scale national scheme, regarding demand-side interventions, various States make special provisions for SCs and STs by providing financial schemes, scholarships, special hostels, concessions in fees and grants for books.[57] In this context, it is said that a number of attempts have been made to bridge the divide between SC, ST children and other sections of children in elementary school. But the important facts related to their inclusion in elementary education could be categorized into initiatives which focus on the supply side (i.e. making schools more accessible, improving quality or providing a supplementary service for SC and ST children) and initiatives which promote greater demand for education (i.e. by providing incentives). Regarding supply side interventions, there are two basic approaches to addressing social exclusion in education, targeting excluded groups with supplementary service or focusing on universal improvements of the system. 'Universalist approaches are essential to building a sense of social solidarity and citizenship.'[58] Targeted programs have generally served as a means of compensating for government weakness in delivering on universal services, and may actually be marginalizing those they are intending to reach if they result in labeling of particular groups and don't act as a bridge to mainstream education services. Kabeer concludes that such approaches 'need to go beyond "ameliorative" approaches that address the symptoms of the problem to "transformative" approaches that address its causes.'[59]

However, recently the Government of India has proposed a new Bill the 'Free and Compulsory Education Bill, 2004' and passed it as Right to Education Bill, 2005. The most important points of Right to Education Bill are as follows:[60]

- Every child between the ages of 6 and 14 years has the right to free and compulsory education. This is stated as per the 86th Constitution Amendment Act that added Article 21A. The right to education bill seeks to give effect to this amendment.
- The government schools shall provide free education to all the children and the schools will be managed by school management committees (SMC). Private schools shall admit at least 25 per cent of the children in their schools without any fee.
- The National Commission for Elementary Education shall be constituted to monitor all aspects of elementary education including quality.

But a careful study of the Bill raises several concerns that have serious implications of almost all the educationally backward sections of our country. The Bill is most likely to be dangerous for the educationally deprived sections and other minorities.[61] Some of the fundamental problems of the Bill include lack of national consensus and political debates. Parents are held accountable for child's education even though it is the responsibility of the State. The Bill ignores children less than six years by referring to the Directive Principles of State Policy (Part IV of the Constitution), which is a non-justiceable right.[62] Salam, in this context, rightly points out as follows:[63]

> The Bill has not addressed the issues of access, quality and equity of education for all children. For example, EGS/AS/TS recommended for disadvantaged children do not meet even the least desirable condition of quality aspect of school. The discrimination is further reinforced by constant references to providing essential levels of learning for the elementary stage and its sub-stage specially meant for districts partly consisting of scheduled areas and is to be followed in all transitional schools. It clearly indicates that poor quality schools must be continuously provided exclusively to SC and ST children.

Additionally, this amendment has also been criticized on civil society front: the National Alliance on the Fundamental Right to Education (NAFRE). NAFRE decried the amendment as a retrograde step to the exclusion of the 0-6 groups in the provision of free and compulsory education that had been provided in a Supreme Court judgment of 1993 (Unnikrishnan vs. the state of Andhra Pradesh). NAFRE and FORCES (Forum for Child Care and Crèches Services) argued that although it is well established fact that the development of a child in the age group of 0-6 is critical, the provision for free primary education including crèche facilities in the country has been very limited. Moreover, the campaign united CSOs (Civil Society Organizations) involved in education and brought education issues to the fore in public consciousness and policy debates. This argues well for enhanced accountability in the future. Furthermore, the inclusion of ECCE in Article 45, albeit as a Directive Principle of the State Policy (implementation is discretionary), recognized the critical links between preprimary education, childcare and development, thus opening some space for a prospective convergent.[64]

Notwithstanding these and other facilities, the underprivileged sections of Indian society, particularly the Scheduled Tribes reveal distressing and tardy progress in education. In this context, Kundu[65] and Haimendorf[66] have made some critical points regarding the government attempts to the inclusion of tribal children in elementary education. According to them, despite governmental efforts, tribal education has suffered from poor quality of teaching, problems of medium of instruction, irrelevant curriculum and text book, more number of single teacher schools, uneven teacher-student ratio, etc. and resulted in high dropout rate, wastage and stagnation, and ultimately ended in slow growth of tribal education.

With regard to financial assistance provided by the government, Rajagopalan[67] found that a majority of ST students complained that they were not getting scholarships due to the unknown reasons and those who were getting the said amount of scholarship was not adequate. Nayar[68] found that nearly 80.65 per cent of SC and 79.2 per cent of ST students considered the scholarship as inadequate. However, Sachchidananda[69] and Singh[70] found a positive attitude towards governmental help but they also found that most of the SC and ST students expressed dissatisfaction with regard to implementation of these programmes. Thus, on the basis of the above discussion, it can be said that poor economic background together with inadequate financial assistance and malfunctioning of the governmental programmes constituted the major factors responsible for the exclusion of SC and ST students in education.

In the recently finalized Approach Paper to the 11th Five Year Plan of the Government of India, which will provide the overall framework for the Government's work during 2007-11, the Government reiterated its commitment to addressing disparities in education between castes and tribes. The Approach paper states:[71]

> Development and empowerment of socially disadvantaged groups is a commitment enshrined in the Constitution, and education is the most effective instrument of social empowerment. Schemes for the educational uplift of the SCs and STs have borne fruit although the gap between the general population and SCs and STs are still at unacceptable levels... Some minorities have fallen far behind the national average in education. It will be necessary to go to the root of the problem and examine the reasons for the decline so that remedial measures can be taken during the 11th Plan.

Then, the question here arises: what needs to be done to include SC and ST children in education, more especially at the level of elementary education. At broader level, addressing social exclusion requires a holistic approach which promotes involvement of excluded populations in community life; ensures access to all basic services; promotes behavioral change; increases income; and addresses other key elements of exclusion. Similarly in education, a holistic approach is necessary based on an analysis of the various components of the decision-making process related to regularly attending school for an SC and ST child and, from the supply side all elements of the education experience must be addressed.

Concluding Remarks

The above discussion leads us to go beyond what we call government schemes and programmes for the inclusion of Scheduled Tribe children in education. So far as governmental efforts are concerned, for the inclusion of ST children in education, the Government of India has taken a number of steps to provide equality of educational opportunity, such as setting up of primary schools, exemption from tuition fee for scheduled tribe students up to senior secondary school level, incentives such as free textbooks, uniforms, scholarships, mid-day meals under the banner of SSA, to them. It was also realized that importance has to be given to the tribal cultures for effective schooling of children from these communities in terms of the use of tribal language as a medium of instruction in early years of schooling, recruitment of teachers from within tribal communities and a curriculum that portrays tribes positively. However, this perspective was not emphasized at large in actual program for action. And that is why the tribal education in India suffers from a multiplicity of problems. Little is being given to preserve their culture; more stress is being given to concessional provisions of education, and little attempt is made to equip them with knowledge and skills through special training so that they can compete with their non-tribal counterparts on equal terms. Also, little attention is paid to the development of tribal languages and culture. There is need to think on multi-level attempts which obviously open broader horizon than education, and factors outside the education sector will relate to the education opportunities available to SC and ST children. At this point, a need arises to tackle the tribal problems through civil society organizations, i.e. through NGOs and voluntary organizations and fulfill the long cherished goal of Universalization of elementary education.

A comprehensive response, based on innovative programmes, is necessary to bring and keep children into the mainstream school system by making schooling attractive to them and also worthwhile for the parents. The fact is consistent with the outcome of the Joint Review Mission of the SSA in 2006 which stated that 'in certain groups like SC, ST and minority children, the number of out-of-school children is still high. It is necessary to identify specific contextual aspects including socio-cultural reasons that inhibit the enrolment and retention of these groups. This requires building of appropriate capacity and resource support at the sub-district level to develop relevant strategies and interventions.'[72]

In order to address all of the determinants of social exclusion, it is important to reduce disparities by applying strategy to include communities in the process and undertake an analysis of causes and factors which lead to social exclusion of children from elementary schooling. Consistent with this fact, the 73rd Amendment of the Constitution, which was enacted in 1992, delegated various powers and responsibilities to the locally elected bodies called the Panchayats, which provide a platform for strengthening a process to address social exclusion. One of the main recommendations from the review of SSA in 2006 was that 'Greater use of Innovation Funds should be encouraged for interventions to boost the performance of first generation learners, especially SC and ST children and older girls.'[73] The innovation funds should be managed locally and based on an analysis of the barriers faced by SC and ST children within the household, the community and in the school (and the interplays between these). In a nutshell, the following policy recommendations and implementation for action should be addressed.

I. Policy Recommendations

1. The Government, local authority, civil society and NGOs should work together and cover actions and programmes of various ministries such as Sarva Shiksha Abhiyan, National Literacy Mission, and Tribal Affairs and Tribal Welfare Projects and programmes of tribal children, to effectively implement these programmes in a unified manner. An integral component of these programmes should be partnership with the community leaders to create mass mobilization and community awareness which is the key to the formation of social capital.

2. The Government of India in consultation with civil society and NGOs must formulate a National Plan of Action incorporating details of programmes for achieving Education for All (EFA) as stipulated under the Dakar Framework of Action by 2002 and UN support for the National Plan of Action.
3. The Government of India must increase budget allocations for education at the level of 6 per cent to the total GDP to show its commitment for achieving Education for All at the earliest.
4. Non-formal education and other alternative education programmes should be viewed as a supplementary support for the formal education system in the initial stage. Ultimately mainstreaming of tribal children in formal education is the ultimate goal and NGOs should act as pressure groups to improve quality of education in the formal schools.
5. Accountability of NGOs and regular monitoring of activities must be made an integral component of funding for educational programmes under various government schemes.

II. Implementation for Action

1. Development of a uniform core content of curriculum along with area-specific curriculum and identification of area-specific teaching-learning materials. The curriculum should be introduced by taking tribal languages into consideration. A committee of experts from central and state education departments, NCERT education experts, area specific NGOs and experts could be given the task of developing the curriculum for various levels.
2. A teacher-learning guide with details of methods of teaching, methodology for preparation of lessons for teachers and monthly targets of curriculum to be completed by the teachers should be prepared by the committee in consultation with the teachers from successful NGOs.
3. Regular training upgrades to the recruited teachers must be provided by government education training institutions and other technical training institutes.
4. Committed and motivated teachers, preferably from local areas and dominant existing social groups even with less formal education but with regular training upgrades should be given priority in recruitment.

5. The Sarva Shiksha Abhiyan programme for the Government of India must incorporate provisions facilitating education for tribal children with more amount of scholarship in the villages. If possible, computer education should be provided in the school.
6. More number of teachers must be appointed, especially from the particular community of the area.
7. Classrooms must be built at the ratio of at least one class-room per class and the facility of toilets must be provided.
8. A mapping exercise must be undertaken to identify suitable locations and target groups, especially children from deprived sections.
9. Simplify the bureaucratic system and make accountable to society. They must work rather as civil servants than as the owner of the districts or blocks and work towards the development in cooperation with the people.
10. Government funded NGOs must be assessed before funding. The assessment should consider NGOs' performance in the field of community awareness and its rapport with the community.
11. Accountability of the NGOs must be ensured through regular monitoring of their work with the help of evaluation studies conducted by researchers.
12. Funds should be released regularly without delays to the NGOs for smooth pattern of their working.
13. Specific funds should be allocated for infrastructure development and procuring adequate teaching-learning materials to the NGOs.

On the whole, the forgoing discussion recapitulates that the government has failed to include tribal children in education, especially in villages, because lack of infrastructure and motivation of teachers towards teaching. In addition, community participation is also necessary in the process so that education would be materialized at larger scale. Hence, it needs to work through social networking and social cooperation with collaborative approach of government, civil society organizations, missionaries and community to include tribal children in elementary education with positive spirit and direction.

Finally, the paper ends with Dr. Ambedkar's views on education: He upheld that education is good only if it promotes and preserves the interests of mankind as a whole. True education, he argued, creates equality in society, provides food to the hungry people and satisfies thirst for knowledge. He was an ardent supporter of public education. He was fully convinced that it is only education that breeds and nourishes the noble sentiments of unity, fraternity and patriotism. Education alone humanizes man. Man, sans education, is no better than beast. He held the unequal opportunities, prevalent in the educational arena, the root cause of misery and rivalry in society. He wanted to strengthen the national unity and integrity through education. He was of the view that 'Education is such an indispensable thing that it should necessarily be within an easy reach of all. It should be available at the cheapest so that the poorest of the poor may receive it. He thought so highly of education that in his tri-worded slogan: Educate, Organise and Agitate, he gave top priority to it.

NOTES AND REFERENCES

1. David Byrne, Social *Exclusion* (Philadelphia, Open University Press, 1999), pp. 1-2.
2. Mayra Buvinic, 'Social Inclusion in Latin America' in Mayra Buvinici and Jacqueline Mazza (eds.), *Social Exclusion and Economic Development* (Baltimore, Johns Hopkins University Press, 2005), p. 332.
3. A. Madnipour, G. Cars, and J. Allen, *Social Exclusion in European Cities* (London: Jessica Kingsley, 1998), p. 22.
4. Bill Jordan, *A Theory of Poverty and Social Exclusion* (Cambridge, Blackwell Publishers, 1996), p. 5.
5. *Ibid.*, p. 164.
6. *Ibid.*, p. 26.
7. A Walker, and C. Walker (eds.), *Britain Divided: The Growth of Social Exclusion in the 1980s and 1990s* (London: Child Poverty Action Group, 1997).
8. T.H. Marshall, *Citizenship and Social Class* (Cambridge: Cambridge University Press, 1950).
9. J. Veit-Wilson, *Setting Adequacy Standards* (Bristol: Policy Press, 1998), p. 450.
10. S. Bessis, 'From social exclusion to social cohesion: a policy agenda', MOST Policy Paper no. 2, http://www.unesco.org/most/besseng.htm, 1995, p. 13.
11. *Ibid.*, p. 13.
12. David Byrne, *Social Exclusion* (Philadelphia, Open University Press, 1999), p. 58.

13. Arjun de Haan, 'Social Policy: Towards Inclusive Institutions', University of Guelph and Department for International Development, UK. Paper at the World Bank Conference 'New Frontiers of Social Policy: Development in a Globalizing World': December 12-15, 2005.
14. Government of India, *India 2000* (New Delhi: Publication Division, Ministry of Information and Broadcasting, 2007), p. 15.
15. R. Govinda, *India Education Report* (New Delhi: Oxford University Press, 2002).
16. Census of India (2001), *(New Delhi: Registrar General and Census Commissioner, Government of India).*
17. Department of Education (2001-02), *Selected Educational Statistics* (New Delhi: Ministry of Human Resource Development, Government of India).
18. Department of Education, *Sarva Shiksha Abhiyan: Fourth joint Review Mission* (New Delhi, Aide *Memoire,* 2006).
19. MODE Research (1995), *Attitudes Study on Elementary Education in India – A Consolidated Report* (New Delhi: UNICEF).
20. R. Govinda, *India Education Report* (New Delhi: Oxford University Press, 2002), p. 90.
21. Murray and Russalie Wax (1964) cited in G. Ananda, *Educating Tribals* (New Delhi: Commonwealth, 2000), p. 6.
22. Naila Kabeer, 'Social Exclusion and the MDGs: The Challenge of 'Durable Inequalities' in the Asian Context', Institute of Development Studies, paper presented at the Asia 2015 Conference (March, 2006), p. 11.
23. S. Toppo, *Dynamics of Educational Development in Tribal India* (Delhi, Classical, 1979).
24. Sachchidananda, *Educational Problems of the Scheduled Castes and Scheduled Tribes in Bihar,* ICSSR Project Report (A.N.S. Institute of Social Studies, Patna, 1975) (Mimeo); Sachchidananda, *Education and the Disadvantaged* (Delhi: Uppal, 1989).
25. C. Rudolf Heredia, *Tribal Education for Community Development: A Study of Schooling in the Talasari Mission Area* (Delhi: Concept, 1972).
26. K.R. Sharma, 'A Study of Educational Backwardness of Tribal Students', *The Education Quarterly,* 35(2), (1983), pp. 33-38.
27. Government of India reports cited in G. Ananda, *Educating Tribals* (New Delhi: Commonwealth, 2000). p. 2.
28. Government of India, *Report of the Backward Classes Commission* (New Delhi: NCERT, 1956).
29. Government of India. *Report of the Scheduled Areas and Scheduled Tribes Commission* (New Delhi: 1962).
30. L.R.N. Srivastava, *The Gallongs* (Research Department, Adviser's Secretariat, Shilong, 1962), pp. 6-7.
31. Renuka Ray, *Committee on Social Welfare and Welfare of Backward Classes* (New Delhi: Government of India, 1959).

32. M. Revellow (1978) cited in G. Ananda, *Educating Tribals* (New Delhi: Commonwealth, 2000), p. 5.
33. P. Vimal Shah and Tara Patel, *Social Context of Tribal Education* (New Delhi: Concept Publishing House, 1985).
34. R.F. Thompson, 'From Elitism to Egalitarianism in Swedish Education', *Sociology of Education*, 38 (Sweden, 1962).
35. Government of India, *Verrier Elwin Committee Report on Multipurpose Tribal Blocks* (New Delhi: Government of India Publications, 1960).
36. U.N. Dhebar, *Report of the Commission for Scheduled Tribes*, Vol. I (New Delhi: Ministry of Home Affairs, 1962).
37. K. Sujatha, 'Socio-Economic Constraints of Development of Education of Tribes in India – A case study of Yanadis in Andhra Pradesh' (Paper presented in the third Annual Conference of the Comparative Education Society of India), Jamia Milia Islamia, New Delhi (1984).
38. Abbasayulu (1977) cited in S.N. Mohapatra, and B.C. Mishra, *Qualitative Education for Tribals: Agenda and Problems* (New Delhi: Deep & Deep Publishers, 2000), p. 65.
39. N.K. Dasgupta, Problems *of Tribal Education and the Santhals* (New Delhi: Bhartiya Adamjati Sevak Sangh, 1963).
40. Sachchidananada, 'Socio-Economic Aspects of Tribal Education' in *Tribal Education in India*, Report of National Seminar of Tribal Education in India (New Delhi: NCERT, 1967).
41. S.K. Kaul, 'Existing facilities, coverage, wastage, stagnation and utilization of Financial Assistance in respect of Tribal Education', *Report of the National Seminar of Tribal Education in India* (New Delhi: NCERT, 1967).
42. K. Sujatha, 'Socio-Economic Constraints of Development of Education of Tribes in India – A case study of Yanadis in Andhra Pradesh' (Paper presented in the third Annual Conference of the Comparative Education Society of India), (Jamia Milia Islamia, New Delhi, 1984).
43. G.C. Medhi, *Education in Jirkedam – A Tribal Institution*, Ph.D. Thesis on Education, Gujarat University, 1980.
44. K.R. Sharma, 'A Study of Educational Backwardness of Tribal Students', *The Education Quarterly*, 35(2). 1983, pp. 33-38.
45. N.K. Dasgupta, *Problems of Tribal Education and the Santhals* (New Delhi: Bhartiya Adamjati Sevak Sangh, 1963).
46. N.K. Ambasht, *A Critical Study of Tribal Education with Special Reference to Ranchi District* (New Delhi, S. Chand and Company, 1970).
47. B.C. Mishra, *Education of Tribal Children* (New Delhi: Discovery Publishing House, 1996).
48. T.B. Naik, *Impact of Education on the Bhils: Cultural Change in the Tribal Life of Madhya Pradesh* (New Delhi: Research Programme Committee, 1969).
49. World Bank, *India: Expanding and Improving Upper Primary Education in India* (Washington DC, World Bank, 2001).

50. Vimala Ramachandran (ed.), *Getting Children Back to School: Case Studies in Primary Education* (New Delhi: Sage Publications, 2003); Probe Team, *India Education Report* (New Delhi, Oxford University Press, 1999).
51. Jyotsna Jha, and Dhir Jhingran, *Elementary Education for the Poorest and Other Deprived Groups* (Manohar Publishers, New Delhi, 2005).
52. *Ibid.*
53. M. Khajapeer, 'Democratization of Higher Education in India with Special Reference to Weaker Sections, Minorities and Women', in *Journal of Educational Planning and Administration,* Volume X, No. 2 (New Delhi, NIEPA, April 1996), pp. 143-152.
54. Kameshwar Choudhary, 'Dalits in Higher Education: Cooption or Domination', *Journal of Higher Education,* Vol. 21, No. 3, Monsoon, 1998, pp. 437-38.
55. *National Policy on Education (NPE) 1986* (Department of Education, MHRD, Government of India), p. 11.
56. *Ibid.* NPE 1986; Revised Document, NPE 1990, etc.
57. Arjun de Haan, 'Social Policy: Towards Inclusive Institutions', University of Guelph and Department for International Development, UK. Paper at the World Bank Conference 'New Frontiers of Social Policy: Development in a Globalizing World': December 12-15, 2005.
58. Naila Kabeer, 'Social Exclusion and the MDGs: The Challenge of "Durable Inequalities in the Asian Context"', Institute of Development Studies, paper presented at the Asia 2015 Conference (March 2006), p. 14.
59. *Ibid.*, p. 16.
60. http://www.ilpnet.org/rte
61. Jeebanlata Salam, *Social Exclusion and Education* (New Delhi: Indian Social Institute, 2004), p. 33.
62. *Ibid.*, p. 34.
63. *Ibid.*
64. Excerpts from UNESCO, 2004. *EFA2003/4.* Paris: UNESCO. P. 208
65. M. Kundu, 'Tribal Education in India, Some Problems', *Journal of Indian Education.* Vol. X, No. 2, July 1984.
66. C. Haimendorf, Von Furer, *Tribes in India: The Struggle for Survival* (New Delhi: Oxford University Press, 1984).
67. C. Rajagopalan, cited in S.N. Mahapatra and B.C. Mishra, *Qualitative Education for Tribals: Agenda and Problems* (New Delhi, Deep and Deep Publications, 1970), p. 70.
68. Nayar (1975) cited in *ibid.*, p. 70.
69. Sachchidananda (1989), *Education and the Disadvantaged* (Delhi: Uppal).
70. N.K. Singh, *Educational Problems of SC and ST School Students in Rajasthan* (Jaipur: Department of Sociology, Rajasthan University, 1975).

71. Planning Commission, *Approach Paper to the 11th Plan* (New Delhi: Planning Commission, Government of India, 2006), p. 64.
72. Department of Education, *Sarva Shiksha Abhiyan: Fourth Joint Review Mission* (New Delhi, Aide Memoire 2006), p. 2.
73. *Ibid.*

14

Combating Social Exclusion in Education: Re-examining the 'Inclusive' Framework

JAGANNATH AMBAGUDIA

One of the greatest problems facing the world today is the growing number of persons who are excluded from the meaningful participation in economic, social, political and cultural life of their communities. Such societies are neither efficient nor desirable. So, the current national and international concern with social inclusion has emerged in response to the challenges posed by persistent and increasing marginalization, discrimination and exclusion of vulnerable groups, including the STs, in all societies. As interrelated and multidimensional processes, inclusion and exclusion 'describe how people's opportunities for full and meaningful participation in the main spheres of social life may be differentially facilitated or blocked. These processes, in turn, contribute to unequal prospects that people have to achieve socially and economically valued resources, capacities, and credentials.'

Policies and Programmes for Inclusion

The policy in which various welfare measures and provisions pertaining to protect the interests of historically disadvantaged sections have been incorporated is known as 'protective discrimination'.[1] The term 'protective discrimination', thus, refers to a wide variety of inclusive policies designed to meet out special or preferential treatment, or grant concession to the weaker sections such as the STs. To put it differently, protective discrimination insists not only preferences in education, politics and public services for STs, but also some other welfare measures adopted by the government. Hence, the theory of protective discrimination is nothing but an instrument of helping those who have remained disadvantaged, marginalized and deprived of opportunities.

The policies and programmes of the Central and State Governments for the benefit of STs cover several areas and they vary from State to State. While STs are legally entitled to preferences nation-wide, they are also entitled to preferences within their own respective States. Now the questions need to be asked are: Does the programme actually deliver the goods (for instance, more jobs or better performance in schools)? Has the programme produced the results that it is supposed to achieve? Against this backdrop, this chapter begins by analyzing preferences in education for STs in Orissa. It also attempts to provide clear understanding of consequences of institutional support for the development of STs in Orissa. To glean the clear picture of implementation of these policies, it tries to show periodical review of benefits in the sphere of education. This paper also explores the educational constraints faced by the tribal communities of Orissa.

One of the modalities of tribes is affirmative action that is providing for reservation in jobs and legislative bodies. Such preference is meaningless unless tribes have education. How can tribes without education get recruited to public services even within the reserved quotas? How can tribal legislators discharge their functions unless they have education and understanding? Therefore, the Indian State has adopted preferential policies and programmes for educational development of STs since independence with the purpose of not only to bring socio-economic transformation in tribal societies but also to reduce the gap between the tribals and non-tribals. The main purpose of this programme is to remove or minimize social and economic disabilities of tribes and to bring them at far with other sections of the Indian society. This is clearly documented under Article 46 of the Indian constitution. The policy for removal of educational backwardness of STs along with other weaker sections appeared to be an integral part of Indian planning and avowed goal of development.[2] Education was envisaged as one of the most powerful engines of the social and economic liberation of STs through awakening and creating awareness. When the educational facilities are extended to the tribes, they will articulate with the new and consequently, new facilities will be made available to them and that will help to change their stereotyped way of life. Education has appeared as one of the most viable means of inclusion of STs in the mainstream society.

Guided by this understanding, the village level study done by National Council of Applied Economics in Orissa claims that all social groups have experienced a secular increase in the level of awareness about sending children, particularly girls to school.[3] However, it maintains striking differences in perception among the parents of different castes about the advantages of educating their children. The scheduled groups perceive only the market benefits of education such as higher wages, availing of loans, tracing land registration papers, etc. The higher castes such as Kuttas and Kumhars, on the contrary, perceive non-market benefits also. The tribal society of Orissa looks at education as 'investment' in human resources for income generation. It is in the sense that in a particular agricultural society, it helps to build up a member of the family capable of earning money from sources other than agriculture. They believe that benefits of education include better sanitation, more efficient consumption, a better choice of marital partner, sound health and so on. Education makes one more civilized, and helps in earning respect and regard in the society and improves employment prospects. While conducting research, a consensus emerged among all groups irrespective of their caste and income that their educated children will look after them safely in their old age.[4] Within this framework, it makes easy to confront the questions such as: To what extent are the parents influenced by the prospects of higher education? And, in what way they want their children to come up? It explains the students' understanding about hopes and aspirations of the parents. Though many parents come from poor and often degrading circumstances, they have definite and positive hopes and aspirations about the efficiency of education. Higher education, however, modifies not only the outlook of tribal students but also that of their parents. In other words, the impact of education does not confine itself to the students or the direct receivers of education but spreads also to others who are related to them.

Thomas E. Weisskopf claims to maintain secular position on the impact of education in India, but it fails to keep the purpose.[5] The major part of the work has been devoted to SCs or its comparison with non-SCs but very little attention has been paid to the STs. This is because of either disinterest or lack of relevant data on STs in India. Weisskopf is less supportive of a quota policy unless it is constrained by size, the period for which it is to be applied and merit bars. He, however, draws two inferences about the consequences of preferences in the higher education. Firstly, virtually all the 'scheduled' students at the most elite Indian universities and institutions for profession and technical training (most of which are centrally controlled) would not have been admitted in the absence of reserved seats. Secondly, admission to a reserved seat enhances the ability of scheduled students to gain access to financial and other forms of government aid without which staying in schools may prove to be very difficult. Scholars who have studied the experience of the tribal students in higher education report widely that they lag well behind non-tribal students in their performances in examinations. Moreover, we speculate that the performance rate of tribal students has likely increased since the period of their study because the cut off marks for admission of students to ST reserved seats have been rising over the years. Thus, Indian preferential policies adopted the educational system that is inclusive in nature.

Indicators of Literacy

There are a number of indicators that determine the literacy level of the tribal society in Orissa. Those indicators can be discussed on the following heads:

- A study has noted that the rate of literacy among middle and rich cultivators is greater than that among the poor cultivators and laborers. The association of educational benefits with land holdings and class positions appears rather very strong in Orissa.[6]
- The study of National Council of Applied Economic Research shows that literacy is closely related to land size. For instance, large farmers have attended higher percentage of literacy (74.3%) than the landless wage earners (only 29%). The reason is that the large farmers could have offered money for their children's education, while the landless laborers could not.[7]
- The literacy rate improves with an increase in household size. For example, the rate is 22.5 points higher for households consisting of eight or more members than households with up to four members.

- The literacy rate is high in the more developed villages. For example, the literacy rate is 66 per cent while it is only 45 per cent in low developed villages.
- Literacy is high among salaried, professional and self-employed groups and least among wage earners.
- It has been seen that there is close relationship between socio-economic status and literacy rate as well as academic performance in higher educational institutions.[8]

The studies, therefore, reveal a positive connection between the size of the family of a tribe, socio-economic status, educational attainment of the parents, occupation, landholding pattern and the level of literacy in the tribal society of Orissa.

Education is the most important thrust area for the socio-economic development of the tribal society in Orissa. To achieve the aims and the objectives stated under Article 46 of the Indian constitution, the Government of Orissa has undertaken a number of important measures to improve the educational levels of STs through steps like provisions of scholarships, boarding facilities, free distribution of Nationalised text books (NTBs), uniforms, and imparting special coaching for appearing in various competitive examinations.[9] Orissa has also introduced mid-day meals in all primary schools to check the dropout rates among the tribal students. Planning Commission shows that Orissa government distributed 60,57,000 NTBs during academic year 1998-99 that benefited 15,14,353 SC and ST students.[10] But the figure of book distribution comes down by 8,62,389 during academic year 1999-2000 and the number of beneficiaries correspondingly decreased by 1,97,421 as well. Besides, there is also a book bank scheme for tribal students, who are pursuing professional courses. This is a centrally sponsored scheme and the expenses are shared between the Centre and the State on 50:50 basis. Under this scheme, Ministry of Tribal Affairs (MTA) released Rs. 5.02 lakh and Rs. 5.62 lakh, which benefited 326 and 350 tribal students of Orissa during the years 2002-03 and 2003-04 respectively.[11] This scheme operates in two different ways: first, two students will be provided with one set of books in case of professional courses and one set for each student in respect of postgraduate courses and Chartered Accountancy.

The Government of Orissa has undertaken measures to provide residential facilities to the STs along with the SCs. Sevashrams and residential sevashrams and Ashram schools and Kanyashrams are established for the aforesaid purpose. During 2002-03, 919 Sevashrams and 143 Residential Sevashrams (up to class V) were functioning in the State under SC and ST Development Department. During this period, the enrollment in these Sevashrams was 1.22 lakh and 0.27 lakh respectively, out of which 61.3 per cent were the tribal students. Similarly, during the same academic year, 112 Ashram schools and 37 Kanyashrams were functioning and the total number of students directly benefited was recorded 27,819, out of which 79.6 per cent belonged to the tribal community. During 2002-03, Rs. 3.70 crore was released for the construction of 55 Ashram schools, 10 Kanyashrams and 15 Residential Sevashrams under 11th Finance Commission. This amount was raised to Rs. 5.01 crore for the year 2003-04 for this purpose. The Government of Orissa is also providing hostels at pre-matric and post-matric levels. At present, 1,548 primary school hostels (40 seats each) and 510 residential institutions are functioning in the TSP areas of the State. Notwithstanding, there are seven special Adivasi hostels including two for women (Bhubaneswar and Raurkela). MTA released Rs. 55 lakh for the construction of seven hostels for STs during 2001-02 and Rs. 41.46 lakh during 2003-04, which benefited 200 and 100 tribal students respectively. It has been observed that Malkangiri district has the highest concentration of tribal population in proportion to the district population, but there is not a single hostel exclusively for STs, where maximum of tribal students continue their post-matric education. There are ten Modern schools (class VI-XII) to provide quality education to meritorious tribal students with residential facilities for 60 students including 30 girl students in each class. This different attitude of the Government of Orissa towards the tribal communities is also partially responsible for different levels of literacy and socio-economic development of tribal communities.

The Government of Orissa also introduced vocational training centres (VTCs) in 1993-94 to develop the skills of tribal youth for a variety of jobs and self-employment as well. To achieve these aims and objectives, MTA released Rs. 64.15 lakh during 2002-03. As a result, by the end of 2002-03, 17 VTCs have been established in 15 ITDAs of 12 districts. Special coaching scheme is being introduced in five junior colleges in the State for 136 ST students to get into engineering course at +2 level and Rs. 12.40 lakh has been released by MTA for the implementation of the scheme. Special attention has also been given to tribal boys to get into military and para-military services in Orissa. The Post-matric scholarship, a centrally sponsored scheme, was introduced in 1944 and extended to the STs in 1948. The Government of Orissa also provides financial assistance to STs in the form of Pre-matric and Post-matric scholarships under the banner of the SC and ST Development Department, Bhubaneswar, Orissa. This scheme operates in two ways: firstly, for boys, this scheme provides scholarship only to two children of same parents/ guardian; and secondly, this condition has been relaxed for girls and now any numbers of girls of the same parents/guardian can get benefit of the scheme.

Pre-matric scholarship and stipend are awarded to all ST students from classes VI to X @ Rs. 300 per month to boy hostler and Rs. 325 to each girl hostler. Similarly, for day scholars, financial help is provided @ Rs. 10 to boys and Rs. 15 to girls reading in class VI-VII and Rs. 15 to boys and Rs. 20 to girls reading in class VIII-X, per month. During 2002-03, an amount of Rs. 62.43 crore was distributed to 7,09,308 SC and ST students out of which 3,67,337 were ST students. Post-matric scholarship is also given to all tribal students. But the amount of scholarship for Post-matric study is determined on the basis of the courses they offered.[12] For this purpose, Post-matric scholarship to the tune of Rs. 8.45 crore was awarded to 80,279 SC and ST students out of which 34,788 were ST students. Similarly, the ST students who are undergoing training in different Industrial Training Institutes (ITIs) of the State are being provided scholarship @ Rs. 60 per month for ten months. During 2002-03, 964 ST students were able to get this benefit. Similarly, central universities also partially try to bring balanced educational development among the districts by giving weightage on the basis of their representation to the educational institutions. For instance, Jawaharlal Nehru University identified 19 districts of Orissa as quartile-1, seven districts as quartile-2 and the rest has been left out.[13] Consequently, quartile-1 districts will get additional points over quartile-2 districts and similarly, quartile-2 districts will get some weightage over the left out districts of Orissa. This notion clearly argues for the inclusive as well as exclusive nature of the Indian educational system.

The collective impact of these inclusive policies for the tribal society in Orissa could be glanced by examining the changes in the literacy rate, dropout and enrollment at different levels. If different census reports of 1961, 1971, 1981, 1991 and 2001 are compared, it is clear that all social groups have experienced a secular increase in levels of education. Consequent upon the expansion of formal schooling, provision of limited residential schools, scholarships and stipends, supply of books, stationery, uniform, mid-day meals, special tutorials and remedial programs, etc., the literacy status of the tribal communities of Orissa has increased from 7.36 per cent in 1961 to 37.37 per cent in 2001 (see Table 1). That the percentage of literacy has increased by five times in four decades is a pleasing statistics, especially when the literacy in the general population has just tripled from 21.66 per cent in 1961 to 63.61 per cent in 2001. Nonetheless, it also points out the enormous existing gap between tribals and non-tribals of Orissa, but this must be seen against a starting point of almost total exclusion from educational opportunities until fairly recently. Ironically, even the two constitutionally identified scheduled groups of Orissa such as SCs and STs maintain the disparity of 4.21, 5.70, 8.55, 14.47 and 18.16 per cent over the successive decades from 1961 to 2001.[14] In short, substantial variation exists in literacy across the social groups in Orissa and this gap is widening over the decades.

The 2001 census demonstrates that across all districts, Puri achieved the highest literacy rate (58.72%), whereas Malkangiri has recorded the lowest literacy rate of only 14.49 per cent (see Table 2). This shows the negative relationship between the concentration of tribal population and literacy rate. It is disheartening to note that the female literacy of STs in Orissa is only 10.21 per cent in 1991 as against the general female literacy rate of 34.68 per cent and the SC female literacy rate of 20.74 per cent. In all the decennial census years, the disparity value has been found to be increasing between these three groups. Paradoxically, the STs are easily outnumbered the SCs in terms of numerical strength in Orissa but their literacy rate is invariably worse. In short, STs are lagging behind SCs in Orissa.

According to 1991 census, literacy rate among the males is higher than that of females across all districts. The highest disparity is seen in Phulbani (33.28%) followed by Balangir (32.46%) and lowest in Koraput (13.29%). It is observed that gender disparity is low in districts with very low literacy rate and vice versa. The highest literacy rate of STs among males is reported in Sundergarh (50.13%)

and lowest in Koraput (15.68%). The highest literacy among females is observed in Sundergarh (24.52%) and lowest in Koraput (just 2.39%). Ironically, all undivided districts lie below the average female literacy of the State (25.56%). Urban and rural disparity in the level of literacy is quite widespread. The disparity is high in Ganjam (46.79%) and low in Keonjhar (8.63%). Urban literacy is almost double the rural literacy. While one out of ten rural females can read and write and three out of ten urban females can do so. It is apparent that rural literacy and female literacy are dragging down the average performance of SCs and STs in Orissa.[15] It is true that the growth of literacy has been accelerating steadily over the years, but the trend of ST literacy shows that despite many schemes being implemented, their literacy and education level is far from being at par with other sections of the society. It is, therefore, safe to comment that the nation has reneged on its constitutional commitment to draw this section into its mainstream.[16]

The reports of NCSCST show that the enrollment ratios of ST population at school levels were 99.14 per cent in the classes I to V (6-11 years) and 39.32 in classes VI to VIII (11-14 years) respectively in 1994-95.[17] The report also depicts that the enrollment rate of girls is less than boys, as the ratio is 68.83:129.48 and 25.31:52.57 in class I-V and class VI-VII in the same year. This indicates that while they move to the higher level of education, their enrollment rate is substantially decreasing. Against these enrollment ratios, the dropout rate was 88.56 per cent in 1990-91. The existing data show that 57.42, 74.0 and 78.48 per cent and 57.36, 81.24 and 86.47 per cent of boys and girls have dropped in 1990-91 at primary, middle and secondary stages respectively. Datasheet on tribes prepared by SCSTRTI shows that the dropout rate of STs in Orissa was 74.5 per cent as against the total dropout rate of 58.0 per cent (class I-VII) in 1998-99.[17a] Unlike the enrollment ratio, the dropout rate increases at the successive higher stage of education and girls are the most victims in this case.

Turning to higher education, it is found that the representation of tribal students is much below than the desired level. In the case of higher educational institutions controlled at the State level, the percentage of ST reserved seats is determined by the (approximate) proportion of this group in the State population. On the basis of this logic, the STs should have represented in the State run universities according to their numerical strength in Orissa. But this principle of Indian constitution has been grossly violated. For instance, the STs represented only 3.73 and 6.00 per cent as against their population of 22.19 per cent (1991 census) in Berhampur and Utkal Universities in 1994-95.[18] It certainly helps us to counter the argument that the higher education through preferences in Orissa helps only to the economically and politically strong within the ST groups.

But this must not be seen at the cost of other vulnerable tribal communities of Orissa. This argument will be more strengthened when we say that the prescribed quota of 23 per cent has not been fulfilled in the State run universities such as Utkal and Berhampur Universities. It is also clear that no enrollment has reportedly been done in courses such as Science, Education and Law in Berhampur University from tribal communities in the same academic year. It is also revealed from the available information that though in the central universities 7.5 per cent seats are reserved for STs, the representation of tribal communities is negligible. Although a large number of students apply to these universities, a few of them are admitted. In Jawaharlal Nehru University, for instance, 1145 ST students applied for admission in 1994-95 out of which only 75 (6% of all students) were admitted. It is worth mentioning that higher is the grade the lower their representation.

Explaining the Phenomenon

Welfare and development already reached to a height on a unilateral plain, mostly in the line of the problems of tribals (external aspects such as social, economic, etc.), but leaving least emphasis on the problems with the tribals (internal aspects like psychological, philosophical, religious, ideological, etc.). A holistic diagnosis of tribal problems in the context of preferential treatment, however, remained unexplored. This section would explore both the internal as well as external constraints that contribute to the discriminatory nature of the Indian educational system. Planning Commission of India states:

> Development and empowerment of socially disadvantaged groups is a commitment enshrined in the Constitution, and education is the most effective instrument of social empowerment. Schemes for the educational uplift of the SCs and STs have borne fruit although the gaps between the

> general population and SCs and STs are still at unacceptable levels... Some minorities have fallen far behind the national average in education. It will be necessary to go to the root of the problem and examine the reasons for the decline so that remedial measures can be taken during the 11th Plan.[19]

Inequality in educational opportunities is not specific to one group in India; the SCs and STs, who are historically deprived both socially and educationally, make the situation quite complex. They did make use of the educational opportunities that colonialism provided but in a manner. The low educational achievements of STs that we encounter today are totally inconsonant with the fact that this group was recently debarred from traditional knowledge or learning. It is, therefore, not surprising that in India today the State, entirely dominated by the so-called upper castes, does not care enough about the literacy of these groups and these groups themselves have not developed a powerful drive to force the State to provide better educational services. This kind of monopoly of the dominant values in the Indian educational system reflects the exclusive nature.

Needless to emphasize that poor economic condition of tribal societies enables them to show the lack of interest in education. Several evaluators have noted that most of the tribal people in Orissa are living in abject poverty under subsistence economy and it is not easy for most of them to send their children to schools. The scholarships paid to these disadvantaged students are totally inadequate to meet the basic minimum requirement of the students. This compels the students to make frequent demand on their parents and, sometimes, parents do not feel reluctant to call their children back to home. Even the disbursement of the scholarship is irregular and creates delay and inconvenience.

Empirical studies indicate that one of the major reasons contributing to the low literacy level of tribes in Orissa is the unsuitable scheduling of the school timing, which clashes with the work schedule of the economic activities of tribal families in which even the potential school going children participate. Thus, Verrier Elwin very appropriately sums up the situation that: 'For a tribal family, to send its grown up girls or boys to school, is essentially a matter of economics; and entails dislocation in the traditional pattern of division of labour... many parents cannot just afford to send their children to school'.[20] Supporting this position, the 42nd Round of National Sample Survey claims that the dropout rate among the tribes is mainly for participating in household economic activity and for other economic reasons. There are various difficulties at home that prevent them from devoting enough time for study or they are forced to help their parents in agricultural and household works, leaving them little time for studies. This leads to the poor performance of the tribal children compared to non-tribal children in Orissa.

It is noteworthy to mention that, as Planning Commission points out, most of the educational programs for tribes in Orissa are aimed at quantitative expansion, sometimes at the cost of erosion of qualitative aspects, which in turn inhibited dissemination and growth of literacy in tribal areas.[21] This notion of education in Orissa is quite contradictory to the dominant principle adopted at the World Education Forum (WEF) held at Dakar in Senegal, in April 2000. While emphasizing the importance of quality, relevance and effectiveness of education, it states: 'Education for all has to be about quality, not just filling in the classrooms'.[22]

Quality education in Orissa is still a privilege for a few. Good education, instead of being available to all children from every stratum of society, is available only to a small minority, which is usually selected not on the basis of talent but on the basis of its capacity to pay fees. The rich and poor are segregated in Orissa, the former attending better type of private schools, which charges fee while the latter are forced by circumstances to attend free government or local authority schools of poor quality. In other words, the children of the masses are compelled to receive substandard education, while the economically privileged parents are able to buy good education for their children in Orissa.

The crucial problem is the language of instruction in which elementary education is to be provided. By going through the deliberations in the Constituent Assembly and Indian Parliament, it becomes clear that neither the Constituent Assembly nor the Indian Parliament debated the language question of the country as a whole. What had been debated is whether English or Hindi would be the national official language and sometimes regional languages and what role Sanskrit should play in the scheme of languages. In short, the idea of the Constituent Assembly at large was to evolve a common language to preserve the unity and integrity as well as to develop a common culture of the country. Without bothering the languages of the marginal tribes, Nehru's recommendation for the use and protection of tribal languages fell on deaf ears.[23]

If we examine the section on language (part XVII of the constitution), certain provisions like Articles 347, 350, 350 (4) and 350 (B) have been dealt with minority languages. But the manners in which these Articles are framed make them ineffective in protecting these languages. Thus, Article 347 reads: 'On a demand being made in that behalf of the president may, if he is satisfied that a substantial proportion of the population of a State desire the use of any language spoken by them to be recognised through that State or any part thereof for such purpose as he may specify'. As of now 22 languages are included in the Eight Schedule of the constitution, but the languages of the eight per cent tribes found no place. This is due to the pretext that those languages are spoken by a small number of people and have no scripts. This is factually incorrect. For instance, over 3.5 million persons speak Santal, spread over a wide area in Bihar, Orissa, West Bengal, Tripura and Assam, and has a well developed script, known as '*Ol Chiki*' and yet not been recognized. While Sindhi spoken by less than two million people and without a linguistic territory and Sanskrit spoken by only a few hundreds, have received official recognition. Similarly, Kuvi language spoken by over one million people in Orissa is still to get State recognition. Thus, in spite of the fact that the Indian constitution in 1956 recognized through Article 350-A the need to provide primary education to linguistic minorities in their mother tongue, millions of tribal people are unable to avail education in their mother tongue.

The tribal languages appear to have given the tribal membership a readily available means through which they could invest in the continuing vitality of the tribal lifestyle and its cultural and social uniqueness. In Orissa, the tribal children speak their language at home with parents and friends and have to learn alphabets of State language in which they are situated. The monolingual tribes face cognitive and communicative problems, where the institutions are in the major regional language and this is what T.K. Oommen has described as 'teaching through an alien language.'[24]

Virginius Xaxa also supports this view by stating that language is one of the most serious handicaps before tribes to get the benefits of the preferential treatment policy as compared to even the SCs.[25]

The poor response of tribal children to formal education and their higher rate of attrition especially in the first few years of schooling relate to the language problem. As D.P. Patnayak claims, 'Where multiple languages and cultures co-exist, the notion of one dominant language as the medium of instruction leaves thousands illiterates in their mother tongue and fosters low achievement levels in the dominant language itself.'[26] Therefore, it is felt that the pronounced lapse is the medium of instruction which is invariably Oriya in Orissa; even the local tribal people did not understand it.

Several studies have also noted that the schools with non-tribal teachers have little meaning and usefulness for the rural and tribal areas. For instance, a survey of 100 primary schools in the tribal belt of Ganjam and Koraput districts of Orissa during 1981-83 shows 93 primary schools were not operating at all. Only seven schools run by tribal teachers under the shade of trees in the villages situated a top hills were functioning.[27] The tribal teachers in general are more sensitive towards tribal children, though those from the same community extend themselves more. They are more likely to bring with them the cultural empathy necessary to understand tribal pupils to entice them to schools and make them stay. The real problem seems to be the lack of cultural empathy, which is often misunderstood by non-tribals simply as different language in Orissa.

In any community, the teacher acts as a friend, philosopher and guide to the educational development process. He will be so, if he has command over language, culture and value system of the concerned community. Unfortunately most of the teachers employed for imparting education to the tribal children lack the language, skill and training to teach tribal children and to motivate them towards education. As Mishra mentions, 'Surprisingly, there are some teachers, teaching for many years in the schools, especially in tribal dominated areas, who have never felt (the need to learn) the tribal language.'[28] Therefore, it is not at all surprising to find an overwhelming number of children languishing sometimes more than one year in class I compared to the bare tickle in higher classes in Orissa.

In the remote villages, schools exist only for namesake. Empirical studies show that teachers are very irregular in the schools located in tribal areas as compared to general schools. Due to their illiteracy and ignorance the parents felt helpless. Planning Commission finds that sometimes when they complain to the authority, action is rarely taken against the teachers due to close bureaucratic and political networks of the teachers in Orissa.[29] This creates problems for the poor parents and children, and the vindictive attitude of the unprincipled teachers sometimes stands on the way of poor and meritorious students to flourish their educational career further.

When it comes to higher education, STs in Orissa suffer from what Weisskopf calls as 'cultural capital' deprivation.[30] This is evidenced by low level of education among family members, lower level of participation in edifying cultural activities and in general, a home environment less conducive to learning. Most critically, ST students typically lack the most important source of 'cultural capital' in Orissa, that is, good command of the English language. On the contrary, though many upper caste families have low level of socio-economic status, they are likely to be much richer than the tribal families in cultural capital. The general entry students not only enjoy the more conducive environment to educational success but also have obtained a secondary education at schools with better non-academic facilities as well as better academic environment. This partly helps to explain why STs perform poorly than general students in Orissa.

Several reports and number of studies demonstrate wide gender disparity in ST literacy in Orissa.[31] This is also supported by the fact that many parents still do not send their daughters to school. This is because the educational investment in girls is likely to be seen by the tribal parents as lower than that of the boys because of their mere limited opportunities in the labor market and near certainty that they will be married out of the family and devote their future time and earnings to their husband's family. It is also observed that girls from the concerned community perform worse than that of the boys. This is because the parents are expected to invest in their sons more than their daughters especially when resources are low. East India Human Development Report, a survey conducted by National Council of Applied Economic Research, claims that social reasons are responsible for the high rate of dropout among girls in Orissa.[32] For instance, when a girl attains puberty, parents become concerned about her chastity and she is restricted to the house. Inter-regional educational disparities are also striking due to uneven economic development and productive variations as well as the presence of missionary activities in coastal areas.[33]

Like other parts of India, preferences in education in Orissa operate through market principle. So, it depends on the parents to send their children to school. It also requires awareness about the need of education on the part of the parents. Sometimes, the parents show lack of interest in formal education. This is because of the way in which the present educational system in Orissa has been structured and operated. It has been designed in an urban middle class milieu and imposed on the entire State both in terms of structure and content. As the tribal communities of Orissa are conservative in nature, their culture, tradition and value system clash with modern culture and values that are the products of the present educational system. The higher educational system creates tensions and adjustment problems due to differences in outlook. If the adjustment problems are serious within the family, it would lead to alienation and consequent separation of the educated from their families. This demonstrates their apathy towards modern educational system. So, Indian educational system is also characterized by its unique feature that excludes the tribes of Orissa from the mainstream society.

Conclusion

The role of school education is connected with the phenomenon of a social exclusion. The present educational system has adopted various strategies with a purpose of rising level of social inclusion and cohesion but the effect is still opposite. Strategies to tackle social exclusion in terms of education have to take this existing complexity into account. Dominant values marginalize the values and experiences of different social groups. This marginalization is reflected in the way education is offered through, for example, its curriculum and teaching styles. These policies disregard people with no perceived economic value and can continue to marginalize others by failing to give value to their different identities or experiences which may challenge the status quo. In this context, the present educational system failed to recognize values of vulnerable tribal communities of India in general and Orissa in particular. So, it must be based on the ethos of the educationally inclusive school. An educationally inclusive school is one in which the teaching and learning, achievements, attitudes and well-being of every individual matter. Effective schools are educationally inclusive schools. This shows, not only in their performance, but also in their ethos and willingness to offer new opportunities to students who may have experienced difficulties. This does not mean treating all students the same way. Rather it involves taking account of student's varied life experience and needs.

Table–1
Progress of Literacy Rate (Per cent)

Year	*General*	*SC*	*ST*
1961	21.66	11.57	7.36
1971	26.18	15.61	9.46
1981	34.23	22.41	13.96
1991	49.09	36.78	22.31
2001	63.61	55.53	37.37

Sources: Census Reports.

Table–2
District-wise Literacy Rate (2001)

Districts	*General*	*SC*	*ST*
Angul	69.40	56.99	45.35
Balasore	70.94	59.41	31.88
Bargarh	64.13	55.56	50.21
Bhadrak	74.64	59.35	27.44
Bolangir	54.93	53.54	43.64
Baudha	58.43	49.92	46.65
Cuttack	76.13	61.40	35.75
Deogarh	60.78	52.84	45.26
Dhenkanal	70.11	56.23	39.41
Gajapati	41.73	37.14	27.77
Ganjam	62.94	44.56	35.54
Jagatsinghpur	79.61	66.30	48.62
Jajpur	72.19	54.61	31.41
Jharsuguda	71.47	63.97	57.23
Kalahandi	46.20	47.12	34.17
Kandhamal	52.95	53.36	44.47

Contd...

Districts	*General*	*SC*	*ST*
Kendrapara	77.33	60.73	40.07
Keonjhar	59.75	64.38	40.30
Khurda	80.19	64.98	49.91
Koraput	36.20	35.43	18.68
Malkangiri	31.26	49.94	14.69
Mayurbhanj	52.43	53.56	38.80
Nawarangpur	34.26	45.36	24.00
Nayagarh	71.02	57.27	47.09
Nuapada	42.29	43.99	33.12
Puri	78.40	64.05	58.72
Rayagada	35.61	35.18	20.23
Sambalpur	67.01	61.49	52.67
Sonepur	64.07	56.77	52.16
Sundergarh	65.22	61.54	52.75
ORISSA	63.61	55.53	37.37

Source:

htt://www.censusindia.net/cendata1/show_ data54. php3?j= 100 &j 1= 21 &j 2=4&j3=Orissa (Accessed on 10th July 2007). Director of Census Operation (2001), Census of India (Orissa), Bhubaneswar.

NOTES AND REFERENCES

1. Jagannath Ambagudia 'Reservation Policy: Continuity and Change', *Social Change and Development*, vol. 3, Annual Journal, July 2005, pp. 166-167.
2. Marc Galanter, *Competing Equalities: Law and Backward Classes in India* (Delhi: Oxford University Press, 1984), p. 56.
3. National Council of Applied Economic Research, *East India Human Development Report* (New Delhi: Oxford University Press, 2004), p. 242.
4. *Ibid.*
5. Thomas E. Weisskopf, 'Impact of Reservation on Admissions to Higher Education in India', *Economic and Political Weekly*, vol. XXXIX, no. 39, September 25, 2004, pp. 4339-4349.
6. National Council of Applied Economic Research (2004), *op. cit.*, pp. 203-206; Sachidananda, 'Structural Constraints in the Education of

Scheduled Tribes and Scheduled Castes' in B.B. Chaudhari (ed.), *Tribal Development in India* (Delhi: Inter-India Publications, 1982), pp. 403-408.

7. National Council of Applied Economic Research (2004), *op. cit.*
8. Thomas E. Weisskopf (2004), *op. cit.*, pp. 4339-4349; Sudha Pai, 'Affirmative Action, Group Rights and Democracy: Caste Conflict in Andhra Pradesh', Paper presented at the seminar on *Indian Democracy and Cultural Nationalism: Critical Perspectives*, Centre for Political Studies, JNU, New Delhi, 17-18 March, 2004, pp. 1-19.
9. Planning Commission, *Orissa Development Report* (New Delhi: Government of India, 2002), p. 450.
10. *Ibid.*
11. Ministry of Tribal Affairs (2004), *Annual Report 2002-03*, New Delhi: Government of India, p. 134 (Annexure-XI).
12. In case of degree and post-graduation level course in science stream, each hostler and day-scholar will get @ Rs. 450 and 190 P.M. respectively. Group B courses like, diploma level courses in medical, engineering etc., Rs. 290 and Rs. 190 P.M.; Group C courses such as, certificate courses in engineering and technology and post-graduation in arts and commerce, Rs. 290 and Rs. 190 P.M.; Group D courses-general courses up to graduate level (2nd year onwards), Rs. 230 and Rs. 130 P.M.; and Group E-class XI-XII in 10+2 system and intermediate courses and first year of general courses up to graduate level, Rs. 150 and Rs. 90 P.M. to hostlers and day-scholars respectively, National Commission for Scheduled Caste and Scheduled Tribe, *Fourth Report, Vol. I, 1996-97* and *1997-98* (New Delhi: Government of India, 1998), p. 52.
13. Jawaharlal Nehru University, *Prospectus: Admission Session*, New Delhi, 2005-06, pp. 52-53.
14. Respective Census Reports.
15. National Council of Applied Economic Research (2004), *op. cit.*, pp. 180-181.
16. P. Radhakrishnan and R. Akila, 'India's Educational Efforts: Rhetoric and Reality', *Economic and Political Weekly*, vol. XXXVIII, No. 48, 1983, p. 2614.
17. National Commission for Scheduled Caste and Scheduled Tribe (1996), *Third Report, Vol. I, 1994-95* and *1995-96*, New Delhi: Government of India; National Commission for Scheduled Caste and Scheduled Tribe (1998), *op. cit.*

17.*(a)* Scheduled Castes and Scheduled Tribes Research and Training Institute (SCSTRTI), Tribes in Orissa: A Data Sheet, (Bhubaneswar: Government of Orissa, 2001).

18. National Commission for Scheduled Caste and Scheduled Tribe (1996), *op. cit.*, p. 51.

19. Planning Commission (2002), *op. cit.*, p. 64.
20. Quoted in Nadeem Hasnain, *Tribal India Today* (New Delhi: Harnam Publications, 1983), p. 105.
21. Planning Commission (2002), *op. cit.*
22. Quoted in Nitya Rao, 'Education: Quality with Quantity', *Economic and Political Weekly*, vol. XXXV, no. 48, November 25, 2002, pp. 4181.
23. J.L. Nehru's position was very clear on tribal languages, when he lucidly spelt out: 'It is absolutely clear to me that the Government must encourage the tribal languages. It is not enough to allow them to prevail. They must be given all possible support and conditions in which they flourished must be safeguarded. We must go out of our way to achieve this', quoted in K. Mohapatra, 'The Ethno-Linguistic Identity of the Tribal of Orissa' in Kishore C. Padhy (ed.), *The Challenges of Tribal Development: Essays in Honour of Dr. N. Patnaik*, New Delhi: Swarup and Sons, 2000, p. 169.
24. Quoted in Jaganath Pathy, 'Indian State and the Tribal Question' in J.P. Singh and N.N. Vyas (eds.), *Tribal Development: Past Efforts and New Challenges* (Udaipur, Himanshu Publications, 1989), p. 25.
25. Virginius Xaxa argues that SCs had been the integral part to the dominant community whether in a village or in a town, the only difference being that untouchables were unjustly segregated from the community and subjected to all forms of disabilities and discrimination. The SCs were extended reservations because they suffered certain disabilities arising from life of segregation from the dominant community. The STs, on the other hand, were given reservations not because they were segregated from the dominant community but because they lived in isolation from the dominant community. Though SCs divided on the basis of castes, they share language, culture and tradition of the dominant community and constitute a part of the dominant nationality of the region. On the contrary, tribes are invariably seen as outsiders, ones who not only do not speak their language but also do not share their customs, traditions and values. In short, SCs have, therefore, had a greater exposure to the larger society as compared to STs, Virginius Xaxa, 'Protective Discrimination: Why Scheduled Tribes Lag Behind Scheduled Castes', *Economic and Political Weekly*, vol. XXXVI, no. 21, July 21, 2001, pp. 2765-2772.
26. D.P. Patnayak, *Multilingualism and Mother Tongue Education* (New Delhi: Oxford University Press, 1981), p. 43.
27. Neeti Mohanty, 'Traditional and Modern Educational Institutions' in Kishore C. Padhy (ed.), 2000, *op. cit.*, p. 195.
28. Dinabandhu Mishra, 'Adivasi Siksakhetrare Odisara Sikshaka O Semanakara Samasya (Oriya) (The problem of Teachers in the Education

of the Tribals in Orissa)', *Sikshaloka*, no. 2, 5th year, September 1970, p. 8.

29. Planning Commission (2002), *op. cit.*
30. Thomas E. Weisskopf (2004), *op. cit.*, p. 4344.
31. Planning Commission (2002), *op. cit.*; National Commission for Scheduled Castes and Scheduled Tribes (1998), *op. cit*; Directorate of Economics and Statistics (2004), *Districts At a Glance*, Bhubaneswar: Government of Orissa; National Council of Applied Economic Research (2004), *op. cit.*; B.B. Mohanty, 'Educational Progress of Scheduled Tribes: A Discursive Review', *Man and Development*, vol. XXV, no. 2, June 2003, pp. 91-106; Sailabala Debi (1996), 'Regional Inequalities in Education in Orissa', *Indian Journal of Regional Science*, vol. 28, no. 2, pp. 11-23.
32. National Council of Applied Economic Research (2004), *op. cit.*
33. Sthobir Khora, 'Continuity Low Literacy: The Case of Orissa', *Economic and Political Weekly*, vol. XL, no. 10, March 5, 2005, p. 928.

15

Poverty, Social Exclusion and Basic Education: The Tamil Nadu Experience

POORNIMA M.

Poverty is a kind of social exclusion that retards the growth and development of an individual. Poverty is often seen as a reflection of inequality as some section of the society is deprived of their basic needs and rights in certain aspect. In order to bring a person out of social exclusion one should be empowered and to eradicate poverty, there should be promotion of equality. To set right the inequalities of poverty, the seed of equality of opportunities and equality of access should be sown. In this regard, education serves as a means to attain equality. This paper brings out the issues of poverty, exclusion and development and highlights the strategic importance of basic education in order to eradicate poverty and move towards sustainable development. Further the paper also discusses the capability approach and human rights-based approach in particular, which talks about the importance of empowering the poor through education so that the voices of the poor can be heard. This paper, through a case study of Chennai district of Tamil Nadu, makes a study of the extent of exclusion and the inclusive measures taken by the government in providing education for all and also identifies the lacunae in it.

Poverty

Poverty is perhaps the most serious challenge in terms of human rights and human development, faced by the developing countries in the world. The multi dimensional nature of poverty affects the lives of millions of people making them deprived of all the basic necessities of life. The magnitude of poverty in today's world is indeed alarming. Human Development Report 2000[1] points out that about 1.2 billion people continue to live below the poverty line on less than $1 a day; more than 2.4 billion people are without basic sanitation; about 100 million are homeless; about 1 billion adults are illiterate; nearly 100 million children live or work on the street. Poverty does not mean lack of income or lack of consumption alone, which is one of the aspects of poverty. Poverty is multi-faceted and encompasses all forms of deprivation – social, economic and political. People lose the capacity and capability to fight for their rights in all these spheres and they are unable to participate in the developmental process. Dealing with poverty is a precondition for India's survival as a democratic nation. Staggering poverty afflicts a large proportion of the population, which is denied basic rights as citizens by their deprivation.[2]

Analysis of poverty is done at two levels: One goes on to define poverty and the other involves in measuring poverty.[3] There is no universal definition of poverty. The World Development Report (WDR) 1990 defines poverty as the 'inability to attain a minimal standard of living'. The United Nations views poverty as 'a human condition, characterized by the sustained or chronic deprivation of the resources, capabilities, choices, security and power necessary for the enjoyment of an adequate standard of living and other civil, cultural, economic, political and social rights.'[4] Measuring poverty seeks to put the aggregate of people living in poverty in statistical terms.

The issue of poverty has been constantly debated for the past few decades. While some differentiate it as urban poverty and rural poverty, there are some people who make the distinction between income poverty and non-income poverty. Income poverty is the deprivation in monetary terms which denotes the lack of purchasing power to secure the basic needs and non income poverty is the deprivation in the elements of well being like shelter, food, nutrition, education, health, etc. Apart from this, there is one more aspect of deprivation, that is, social exclusion. When people are marginalized, discriminated or left out in social relations, they lack basic security and the capability to lead a life of value. With or without adequate income or human development, a socially excluded individual is unable to access the basic amenities of life or participate in social life.[5]

The pressing need of the hour is to eradicate poverty which acts as a stumbling block to development. In the process of eradicating poverty, there is no single recipe available that leads to poverty reduction on the whole. There are many indicators for its eradication like employment, education, health, etc. Among these indicators, providing basic education serves as an indispensable tool that contributes to poverty reduction in the long run, as it helps in treating the root cause of poverty. It helps in breaking the vicious circle of poverty and also it builds the capability of the poor people thereby making them participate in the developmental process.

Poverty Among Children

The severity of poverty is more aggressive when it comes to children. Poverty is so harsh on children that it pushes them into the modern forms of slavery like child labour, bonded labour and child prostitution. Poverty threatens all aspects of a child's life by depriving children of the capabilities needed to survive, develop and thrive. Children in the developing countries spend most of their childhood struggling to survive, without much hope for a secure, productive life. They have limited access to education, which limits opportunity and reduces potential.[6] Children living in poverty are deprived of many of their rights—survival, health and nutrition, education, and so on. A child's experience of poverty is different from that of the poverty of an adult. UNICEF argues that children are often hardest hit by poverty. Poverty in childhood does not end with one generation, it often continues to the next one as well.

Dimensions of Child Poverty

The dimensions of poverty in children are multi-faceted. Children living in poverty experience various types of deprivation. The notion of deprivation implies various aspects in life that a child is denied, including material and emotional resources. One form of deprivation accentuates another form of deprivation and such deprivation causes suffering in the short run and hinders individual development in the long run. The forms of deprivation are of various kinds like health deprivation, nutrition deprivation, education deprivation, shelter deprivation and information deprivation. Over 16 percent of children under five in the developing countries are severely malnourished. Nearly half of these 90 million children live in South Asia and they remain among the poorest of the poor throughout their lives. In case of basic education, over 140 million children in developing countries have never attended school. Worldwide, 16 per cent of girls and 10 per cent of boys miss out of school completely.[7]

Poverty in childhood perpetuates poverty in adulthood. In order to break the generational cycle of poverty, poverty reduction must begin with children. For this purpose the education deprivation of children should be solved. Education keeps the children aware of the opportunities available at their disposal which help them to build up their capabilities thereby breaking the cycle of poverty. The development of the human capabilities in childhood depends greatly on the ability of the family and of the State to ensure that children are free from deprivation.[8] Thus, the various types of deprivation faced by children can be addressed by way of providing access to basic education. The developing countries spend most of their money for repayment of debt or for maintaining the military forces. Even if fraction of the amount spent on it is diverted to the basic education of children it would be a step forward in wiping out poverty.

Effects of Poverty on Children

Children are perhaps their mother's best helpers, especially girl children who assist their mothers in household work, collect fuel wood and water and take care of their younger siblings that in turn affect their education and often result in dropping out of school. Children leave school prematurely for a variety of other reasons also, including the cost of schooling, the need to supplement family income, or unfriendly school environment and poor education quality. The Education For All (EFA) Report[9] brings to light that, while all other developing countries had common reasons like family background, gender bias, household wealth, and mother's education for children being out-of-school, in India in addition to the above mentioned reasons other reasons were also responsible like children being orphans, child laborers, children of Scheduled caste and tribe household, children belonging to a particular state, class, caste or religion and so on. The EFA Report states that among 112 developing countries for which information was obtained, 4 countries alone accounted for about 23 million children out of school. The largest number of out of school children in 2004 was in Nigeria, Pakistan, India and Ethiopia.[10] Tables 1 and 2 give a picture of the number of out-of-school children in the world and the position of India in relation to out-of-school children.

Table–1
Developing Countries with Over 500,000 Out-of-school Children, 2004

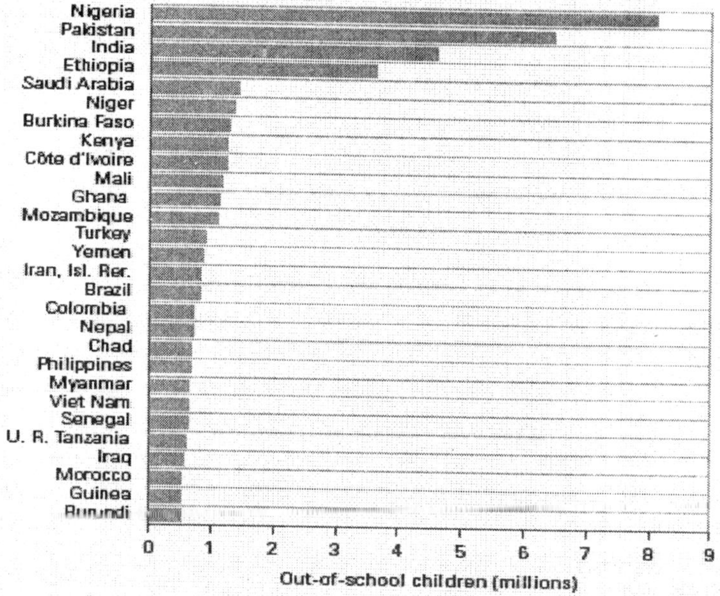

Note: These countries together account for 43.3 million out-of-school children, out of the global estimated total of 76.8 million.
See source table for detailed country notes.
Source: Annex, Statistical Table 5.

Table–2
Out-of-school Children in Select Countries in 1999, 2002 and 2004 (thousands)

	1999	2002	2004
Mali	1 113	1 089	1 172
Cote d'Ivoire	1 253	1 144	1 223
Kenya	1 833	1 868	1 225
Burkina Faso	1 205	1 264	1 271
Niger	1 393	1 381	1 326
Ghana	1 329	1 307	1 357
Saudi Arabia	1 345	1 371	1 630
Mozambique	1 602	1 572	1 089
Ethiopia	4 961	4 633	3 615
India	...	15 136	4 583
Pakistan	...	...	6 463
Nigeria	...	...	8 110

Note: See source table for detailed country notes.
Sources: Annex, Statistical Table 5; UIS database.

Street children are also found in substantial numbers in India. Street children are the most commonly visible sight in the metropolitan cities of India who are found on the streets selling toys, books, flowers and newspapers. They are also the most difficult group to reach as the cruelty of exploitation and poverty makes them tough and aggressive.

The challenge for governments regarding these groups is to increase opportunities and incentives for them to re-enter the education system, which often necessitates new forms of initiatives in meeting their needs. The country has to continue its relentless struggle, to eradicate illiteracy and ensure that every child will benefit from the provision of basic education without exception of caste, creed, language, religion, or any other social, economic and regional consideration.[11]

Education can be made acceptable to the children and adults of poorer classes only when it is accompanied by other things which fulfill their immediate and vital needs.[12] Hence basic education must correspond to the actual needs, interest and problem of the children in the learning process. Investment in education at any time has a multiplier effect, yielding additional benefits for the future. In summary, education is a powerful tool for reducing poverty, unemployment and inequality, improving health and nutrition and promoting sustained human development led growth.[13]

Impact of Education on Poverty and Development

Poverty removal is the central objective of the Millennium agenda. The primary aim is to reduce income poverty by cutting in half the proportion of people living on less than a dollar a day.[14] For this purpose a massive push is needed to boost access to essential services for the children which will provide a vital kick-start to human development and poverty reduction. Basic education is the key to sustaining growth and poverty reduction. All over the world basic education has been given its due recognition which is well evident from the Declaration on Millennium Development Goals,[15] Conference on Education for All, and World Education Forum.[16] Hence it can be said that basic education would facilitate in contributing to social, economic and cultural progress free from hunger, malnutrition and poverty. Education is an indispensable tool for personal and social improvement.

Education not only enriches the life of an individual but also enriches the whole nation. A nation cannot be said to have developed only if few of its elite groups are educated. It is considered to be developed only if education is imparted even to the poorest of the poor sections of the society. The poor people, having education as a means, come up in life acquiring other aspects of life like sound health, secure job, etc. However, we cannot expect a sudden change in the way of life of the people.[17] Education takes its own pace of time to develop the people which can be realized only in the long term. Assurance of basic minimum needs found an expected and prominent place in the Fifth Plan period for the first time in India. The basic minimum needs not only meant the day to day needs of the people in terms of income and consumption but it also meant education for all children up to 14 years of age, minimum public health facilities, nutrition for children, protected water supply, etc. However, there has always remained a gap between so called motivations to remove poverty and the slogans made about it.[18]

Hence the powerful instrument of education which makes its impact in poverty reduction and human development should be improved qualitatively and it should be very well designed keeping in mind the poverty issue, the prime objective of the Millennium Development Goal (MDG) and it should be made accessible to all the children in the country.

Strategic Importance of Basic Education

Basic education brings about a remarkable change in the society as it acts as a facilitator of social change and also it is an element for bringing about values and quality in life. A firm commitment to the spread of basic education is vital because of its strategic importance. The strategic importance that basic education offers can be understood in five distinct ways as put forward by Amartya Sen and Jean Dreze.[19]

1. Intrinsic Importance: Basic education is a valuable factor for development and it can bring about a direct change and a positive change in a person's life. The art of learning has got its own intrinsic values that help an individual in the realization of his personal goals, in building confidence and moving towards self improvement.
2. Instrumental Personal Roles: A person's education motivates him to generate and utilize his potential to the fullest as it

makes a drastic change in his personality also. If a person is educated he can be more confident of getting a well secured job that would make him economically sound and that makes him to participate actively in various activities in the society.

3. Instrumental Social Roles: Basic education also enables a person to take part in various activities and issues that are raised in the society. As information is well furnished to an educated person he is able to take part in the discussion in relation to the social needs and he is able to voice out his stand in it, which enables him to make full use of his privileges and rights in a democracy.
4. Process Roles: The process of schooling, apart from individual gains extends its benefits to the society in other consideration also. Process of schooling helps in expanding its activities to all type of children and thereby tries to help child laborers and offers education to them. Apart from this, schooling helps on widening the horizon for the children.
5. Empowerment Roles: Educational achievements of poor children and other disadvantaged groups empower them and help them come out of poverty trap. It helps in reducing inequalities and serves as a means of attaining equality as it promotes equal opportunities to all sections of the people.

Analysis of Basic Education in India

Basic education refers to a whole range of educational activities that take place in different settings and aim to meet basic learning needs as defined in the World Declaration on Education for All in Jomtien. Basic education is an indispensable 'passport to life' that will enable people to choose what they do to share in building the collective future and to continue to learn.[20] Basic education is essential if social exclusion and the resultant inequality is to be successfully challenged. The significance of basic education especially to the downtrodden was recognized in the Jomtien conference,[21] which stated that education should be imparted to the socially, culturally and economically deprived groups.

India has understood the strategic importance that basic education offers to an individual and how it helps in motivating the people to take part in the process of development. Recognizing its importance, the framers of our Constitution has made elementary education free and compulsory for children from 6 to 14 years of age under Article 45 of the Directive Principles of State Policy. The 86th Constitutional Amendment Act was passed to make the Right to Elementary Education a fundamental right and a fundamental duty.[22]

Right from the Jomtien Conference in 1990 to the Dakar Framework in 2000, education has been given a prime consideration which contributes to human development and it is a global concern and commitment to universalize elementary education. Education for all has become an obligation and a prerogative for India to accomplish the goal by 2015.

But though the importance of education is felt, it has not been given the due consideration that is needed for bringing the Constitutional obligations into reality. There is one field in which India has done worse than even the poorest of the poor countries in the world and that is elementary education. India has been left behind in the field of basic education even by countries which have not done better than India in many other developmental achievements such as Ghana, Zambia, Kenya and Philippines.[23]

A major objective articulated by Jomtien was universal access to and completion of basic education. The number of children enrolled in school rose from an estimated 599 million in 1990 to 681 million in 1998.[24] This means that some 10 million more children have been going to school every year, which is nearly double the average increase during the preceding decade. However, this statistics is for the whole world and India has to catch up with its neighboring countries in the field of basic education.

In order to achieve Universal Primary Education by 2015, at a global level two steps are needed.

(a) Identifying all hard-to-reach children and assessing their characteristics, extent of exclusion and the obstacles to their attending school; and

(b) Devising strategies and policies to reach them, and obtaining and allocating financial resources.

As per the goal of Education For All (EFA) discussed in the World Education Forum (WEF) the above mentioned steps are to be taken by India to universalize education within 2015. A firm commitment to the widespread and equitable provision of basic education is the first requirement of rapid progress in eradicating educational deprivation in India.

Development in Relation to Poverty Reduction and Basic Education

Development can be regarded as an activity, a process, an event or a condition that often takes the form of reaching a better position from the state of being. Traditionally development meant only the growth of a nation in terms of per capita income or economic stability.[25] Measuring development in terms of money fails to recognize other aspects of human life that are very crucial to the growth of people that builds the quality of one's life. Economic growth alone cannot be regarded as development. A society can be called developed only if sufficient opportunities are available to an individual that contributes to his/her empowerment, participation and job security.

The human development approach is gaining predominance in the human development paradigm in the recent years.[26] This can be very well understood by making an analysis of the Human Development Reports (HDR). While the earlier HDR of 1992 and 1997 is concerned about opportunities available for human development and political freedoms for human development whereas the HDR of 2000 is concerned about the human rights for human development. The human rights approach started gaining momentum as it serves as a base for providing opportunities to the people.

At the global level, development regime focuses on various issues for women, poor people, indigenous people, environment, health, micro credit, basic education, governance and so on. In the international arena people take up a particular issue and they specialize in it and work towards it. The poor people now represent a global population living in countries saddled with MDG performance targets under global surveillance.[27] Poor people are thus no longer conceived primarily as national citizens. They are targets, beneficiaries, and participants in a development process.

The notion of poverty as well as the notion of basic education has both been taken up in the development agenda worldwide. Whether it be poverty reduction or providing basic education, both depends upon the provision of opportunities to the people that make them take part in the development process with improvement in quality of their lives. While talking about making opportunities available to the people in the development paradigm the aspect of poverty reduction or basic education that contributes to development should not be viewed in isolation as they are interrelated to each other.

In the process of development, scholars from the various fields of economics, sociology and governance talk about various approaches in expanding the opportunities for the people. When one argues about increasing the per capita income, others talk of expanding the capabilities of people. When some intellectuals are concerned about the basic needs of the people others are worried about the human rights of the people. The next section makes an analysis of the capability approach put forward by Sen and the human rights based approach in the context of poverty reduction and basic education as a measure to move people away from social exclusion. The current discussion in the debate of development discourse is not simply about development but about sustainable development. The nagging problem of poverty also stresses on sustainable development. The concept of sustainable development which may be seen as an alternative to the traditional concept of development implies an interlinking and balanced relationship between economic, social and environmental factors.[28] Development strategies based on industrialization may help in satisfying economic needs of the poor people but not in reducing poverty in the long run. There should be an integrated mix of economic, social and environmental dimension so as to move towards sustainable development.

Poverty and Capability Approach

Sustained development requires development of capabilities in people so that they are eventually able to take care of themselves.[29] The human capability approach has intrinsic value for the well-being of people and plays an indirect role in influencing social change and in influencing economic output. Sen argues that the expansion of human capability can be seen as the central feature of the process of development. Capability refers to the alternative combinations of 'functionings' from which a person can choose. Functionings refer to the sequence of things that a person does to achieve something.[30] Hence the capability approach is focused on the individual's capabilities and functioning. But the marginalized people are ignorant even to realize their capabilities, no matter how hard the government or voluntary organizations try to empower them. Therefore participation by the poor has to be at the collective level. Without collective action, the voices of the poor can rarely be heard.[31] Various institutions and NGOs should come forward in support of the poor and give a voice to the voiceless.

Capability approach focuses on improving people's capabilities over a period through the design of 'human development' strategies and it leads to the improvement of access to health and education services, to adequate nutrition and safe water supply, thus improving the level of human capital on the whole. Development paradigm should include a broad range of freedoms or rights such as the basic capabilities to avoid starvation, undernourishment or premature mortality, as well as rights to education and being able to engage in participation in the political process.[32]

Basic Needs Approach and Human Rights Approach

The basic needs approach states that development can be realized only if it is focused on the needs of the people. Under this concept households are defined as poor if their food, clothing, medical, educational and other needs are not met. Basic needs approach do not seem to attempt to put various aspects of basic needs in to a single factor. This approach involves some elements of subjectivity in determining 'satisfactory' levels of healthcare, housing, education, cultural amenities and other aspects.[33]

In contrast to the needs-based approach, human rights-based approach focuses on the empowerment of the people as a core strategy in ensuring that the system of governance is reformed to respond to issues that affect their lives, including poverty.[34] Poverty recognized only as a matter of satisfying basic needs reflects on economic factors alone and calls for the response of only the government officials at the top level. When poverty is regarded as a human rights approach, the economic, social and political factors are considered and it gets a wider response from the various actors in the society like the government, private players, NGOs, local communities, etc.

A rights-based approach has wider advantages when compared to the needs-based approach. In the rights-based approach the focus shifts from the government to the citizens. Human rights-based approach recognizes that poverty is not just a matter of being economically deprived. It is defined and sustained by a sense on the part of the poor of helplessness, dependence, lack of opportunities, and lack of self confidence and self respect. The language of rights makes clear that poor is not subject of charity and benevolence by governments or rich people. They are entitled to a decent standard of living and that rights are the vehicles for their participation and empowerment.[35] These discussions are raised having the development discourse in relation to poverty reduction alone. Approaches in relation to basic education can be understood by analysis of the various phases of development approaches.

Phases of Development Approach and Basic Education

There are various approaches to development that developed in different phases.[36] In the early 1960s development was more oriented towards projects and the project approach was an exercise which was developed for the people by the officials at the top level. This approach focuses more on the development for the people. The next phase in late 1960s created the sectoral approach to development, in which various programmes were developed by the government for the development of the people.[37] This approach stressed the value of decentralizing authority to lower levels of government organization in order to enhance the management of the sectoral programmes. There was growing emphasis on education, training of masses, adult education and universal primary education. The main idea of this approach was *development of the people.*

The growth of basic education during the 1960s was more based on the rules and regulations of the government. Based on the constitutional commitment of providing free and compulsory education to all children below 14 years of age, the government framed the educational policies and the government chose to educate the children through vast, centralized machinery designed by the government with superstructure, staff, infrastructure and resources.[38] But the project approach failed to realize improvements especially in the conditions of the poorer segments of the population in terms of basic education. The analysis of the educational developments in India in the late 1960s from the point of view of the phases of development brings out clearly that it was more based on the sectoral approach. The Kothari Commission made many recommendations to the improvement of education in India and the committee stated that there should be intimate contact between the schools and the local communities.[39] Mid day meal schemes were also launched in some states and the educational programmes were designed for the development of the people.

The third phase of development was oriented towards policy approach which was developed by the end of 1970s. Under this approach the challenge was no longer on how to administer or manage the development; it was much on identifying the avenues that may facilitate it. Market, private and voluntary organizations could play a more significant role in working with people to realize their aspirations. NGOs were able to do with the people what the government had failed to do for the people. The perception of development under this approach is an exercise done with the people.[40] The fourth phase of development, the political approach or bottom-up approach in 1990s realized that development is not only about the projects, programmes or policies but also about politics. People must be given the right incentives and opportunities not only in the economic but also in the political arena. Development is the product of what people decide to do to improve their livelihoods. People constitute the principal force of development and must have the chance to create institutions and organizations that respond to their needs and priorities. Development in this stage was regarded as something done *by the people*.[41]

The development of education system in India started gaining momentum only after 1980s. The National Educational Policy of 1986 has been guiding education all through. Many programmes like Operation Black Board, District Institutes on Educational Training (DIET), Non-formal Education and Mid Day Meal Scheme (MDMS) were established after the policy was framed.[42] Educational development was viewed from the point of view of the needs of the people. As per the human rights-based approach, the Right to Education Bill 2005 has made it a right to every child to have compulsory education. From the Jomtien conference to the Dakar Framework, various actors other than the government took part in the conference to voice out the needs, aspirations and rights of the poor people in the World Education Forum.

Thus it can be said that the rights-based approach applied to development regime would make a significant contribution to poverty reduction. Basic education acts as a catalyst for social change and development of the nation as a whole. In order to eradicate poverty and promote development, imparting basic education to the children is essential. The next section makes an analysis of the extent of exclusion in Chennai district of Tamil Nadu and the critical gaps and inclusive measures taken in combating poverty in the context of basic education.

Exclusion, Poverty and Education in Chennai, Tamil Nadu

In a vast country like ours educating the children should be given the prime focus, especially the education to poor sections of the society. Exploration for the field study started with a series of queries. In spite of the steps taken by the government why does our country still lag behind when compared to our neighbouring countries in the mission towards basic education? When various programmes are available for the poor to promote their education why are more children found on the streets in the metropolitan cities of India selling flowers and newspapers? All such queries make one skeptical about the initiatives of the government, private players, civil society and other institutions in meeting the requirements of the poor people.

The research is based on the field study in 2007conducted in two zones, Vyasarpadi and Taramani, which are in the north and south zones respectively in the Chennai district of Tamil Nadu. This is basically a qualitative enquiry which combined observations, in-depth interviews, focused group discussion and administering of structured and semi-structured questionnaire to the respondents to collect the data. The study is explorative, focusing on the lives of children living in extreme poverty, the structure of the family and the primary education as facilities available for them. Parents, children in the age group of 6-14 years, government schools and even NGO run schools were visited for the purpose of the study. Private schools were beyond the purview of the study as the education imparted in such schools was not accessible to the poor. The sample in this study is skewed in favor of the families in the BPL category whose socio-economic status is very poor so as to find out the extent of exclusion.

Scenario of Education in Chennai

In general Chennai can be regarded as an education centre as people from all over Tamil Nadu come to Chennai for their higher studies. The overall picture of educational scenario in Chennai shows a positive trend and especially basic education in particular is taken care of by various actors. Children get themselves enrolled in various schools like government schools, NGO-run schools, private schools, Municipal and Corporation schools, Anglo-Indian schools and schools run by panchayat unions in the suburban belt of Chennai. Now there are growing numbers of residential and international schools in Chennai where only elite enroll their children. The Directorate of Education in Chennai looks after the schooling system in Chennai and the Corporation of Chennai manages the education of government and corporation schools. The State Project Directorate in Chennai takes care of the execution of the schemes and programmes.

As per the 2001 Census of India the literacy level of Chennai is 80 per cent which is higher than the State average of 73 per cent and national average of 65 per cent. Though the statistics of the literacy rates of Tamil Nadu in General and Chennai in particular shows a progressive trend, the State and the State capital still lags behind when compared to the neighboring state of Kerala where the literacy rate crossed 90 per cent. Many of the children in Chennai still remain out-of-schools. In spite of establishing primary schools at a distance of 1 km in each locality, the problem still persists and there exist more out-of-school children. The pupil-teacher ratio for primary schools is high as 38 when compared to the national average of 40.[43]

The poverty levels in Tamil Nadu have declined from 45.80 per cent in 1987-88 to 21.12 per cent in 1999-2000. However, the incidence of poverty is still high which has to be given consideration even though it is less than the all-India average of 26.1 per cent.[44] The incidence of poverty has to be treated which is the root cause for the lack of capability in the people and it affects the education of children too which causes exclusion, thereby retarding the overall growth of the children.

Determinants to Measure the Extent of Exclusion

In order to measure the extent of exclusion, the socio-economic background of the poor children and their families is to be analyzed. The risk of exclusion is not shared evenly in the society and is often concentrated more among the poor communities, who suffer from a combination of linked problems such as unemployment, poor skilled work, low income, unfair discrimination, poor housing, bad health and family breakdown.

Family Structure and the Number of Children

Nearly thirty families were visited to know about a children's family background. Evidence in the field shows that majority of the dwellers in filed area live in a single nuclear family as the size of their house and the economic status of their family does not permit them to live in an extended family. Almost all the people in the field area live below poverty line (BPL), and have to struggle to earn their basic necessity. The table gives a clear picture that children of these families are definitely in disadvantage in meeting their educational needs. In spite of their economic position, majority of the people interviewed have 2 or 3 children and only 2 families followed a single child norm while there are 4 families that even have 4 children each. Naturally the parents are in disadvantage to meet the educational needs of all their children and education becomes secondary to them.

Table-3

Amount Spent for Education of Children

Children in the Family	*Amount Spent Per Annum*			
	Family	*0 -500*	*500-1000*	*1000-2000*
1 child	2	2	3	1
2 children	12	4	5	2
3 children	12		4	7
4 children	4		2	
Total	30	6	14	10

As the size of the family is too big, the income to support the education of children and to provide other facilities to the children is not sufficient. They live in extreme conditions of poverty and they need to feed too many mouths with their meager earnings.

There are 14 families who spend around Rs.1000 for the education of their children out of which only 3 families have single child. All the rest have more than 2 children. Families with 3 children are spending nearly Rs. 2000 for the education of all the three children. On an average, a family is able to spend only Rs. 250 for the education of a child per annum which is definitely not sufficient to meet the requirements of the child. Families with one child are able to spend more on the child's education which ranges from Rs. 500 to Rs. 1500 on an average.

Economic Status of the Family

Nature of Occupation

Among the thirty families visited, 3 of the fathers are jobless and 11 of the mothers are housewives. Most of the fathers are addicted to alcohol and few engage in gambling. The children in 4 of the families did not have father. Most of the parents work as coolies and they depend on their daily wages that will have to forgo the wage if they don't go for work for a day. And many of the mothers work as servant maids and they are paid very meager amount as salary.

Table–4
Nature of Occupation of the Parents

Father		*Mother*	
Watchman	2	Housewife	11
Tiffin shop	1	Tiffin shop	3
Tea shop	1	Servant maid	8
Coolie	12	Sell flowers	1
Rickshaw	4	Coolie	5
Vendor	3	No mother	2
No job	3		
No father	4		
Total	**30**		**30**

Table–5
Economic Status of the Family

Level of Income		*No of Families*
0-1000	1	
1000-2000	20	
2000-3000	8	
3000-4000	1	
Above 4000	-	
Total	**30**	

As stated earlier, most of the families depend on daily wages and the Table 5 shows the level of income of a family per month. None of the families earns more than Rs. 4000 per month and there is only one family whose earning is below Rs. 1000.

The monthly income of majority of the household is between 1000 and 2000 rupees. When such average income is equated with that of the family size the income will be insufficient even to meet the basic needs of the family. While most of the earning is spent on food items, only a small amount remains for meeting the educational needs of their children.

Educational Status of the Family

The education of the parents makes a difference in the progress of education of their children. The data illustrates that majority of the parents are illiterates and the female literacy rate is poor than that of the male. Not even a single mother in the sample had passed the upper primary education while there was only one male respondent who had passed his higher secondary schooling.

Table–6
Educational Status of the Family

Sl. No.	*Level*	*Father*	*Mother*
1.	Illiterate	13	16
2.	Primary education	3	5
3.	Upper Primary Education	5	7
4.	High School	4	-
5.	Higher secondary	1	-
6.	Higher education	-	-
	Total	**26**	**28**

All aforementioned factors are to be taken into consideration while making an analysis of the state of exclusion because they have strong impact on the education of the children. Even the presence of one of the factor will have adverse effect on the family. When such conditions occur in combination, the life of children gets more affected than the adult. The children tend to lose their childhood and they begin to play the role of an adult in order to support their family. There are some children who go for work both in the morning and evening, before and after school hours. The burden of work is more in case of girl child, who engages herself in all kinds of work at home, like cooking, collecting fuel woods, taking care of young siblings, etc. Hence children from poor households are not regular to schools and they give a wide range of reasons for their absenteeism.

Such conditions of the downtrodden and the impact of poverty on the lives of the people make one look back at the questions raised by UNESCO.[45] What opportunities are there in a world of continued environmental degradation and poverty, a world where 1.3 billion people live by less than US $1 a day (UNDP) and where 884.7 million adults are illiterate (UNESCO) and caught, for the most part, in a cycle of educational failure, poor health, social exclusion and exploitation?

In order to make the poverty ridden families come out of the vicious circle, the mental problems of such group should be addressed, as their vulnerability makes them more aggressive, which passes on to next generations too. Apart from this, a solution in the long run can be put in place by educating the poor. Basic education serves as a means to overcome exclusion and bridge the gap, which cleaves the society into two. However, mere enrollment of children in schools can never be helpful in any way to overcome poverty and exclusion. Children should be prepared in schools to meet the future challenges of life. For this purpose, the schools should be better equipped and proper facilities and infrastructure should be made available for the children at schools. The following section makes a study of the inclusive measures taken at the micro level, in the field area and also identifies the critical gaps in it.

Measures Taken to Reach Out to the Poor and the Critical Gaps in it

Exclusion and deprivation form the bases for all kinds of mishaps that take place in the life of a poor child and these affect the state of living of children. While the majority of the in-school children comes from the economically well off background, majority of the out-of-school children comes from the poor and marginalized sections of the society. When such deprivation factor is analyzed a sweeping statement that income and expenditure poverty attributes to deprivation will not yield a good result. Poverty cannot be understood by looking at income and expenditure factor alone. Food insecurity, vulnerability to crisis and lack of access to basic services like safe drinking water, school or health facilities are also some other aspects of deprivation.[46]

Evidence from the field suggests that some of the aspects of deprivation are considered by the service providers when meeting the needs of the economically deprived classes. To cater to the needs of the deprived classes, various service providers like government schools and NGOs run transit schools for school dropouts and formal and non formal institutes for such children. Homes are provided to the needy children, and night schools are also held for children who are unable to attend regular schools. Free tuitions are given to the poor children in the evening and they are also provided with text books, note books, meals etc. Awareness is also created among the illiterate parents about the importance of education of their children and the mental make up of the children is also strengthened.[47] In order to meet the financial constraints of the poor children, the government provides education free of cost and supplies free books and uniforms to the children. The government officials who are executing the scheme of SSA in the city claim that the specially focused groups are given life skill programmes and they are also taken to exposure visits.

Enrollment, Retention and Mainstreaming

Enrollment is the first step in the process of bringing the out-of-school children to school. It is clear from Table 7 that the rate of enrollment in the age group of 6-14 years is very high showing a positive trend towards Universal Elementary Education (UEE). However, the real challenge lies not in enrollment of children, but in retaining and mainstreaming the children by adopting attractive and innovative measures.

Table–7
School Age Children and Enrollment in Tamil Nadu, 2003-04

Age Group	*Sex*	*School Age Children (in lakhs)*	*Enrollment*	*% of Enrollment*
6-11	Boys	34.45	34.10	98.98
	Girls	32.15	31.81	98.94
	Total	**66.60**	**65.91**	**98.96**
11-14	Boys	19.18	18.71	97.55
	Girls	18.98	17.30	91.15
	Total	**38.16**	**36.01**	**94.37**
14-16	Boys	12.95	9.20	71.04
	Girls	11.98	8.40	70.12
	Total	**24.93**	**17.60**	**70.60**

Source: http://www.tn.gov.in/schooleducation/statistics/table2-event.htm

According to a non-governmental organization, Oxfam, today up to '150 million children start primary school but drop out before they have completed four years of education, the vast majority before they have acquired basic literacy skills'.[48] The trend of dropping out of schools is often more rampant in government schools where almost all the children come from a very poor background who think education does not offer any return. Moreover, the school system of today, especially those for the poor children, fails to develop the skills of children. Sengupta is of the view that the government schools create large and impersonal school spaces with limited meaningful interactions between students and teachers.[49] The interaction between the children and teachers should be strengthened. Dealing with the needs of the children who drop out from school requires special concern as it is necessary to understand the problem of children. In Tamil Nadu, it was observed that the instructors of the NGO-run schools go for a field visit to identify the target children and they are put in transit school or a bridge course under the SSA.[50] Parents of such children are contacted and given counseling for their family problems. Children are retained in school by play way method[51] followed in the transit school and they are exposed to different areas like music, TV, computer, sports, arts, painting, etc. Finally after keeping them in the bridge course for a short period of time they are put in regular schools. In order to bring back out-of-school children to the mainstream, the public schools in Tamil Nadu have formulated various initiatives like bridge course, back-to-school scheme, and residential camp to enroll and mainstream the children into schools. Door to door canvass is done and enrollment campaign is also conducted. In order to cater to the educational needs of all the children, as a step forward to realize the goal of EFA, the government works in partnership with several NGOs so as to meet the target group which is excluded from education.

Facilities in Schools

The schooling facilities form a major component for evaluating the effectiveness of schools as the school environment forms the basis for increasing the enrollment and also for minimizing the dropouts. If this aspect is not given due consideration then no purposive educational progress could be achieved. Both the physical and academic facilities should be taken into consideration and the availability of well equipped study environment is a necessary prerequisite.

According to a PROBE survey in 1999 conducted in five selected states of India, 63 per cent of the schools had leaking roofs, 52 per cent had no playground, 58 per cent had no drinking water, 89 per cent had no functioning toilet, and 27 per cent had no blackboards. Only 2 per cent had all the facilities while 8 per cent had none at all.[52] This is the state of affairs of the government schools all over the country. However, with the commencement of the programme SSA in 2000, there has been a remarkable change in the infrastructure of the government schools. If not all, many schools have started functioning under a well equipped building which earlier had to function under a small shed, thatched roof or under a tree. In the study area in Chennai, observation was made on the infrastructure and other facilities available in the government schools as well as NGO-run schools which are depicted in Table 8.

Table-8
Observation Schedule for Infrastructure in Schools

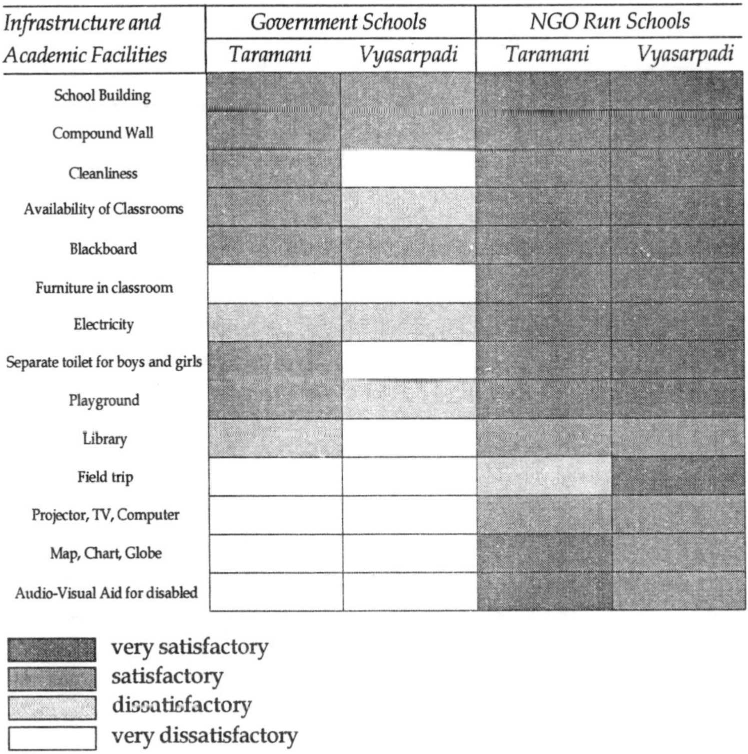

A lump sum amount is allocated for the construction of school buildings so that all the government schools get a well equipped infrastructure. Electricity facility is available but it works occasionally. Both the government schools in the field area did not have either desk or chairs for the students. Drinking water is available and there are common toilets for both boys and girls and it is poorly maintained and at times there is water crisis. Toilet facility is there and there is a compound wall also for the schools. But the tragedy is that there is no staff to maintain it. The toilets are to be maintained by the teachers themselves. There is no security guard to take care of the schools at night time and common people in the locality are using the school premises to dry their clothes.[53]

From the table it is clear that in spite of the efforts taken by the government, the government schools still lag behind even in the provision of basic amenities. In one of the government school though electricity facility is available it is not found to be in working condition or even if power supply is available it is only for two hours in a day as stated by the school teachers. While the NGO-run schools are providing purified and filtered drinking water to the children the government schools do not have pure drinking water and most of the time the drinking water is very dirty. In contrast to the government schools the NGO schools had a well constructed school building with sufficient space and rooms. Safe drinking water with water purifiers and proper toilet facilities for both boys and girls are also available. Children are also provided with large play areas. Dedicated clinics, doctor and nurses are also available in the campus for any medical assistance. The classrooms are well furnished with proper electricity facility. Such comparison has been made with the infrastructure of the NGO schools so as to find out whether availability of proper facilities makes any impact on the learning outcome of children and their motivation to attend school. Children in the NGO-run schools showed better performance and seemed highly motivated than those in the government schools, even though children in both the schools are from the same socio-economic background. This shows that a well functioning and attractive school with basic facilities and infrastructure makes a major difference in the lives of the poor children. This is of particular importance in government schools that cater to the majority of poor children in rural and urban areas.[54]

Awareness Among Parents

Parental care is the most important attribute which is very essential for a child for the enrollment and regular schooling. As most of the parents are illiterates and as they live under the poverty line, their critical need is to have atleast one meal per day and education becomes secondary to them. But still there are some parents who in spite of all their sufferings want to educate their children.

Most of the parents do not have awareness about the education system or the importance of education. Measures are taken by the government to spread awareness about the importance of education to the parents. The government reaches the parents through door to door canvass for enrollment drive, but this is done once a year at the time of admissions. However, in Vyasarpadi area of Chennai it was noticed that with the support of NGOs and local community, the government schools organize cultural programmes with specific themes to stimulate the attention of the parents and to spread the awareness about importance of education to them. The parents are attracted by such programmes and try to participate in the school activities. In the initial stage the parents who were disinterested in sending their working children to school, later became very happy to see the improvement in their children. However, every school, NGO or local community does not come forward to stimulate the attention of parents. The enrollment drive and awareness activity seems to be active only at the beginning of the academic year, after which the follow up programmes in reaching the target group is absent.

Mid Day Meal

The Mid Day Meal Scheme has been in operation in Tamil Nadu since 1982 which is the largest school feeding programme in the country. The main objective of the scheme is to provide adequate nutrition to the economically underprivileged children to develop their mental and physical ability and to increase the enrollments in schools and to reduce the dropouts.[55] But there are allegations of corruption, bureaucratic hurdles and mismanagement of funds which are said to be major obstacles and prevents the benefits of the scheme from reaching the needy children.[56] And also, the quality of the food supplied is sometimes so bad that it neither lures the poor children nor does it provide nutritional support to them. Most often these children suffer from temporary hunger, which can affect the child's ability to pay attention, and so has detrimental effects on learning.[57] But in spite of all such flaws this scheme seems to be the major scheme that covers large number of beneficiaries and most of the poor children take their meals in school only. Some of the parents when enquired in the field say that though the food is of poor quality, their children take lunch only from the noon meal centre as they cannot afford three meals a day. In each noon meal centre there is an organizer, who coordinates proper management of the scheme in their respective schools and every teacher takes turn to supervise whether the food is properly cooked or not. Proper care has to be taken for monitoring the distribution of rice in the scheme so that measures taken by the government for the poor reaches them.

Distribution of Uniforms

Distribution of free uniforms to the children also forms important part of the initiative taken by the government to reach the excluded children. A shirt and a half-pant for boys and a blouse and a skirt for girls are freely distributed in the schools in the beginning of every academic year. However, survey in the field and discussions with parents and children revealed that only one set is distributed at the beginning of the year and the uniform distributed is of poor quality which lasts not even for a month. After this, it becomes an extra burden for parents from low economic status to stitch new uniforms for their children and it is beyond their means.

Though the government takes a lot of effort to improve primary education, it is not up to the mark. Since independence, the goals are determined by the government for every ten years but the targets shift every time there is change of authority and it hardly keeps its promises. The 1999 PROBE report points to the existence of 'multi tracks' — different types of schooling for different sections. The poor and the disadvantaged go to public schools; the middle-class and those in the lower socio-economic ladder to private schools that are either aided, unaided, recognized or unrecognized; the rich to the high fee-charging private schools; the elite to schools offering international certifications; and some to informal or non-formal schools. This is a response not merely to the differentiated market demand, but to government policy. Evidence from the field also shows similar type of arrangement in which almost all the children studying in the government schools or NGO-run schools are living below poverty line and they are put in different types of school based on the income level of the family. In a focused group discussion in Taramani area of Chennai, for instance, a child of 8 years old stated that

> My mother is a maid servant working in a high-class house. Even I assist my mother in her work before school hours. In that house an *akka*[58] is studying class IV in a big school. She goes to school by car and I like the uniform that she wears. I asked my mother to put me in that school. But she scolded me.[59]

This clearly brings out the hierarchy of schools existing in the state and as put forward by Jalal such school system creates a new 'caste of educators' creating hierarchy of education within educational system.[60] Thus, now not only children but also schools are socio-economically differentiated.

Conclusion

Educational opportunities available in our country are biased and are unequal for the rich and poor. Students from low income families are in great need of proper nutrition or balanced diet, schooling and community support and skills.[61] The public school system has ignored these special needs of students from low income families. Though measures are taken by the government, it cannot be regarded as inclusive measures as still more number of children from poor families are beyond the reach. Mere measures are not sufficient if they are not effectively implemented.

Education is indeed a fundamental right to every child and it should not be denied to any child just because of the lack of opportunities or the lack of resources to avail the services due to the condition of extreme poverty of the child.

As discussed earlier still there are millions of people in our country who suffer from extreme poverty and every day survival is a threat to them in spite of the steps taken by the government to eradicate poverty. The people who have got the capabilities in economic terms are able to get their children educated with their economic well being. Other set of people who are deprived of their capabilities though they realize the importance of education and are economically sound, are not aware of the opportunities and means available for educating their children. Apart from this, there are one more set of people who are economically weak and do not realize the value of education and hence for generations their children are neglected and continue to live in poverty.[62]

Capabilities of the people need to be improved so that they are able to make their choice from the available opportunities. For improving the capabilities of people rights of the people need to be realized. Once the rights of the people are recognized, steps will be taken by the institutions in governance to empower the people based on such rights. In a world where poverty and human rights are much debated, the human rights-based approach combined with capability approach that helps in human development is regarded as the vital factor to elevate the people living in extreme poverty.

A zone or council of education can be set up for every district and the members for the zone or council should be from diverse sections like NGOs, government officials, teachers, parents of children, representation from the ward, representation from slums, private players and media and once in every month they can have a review meeting of the steps taken in providing education to all sections of the society. By doing so, the question of inequalities and exclusion in basic education can be addressed.

It is necessary to point out the role of teachers in schools, who are burdened with non-teaching tasks like the census work, administrative work, literacy campaign, vote counting and so on. All such tasks finally bring a passive response from the teachers in meeting the educational needs of children. Hence extra personnel should be recruited in schools to perform various tasks so that teachers in government schools are free from other tasks and can give their utmost attention to the needs of the poor children.

Provision of mid day meal to children should be regulated and monitoring mechanism should be strengthened so as to prevent unscrupulous activities. Measures should be taken to provide breakfast to the poor children. Mostly children in the government schools come to school empty stomach in the morning which prevents them from learning as they don't have energy. The children needs to have some energy to sit in the class and learn the lessons taught. If breakfast is provided in the morning, it would enhance the ability of children at schools who can perform in a better way.

When education is imparted to children in schools, apart from academics they should be trained in other areas also. As M.K.

Gandhi said knowledge undoubtedly adds grace to life, but it is in no way indispensable for man's moral, physical and material growth.[63] The children should be encouraged in extra curricular activities. Children should be given vocational training in schools so that they are prepared to some extent to face the challenges of the world.

There is a need for a broad understanding of the problems of poverty and exclusion, so that proper measures can be formulated. Every such measure taken by the government should take into account the developmental needs of poor children. Each such measure should be aimed at creating an egalitarian society and should concentrate on preparing every child in terms of vocational skills so that it expands the opportunities of every child.

In an era of Information and Communication Technology (ICT), almost all the government schools and teachers are still unaware of the use of ICT. Knowledge of ICT should be imparted to the teachers, so that it reaches children through them. Each and every government school should have a website on its own and all the activities and state of affairs of the school should be updated on the website. By doing so, the condition of every school will be available to everybody, which might serve as a means for getting help and assistance for poor students.

With the emergence of new institutions in the sector of education, the scenario of education has changed. Both the capability aspect and human rights are much debated and has been recognized in the international arena in recent years. If the government works in collaboration with the other institutions like civil society, community groups and rural and urban local bodies, then the goal towards attainment of Universalization of Elementary Education (UEE) by 2015 is not a distant dream. Thus a combined and a coordinated effort can help the poor children in actualizing their capabilities and rights which will thereby provide them the voice to debate in the developmental discourse in their later phase of life. Synergy among various institutions can contribute to holistic development free from poverty and exclusion. Thus, what is needed is the commitment on all fronts to arrive at a strategy to work in collaboration towards a common goal for making our country a better place to live in with high level of human development.

ANNEXURE
District-wise Performance on Literacy Rate in Tamil Nadu for the Year 2001

District Name	*Literacy Rate*			*Deviation from State Average*		
	Person	*Male*	*Female*	*Person*	*Male*	*Female*
STATE Average	**73.47**	**82.33**	**64.55**	**0.00**	**0.00**	**0.00**
1. Kanniyakumari	88.11	90.88	85.38	14.64	8.55	20.83
2. Thoothukudi	81.96	88.66	75.64	8.49	6.33	11.09
3. Chennai	80.14	84.71	75.32	6.67	2.38	10.77
4. The Nilgiris	81.44	89.63	73.39	7.97	7.30	8.84
5. Tiruchirapalli	79.16	87.16	71.19	5.69	4.83	6.64
6. Kancheepuram	77.61	84.82	70.21	4.14	2.49	5.66
7. Madurai	78.65	87.24	69.93	5.18	4.91	5.38
8. Coimbatore	76.95	83.82	69.80	3.48	1.49	5.25
9. Tirunelveli	76.97	85.89	68.50	3.50	3.56	3.95
10. Thiruvarur	76.90	85.59	68.36	3.43	3.26	3.81
11. Nagapattinam	76.89	85.61	68.35	3.42	3.28	3.80
12. Thiruvallur	76.54	84.62	68.23	3.07	2.29	3.68
13. Thanjavur	76.07	85.45	66.95	2.60	3.12	2.40
14. Virudhunagar	74.23	84.56	64.09	0.76	2.23	-0.46
15 Ramanathapuram	73.05	82.96	63.55	-0.42	0.63	-1.00
16. Vellore	73.07	82.67	63.53	-0.40	0.34	-1.02
17. Sivagangai	72.66	83.70	62.12	-0.81	1.37	-2.43
18. Theni	72.01	82.50	61.41	-1.46	0.17	-3.14
19. Pudukkottai	71.96	83.22	60.94	-1.51	0.89	-3.61
20. Cuddalore	71.85	82.76	60.85	-1.62	0.43	-3.70
21. Dindigul	69.83	80.29	59.30	-3.64	-2.04	-5.25
22. Karur	68.74	80.42	57.30	-4.73	-1.91	-7.25
23. Nammakkal	67.66	78.02	57.04	-5.81	-4.31	-7.51
24. Tiruvannamalai	68.22	80.14	56.31	-5.25	-2.19	-8.24

Contd...

District Name	Literacy Rate			Deviation from State Average		
	Person	Male	Female	Person	Male	Female
25. Salem	65.72	75.25	55.61	-7.75	-7.08	-8.94
26. Erode	65.51	75.49	55.26	-7.96	-6.84	-9.29
27. Perambalur	65.88	77.68	54.26	-7.59	-4.65	-10.29
28. Villupuram	64.68	76.02	53.16	-8.79	-6.31	-11.39
29. Dharmapuri	59.23	68.82	49.10	-14.24	-13.51	-15.45

Source: http://www.tn.gov.in/schooleducation/statistics/table2-event.htm

* Part of the MPhil dissertation submitted on the topic, *Role of Non Governmental Organisations (NGOs) in Basic Education: A Study of NGOs in Chennai District of Tamil Nadu*, in Centre for the Study of Law and Governance, Jawaharlal Nehru University is revised and used in this paper.

NOTES AND REFERENCES

1. *Human Development Report 2000: Human Rights and Human Development*, (New York: UNDP, United Nations Publication, 2000).
2. David Ludden, 'Review of Poverty: Human Consciousness' and the Amnesia of Development by Rajni Kothari' in *The Journal of Asian Studies*, Vol. 56, No. 3. August 1997, pp. 822-824.
3. Adil M. Khan, *Economic Development, Poverty Alleviation and Governance: The Asian Experience* (USA: Ashgate Publishing Company, 1996).
4. Human Development Report 2000, *op. cit.*
5. Arjun Sengupta, 'Extreme Poverty and Human Rights A Mission Report on the US' in *Economic and Political Weekly*, April 7, 2007, pp. 1298-1307.
6. http://www.care.org/campaigns/childrenpoverty/index. asp?source=170740250000&WT.srch=1, visited on 24th September, 2006.
7. *The State of World's Children: Childhood under Threat* (New York: UNICEF, 2005).
8. *Ibid.*
9. *EFA Global Monitoring Report 2007, Strong Foundations: Early Childhood Care and Education* (France: UNESCO Publishing, 2007).
10. *Ibid.*
11. R. Govinda, *Status of Primary Education of the Urban Poor in India: An Analytical Review*, Report no. 105 (Paris: UNESCO, International Institute of Education Planning, 1995).
12. Ernest E. Neal, 'Review of Compulsory Education in India by K.G. Saiyidain, J.P. Naik and S. Abid Husian' in *Phylon (1940-56)*, Vol 14, No. 2, 1953.

13. *World Development Report 2004: Making Services Work for Poor People,* (New York: *World Bank*/Oxford University Press, 2004).
14. *United Nations Millennium Declaration 2000* (New York, Resolution adopted by General Assembly Summit, September, 2000).
15. UN's Millennium Declaration came up with 8 Millennium Development Goals, the chief being eradication of extreme poverty and providing universal primary education. The other goals are to promote gender equality, reduce child mortality, improve maternal health, combat HIV/AIDS, malaria and other diseases, ensure environmental sustainability and to develop a global partnership for development.
16. The vital importance of basic education was much felt and the World Education Forum adopted the Education for All Framework in 2000 in Dakar, the goal of which is to provide education to all children, that can tap the talents and potential of every individual so that they can improve their lives and transform their societies.
17. Walter McMahon, *Education and Development: Measuring the Social Benefits* (New York: Oxford University Press, 2001).
18. R.K. Mishra, *Poverty and Exclusion: The Indian Experience,* Draft Paper presented in the Conference on Poverty, Inequality and Access to Justice for the Poor in South Asia, New Delhi: Centre or the Study of Law and Governance, JNU, November, 2006.
19. Amartya Sen and Jean Dreze, *India: Development and Change* (New Delhi: Oxford University Press, 2002).
20. Disha Nawani, *Role and Contribution of NGOs to Basic Education,* Year 2000 Assessment: Education For All (New Delhi: National Institute of Educational Planning and Administration, 2000).
21. The World Conference on Education for All was held at Jomtien in 1990, which represents a worldwide consensus on expanded vision of basic education and a renewed commitment to ensure that the basic learning needs of every individual are met effectively in all the countries.
22. Government of India, *India 2008: A Reference Annual* (New Delhi: Ministry of Information and Broadcasting, 2008).
23. Amartya Sen and Jean Dreze, *op. cit.*
24. *Final Report of World Education Forum in Dakar, Senegal,* France: UNESCO, 26-28 April 2000.
25. John M. Alexander and Koen Decancq, 'Measuring human development' in *Frontline,* Vol. 22 (04), February 12-25, 2005.
26. *Ibid.*
27. David Ludden, 'Development Regimes in South Asia History and the Governance Conundrum' in *Economic and Political Weekly,* September 10, 2005, pp. 4042-4051.
28. Adil Khan, *op. cit.*
29. S.N. Pawar *et al., NGOs and Development: The Indian Scenario* (New Delhi: Rawat Publications, 2004).

30. Amartya Sen and Jean Dreze, *op. cit.*
31. Santosh Mehrotra, 'Human Capital or Human Development? Search for a Knowledge Paradigm for Education and Development' in *Economic and Political Weekly*, January 22, 2005, pp. 300-306.
32. Amartya Sen, *Development as Freedom*, New York: Random House, 1999.
33. Adil Khan, *op. cit.*
34. C. Raj Kumar, 'Poverty, Human Rights and Development', *The Hindu*, New Delhi, February 22, 2007.
35. Goran Hyden, and Julius Court, *Governance and Development: Trying to Sort out the Basics*, Draft Paper, presented at the Conference on 'Poverty, Inequality and Access to Justice for the Poor in South Asia', New Delhi: Centre for the Study of Law and Governance, JNU, November 2006.
36. *Ibid.* This paper has elaborated in detail the different phases of development.
37. *Ibid.*
38. Baidyanath Saraswati, ed., *The Cultural Dimension of Education* (New Delhi, IGNCA & D.K. Printworld Pvt. Ltd., 1998).
39. Feroz Ahmed and Suresh Garg, *Forty Years of Kothari Commission: Reforms and Reflections* (New Delhi. Viva Books Private Ltd., 2000).
40. Goran Hyden and Julius Court, *op. cit.*
41. *Ibid.*
42. K. Sudha Rao, *Educational Policies in India: Analysis and Review of Promises and Performance* (New Delhi: NIEPA, 2002).
43. *Tamil Nadu Human Development Report 2002*, Government of Tamil Nadu, available at http://www.tn.gov.in/schooleducation/statistics/table2-event.htm accessed on 4th January, 2007.
44. *Ibid.*
45. Education to Fight Exclusion: The UNESCO Special Project for the Enhancement of Learning and Training Opportunities for the Youth, UNESCO Education Sector, 1999.
46. Jyotsna Jha and Dhir Jhingran, *Elementary Education for the Poorest and Other Deprived Groups: The Real Challenge of Univerzalisation* (New Delhi: Manohar Publishers, 2005).
47. Through direct observation and interview with the focused groups in the field.
48. Education to Fight Exclusion, *op .cit.*
49. Arjun Sengupta, *op. cit.*
50. It was observed by the researcher when the researcher accompanied the NGO instructor when she went for her field visit.
51. Play way method is used by the NGOs under which children are taught by way of games. Play way Method was recently introduced by the

Government of Tamil Nadu, under Activity Based Learning, to facilitate the learning of children. For instance, in order to familiarize rhymes, numbers and vocabulary to children such learning aids are displayed by way of games in front of children, who learn from it when they play with it.

52. Anuradha De, Jean Dreze *et al.*, *Public Report on Basic Education in India* (New Delhi: Oxford University Press, 1999).
53. Through focused group discussion with the teachers in the field.
54. Vimala Ramachandran, Kameshwari Jandhyala and Aarti Saihjee, 'Through the Life Cycle of Children: Factors that Facilitate/Impede Successful Primary School Completion', *Economic and Political Weekly*, November 22, 2003, pp. 4994-5002.
55. Padmini Swaminathan *et al.*, 'Tamil Nadu's Mid Day Meal Scheme: Where Assumed Benefits Score over Hard Data' in *Economic and Political Weekly*, October 30, 2004.
56. Sunita Chugh, *Why Children Drop Out? Case Study of a Metropolitan Slum* (New Delhi: Bookwell, 2004).
57. M.D. Usha Devi, 'Poverty Database in Education: Strategies for Monitoring Poverty Reduction', *Economic and Political Weekly*, July 21, 2001, pp. 2779-2283.
58. *Akka* is a Tamil word which means elder sister.
59. Focused Group Discussion, Kavitha, February, 2007.
60. Jennifer Jalal, 'Exploring the Dynamics of 'Choice', 'Voice' and 'Responsiveness' in Education Services in Delhi', Draft Paper presented in the Indo-European Research Programme on *Urban Actors, Policies and Governance in four Indian Metropolitan Cities,* New Delhi: Organized by Centre de Sciences Humaines de and India International Centre, 23-24 January 2007.
61. Arjun Sengupta, *op. cit.*
62. Abdul Kalam, 'For Dignity of Human Life' in *Yojana*, vol. 49, September 2005.
63. M.K. Gandhi, *India of My Dreams*, (Ahmedabad: Navajivan Publishing House, 1947).

PART–IV
FACING THE CHALLENGES

16

Indian Judiciary and Problems of the Poor: Where do the Marginalized Find Place?

PALLAVI BAHAR

The presence of law and legal institutions is a necessary condition for the protection of the rights of rich and poor alike. It is, however, not a sufficient condition to guarantee equal justice to all sections of the society. The accessibility of these arrangements to citizens constitutes real justice[1] enabling even the weaker sections of the society to preserve their freedom and liberty. However, the requirements of freedom and justice have been so demanding and complicated, and the procedures of courts so slow and expensive, that only people with adequate means and resources at their disposal can reach them to take advantage of these arrangements. As a result, the poor and weaker classes get excluded from the scope of securing basic rights for themselves despite the presence of a judiciary which claims to be the paramount superstructure guaranteeing the rights and liberties of all, especially the weak and deprived.

It is a well-evident fact that the history of human society, from feudal set up to capitalist mode, has been marked by various forms of inequalities and atrocities over the poor and the weak and in favour of the rich and the resourceful. Imperialism and colonialism gave way to new forms of inequalities and immense socio-economic disparities among nations and people within nations emerged.[2] Though the concerns for the rights of the man were time and again raised[3] and fought for through various reform movements,[4] however, it was with the emergence of the United Nations that the protection of individuals and their rights became a matter of concern for the legal machinery. Until the emergence of the UNO, the problems of the poor and disadvantaged were overlooked as the state concentrated solely on economic development. Radical change towards accommodation of the needs of the deprived was expected to come with the formulation of the UN Charter which established 'universal respect for, and observance of human rights and fundamental freedoms for all without distinction as to race, sex, language or religion'.[5] However, the Charter did not define the contents of Human Rights. The task was accomplished through the UN Universal Declaration of Human Rights (UNDHR),[6] 10th December, 1948, wherein the fundamentals of human rights and freedoms were institutionalized and the judiciary became a crucial instrument in this direction.[7] Earlier, the functions of the courts were limited to law making, imparting decisions and settling disputes. But with the UNDHR, the judiciary became more sensitive to the issues of rights.

The Indian Constitution embraced the goals of UNDHR, aiming to secure rights, liberty, equality and social justice for its citizens. It included freedom from arbitrary arrest, fair criminal trial, equal pay for equal work, provisions for securing adequate livelihood, education, etc. The Indian Constitution laid certain provisions for the protection of and guarantee of rights to the citizens. The Preamble of the Indian Constitution set the aim to secure for all its citizens justice, social, economic and political; liberty of thought, expression, belief, faith and worship; equality of status and of opportunity; and to promote among them all fraternity assuring dignity of the individual and unity of the nation. The Constitution enlisted various articles such as Article 14, 22, 32, etc. which sought to secure legal equality and enhance equal access to judicial institutions. These articles were included to ensure a just and egalitarian social order. The Constitution also provided for distributive and corrective justice.[8] Under the Constitution, it became the duty of the Supreme Court to enforce the Fundamental Rights of the citizens and the provisions of the Constitution. The Indian judiciary was designed to serve as the most potent force to check the anarchic tendencies of the governing authority within the limits prescribed by the Constitution of India and also assigned the task to defend the rights and liberties of the citizens of the country. It was marked by certain values such as free and fair trials, speedy justice, impartiality, moral uprightness of the decision[9] and so on.

Even though, the Indian judiciary attempted to establish an egalitarian legal system where all were equal in the eyes of law, the limitations of the judicial system, which was inherited from the British, came to the surface within a short period of time. The British India legal system had always remained averse to the claims of the weak and the deprived. Their court system was characterized by lengthy judicial procedures and excessive formalism in terms of language, etiquettes and outfits which made it imperative to hire a lawyer. This made the judicial system complicated and expensive. These features distanced the poor from the legal machinery and the possibility of attainment of justice was occluded. Also individual rights were never a concern for the British courts. The only right to be protected was the right to property[10] and the fight for justice was largely covered by the Indian reform movements, such as those against Sati, and for the education for girls, removal of untouchability, etc. Only those cases involving higher officials were dealt with in the British courts.

However, attempts were made to counter the defects of the inherited legal system. Though the judicial structure continued to follow the British pattern of judiciary, the Constitution did try to make justice readily available for the citizens. Whereas the scope of the judicial functioning was initially limited to interpreting laws of the Constitution and restoring justice to the contesting parties and the importance of the judicial system relegated to the background as the executive assumed major power, revolutionary changes emerged during the post-emergency phase. It saw the judiciary in its most active forms which performed more promising functions with regard to protecting and safeguarding the rights of the individuals for whom justice seemed to be a distant dream. Various laws were amended and reframed to cater the needs of the victims of violation of human rights. On the civil rights front, the judicial system adopted a more benevolent approach. While propagating the doctrine of 'equal justice to all', which forms the base of the entire edifice of the legal machinery, it took a step further in establishing 'equal access to justice'.

Indian Legal System and the Systematic Marginalization of the Poor

Despite the concerns of the national political leadership for the poor, the administration of justice has tended to neglect the needs of poor citizens[11] and its main beneficiaries have been persons with money, political power and bureaucratic influence, and lately, connections with musclemen. This has nullified the aim of Article 14[12] of the Indian Constitution as the legal system has unintentionally turned in favour of the affluent sections and hampered the notion of legal equality. Even Article 22[13] was restricted in terms of providing equal access to justice as even it did not guarantee any right to legal assistance from the state. Similarly, Article 32, which confers a right to move the court, is limited as only those who can afford expensive justice can reach the courts, thus making justice unaffordable for the poor.

The biggest paradox lies in the fact that the judiciary, which is the protector of the people against arbitrary state action, is itself a state organ. When the court is an umpire between two parties, one of which is the state, its neutrality is vulnerable to erosion. World Bank Report of 1997 mentions that the courts were created to protect people from 'arbitrary government actions – ranging from unpredictable, ad hoc regulations and taxes to outright corruption,' and of the influential leading to further marginalization and victimization of the poor. They were needed for protection from unchecked political and administrative action which could lead to denial of basic services such as rehabilitation, unhygienic surroundings as in slums, problems of water and electricity, etc. The logic of courts was to have a neutral third party for resolving disputes and imparting impartial and just judgments. But the court does not remain a neutral party when one of the contending parties is the state itself. This limitation was highlighted in cases such as Narmada Bachao Andolan where the concerns of the poor have been neglected and unattended by government, and there is little evidence that restraints are being placed on arbitrary state action. The poor are most likely to lose their property or land arbitrarily seized or confiscated by the government for its developmental purposes and projects, e.g., the Land Acquisition Act which granted to the state the power to expropriate property or land from farmers for housing by providing only minimal compensation. The squatters and other poor people living in conditions of illegality are often the consequence of such government acts.[14]

The conditions for obtaining justice have been so demanding that only socio-economic elite could gain access to them. Thus, the mere existence of law and legal institutions is not a sufficient condition for the preservation of freedom and liberty, and for guaranteeing equal protection to all sections of the society.

The formal legal system goes by certain assumptions like treating all persons subject to law as equals and legal system working as a neutral third party. It assumes that the consumers of law are conscious about their rights and interests and are capable of seeking appropriate remedies offered by the legal system. Such a system fails to recognize the legal incompetence of the 'handicapped population'.[15]

The present day world presents a very dismal picture where cases between two parties, be it laborer versus master or tenant versus landlord, are fought but on unequal terms. The affected party is generally weaker than the claimant and has lesser resources at its disposal. Similar is the condition in criminal cases where the victim does not even get an opportunity to appropriate justice and enforce his constitutional rights. The fact is apparent in the case of undertrials, women, poor, children, etc.[16]

Thus, one of the main causes for the failure of the legal system in serving the cause of the backward and economically weaker sections is the limited accessibility to institutions of justice for the disabled population who are not efficient enough to use the judicial system to their advantage. The deprived sections continue to suffer at the hands of the law enforcement agencies, the judicial system remained expensive and time consuming, and the affluent sections continue to exploit the legal system to their advantage, thus preventing the poor and illiterate masses from equal access to justice.

In a country, where nearly 80 per cent of the population lives in villages and where 70 per cent of the population is illiterate, treating rich and poor alike is not a viable option towards securing equal justice for both. Such an insensitive and limited approach towards the needs of the disadvantaged further deteriorates their condition, hence distancing them from the justice system. Let us examine some of the major impediments in the path of attaining fair and equal justice by the marginalized section of the society.

There is the entire section of refugees, urban poor migrants, vegetable sellers, etc who live under severe conditions of illegality due to no available alternative. These communities, who live under constant threat of harassment or arrest by police, fear getting noticed and so avoid getting voluntarily entangled with the legal machinery to enforce their basic human rights. Moreover, due to the increased incidents of victory of big landowners and wealthy section of the society owing to the resources available with them, the poor section generally assumes that law is a tool which can be used efficiently only by the affluent category.

There are certain other barriers such as official (in case of India, English) and legal language (very formal and not easily comprehensible) which require great amount of clarity in the usage of the terms. Due to excessive formalism in the language and procedure, the need of a legal professional becomes inevitable which acts as an additional burden due to the high fees charged by them. These factors act as major stumbling blocks in poor people's access to justice and thus make them reluctant in approaching the legal system altogether.

Thus, the helplessness of the deprived sections is further reinforced by the way legal procedures are structured and their condition further degenerates in the process of demanding their basic minimum rights as humans.

Insensitivities of the Legal Practices towards the Poor

1. ***Lack of Awareness Regarding Legal Claims***

The poor are generally unaware whether the problems they are facing could be challenged. This happens mainly due to the dearth of legal empowerment programmes for the poor, who are, in reality, in most urgent need of such schemes. Often, the slum dwellers, squatters and also the migrant labourers are unaware of the provisions enlisted for them in various acts such as Inter state Migrant Worker Act, 1979, Contract Labour Act, 1970, and the Minimum Wages Act, 1948. These Acts included provisions for drinking water, toilet facilities, blankets in winters, proper accommodation, crèches, etc. to the workers by the contractors.[17] While the minimum wages range from Rs. 125 to Rs. 132 per day, the contract laborers are given only Rs. 17 to Rs. 100 per day by their contractors.[18] They are incompetent in constructing their legal claims. Moreover, they are under fear of losing their jobs if they raise their voices against these contractors. Thus, the ignorance about identifying their problem, in the first instance, and thereafter questioning it on legal terms, is the starting point of the denial of social justice. Moreover, there are very limited attempts on the part of the government in the direction of implementing such schemes as setting up of law clinics and appointing legal luminaries to impart legal education to poor people.

2. Police Misconduct

Once entered in and involved with the machinery of justice, the poor are faced with problems of a more serious kind. The poor are most likely to suffer harassment and arbitrary treatment by the government officials as they have no money to bribe or influence the system. As such, the poor, who are often victimized by the police, are reluctant to approach it. They see all outside the police station—various atrocities and injuries inflicted upon the poor by the government officials through torture, arbitrary seizure of their land and confiscation of their goods, etc. Moreover, in most places, it is the poor who are pressurized to pay for basic services and necessities for livelihood, such as access to water, healthcare facilities, education, electricity, etc., despite fact that it is clearly beyond their capacity to pay for these. Moreover, these are still not adequately provided to them.[19] Again nothing is done to protect the sufferers of massive developmental projects, e.g. the Piparwar Case.[20] These examples display how the violation of social justice and human rights goes unnoticed and unchecked by the entire legal system. Despite all the torture and fear, if they do approach the police to file their complaint, their case is treated with little attention and more often than not they are put to harassment and humiliation by the police officials. Related to this is the problem of living in conditions of illegality. Due to Acts such as Land Acquisition Act, 1894 (amended in 1984), the lands of small farmers and rural poor have been expropriated by the state without providing any compensation or alternative arrangement to them. When the government fails to provide living space to the poor and immigrants they set up illegal residences or 'Jhuggis'.[21] Thus, they are reluctant in raising their voice for the protection of their rights as they are likely to get defeated for being violators of law themselves. This also generates fear among the poor that raising voice to claim their rights would debar them from the welfare programmes on which their survival is based.

The position of the marginalized is more vulnerable to getting subjected to police misconduct. Institutionalized tolerance of such deviant behaviour of officers aggravates the problem. In such a circumstance, police behave as tools of oppression rather than protectors of rights of citizens. Most of the poor people fear approaching the police due to past experiences of torture and a fear of further harassment and humiliation. Factors which restrict the poor from reaching out to the enforcement agencies include brutality, harassment, improper investigation, corruption, bribery and ill treatment, etc. Even the women undergo physical violence by male police officers.[22] Thus, for the poor, this pattern of approaching the machinery of justice through police and the complicated process of filing FIRs discourages the use of government services. Approaching the law enforcement agency for protection is the first step from where the citizens enter the doors of the judicial system. However, one can observe that it also forms the first step from which the distance between the poor and the system of justice is increased. The *biased treatment*, by the police, of the rich and the poor, is quite evidently tilted favorably towards the rich.

3. *Financial Obstacles*

'Everybody is equal in the eyes of the law but not in the courts of law.'[23] The Court Fees Act, 1870[24] was designed to restrict the use of judicial benefits by the poor and to discourage litigation, in general. Our post-independence judicial system chose to continue the practice and even today the court fees has to be paid by the party concerned who seeks to get assistance from the judicial departments and for the redress of its grievances. The court fee starts with Rs. 250. Though it says that no court fee is payable in matters filed by Supreme Court Legal Aid Committee, it was inferred from the survey that almost all the indigent population who are unaware of the Legal Aid Provision itself, end up paying the court fee.[25]

On similar lines was the Legal Practitioners Act, 1846, which gave the lawyers the freedom to charge any fees for the professional services rendered by them, regardless of the nature of the client, be it rich or poor. Even the Advocates Act, 1961 (of independent India) concentrated only on professional quality and discipline, totally ignoring this crucial aspect of making available to all, the opportunity of obtaining justice. With such freedoms, lawyers are often found furthering only their own social status and market advantage. Moreover in legal systems, such as that of India, private citizens are not even allowed to appear in court to present their case, which makes the need for lawyers unavoidable.[26] Lawyers exploit the helplessness of the people and charge exorbitant amount from clients to amass wealth. As quoted by Carlin in his study of the ethics of New York City bar of 1966, 'The best trained, most technically skilled, and ethically most responsible lawyers are reserves to the upper reaches of business and society. This leaves the least competent, least well-trained, and least ethical lawyers to the smaller business concerns and lower-income individuals. As a result, the most helpless clients who most need protection are less likely to get it.'[27] These lawyers, however, are deemed necessary as they are the only guides available for any legal remedy.

Not only this, even the Code of Criminal Procedure shows its inherent anti-poor bias by providing that after depositing the security amount, the accused can be released on bail. This establishes inequality as the price of the bond is usually beyond the capacity of the poor.[28] Thus, one can see that there is an anti-poor bias not just in legal structure but in the law itself. Due to such limitations the legal machinery remains underused by that section of the society which is in most need of it.

4. ***Excessive Formalism***

The use of official (in the case of India, English) and legal (very formal and not easily comprehensible) language, which requires great amount of clarity, has made the employing of lawyers inevitable for parties involved. Lawyers tend to exploit the situation charging high fees from their clients. Along with the use of specialist language and such formal practices, the elitism of the justice system is also displayed by the fact that courts are located in urban areas which further isolates the poor who are in any case hesitant to approach the judiciary. Distance from the court has proved to be a crucial factor causing discomfort in approaching the legal system.[29] The use of foreign language, formal procedures and practices, prescribed dress code, etc. create a feeling of cultural alienation among the poor as they are not able to identify with the system. The Bar Council Rules under the Advocates Act, 1961, lay that 'An advocate shall appear in court at all times only in the prescribed dress code and his appearance shall always be presentable.' Such practices create an aura which intimidates ordinary people. The poor people lack the confidence to face such huge and formal machinery. There needs to be an emphasis on increasing the efficiency of the lawyers and clients in presenting their case and not on how they should appear.

5. ***Delays***

The research work of Maja B. Micevska and Arnab K. Hazra[30] shows that about 20 million cases are pending in lower courts and another

3.2 million in High courts. Such huge pendency and congestion of cases is the outcome of infinite delays in the trial process due to financial constraints for establishing more legal structures, huge unfilled vacancies of judges, delay tactics used by lawyers and litigants on irrational grounds, etc.[31] Moreover, the number of holidays per year are another cause for huge pendency of cases.[32] The real sufferers of delays are obviously not the affluent and resourceful but the poor for whom each day spent in court affects adversely their daily livelihood and wages. For the poor person, every hour that he spends in the court matters as it means time away from his income generating activity and a cut in his income. 'Their fundamental components of livelihood are at stake.' For property and business cases, unending court hearings and delays in judgments are a matter of profit and loss. However, for the poor it is a matter of their means of survival.[33] It is most commonly observed that it is the poor and ignorant who linger within the boundaries of jail for several years for petty crimes while the influential move about freely owing to sufficient means to get bail.[34] The influential, rich and empowered sections of society are in a better position to claim their rights, even if this involves time spent in visiting courts and hearings.

The poor are worst affected by such a system which works 'haltingly, partially and occasionally.'[35] Thus, one can realize that in order to ensure equality of justice, it is not only sufficient that a law treats rich and poor equally, but is also necessary that the poor must be in a position to get their rights enforced.

Legal Aid and Assistance Reforms in India

In a society with embedded socio-economic inequalities, the role of an impartial, fair, supportive and proactive judiciary becomes inevitable. Social justice in such societies can be achieved only through impartial substantive law. The attainment of true justice can be realized only by making appropriate and additional mechanisms to assist the deprived in reaching the judicial superstructures in the first instance. As per the norm, true justice implies a system in which rich and the poor are able to access justice equally. Access to justice is in a very limited sense understood as access to justice in courts of law. However, it involves an improvement in the usage of every legal mechanism which would enable citizens to protect their rights and attain appropriate legal justice.

Recognizing the limitations of the formal legal system, the courts have begun to 'democratize legal remedies' to counter injustice and the role of the state extended to providing legal assistance to the indigent persons towards increasing accessibility to justice.[36] It has generated as a systemic necessity and sought to establish socio-economic legal justice by reducing the impossibilities in the legal system with respect to the poor through the creation of awareness about the legal rights and processes, rendering legal advice, helping the enforcement of court verdicts, etc. This is being brought into practice through the 'Access to Justice' Movement which is based on the twin principles of:

- Ensuring that every person is able to invoke the legal processes for redressal, irrespective of social or economic status or other incapacity.
- Ensuring that every person should receive a just and fair treatment within the legal system.[37]

The reform movement has been classified into three waves by Cappelletti:

- Legal Aid—Legal Aid Movement (1960-80) was focused to increase the availability of formal legal institutions and peoples' access to justice. It sought to increase state's role in making justice accessible to all equally.
- Public Interest Law—It implied justice for groups, that is, legal representation for diffuse interests, especially areas of consumer, environmental protection, etc.
- Alternative Dispute Resolution—It was precisely the 'access-to-justice' approach aimed at removing barriers in the attainment of access to justice, without abandoning the first two reform waves. It went beyond legal representation and towards creating new court structures, use of lay persons or para-professionals (both on Bench and Bar), modification in substantive law, and use of informal and formal dispute resolution mechanisms. Cappelletti and Garth refer to the third wave as the emergence of a fully developed access to justice approach.[38]

The access to justice reforms started in the backdrop of the need to improve the judicial pattern, check delays, develop mechanisms for the speedy disposal of justice, overcome financial constraints, simplify rules and procedures, create awareness among the disadvantaged and assist them in claiming their rights and accessing justice. Recognizing the inadequacies in the implementation of the set goals, the Government of India started exploring ways of providing legal aid to the poor. Thus, Legal Aid becomes an imperative social service which a welfare state owes to its citizens. The chief purpose of the legal aid scheme, therefore, is to enable the oppressed and disadvantaged community to enforce their rights and corner justice against their influential opponents who have all the necessary resources to approach the legal machinery and fight the case.[39]

The groundwork for establishment of legal aid, however, had already been done by various commissions, such as Justice N.H. Bhagwati Committee 1950, 14th Law Commission 1958, Justice P.N. Bhagwati Committee 1971, Justice V.R. Krishna Iyer Committee 1973, etc. The legal aid scheme was also floated in different states, like Madhya Pradesh Legal Aid and Legal Advice Act 1976, Uttar Pradesh Legal Aid to the Poor Scheme 1975, etc. The efforts, however, remained dormant until the 42nd Amendment Act, 1976. Legal aid then came to be recognized as a constitutional imperative arising from Articles 14, 21, 22,[40] 32 and Article 39 (A).[41] Article 39 (A) of the Directive Principles of State Policy states:

> The state shall secure that the operation of the legal system promotes justice on a basis of equal opportunity, and shall in particular, provide free legal aid, by suitable legislation or schemes or in any other way, to ensure that opportunities for securing justice are not denied to any citizen by reason of economic or other disabilities.

As a result, legal aid to the poor acquired the status of a fundamental right.

Various other developments have been in motion to improve the provisions of equal access to justice for all on an equal basis. Crucial in this direction were the judgments in Hoskot,[42] Hussainara Khatoon,[43] and Khatri cases;[44] the enactment of the Legal Services Authority Act, 1987 which works at National (under Justice J.S. Anand since 1998), State, District and Taluk Legal Services levels; provisions of rules for refunding court fees; appointment of 'Legal Aid Counsel' and Free Legal Aid Centres, etc. More recently, in 2005, new forms of legal aid for newer categories defined as in need of the service have come up. These are Crime against Labour Cell, Legal Aid Resource Centre for Workers, Jal Adhikari Abhiyan and Jal Lok Adalats for Farmers.

Conclusion

A legal system is regarded as unjust and biased when, knowingly or unknowingly, it creates socio-economic inequalities between different sections of the society, that is, one which grants protection to one section of society and denies the same to the other. Contrary to that, a just system is one in which there is equal recourse to law available to all sections of the society and where justice is done to rich and poor alike.[45] It requires, as its prerequisite, the existence of predetermined rules of law and where an equal distribution of rights and responsibilities, benefits and burdens takes place among citizens. However, in a society where deep rooted divisions between various classes, castes, races, etc. exist, mere prevalence of laws and legal institutions is not sufficient to secure justice to all. It requires additional measures to enable the deprived to make their voices heard and prevent the resourceful from taking undue advantage of the legal machinery. In cases between two parties, be laborer versus master or tenant versus landlord, the judicial battles are fought on extremely unequal terms. It is with this understanding that the reforms in the direction of guaranteeing equal access to justice to all were initiated and provisions were designed where the poor and the disadvantaged could be brought within the purview of equal attainment of legal and social justice.

However, the current situation reveals contrary facts. The results of the reforms have been far from satisfactory due to various structural and procedural weaknesses such as below average performance of the legal aid lawyers owing to their low salaries and inexperience; the lack of genuine intentions of serving the needs of the poor rather than aiming at lessening the burden of the courts; the inability of the reform measures to sensitize the lawyers towards the needs of the disadvantaged. Speaking at the function, Union Minister of State for Law and Justice K. Venkatapathy said that some of the States were not keen on providing free legal aid to the needy. In fact, certain State Governments had stopped asking funds for legal aid.[46] It is extremely necessary to maintain high standards of professional conduct by the Bar members and take their responsibilities seriously by making provisions for bringing legal services to the doorsteps of the poor through means of legal literacy, etc. Analysis of the reforms reveal that these have been mostly focused on increasing efficiency of the courts and legal system in terms of managing market mechanisms, financial autonomy of the courts, etc.[47]

The access to justice has been functional largely to the benefit of the business and corporations rather than its much proclaimed purpose of access to justice by the poor.[48] The Piparwar case in which a large number of tribes were tortured by the law enforcing machinery due to their refusal to leave their land of residence, the Clean Delhi project which led to forceful evacuation of slums for beautification of Delhi for the Commonwealth Games in 2010 and such other measures have rendered thousands homeless. One of the victimized residents said: 'We had two hours' warning that our homes would be destroyed. That's about all we know about the games. Because we're poor and have no influence, that's all they needed to tell us'.[49] The judiciary has remained a silent observer and at places consented to such violation of rights of the underprivileged. These cases are a sufficient proof of the systematic marginalization of the poor through the insensitive government policies that have received judicial consent and displayed severe unconcern and biases of the judiciary against the weak masses. The judiciary rather than bridging the gap has fuelled the problem as most of its provisions have proved more beneficial to the upper strata of the society consisting of those who are in a better position to afford justice through muscle and money power. The poor continue to be deprived from taking advantage of the judicial system to preserve their rights while those who possess money, connection and muscle power find it easier to access the legal system.

K.G. Balakrishnan, the Chief Justice of India, expressed: 'The poor generally has less voice, less income and less access to services than most of other people. We have to create and shape the public action so that acquisition of human capacity is not driven by circumstances such as birth.'[50] Thus, it is the poor and disadvantaged people who are in desperate need of an approachable and comprehensive legal system. Of course, such a system is the requirement of all, but unfortunately the poor are the ones who are deprived of access to the machinery of justice.

*Earlier version of this paper has been presented at the SAARC International Conference, November 2006.

NOTES AND REFERENCES

1. Christine Parker, *Just Lawyers: Regulation and Access To Justice* (Oxford: OUP, 1999), pp. 46-47.
2. The colonial masters completely drained the wealth and ruined the economies of the subject nations, thus, rendering the condition of the masses deteriorated to the worst extent.
3. For instance, Locke stressed upon the natural rights to life, liberty and property of individuals and the creation of the state for their protection.
4. The concerns for rights of man were also raised with the revolutionary movements in France, India, etc.
5. Mamta Rao, *Public Interest Litigation in India: A Renaissance in Social Justice* (Lucknow: Eastern Book Company, 2002), p. 8.
6. UNDHR, 10 December 1948, declared that human beings are born free and have equal dignity and rights without distinction of any kind such as race, religion, colour, creed, sex, language, political or other opinion, national or social origin, property, birth or states.
7. J.L. Kual, 'Human Rights in Developing Countries: Some Policy and Legal Considerations', in B.P. Sehgal, *Human Rights in India* (New Delhi: Deep and Deep Publications, 1995), pp. 621-632.
8. Distributive justice implies securing balance of benefits and burdens. Corrective justice is understood in terms of restoring the status quo through redressal of imbalances between benefits and burdens.
9. The term 'moral uprightness' has been used in A.A.S. Zuckerman ed., *Civil Justice in Crisis: Comparative Perspectives of Civil Procedure* (New York: OUP, 1999).
10. Court Fees Act, 1870, Act No. VII of 1870.
11. The usage of the term 'Poor men' implies those who are socio-economically deprived, mentally ill, old age, women, children, weak, disabled, undertrials, etc.
12. Article 14 provides that state will not deny to any person equality before law or equal protection of laws.
13. Article 22 provides right to consult and to be defended by a legal practitioner of one's choice by a person who has been accused and detained in custody.
14. Michael Anderson (2003), 'Access to Justice and Legal Process: Making Legal Institutions Responsive to Poor People in LDCs', *IDS Working Paper 178*. Feb. (Sussex: Brighton, 2003), p. 16.
15. Carlin Howard and Messinger ,'Civil Justice and the Poor: Issues for Sociological Research', *Law and Society Review*, 1967, pp. 69-71.
16. A.P. Reddy, 'Right to Free Legal Aid: Judicial Activism', *Supreme Court Journal*, Vol. 1, 1989.

17. Inter state Migrant Worker Act, 1979; Contract Labour (Regulation and Abolition) Act, 1970; Minimum Wages Act, 1948.
18. Survey conducted by Venkat, 'Living Under Bondage', 2006.
19. *Ibid.*, p. 3.
20. In Piparwar Case the displaced tribal community was thrashed by the police brutally on demanding their rights for rehabilitation granted by the court of law in Bihar.
21. The term *jhuggis* is used to denote squatter settlements where basic human rights for decent living are violated in terms of dilapidated households, unsafe drinking water, unhygienic living conditions, food scarcity, etc. and where they live under constant threat of losing their livelihood means and atrocity of police.
22. Conclusion derived out of the interview conducted with poor litigants in various courts in Delhi, 2006.
23. Shivraj Patil (2003), 'The Litigation and Performances of the Judiciary', in Kashyap (ed.), *The Citizen and Judicial Reforms: Under Indian Polity* (Delhi: Universal Law Publishing Company, 2003), p. 86.
24. Through the Court Fees Act, 1870, a number of measures to extract money out of the pockets of Indian plaintiffs were provided. For instance, in cases of land revenue, the fees payable in such suits extended to fifteen times the net profit arisen form the land before the date of presenting of the plaint. 24 Also the Courts Fee Act 1870 required that any person filing suit for money damages was to pay in advance a non-refundable court fee amounting to 7-11 per cent of the damages sought. Michael Anderson, *op. cit.*, p. 16.
25. Conclusion derived out of the interview conducted with poor litigants in various courts in Delhi, 2006.
26. The Supreme Court Rules explicitly mention that all plaints, petitions, applications and other documents are required to be presented by the plaintiff, petitioner, applicant, appellant, defendant or respondent in person, by his duly authorized agent or by an Advocate-on-Record duly appointed by him for the purpose, at the Filing Counter of the Court, which proves that the need for a lawyer is imperative.
27. Christine Parker, *Just Lawyers: Regulation and Access to Justice* (Oxford: Oxford University Press, 1999), p. 25.
28. Michael Anderson, *op. cit.*, p. 19.
29. Conclusion derived out of the interview conducted with poor litigants in various courts in Delhi, 2006. 90 per cent of the poor litigants expressed their discomfort in approaching the legal set up due to the distance from the court.
30. Hazra and Micevska, 'The problem of court congestion: Evidence from Indian lower courts', 2004.
31. Venkatesan, 'For Judicial Transparency', *Frontline*, Vol. 21 (17), August 2004, pp. 14-27.

32. In terms of working days per year, the Supreme Court of India is operational for only 180 days, the High Courts for 200-210 and the lower courts for 240-270 days.
33. Michael Anderson, *op. cit.*, p. 20.
34. Observation of the survey conducted with Tihar Jail women inmates, 2004, Delhi.
35. Marc Galanter and J.K. Krishnan, paper on 'Debarred Informalism: Lok Adalats and Legal Rights in Modern India', in First South Asian Regional Judicial Colloquium on Access to Justice, New Delhi, 13 November 2002, p. 6.
36. A.P. Reddy, 'Right to Free Legal Aid: Judicial Activism', *Supreme Court Journal*, Vol. 1, 1989, p. 4.
37. S. Murlidhar, *Law, Poverty and Legal Aid: Access to Criminal Justice* (New Delhi: Lexis Nexis Butterworths, 2004).
38. Christine Parker, *op. cit.*
39. Sudhakar Reddy, 'Legal Aid to the Poor', *SCJ*, Vol. 1, 1989, p. 47.
40. Article 22 (1) guarantees to an arrested person the right to consult and to be defended by a legal practitioner of his own choice. With the Hussainara Khatoon case, 1979, it became the duty of the state to provide lawyer to an accused unable to afford counsel.
41. Article 39 (A) of the Directive Principles of State Policy states: 'The state shall secure that the operation of the legal system promotes justice on a basis of equal opportunity, and shall in particular, provide free legal aid, by suitable legislation or schemes or in any other way, to ensure that opportunities for securing justice are not denied to any citizen by reason of economic or other disabilities.'
42. The Hoskot vs. State of Maharashtra case established that when the accused is sentenced to imprisonment, a copy of the judgment shall be given to him free of cost immediately after the pronouncement of the judgment, whether or not he applies for the same.
43. In the case of Hussainara Khatoon vs. State of Bihar in AIR 1979 S.C. page 1371, the Supreme Court held that the right to free legal services is an essential ingredient of reasonable, fair and just procedure for a person accused of an offence and it must be held to be implicit in the guarantee of Article 21. This was a case where it was found by Mr. Justice P.N. Bhagwati and Justice D.A. Desai that many undertrial prisoners in different jails in the State of Bihar had been in jail for period longer than the maximum terms for which they would have been sentenced, if convicted, and that their retention in jails was totally unjustified and in violation of the fundamental rights to personal liberty under Article 21 of the Constitution.
44. In the Khatri vs. State of Bihar AIR 1981 SC 9288, it was held that Legal Aid must be made available to an accused from the stage of first production before the magistrate. It is at this stage that the accused

needs competent legal advice and no procedure would be reasonable, fair and just which denies legal advice and representation to him at that stage.

45. Heber Smith, *Justice and the Poor* (Patterson, Smith Publishing Corporation, 1972), p. 3. The idea is borrowed from Pound, 'Causes of Popular Dissatisfaction with the Administration of Justice', 29 American Bar Association Review, 1906, p. 395 quoted in ibid., p. 3.
46. The Hindu, 'Provide Legal Aid to The Poor: CJI' (Online edition). February 18, 2007. http://www.hinduonnet.com/thehindu/thscrip/print.pl?file=2007021804180500.htm&date=2007/02/18/&prd=th&
47. Bikram Jeet Batra, *India Together*, July 7, 2008. http://www.indiatogether.org/ 2007/may/rvw-judreform.htm.
48. Upendra Baxi, 'Access to Justice in a Globalized Economy', in Golden Jubilee Conference, Indian Law Institute, New Delhi (August 2006).
49. Amelia Gentleman, 'The poor Lose Homes as Delhi Cleans Up', 1st January 2007. http://www.iht.com/articles/2007/01/01/news/delhi.php.
50. The Hindu, 'Provide Legal Aid to the Poor: CJI' (Online edition). February 18, 2007. http://www.hinduonnet.com/thehindu/thscrip/print.pl?file=2007021804180500.htm&date=2007/02/18/&prd=th&.

17

Disability, Inclusiveness and PRIs in India

VIKASH KUMAR

The literal meaning of the Panchayat is a council of five persons and with its present connotation it is a democratic institution, which has tremendous possibilities of new avenues in the field of decentralization, development, mass participation and grassroots democracy.[1] The 73rd amendment of the Indian Constitution in 1992 was marked as a milestone in the history of Indian federal democracy. It began an era of strengthening participatory democracy and enabling those sections of society, hitherto considered as second-class citizens in their own country, to participate in the process of decision-making. It was none other than the Panchayati Raj Institutions (PRIs) at three levels of District, Block and Village encompassing every nook and corner of the country which catapulted the depressed sections to leadership positions in a society where they have been discriminated since time immemorial.[2]

Iqbal Narain is credited with the view that the study and concept of Panchayati Raj should be approached from two directions namely: normative and empirical. The advocates of normative political approach attempts to construct an *ideal type* or ideal conceptual model of Panchayati Raj based on their own worldview and aspirations. Contrary to this the empiricists endeavour to find out the practical implications of the Panchayati Raj and the gap between the ideal construct and the ground reality. All over the world societies are under the process of tremendous change and thus time may come so as the empiricists may invoke for an altogether new conceptual model and for re-orienting the ideal type in the light of new practical terms at whatever rate that suits so. In Indian context achievement of such stage is yet a far cry; however, the nascent trends in this direction have been initiated by both the Government and Civil Societies which may eventually mutually benefit both the normative and the empirical theorists.

Both the normative and the empiricist thoughts are inevitable for the efficient functioning of the PRIs. But the significance of these thoughts is not positioned in their exclusivity and incompatibility to each other. Rather their mutual benefit in crystallizing the image and the aspirations of the institution and the functionaries of the Panchayati Raj. Through their honest joint partnership in this regard, they can also provide a measuring rod for the evaluation of their functioning as also improving the tone of their working by removing their stereotypes; for example, the normative theorists could warn the empiricists to refrain from being over reactionary and on the other hand empiricists could pinpoint the normative thinkers not to turn their ears from the ground realities.[3]

In the light of the above argument it can be said that with the passage of time the Panchayati Raj Institutions (PRIs) have achieved marginal success by ensuring the proportional representation in its three tier structure to the depressed and marginalized sections of the society, thus endeavoring to minimize the gap between ideal and the reality—such as, the Scheduled Castes (SCs), Scheduled Tribes (STs), Other Backward Classes/castes (OBCs) and the women from SC and ST communities and as a whole. However, the issue of empowering the persons with disabilities (PwDs), i.e., one of the most depressed and vulnerable sections of the society, through equitable representation has not caught the imagination of the policy makers, thereby relegating this issue to the background.

There are 2.19 crore persons with disabilities in India which constitute 2.13 per cent of the total population as per the Census 2001. According to 58th round National Sample Survey, there are 1.85 per cent persons with disabilities in India including persons with visual, hearing, speech, locomotor and mental disabilities. Astonishingly, more than 49 per cent of disabled population is illiterate and only 34 per cent are employed out of nearly 75 per cent of PwDs who live in rural areas.[4] However, conservative approach estimates nearly 6-7 per cent disability population out of the total national population.[5] Also there is incoherence between the definitions and criteria adopted for enumeration by these two premier institutions of data collection in India. The vagueness is, however, foretaste of governmental ignorance and insensitivity towards persons with disabilities.

Hence, the above argument leads to certain relevant questions related to the functioning and activities of the PRIs, especially with regard to empowering the persons with disabilities. Are the provisions enshrined in various domestic legislations including Persons with Disabilities (equal opportunities, protection of Rights and full participation) Act 1995, in conformity with international treaties and legislations? If so, to what extent? What are the pitfalls of the enumeration processes in regard to collect necessary information about the representation of persons with disabilities in PRIs? Do the PRIs strive to minimize the gap between the ideal construct and the real situation through the political empowerment of all discriminated and disadvantaged sections including persons with disabilities at the grassroots level? How could the persons with disabilities be reconciled to the changing pace of disability rights movement in India? These questions, in fact, echo in the minds of the laymen as also all those involved in the process of empowerment.

What are Civil and Political Rights?

In this context G.N. Karna classifies the rights into two headings namely human rights and legal rights. By virtue of their nature and resources, human rights are prerequisite and inalienable for a dignified life which every person are entitled to possess. On the other hand, according to him, legal rights are recognized and legitimized by the state and enjoyed by its citizens. From this viewpoint, it becomes the most solid of all the rights, and therefore perhaps in all democratic political systems there are certain safeguards against the violation of legal rights. He further sub-classifies legal rights into civil and political rights. In every civilized society, civil rights e.g. freedom of association, right to acquire property and contact people, etc. are essential to develop a person's overall character to become a responsible citizen and to lead a decent civic life. On the other hand, political rights are recognized and guaranteed by the law of the State to ensure its citizens the right to vote, contest election and assume responsibilities of public offices.[6] However, these divisions and sub-divisions of rights are complimentary to each other because any right can't be enjoyed in the absence of the other and at the same time they strengthen each other also.

According to Henry J. Steiner, rights can be divided into two parts, namely First Generation Rights and Second Generation Rights. Those rights which provide for certain basic guarantees for an individual in relationship to a state like civil and political rights are generally termed as first generation rights. While state has to provide certain basic amenities to an individual to ensure his or her second generation rights like economic, social and cultural rights. First generation rights of an individual cannot be infringed in any case of invasive action by the state. The distinguishing character of divisions should be highlighted when introducing the concept of civil and political rights. An individual should enjoy freedom from all forms of coercive actions of the state to avail the civil and political rights. On the other hand, economic, social and cultural rights require certain arrangements by the state in order to fulfill its obligations.[7]

Despite the differences between these two sets of rights, they cannot be viewed in separate watertight compartments; rather they are highly fluid and interdependent to each other, as also they are complementary and essential for the proper implementation of the either. Moreover, there could be differences in classification and sub-classification of different rights; civil and political rights predominantly stand as the primary rights.

Various Approaches to Disability

Over the period of time various stigmatic, medical/biological and charity paradigms about disability lost their relevance due to their limitations. Social and medical models and rehabilitation policies, etc., by their very nature and scope, proved to be insufficient in dealing with the issues of persons with disabilities. In the last quarter of the twentieth century disability rights movement got its momentum and disability rights activists and academicians shifted the epicenter towards the rights based perspectives like minority rights approach and socio-political rights approach, etc. There has been an increasing recognition of abilities of persons with disabilities and emphasis on mainstreaming them in the society based on their capabilities. Generalization about disability *in toto* can't be made through a single model of disability. However, in this context a brief discussion of Minority Rights approach and Socio-Political approach would be of worth.

Minority Rights Approach

G.N. Karna pinpoints five elements to study disability from minority group perspective. Firstly, disability and minority could be synonymous in the sense that disabled are equally subjugated and victims of discrimination and exploitation by the majority non-disabled persons. They are compelled to lead a life of second class citizens in this social structure, despite several laws are enacted like Civil Rights Acts and American Disability Act, 1990 in USA and Persons with Disabilities Act, 1995 in India to protect them from various forms of discrimination. People in rural areas, however, are double victims. Secondly, common traits of minority group is paralleled for disabled as their disabilities are seen as common characteristics of defect and labeled indiscriminately as incompetent to assume any public office. They are looked down as non-functional and burden for the family and society at large and more so in rural areas. The spirit of unity and group solidarity is important in the case of minority group identity; however in the case of disability it is somewhat lacking, especially in developing countries like India. Although there are evidences of emergence of group rights consciousness globally, persons with disabilities failed to establish any significant physical existence as pressure groups at domestic and international level. Minority individuals owe a non-voluntary membership of his or her community; likewise, disabilities are inflicted on a person by natural or artificial causes (except some cases of chronic illness and unconsciously motivated disabilities) and hence become involuntary. Lack of awareness, poverty and technological inaccessibility especially in rural areas compelled a person with disabilities in perpetuity and sufferance. Lastly, intra-marriage system is the major distinguishing characteristics of a minority group which is also aptly applicable to the persons with disabilities because even in the era of modernity, educational advancement, disability rights movements, etc., the dogma of disability prohibits a disabled person making a matrimonial union with a non-disabled person. In case if it happens rarely, their fate is looked with suspicion, which generally does not happen in case a person becomes disabled after his or her matrimonial alliance.[8]

Nevertheless, there could be other factors to find out the similarities and dissimilarities between minority group and disabled people, but it is not an objective here to pinpoint the differences and similarities between disabled people and other minority groups. What is rather important here is to ensure the social and political rights of these people in an appropriate and distinctive manner along with other disadvantaged sections of the society such as STs, SCs, OBCs, Women and Minorities.

Socio-Political Approach

The socio-political approach views disability as a byproduct of the interaction between an individual and the social structure. More simply, it is the environment which inflicts several functional prerequisites for a person to be functional or non-functional for the society, which fails to account the needs and aspirations of the disabled. They become the victims of labeling and stigma of being socially incapable. This argument is vehemently supported by the advocates of socio-political approach like Harlan Hahn,[9] Frank Bowe[10] and Mike Oliver.[11] Burdened by '*multiple jeopardy*' of poverty, illiteracy, government expenditures and inflation, etc. they become unable to share the political rights and responsibilities. This truth becomes crueler in the rural political scenario where the local government is already dominated by local political elite who possesses money and muscle power. Strongly supporting the socio-political integration and mainstreaming of the persons with disabilities, Frank Bowe succinctly advocates that 'keeping disabled in dependency is costing us many times more than would helping them to independence.[12]

Echoing more or less a similar view, G.N. Karna observes that:

> Determination is primarily, shaped by legislations and policies, reflecting collective or political choice about the manner in which society should be structured, thus providing a range of opportunities accessible to persons with a variety of physical or other disabilities.[13]

Therefore, the functional requirements of the socio-political and professional structure of the society should be modified in such a way that the abilities of persons with disabilities could be ensured in the society.

Civil and Political Rights of Persons with Disabilities

In the international arena, several arrangements have been made through treaties and other instruments to guarantee the civil and political rights of an individual in general and with specific provisions addressing the rights of persons with disabilities in particular. The International Covenant on Civil and Political Rights, 1996 (ICCPR) finds its place at the centre of all international treaties with its detailed provisions and rather substantive procedures. The Covenant on Economic, Social and Cultural Rights, 1966 has also developed human rights monitoring procedure – in part modeled on the committee under the Civil and Political Covenant, and in part fashioned for own separate needs. In addition Convention Against Torture, 1975 (CAT), the International Convention on the Elimination of All Forms of Racial Discrimination, 1963 (CERD), Convention on the Rights of the Child, 1990 (CRC), Regional Human Rights Conventions, and Convention on the Elimination of All Forms of Discrimination against Women, 1979 (CEDAW) also contain provisions in some way or the other to guarantee civil and political rights of the persons with disabilities.

Along with others, political rights also find prominent place in the purpose and content of the Standard Rules on the Equalization of Opportunities for Persons with Disabilities, 1993 of United Nations.[14] One of the major objectives of it is to ensure same rights and obligation for the persons with disabilities, as it is enjoyed by others. It directs the nation states to take necessary action to remove the obstacles making it difficult for them to exercise their rights and freedom and to participate fully in the activities of their societies.

According to the Preamble of the Standard Rules,

> States should provide models for the political decision making process required for the attainment of equal opportunities, bearing in mind the widely differing technical and economic levels, the fact that the process must reflect keen understanding of the cultural context within which it takes place and the crucial role of persons with disabilities in it.[15]

Further, it adds as the preconditions for equal participation of the persons with disabilities:

> States should initiate and support information campaigns concerning persons with disabilities and disability policies, conveying the message that persons with disabilities are citizens with the same rights and obligations as others, thus

justifying measures to remove all obstacles to full participation (Rule 1, Awareness-raising).[16]

This would help to raise awareness in society about persons with disabilities, their rights, their needs, their potential and their contribution.

The International Covenant on Civil and Political Rights (ICCPR) of 1966 is one of the most important international instruments on human rights which vow a plethora of fundamental rights and freedoms which corroborate the entitlement of all persons to take part in political and public life.[17] It constitutes the International Bill of Human Rights, along with the Universal Declaration of Human Rights of 1948 (UDHR), and the International Covenant on Economic, Social and Cultural Rights (ICESCR) of 1966 as United Nations major arms of human rights and guidelines for the nation states. By endorsing the democratic governments, the UDHR (Article 21) sets one of its ideals as 'the will of the people shall be the basis of the authority of government'.[18]

Gerard Quinn writes that in the last quarter of the twentieth century disability has emerged more as civil and political rights rather than a medical problem. This shift of approach tries to explain that disability should also be seen as a human rights issue in the same way as gender and other depressed communities such as race are seen.[19] According to Quinn, if ICCPR can be divided into four major clusters, and political rights of the disabled people is one of them along with 'rights that refer to human existence', 'liberty rights' and 'associational rights'.[20]

In addition, the ICCPR expects Nation States to guarantee for every citizen the right and opportunity to 'take part in the conduct of public affairs, directly or indirectly through chosen representatives, to vote and to be elected at genuine periodic elections (and) to have access on general terms of equality to public office'.[21]

It is specified that every citizen is entitled on the basis of equality to engage in all forms of natural political rights like standing for elections, right to vote as also right to be appointed to public positions. The inherent meaning of this Article also includes person with disabilities to be righteous, to owe the responsibilities of the public offices and contribute to the nation building as an elected representative like their non-disabled counterparts.

The Vienna Declaration and Programme of Action or the World Conference on Human Rights in 1993 emphasized the relation of Human Rights and Participatory Democracy in reciprocity. Both are symbiotic to each other as being interdependent and mutually reinforcing. Today it is widely accepted in the international arena that the protection of basic rights and general rule of law can best be achieved under the democratic set up. Also, freedom of speech, other political freedom, and equal representation of every section of the society are the pillars for the success of proper functioning of the democracy.[22]

By virtue of being international, these treaties are open to all states and they are supposed to participate in these monitoring procedures. These procedures with the passage of time evolved and are well established under the aegis of ICCPR where the Human Rights Committee has now established a very substantial jurisprudence. Therefore, these provisions and directives stand for much importance for States to make their respective domestic policies in consonance with the international commitments to safeguard the political interests of persons with disabilities.

Fortunately, after independence India became signatory to most of the major international human rights treaties and started endeavoring to fulfill its commitment, although with a slower pace. India also endorses the regional arrangement, for example, declaration on the full participation and equality of people with disabilities in the Asia Pacific Region (ESCAP) as also Biwako Millennium Framework for action towards an inclusive, barrier free and rights based society. Nonetheless, India became signatory to UN Convention on Protection and Promotion of the Rights and Dignity of Persons with Disabilities recently.[23]

Civil and Political Rights of Persons with Disabilities under Indian Constitution and other Legal Provisions

It is quite appreciable that from the very first dawn of the independence Indian policy makers envisaged the vision of ensuring civil and political rights as a fundamental right available to every citizen of this country in the form of right to life and liberty, equality before the law, freedom of speech and expression, association and religion, etc. At the very onset the Preamble to the Constitution declares India as sovereign democratic republic. The democratic form of the country ensures its citizen two kinds of political rights, viz. the right to vote and the right to contest for election. To emphasize the paramountcy of the rights, Article 13 (1) reads as 'all laws in force in the territory of India immediately before the commencement of this Constitution, in so far as they are inconsistent with the provisions of this part, shall, to the extent of such inconsistency, be void.' In this light, state is expected to provide the required basic infrastructure of civil society for the realization of the individual rights. Therefore, clause (2) of the article refrain the state from making any such law 'which takes away or abridges the rights conferred by this part and any law made in contravention of this clause shall, to the extent of the contravention, be void.' The paramountcy of the rights and its obligation will remain the same till the remedies are provided for example under the 'Right to Constitutional remedies'. Article 32 (1) says that 'the right to move to the Supreme Court by appropriate proceedings for the enforcement of the rights conferred by this part is guaranteed.' Adding to the above, Clause (4) states that 'the right guaranteed by this article shall not be suspended except as otherwise provided for by this Constitution.' Article 226 (1) of the Constitution, however, further disseminates the importance of the remedial arrangements to the second line of judiciary. Every High Court shall have power 'to issue to any person or authority, including in appropriate cases, any Government ... directions, orders or writs[24] for the enforcement of any of the rights conferred by part III ...'[25] Article 326 provides for the election to the House of the People and to the Legislative Assemblies of States to be on the basis of adult suffrage, that is to say every person who is the citizen of India and who is not less than the age of eighteen years on such date as may be fixed in that behalf by or under any law made by the appropriate Legislature on the ground of non- residence, unsoundness of mind, crime or corrupt or illegal practice, shall be entitled to be registered as a voter at any such election. [26]

Various Provisions Ensuring Participatory Democracy

Article 243C of Part IX under the head of 'The Panchayats', of Constitution of India clearly outlines the composition of the Panchayat that every citizen of the respective area will have their representation in the prescribed manner. Article 243A elevates the position of the common man at the centre of the PRIs by giving constitutional recognition to the 'Gram Sabha' which acts as the sole platform to ensure direct, participatory democracy. Further, Article 243D reserves not less than one third elected seats and offices of the chairpersons for women at all three levels of the Panchayats. It also provides that in proportion to the population of SCs and STs, seats and offices are to be reserved in proportion to the size of their populations within that Panchayat, i.e. one third seats to be reserved for them and within that, at least one third seats are to be reserved for women belonging to these categories. Other Backward Classes are also provided reservations by other clauses in a same manner. Thus, Article 243D acts as a flag bearer and precursor of equality and justice for the disadvantaged persons and other marginalized communities of the society even in the remote villages of India.[27]

Deriving the straight, inherent and implicit meaning from the text of the Constitution, persons with disabilities can claim their full rights if it is implicit by the provisions that these people lie in the same group for whom, rights are guaranteed. At the same time Constitution doesn't explicitly mention disability as reason to protect persons with disabilities from the discrimination as in the case of other categories like religion, race, caste, sex, place of birth or any of them.[28] As also, Article 14 guarantees equality before law that 'the State shall not deny to any person equality before the law or the equal protection of laws within the territory of India'.[29] Since the bearers of civil and political rights are presumed to be autonomous, capable of exercising their capacity before the law and equally enjoy the protection of the law, the question arises whether or not persons with disabilities can exercise their full legal capacity in the absence of explicit protection?

A landmark step in the direction of ensuring equal opportunities for the persons with disabilities was taken in terms of enacting 'The Persons with Disabilities (Equal Opportunities, Protection of Rights and Full Participation) Act, 1995', in February 1996. This Act claims to be the pioneer in providing both preventive and promotional aspect of rehabilitation like education, employment including vocational training, affirmative action in terms of seat reservations, research and manpower development, establishing research institutes and rehabilitation centers and ensuring various forms of social security. But in reality the most important of this act also doesn't bother to indulge itself into the matter of political empowerment of the persons with disabilities, which is, by and large, the onus of the other forms of the empowerment. For instance, chapter VIII titled 'Non-Discrimination' predominantly deals with the issues of infrastructural barriers. Chapter IX, 'Research and Man Power Development' engages itself with prevention of disability, rehabilitation, development of assistance devices and job identification, etc. Moreover, chapter XIII ('Social Security') of the Act also doesn't look beyond financial security and safeguards.[30]

Thus, it can be said that even this Act fails to signify its major objective even after twelve years of its implementation. The title 'full participation' has very limited scope, chained with mere financial, employment, education and other rehabilitation security. Hence it becomes meaningless as it does not ensure the basic human rights of grassroots decision-making processes for the persons with disabilities.

On the one hand, the Draft National Policy for Persons with Disabilities 2006 has highlighted the role of Panchayati Raj Institutions at various stances, such as, in order to ensure prevention and early detection of disabilities, the assistance of health, education, Panchayati Raj, welfare and rural development organization both in government and non-government sectors will be taken. Further, it had also been suggested that for training and sensitization of community decision makers such as members of Panchayats and head of the families, etc., programs should be undertaken to meet the manpower requirement for rehabilitation of persons with disabilities. Most importantly, at the end of the draft policy it had strongly recommended that the Panchayati Raj Institutions will have representation of persons with disabilities and particularly women with disabilities, as also Panchayati Raj Institutions will be encouraged to participate in the implementation of the national policy to address local level issues and draw up suitable programs which will be integrated with the district and State plan.[31]

On the other, the National Policy for Persons with Disabilities 2006 is still languishing with approach of welfare and charity model. It entrusts the Panchayati Raj Institutions at village level for the welfare of persons with disabilities and setting up of mental healthcare homes for severe mentally ill persons under district level with the involvement of NGOs. The national policy, however, also envisaged the Panchayati Raj Institutions in association with urban local bodies, in the functioning of the District Disability

Rehabilitation Centres and District Level Committees to coordinate the matters relating to the implementation of the policy. But ironically, it keeps mum on the matter of proper representation of the persons with disabilities at the third and basic tier of the decision making institution, thus making it actual participatory and inclusive in nature. Although, it acknowledges and recognizes that persons with disabilities are valuable human resource for the country and seeks to create an environment that provides them equal opportunities, protection of their rights and full participation in the society.[32]

The Constitution of India allows a law to be enacted for the purpose of ascertaining the qualification and disqualification of an individual from the electoral processes. The Representation of People Act 1950 disqualifies persons of unsound mind from his or her right of adult suffrage. Section 16 (1) (b) of the Act declares that a person shall be disqualified for the registration in electoral roll if he or she is of unsound mind and stands so declared by a competent court.' Section 16 (2) of this Act deals with the post registration disqualification that the elector's name to be struck off the electoral roll if he or she becomes of unsound mind. The Representation of People Act 1950 categorically denies a person of unsound mind of right to vote and to be elected because Section 62 (2) of the Act states that the 'entry in the electoral roll not be conclusive on franchise rights if the elector is subject to any disqualification specified in Section 16. The above argument of disqualification under the Act is discriminatory in nature because, as Amita Dhanda argues that 'unsoundness of mind' is very much relative and subjective terminology and courts are required to adopt a multi-dimensional legal approach while pronouncing on the unsoundness of a person. Because one functional requirement may find a person unsuitable to its prerequisites but others may not.[33] This argument of subjectivity is most applicable to rural areas, where bias and prejudice play a major role in all social evils against persons with disabilities.

In the 58th round survey of the NSSO titled 'Disabled Persons in India', various themes and criteria have been covered, including Types of disability, Age at onset of disability, Treatment taken for disability, Type of aid/appliance, Extent of physical disability, Living arrangements for disabled, General Education, Vocational Training if any, Activity Status of disabled persons, Particulars of school enrollment of disabled persons (age 5-18 years), whether attended pre-school intervention program or not, etc. However, NSS does not cover the criteria of enumeration of participation of persons with disabilities in the third tier. However, the above particulars fall under the demographic and other particulars of household members of Block 4 which has seventeen columns. Column 14[34] deals with 'usual activity status', but unfortunately there is not any code regarding the political engagements of this marginalized section of the society.[35]

After a gap of 20 years that is to say 1981 to 2001 in census 2001, question number 15 tries only to identify five types of disabilities, namely, visual, hearing, speech, mental and movement disability, whereas the census report 1981 dealt with the enumeration of totally blind, totally dumb and totally crippled.[36] This shows how discrepancies are embedded in Governmental approach and policies towards persons with disabilities. In spite of this, there should be more buoyant enumerative devices so as to collect the actual information regarding the mainstreaming of persons with disabilities as also provide necessary and varied inputs to the policy makers.

One can delight, however, to know that the Ministry of Panchayati Raj has presented an overview regarding a positive signal about the grassroots political participation of caste, class and gender based depressed sections of the society. The following table shows the percentage of the representatives from different sections.

From the above table, it is evident that at in all the three tiers, PRIs have almost fulfilled respectively SCs, STs and Women representation quota in proportion to their population and legal provisions, that is to say 19 per cent, 10 per cent and 37 per cent. However, even one-third seats are reserved mandatory for the women within SC and ST category for their socio-cultural, economic and political empowerment. It must be noted that at some stances the actual occupancy of seats by women belonging to these categories substantially exceeds the percentage of reservation. For instance in Karnataka, the number of elected women representatives from SC and ST communities is in the ratio of 46 per cent and 65 per cent respectively.[37]

However, despite the fact that the Ministry of Panchayti Raj recognizes the vulnerability of the persons with disabilities, this has not been mentioned explicitly in disability typologies. This lapse

Table-1
Panchayats and Elected Representatives (under Three Tiers of PRIs) in States and Union Territories

Sl. No.	Name of Tiers of Tiers	Number of Panchayats	Non-SC & Non-ST Categories	Number of Panchayats and Elected Representatives in the Three Panchayats in States/UTs as on 01-12-2006						
				Number of Elected Representatives						
				SC		ST		Total	Women	
				Number	%	Number	%	Number	Number	%
1.	Village Panchayats	232913	1851166	490986	18.5	314324	11.8	2656476	975116	36.7
2.	Intermediate Panchayats	6094	112371	32898	21.0	11340	7.2	156609	58094	37.1
3.	District Panchayats	532	11311	2734	17.4	1649	10.5	15694	5779	36.8
	TOTAL	239539	1974848	526618	18.9	327313	9.8	2828779	1038989	36.8

Source: Ministry of Panchayati Raj, India

has been sought to be rectified considerably *inter alia* the National Policy for Persons with Disabilities (2006) announced by the Ministry of social Justice and Empowerment, Government of India. This policy document seeks to entrust the responsibility of issuing disability certificates, apart from managing rehabilitation centers and monitoring the implementation of plans and schemes formulated by the Government of India for empowering the persons with disabilities. The PRIs could accomplish these tasks in close coordination with District Administration and in the light of guidelines laid down by the Government of India in this regard.[38]

Unfortunately, the overview presented by the Union Ministry of Panchayati Raj of India sees the empowerment of the disabled persons in terms of mere issuing of disability certificates, providing them assistance devices and managing rehabilitation centers. In this context, G.N. Karna rightly opines that Indian perspective on disability is still guided by the welfare and charity model to a considerable extent, lacking rights-based framework to understand the whole gamut of issues related to the empowerment of the persons with disabilities. [39]

Lastly, there is a severe failure on the part of disabled people themselves for not mobilizing their huge human resources for their political empowerment. It is evident from the fact that unlike other depressed communities the reliance on numbers for political mileage has failed in the case of persons with disabilities, e.g., Uttar Pradesh (34,53,369) having the largest number of disabled population followed by Bihar (18,87,611), West Bengal (18,47,174), Tamil Nadu (16,42,497) and Maharashtra (15,69,582), they have not been able to organize themselves politically as one community.[40]

The debate gets all the more strengthened with the fact that while rural areas have the largest concentration, e.g., Himachal Pradesh (92.82%) tops the rank followed by Sikkim (91.18%), Bihar (89.66%), Nagaland (88.76%) and Assam (88.27%), even in these areas PwDs have failed to assert their representation and participation in the third tier of governance.[41]

The reason behind this exclusion is the lack of awareness among the disabled regarding their basic human rights particularly political rights. This argument could be substantiated with the fact that in Himachal Pradesh only 50.56 per cent rural disabled people are literate while there is 75.08 per cent rural literacy. Same is the case with Sikkim, Bihar, Nagaland and Assam where total rural disabled literacy is only 39.35 per cent, 34.92 per cent, 26.44 per cent and 42.42 per cent respectively, while total rural literacy there is 66.82 per cent, 43.92 per cent, 62.79 per cent and 59.73 per cent respectively.

Concluding Observations

In the light of above discussion, it would not be preposterous to assert whether the approach and functioning of the Panchayati Raj Institutions are really inclusive in nature? If not so, how could it be reconciled to the changed scenario, especially in the aftermath of the worldwide disability rights movements and several domestic and international commitments by the Government of India?

From the above elucidation, it is clear that the PRIs may have greater role to play in empowering the persons with disabilities at the grassroots level. Considering the gargantuan nature of the problem, it is beyond the capacity of the 'Center Centric' Government agencies and policies alone to mainstream the persons with disabilities. Thus, it becomes inevitable to have decentralized form of government, comprising every section of the society on the basis of equality and justice with special focus on persons with disabilities to ensure their representation. Because the basic goal of establishing an egalitarian society in our Indian context could be achieved only if all sections of the society, especially those who are at the lower rungs, are mainstreamed. By including these people in the third tier as decision makers and not as just passive recipients, would be the only way to fulfill the constitutional and international commitments to ensure the basic human rights of the disadvantaged sections, and thus achieving the basic objective of the Panchayati Raj Institutions. From these vantage points, the following suggestions are offered to accelerate the empowerment process of the persons with disabilities through the three tier PRIs in collaboration with organizations of/for the persons with disabilities.

To begin with, Census and NSS must adopt more comprehensive criteria to collect information regarding disability related issues and problems including political participation, especially in grassroots decision making institutions. Further, classification and criteria adopted by both these organizations should be in coherence and in similar manner, so that it can present reliable inputs, which can serve eventually as guidelines for the policy makers.

Secondly, the role of NGOs is very crucial in this respect because according to an estimate there are approximately 4 to 6 thousand NGOs functional in the field of disability. No doubt over the passage of time, voices of few genuine and honest organizations have yielded some fruits. In India, many organizations are working with various issues of disability, for instance education, prevention of disability, manpower development, vocational rehabilitation, sexual empowerment, physical rehabilitation, employment and nondiscrimination, etc. Unfortunately, none of the organizations has raised voices against the infringement of the political rights of persons with disabilities. Therefore, it is the need of the hour that these organizations must start agitations and persuade the election authorities to ensure at least proportional representation in the Panchayati Raj. They should also endeavor in a collaborative manner so as to implement the laws and policies at the grassroots level.

Thirdly, lakhs of civil society groups across India have also achieved remarkable success in raising and solving their local and native problems, for example, sanitation, small scale industries, primary education, water management, awareness generation as also various forms of community developments, etc. Moreover, civil society groups have played a crucial role in the empowerment of the downtrodden sections of the society like SCs and STs and women. But, there is no significant contribution in finding place in the three tier system for Persons with Disabilities. Therefore, it would be imperative on the part of civil societies to generate awareness and act the needful in this direction to ensure their representation and their periodic enumeration by the national agencies.

Fourthly, hitherto, persons with disabilities have failed to organize a national level pressure group. Therefore, it is the need of the hour that persons with disabilities must unite so that they can raise their voice. Civil society organizations formed by persons with disabilities themselves could play a vital role in building the pressure on the policy makers.

Fifthly, rehabilitation is a multi-dimensional and long drawn process which doesn't mean mere physical rehabilitations. These dimensions or spheres such as social, physical, economic, political, etc. should work in collaboration with mainstream persons with disabilities. By ascertaining the political rights of the persons with disabilities, PRIs could act as a bridge between the Central Government, community, civil society groups, family and the disabled people to ascertain the rehabilitative services.

Lastly, despite of several international and national safeguards protecting persons with disabilities' political rights particularly, there are still many additional barriers hindering these people to enjoy their natural rights. Due to infrastructural and bureaucratic barriers, especially in rural areas, for instance, a person with disabilities may not be able to communicate with his or her political associates or may face difficulties to take part in the political processes which are not complementary with his or her disabilities like a visually challenged person finds difficulty to cast his or her vote in the present ballot system. As also due to infrastructural barriers in rural areas a person with disabilities who wish to be elected for the Panchayat elections, may not be able to convey his message to the voters. Therefore, there is greater need to view these issues in a wider perspective especially in terms of accessibility, management and proper allocation of resources to enable them to enjoy their rights and making Panchayati Raj Institutions inclusive in true sense.

END NOTES AND REFERENCES

1. George Mathew, 'Panchayati Raj Institutions and Human rights in India', Paper Prepared for The International Council on Human Rights Policy Decentralisation, Local Government and Human Rights, Spring, International Council on Human Rights Policy, Versoix, Switzerland, 2002, p. 2.
2. Government of India, *Basic Statistics for Local Level Development – Perspective through Panchayati Raj*, Paper presented in 14th COCSSO held at NASC, Pusa, New Delhi from 10 to 11 April 2007, Ministry of Statistics and Programme Implementation, New Delhi, India.
3. Iqbal Narain, 'The Concept of Panchayati Raj and Its Institutional Implications in India', *Asian Survey*, Vol. 5, No. 9 (September 1965), pp. 456-466, University of California Press, retrieved from http://www.jstor.org/stable/2642495.
4. Government of India, 'NSS 58th round Disabled Persons in India (July-December 2002)', Report No. 485 (58/26/1), National Sample Survey Organisation, Ministry of Statistics and Programme Implementation, New Delhi, December 2003, pp. C4-C5.
5. Government of India (2001), *Population Census of India, 2001*, Registrar General of India, Ministry of Home Affairs, New Delhi, 2001.
6. G.N. Karna, *Disability Studies in India: Retrospects and Prospects* (New Delhi, Gyan Publishing House, 2001), pp. 141-142.

7. Henry J. Steiner, *International Human Rights in Context: Law, Politics, Morals*, 2nd Edition, Oxford University Press, Oxford, note 3, (2000), p. 247; Quoted in, 'Human Rights: Course Module for Indian Universities', SAHRDC, New Delhi, 2005.
8. G.N. Karna, *United Nations and Rights of Disabled Persons: A Study in Indian Perspective*, New Delhi, APH Publishing Corporation, 1999, pp. 60-63; See also I. Robertson, *Sociology* (New York, Worth Press, 1981); also see C. Safilios, Rothschild, *The Sociology and Social Psychology of Disability and Rehabilitation* (New York, Random house, 1970).
9. Harlan Hahn, 'Disability and Rehabilitation Policy: Is Paternalistic Neglect Really Benign?' in *Public Administration Review*, vol. 42, no. 4, July-August 1982, pp. 385-89.
10. Frank Bowe, *Rehabilitating America: Towards Independence for Disabled and Elderly People* (*New* York, Harper & Row, 1980).
11. Mike Oliver, *The Politics of Disablement* (Houndmills, Macmillan, 1990), p. 5.
12. Frank Bowe, p. xv.
13. Note 8, Karna, p. 65.
14. United Nations, *Standard Rules on the Equalization of Opportunities for Persons with Disabilities* 1993, A/RES/48/96 85th Plenary Meeting 20 December 1993: Washington D.C.
15. *Ibid.*
16. *Ibid.*
17. United Nations, *International Covenant on Civil and Political Rights, 1966*, General Assembly resolution 2200A (XXI) of 16 December 1966. Retrieved from http://www.ohchr.org/english/law/ccpr.htm.
18. United Nations, *Universal Declaration of Human Rights, 1948*, General Assembly resolution 217 A (III) of 10 December 1948: Geneva.
19. Gerard Quinn, 'The International Covenant on Civil and Political Rights', in *Human Rights and Disabled Persons*, in T. Degener and Y. Koster-Dreese (eds.) (Dordrecht, Martinis Nijhoff, 1995), p. 81.
20. *Ibid.*, p. 83.
21. United Nations, *Standard Rules on the Equalization of Opportunities for Persons with Disabilities* 1993, Article 25.
22. David Beetham and Kevin Boyle,, *Democracy: 80 Questions and Answers*, New Delhi, National Book Trust, 1996, p. 85. See also United Nations (1993), *World Conference on Human Rights: Vienna Declaration and Programme of Action*, Vienna, 14-25 June 1993, Retrieved from http://www.unhchr.ch/huridocda/huridocda.nsf.
23. Government of India (2006), *National Policy for Persons with Disabilities 2006*, Ministry of Social Justice and Empowerment, No.3-1/1993-DD.III, New Delhi.
24. Writs in the nature of *habeas corpus, mandamus*, prohibition, *Quo warranto and certiorari*, or any of them, for the enforcement of any of the rights conferred by Part III and for any other purpose.

25. Government of India, *The Constitution of India 2006* (Amended and Reprinted), Ministry of Law, Justice & Company Affairs, New Delhi, 2006; See also Government of India (2005), *Disability Manual*, National Human Rights Commission, New Delhi, 2006, p. 160.
26. *Ibid.*
27. *Ibid.*
28. *Ibid.*, Article 15(1).
29. *Ibid.*
30. Government of India, *The Persons with Disabilities (Equal Opportunities, Protection of Rights and Full Participation)* Act 1995 (New Delhi, Parliament of India, 1995).
31. Government of India (2005), *Suggestions/Comments on Draft National Policy for Persons with Disabilities*, Ministry of Social Justice and Empowerment, F.No.3-1/93 DD.III, New Delhi, Dated: 15.06.2005.
32. Note. 22.
33. Amita Dhanda, *Legal Order and Mental Disorder* (New Delhi, Sage Publication, 2000), pp. 301-306; See also Government of India, *Disability Manual* (New Delhi, National Human Rights Commission, 2005), pp. 204-205.
34. Column 14: usual activity status: worked in h.h. enterprise (self-employed): own account worker–11, employer–12, worked as helper in h.h. enterprise (unpaid family worker)–21; worked as regular salaried/wage employee–31; worked as casual wage labour: in public works–41, in other types of work–51; did not work but was seeking and/or available for work–81, attended educational institution–91, attended domestic duties only–92, attended domestic duties and was also engaged in free collection of goods (vegetables, roots, fire-wood, cattle feed, etc.), sewing, tailoring, weaving, etc. for household use–93, rentiers, pensioners, remittance recipients, etc.–94, not able to work due to disability–95, beggars, prostitutes–96, others–97.
35. Government of India (2002), *NSS 58th Round Disabled Persons in India (July–December 2002)*, Report No. 485 (58/26/1), National Sample Survey Organisation, Ministry of Statistics and Programme Implementation, New Delhi, December 2003, pp. C4-C5.
36. *Population Census of India, 2001.*
37. Government of India, 'Overview on Panchayati Raj in India: The Greatest Experiment in Democracy Ever' (Presented by Union Minister for Panchayati Raj Mr. Mani Shankar Aiyar), Union Ministry of Panchayati Raj, Government of India, New Delhi, 24 October 2006.
38. Mani Shankar Aiyar, *Overview on Panchayati Raj in India: The Greatest Experiment in Democracy Ever*, Union Ministry of Panchayati Raj, Government of India, New Delhi, 24 October 2006.

39. G.N. Karna, *Disability Studies in India: New Directions for Future*, Monograph Series – 2 (New Delhi, Society for Disability and Rehabilitation Studies, 2007).
40. Data analyzed from the *Population Census of India, 2001*, Registrar General of India, Ministry of Home Affairs, Government of India, New Delhi, (2001).
41. *Ibid.*

18

The Rhetoric of Exclusive Development

SHAILAJA MENON

When the last tree has died and the last river has been poisoned, and the last fish has been caught, we will realize that we cannot eat money.

— An Indian proverb

The tribals are in a jungle state: we are bringing them into civilization.[1]

Not very long ago, when we went for a film, before the main feature commenced, a newsreel was screened. Inevitably, it showed the inauguration of a dam, which followed a set pattern. The opening shot would show Ramu *bhaiyya* peering anxiously at the sky, begging the rain gods to water his parched lands. Even his forefathers had not expected things to be any different. The narrator queried... 'Would Ramu *bhaiyya's* crop and cattle survive? No one knew. It was one's fate. The camera focussed on the dam. Everyone was waiting for the dignitary. Usually, the Prime Minister would press the button, open the flood gates and behold, sparkling waters would gush out to the thirsty fields. On such a promising note, the film would start. But did we ever pause to ponder whether Ramu *bhaiyya* actually got all the water and electricity as promised. What happened to the people who inhabited the dam site? What was their fate?[2]

The Blueprint of Development

Today, development means massive industrialization and market oriented productivity. A developed nation's agriculture is chemical intensive, technology, energy intensive and trade export maximising.[3] Natural resources have been utilized to the point of no return. Never before in human history were resources exploited in such proportion. The forces of production in historical societies never crossed the limits of minimal resource requirements despite the changing levels of skills, strategies, and managements.[4] The problem is further worsened, when local communities are divested of their customary rights over natural resources. What one fails to realize is that man's cultural traditions have always forced him to show ecological prudence, which basically made him conservation conscious.[5]

Ironically, the assumption is that the common forest dwellers who depend on the biomass are responsible for the vanishing forests. Hence, every effort is made to involve that state to stop such activities. The state with its coercive power, capital and labour is willing to finance the creation of a built environment, displacing millions in the process. But the forest dwellers are unwilling to accept the state's agenda of exclusive development. So, the new catch phrase is 'People's Participation'. The approach is 'I manage, you participate'. What is lacking in the entire design is the understanding that people's participation is the process by which the rural poor are able to organise themselves and through their own organization, are able to identify their own needs, share in the design, implementation and evaluation of the participatory action.[6]

No society whether in the rich industrialized west or in the poor Third World can afford to allow its environment to degrade as the ultimate profitability of its economy depends on the health of its physical environment. Yet the elite political class around the world see economic development as a zero sum game in which improved living conditions can only be achieved at the environment's expense. Indira Gandhi at the 1972 UN Conference on the human environment in Stockholm was loudly endorsed for describing 'poverty as the worst form of pollution'. A Nepali Prime Minister lamented the slow development of his country with the similar sentiment, 'We could do with a little more industrial smog'.[7]

A school of thought believes that environmental degradation is a sign of progress. That environmental protection is better tackled after a country builds an industrial base which generates wealth, still enjoys wide currency. One of the basic necessities for building an industrial base is electricity and with fossil fuels getting depleted, hydro-electric power is the lucrative alternative. This explains why no other capital projects have received more funding, or caused more grief, than energy projects, focussing exclusively on the production of electric power.[8] The hydro-electric dams flood large numbers of rural people off their lands to uncertain and miserable fates. The flooded river valleys tend to be extremely fertile, the majority being tribals with cultures and traditions irreplaceably tied to their land. The electric power produced almost never benefit the local populace but is transported to the industrial centres, where the national government resides primarily for the benefit of state industries and multinational corporations.

The misery these projects have for the local populace is justified by their presumed benefit to the greater national good. 'Threats commonly faced by indigenous people throughout the world include dispossession of land, flooding of land through hydro electric schemes, deforestation and consequent damage to traditional agriculture, armed forces carrying out the policies of distant central governments, desecration of places of worship and ethnocide, and the destruction of a culture. The culprits of indigenous people are MNCs and governments bent on 'development' at all costs.'[9]

The myth that hydro-electric projects are forever has led to the world's foreign aid agencies to promote dam construction above all other energy projects.[10] However, not only these large hydro-dams non renewable themselves, but they also reduce the renewability of their river valleys and destroy the self sufficiency of the entire region. By interfering with the natural flow of the river and trapping the nutrient rich silt in the reservoirs instead of letting it wash over the river banks during the annual flooding; the dams deprive the flood plains of the nutrients needed to maintain their agricultural productivity. So, regions that now have reservoirs for hydro-electricity usually becomes dependent on chemical fertilizers to replenish their soil and on man made irrigation systems to replace the lost irrigation of the annual floods. This leads to a decrease in the area's ability to regulate itself naturally and an increase in the amount of top soil that silts up the river bed and eventually destroys the dam. Ultimately, the river valley is unable to provide hydro-electricity, irrigation, fertilization and flood control for its river valley.

The intrusion of these dams into ecologically sensitive areas upsets the existing equilibrium to claim a human toll. The process of building such projects in the third world creates a malaria problem.

In addition to malaria, which affects more than eight hundred million people annually and kills more than a million infants below the age of two years, bilharzias, a disease which thrives in the still waters of irrigation canals and dams, debilitates some two hundred million people. The Indira Gandhi Canal has ushered in prosperity in the desert region of Rajasthan. But the dream has turned into a nightmare with the deadly plasmodium, falciparum malaria, advancing along the course of the canal, from Sriganganagar district to the interior of the Thar Desert. Due to seepage and water stagnation the area around irrigation projects are vulnerable to malaria.[11]

The Genesis of Dam Building

Water is the prime source of development. In India, the availability of water both for industrial and domestic use has always been a problem. The water resource management strategy in India has so far been guided by the policy that water is strictly a fixed resource and we cannot really destroy it on any significant scale.[12] The idea that water is undestroyable because its' renewable has led to a rapid depletion of water resources in tanks, rivers, lakes and streams. The fact is that water is not automatically a renewable source as its renewability is governed by the ecological processes that maintain and stabilize the water cycle. Disrupted water cycles can turn water from an abundant renewable resource into a vanishing non-renewable resource.

Historically, the exaggerated emphasis on civil engineering at the cost of environmental balance, efficient crop practice and local management, as found in modern irrigation programmes was because the British found that revenue officials were unable to maintain irrigation projects and so army civil engineers were appointed for the purpose.[13] The East India Company spent a modest amount on the repair of irrigation projects and derived handsome profits in terms of revenue earned from irrigated land, milling, watering cattle, transporting timber, selling produce that grew on canal sides and from fines collected on breach of canal regulations[14] To illustrate, in Madras Presidency, the reconstruction of ancient irrigation works brought very high profits, some earning a net annual income of 73 per cent after paying a 45 per cent interest on capital. The revenue from the west Jamuna canal which was about Rs. 15000 in 1820 expanded to Rs. 4.2 million twenty five years later.[15]

For decades, one of the popular techniques for sustaining water is through dam construction. Dams have been a symbol of modernity, a backward nation having freed itself from imperialist rule on the path to modernization. The twin pillars on which a new India was to be erected was modern industry and scientific agriculture.

The government laid down certain criteria when huge multi purpose projects were implemented. A good irrigation policy should by and large result in the following:[16] (1) Maximum agricultural production per unit of water where water availability is a constraint; (2) Maximum productivity per unit of land where land availability is a constraint; (3) Equity in water distribution between large and small farmers; (4) Sustainable irrigation without loss of productivity (this normally means maintaining a sustainable ground water table); (5) Benefits to farmers which include water availability at the required time, required quantity and duration; (6) Economically viable and environmental friendly projects; and (7) Maximization of service areas in drought prone areas.

The case in favour of multi purpose projects is further strengthened by the current economic scenario of the country. This is of special significance for Gujarat, the industrial hub of India. The present urban scene in Gujarat reflects the skewed notions of development prevalent today. With a growing population and an ever mounting backlog related to housing, problems of water supply, sanitation, drainage, sewage, transport, communications, roads, electricity supply have multiplied manifold. The state is forging ahead with capital intensive projects, which would lead to intra-regional disparities, induce discontent and propel migration to the already crumbling cities. Simultaneously, the changing nature of economic enterprises will not only displace workers from specific sectors but would also be more selective in absorbing the incoming ones. Where would the economically displaced and the new entrants live and how would they cope with limited, employment opportunities and low returns from a variety of unprotected and informal sector jobs? Transferred into vote banks, they would be enumerated as participants in the city's governance without having access to basic amenities.

In addition to putting further pressure on urban land, infrastructure and labour market, such a process will generate elements with the potential of disturbing the social ecology of

Gujarat's urban and semi-urban locations. Such jumbled units will create pollutants and disasters, feed on water meant for agriculture, marginalize farmers through the changing logistics in the land market and stir up issues of displacement, rehabilitation and compensation by transferring the land status. In short, while barely drawing any advantage from these condensed growth centres, the common citizen will have to bear the brunt of such a distorted development process.[17] Given such a dismal tale of affliction, it is not surprising that successive State Governments, regardless of party ideology have promoted the Narmada project as a panacea for all the ills of the state, which will usher in a golden era of prosperity.

Displacement and Rehabilitation

There was no definite policy for rehabilitation for the project affected people, in the case of the dams so far constructed. The Government of India formed the Narmada Water Disputes Tribunal (NWDT), to formulate the first ever rehabilitation policy in India. According to the Tribunal's orders, the responsibility of the rehabilitation of the oustees from Madhya Pradesh and Maharashtra rests with the Government of Gujarat. They were to be settled in the Narmada Command Area and provided amenities like roads, schools, etc. as per the standards laid down by the Tribunal. There were no specific recommendations from the Tribunal regarding the oustees. However, the Gujarat Government passed two Resolutions in 1979 for its oustees. It was decided that the Gujarat Government would provide land by way of compensation to the oustees, from the land belonging to the revenue department. It was also indicated in the Resolution that the lands belonging to the Forest Department could also be procured for this purpose.[18]

The Resolution did not contain any clause that the Gujarat oustees should be rehabilitated in the Narmada Command Area. This meant that even non-irrigated land could be given to them. Since the Central Government has banned the use of forest land for non-forest purposes, the question of using forest land does not arise. It was so decided that by this Resolution, the Gujarat oustees would get the same facilities as the oustees of Madhya Pradesh and Maharashtra would get. The oustees also had an option that those who are not willing to get themselves rehabilitated on the land provided by the Government could buy land from the open market for which the Government would provide loans. There are two assumptions: *(a)* It may that the tribal oustees may not find the Government land suitable; *(b)* The amount paid as compensation to the oustees would not meet the requirements of purchasing land with higher prices in the open market. As a result, it would not be possible for the oustees to purchase land against the land they would lose.

However, in this policy the agricultural labour, artisans and such other oustees did not come into the picture as far as their rehabilitation was concerned. Moreover, even if they are paid full compensation against their financial loss, there was no provision for compensation against the loss of their habitat, employment, social networks and emotional bonds.

The World Bank (WB) intervened in the scene by way of financial assistance and stressed proper rehabilitation. The Narmada Control Authority (NCA) formed at the central level organised a sub-group to look into the problem of rehabilitation. In 1985, a special resolution was passed which demanded that the Gujarat oustees should be given the same facilities that were given to the oustees of Madhya Pradesh and Maharashtra like rehabilitating them into the command area. Other salient features of the resolution were as follows:[19]

1. After rehabilitation, the condition of the oustees should improve. It should be arranged at the place of their choice. They should be encouraged to mix with the local people.
2. The participation of the oustees in the planning of their rehabilitation will be ensured.
3. Every land owning oustee will irrigable land equal to the land he loses, subject to the prevailing agricultural land ceiling and he will get this land at the place of his choice. Supposing such an oustee has less than two hectares of land at the site of submergence, even then he will get at least two hectares of land at the new place.
4. Every landless oustee will be rehabilitated in either agricultural or non-agricultural area. The rehabilitation shall be so arranged as to see that he secures permanent means of livelihood. Land owning oustees would get compensation for the land lost, acceding to the prevailing market rates.

Many important resolutions were also passed. For instance, a resolution dated 17 December 1987 stated that even the landless oustees would get two hectares of land. Subsequently, another resolution dated 30 May 1988 pointed out that every major son of a landless oustee as well as the land owning oustee would be given two hectares of land. In yet another resolution dated 2 June 1988, it was decided that a major son of a land owning family would also get two hectares of land. In other words, two hectares of land was promised to all male oustees above 18 years of age. Since, it would take time to get work at the new place; subsistence allowance will be paid at the rate of Rs. 15 per day for 25 days in a month. This allowance will be for a year. In defining a family, every son above the age of 18 is considered a separate family unit. In addition, every family would be allotted 500 metres of plot for residential purposes.

The rehabilitation policy of the Gujarat Government in a nutshell:[20]

1. Full compensation for existing house, dismantled components transported free of cost at the new habitat.
2. Each family will get minimum 2 hectares of irrigable land whether it is land owner or agricultural labourer. Even an encroacher will get his share.
3. Every co-sharer and every major son of co-sharer will get 2 hectares of land.
4. The landless agricultural labourers affected due to the submergence of land will also be entitled to get 2 hectares of land.
5. Every major son of the landed oustees, agricultural labourers, encroachers, co-sharers, who had attained the age of 18 on 1st January 1989, would be treated as a separate family.
6. Free residential plot measuring 500 metres.
7. Facility of temporary sheltered accommodation at the new village site.
8. For constructing the plinth of the houses, a grant up to Rs. 10,000 will be given to the Project Affected Persons (PAPs).
9. To purchase new roof tiles, instead of transporting the old tiles at the new place, Rs. 2000 will be given.
10. Every oustee family will also be paid subsistence allowance of Rs. 4500 for the first year, paid in three instalments.
11. Resettlement grants of Rs. 750 plus escalation in the consumer price index at 8 per cent from January 1980. This is given in bulk after the PAPs shift permanently to the new site.
12. A subsidy of Rs. 500 to PAPs to purchase productive assets.

13. To make the land fit for cultivation, the land is either ploughed or a grant of maximum of Rs. 600 is given to for ploughing/ tracterizing the fields.
14. To derive the benefit of 100 per cent rural electrification, the PAPs are given assistance for electrifying their new houses up to 1.5 points.
15. Apart from being considered for new jobs, there are certain vacancies for the PAPs in the Sardar Sarovar Narmada Nigam Limited (SSNNL).
16. A small cell will ensure that the PAPs get the benefits of the ongoing development schemes.
17. Civic and other amenities like roads, schools, wells, vocational training will be provided at the resettled site.

The Legal Implications

On record, the above mentioned proposals are very comprehensive and provide for proper rehabilitation, but there is another side to the story. And it is this aspect which has leading to dissenting voices and protests regarding such mega projects. Lands were acquired by displacing the people in the interests of the nation. The spirit of 'national good' and 'national development' swayed the people. The social and environmental costs were ignored and voices of disagreement were brushed aside. Developmental projects have been justified on the ground that it is in the 'best interests' of the nation even if it means the virtual decimation of a community inhabiting the particular area. As a Government official has stated that 'the oustees must undergo hardship and distress and face an uncertain future, so that others may live in happiness and be economically better off. For this the community and the nation should be grateful to the oustees.'[21] But the question remains as to who constitutes the 'community' and who constitutes the 'nation'?

This is not the first instance where the state has parroted the argument of 'public interest' to justify the displacement of tribals. When limitations were imposed on the rights of the tribals to use and enjoy forest resources, which they had been traditionally enjoying for generations, it was argued that the forest resources are getting depleted and if this was not curtailed, the forests would vanish. It is in the national public interest to preserve the natural resources and which can only be possible by curtailing the tribals' access to forests. The Forest Act does precisely this, as it vests complete control over the forest area in the state, thus taking away from the tribals what traditionally belonged to them.[22]

The nation states who are signatories to the various international conventions must adhere to certain broad parameters before approving any development projects. The emphasis is placed on the human factor. The understanding is that a human being cannot be sacrificed at the altar of economic growth and the effects of any project on the community should be of prime concern. Hence, the human being becomes the subject and not the object of development and the respect for human rights becomes fundamental and all pervasive. The Universal Declaration of Human Rights adopted by the UN General Assembly in 1948 states in Article 3, 'everyone has the right to life, liberty and security of person'. Article 25 mentions, 'everyone has the right to a standard of living, adequate for the health and well being of himself and his family with all the necessities'. The International Covenant on Economic, Social and Cultural Rights adopted in 1966 and which came into force in 1976 and to which India is a signatory states that equal and inalienable rights derive from the 'inherent dignity of the human person'. Article 1 (sub clause 2) points out that in no case can the people be denied of its means of subsistence. Further, Article 69 of the International Covenant on Civil and Political Rights states that 'every human being has the inherent right to life. This right shall be protected by law. No one shall be arbitrarily deprived of law'[23]

A more specific international resolution which deals with displacement of tribals and which are binding on all states, who are signatories to it; These are the provisions contained in the Convention Concerning the Protection and Integration of Indigenous, Tribal and Semi Tribal Populations in Independent Countries, which was adopted at the General Conference of the ILO on 5 June 1957. The Article 11 of the Convention recognizes both collective and individual rights over the lands, which the indigenous, tribal and semi-tribal population have traditionally occupied. Article 12 proceeds to provide protection to these populations by stating that they shall not be removed from their habitual territories without their free consent, except in accordance with national laws and regulations. If the removal of these people is absolutely necessary, they shall be provided with lands of quality at least equal to that of the lands previously occupied by them.

The situation on the ground is entirely different despite such safeguards. With the population increase, the pressure on land has also increased. Now, relocation has become difficult. Simultaneously, there is a growing awareness of the disparity between the losers and the beneficiaries. A close look at the composition of the displaced population reveals, not surprisingly, that the majority belonged to the poor and backward sections of society. Those who suffered most were of course those who had lost all and gained nothing for their sacrifice. Gradually as the euphoria died down and realization dawned, the muted voices that had expressed doubts about the claims made for dams became louder and more vociferous. Questions were raised and protests broke out.

The genesis of the anti dam protests was the Anandwan Declaration which was issued at a meeting convened by Baba Amte in Anandwan in 1988. The Declaration called for the end to the construction of large dams.[24] It is interesting to note that the protest against Sardar Sarovar and Indira Sagar began as long ago as 1978 when the issue was mainly that of adequate compensation for the lands to be submerged. But as the movement gradually evolved, the focus was on rehabilitation. The Narmada Bachao Andolan (NBA) has also placed an alternative mode of development on the agenda.[25]

Given the growing needs of our society, it is true that not all projects can be brought to a halt. But it has become imperative to make the planning process more interactive so that displacement can be made less horrendous. There are different sets of people who are affected by any project: A) Those who are directly displaced by the project due to the acquisition of their lands and properties; B) People from whom only a part of their property is acquired and who although faced with acquisition are not entitled to resettlement; C) Those who do not face direct acquisition but are nevertheless afflicted due to changes in the land use pattern as a result of the project. The project affected persons are: 1) Those who had lost access to the natural resources on which they traditionally depended, and left with no alternative they are forced to move out of the area and are thereby displaced. 2) Those who are affected because the people on whom they depended for their livelihood are no longer there. 3) Those who are affected by the environmental consequences resulting from the project. Though the Narmada plan envisages an increase in stall feeding and decline in free grazing by cattle, in the guidelines of rehabilitation, there is no provision of any alternative fodder sources. The cattle, their owners and the grazing lands will suffer because of the submergence.[26]

The phenomenon of displacement needs to be situated in a much wider context, when different categories of people are affected in myriad ways. One of the most pertinent factors which tend to be overlooked when any project is initiated is the people's opinion. Do they want it? Do they see it as a solution to their problems? The study of the Baliraja Dam is an instance of how it is possible to construct an irrigation dam with the full participation of the people without any displacement. The solution has to be area and situation specific and based on peoples' needs.[27]

The principal Central Law which deals exclusively with the acquisition of private land by the state is the Land Acquisition Act of 1894 (henceforth referred to as the Act). This Act is applicable to entire India except the state of Jammu and Kashmir which has its own enactment in this regard. As the Act was enacted at the time when the state had a negligible role in promoting public welfare, obviously, its provisions are not in consonance with the current socio-economic realities. It's no longer sufficient for the state to act as the custodian of law and order and as it is expected to actively advance the well being of its citizenry. Increasingly however, both the Central and State Governments have been using the provisions of this Act to acquire land for various projects—thermal stations, nuclear power plants, multi purpose projects, etc.

The gravest shortcoming of this Act is that it provides for cash compensation alone for land compulsorily acquired under its provisions. The landless labour, artisans, collectors of forest produce etc who form an integral part of the socio-economic fabric of the village community and who will also be forced to start the struggle of life afresh, apparently do not need to be recompensed for the destruction of a way of life. Also at risk are religious and cultural symbols which provide meaning to a community. To illustrate, in the Narmada valley, the loss of archaeological and cultural loss has not been assessed. It is virtually impossible to relocate every single structure.[28]

The Act neither contains any provision for allotting alternative land of a comparable quality to those whose land has been acquired nor does it make it obligatory for the authority acquiring the land the assume the responsibility of resettling and rehabilitating those displaced by the acquisition. The state's responsibility ceases with the payment of cash compensation. In addition, by virtue of an amendment introduced in the Act in 1984, both the Central and State Governments can now acquire land for the purpose of providing residential accommodation to those affected because of government schemes, projects undertaken by local authorities or by state owned or controlled organizations. The fact is such a provision has been introduced indicates that the state is aware of the plight of those displaced. But this does not make it obligatory for the government to acquire alternate residential land for those who have lost their homes due to acquisition under the Act. Given that almost all available land is occupied by exercising the power conferred by this provision, the government will only be displacing another set of people who in turn will have to be resettled. Experience has shown that payment of compensation in cash to the displaced is not an adequate solution. The bulk of the displaced being tribals are often not capable of investing the compensation wisely.[29]

At present, a person whose land is acquired under the provisions of the Act and who is consequently forced to uproot himself and put down roots in a new and often hostile environment has no legally enforceable right, except the right to be compensated for the land that he lost, at rates that are generally below the prevailing market rates. The reason for this inequitable situation is that the Act provides for payment for compensation on the basis of the rates prevailing at the time the government issued notification under Section 4 of the Act, announcing that it may consider acquiring the land described in such a notification. Under the provisions of the Act, as many as three years may elapse between the time that the notification is issued and the collector makes his award adjudicating the compensation payable to the displaced. Even if the award is made, there is no guarantee that payment will be forthcoming as the Act prescribes no time frame within which the compensation must be made. There is provision only for payment of interest in the event of delay in payment once the collector takes possession of the land in question. Such a policy always operates to the disadvantage of the displaced as the compensation they receive is generally inadequate and does not enable them to purchase alternate land as the land value appreciates beyond their reach. The position of a displaced person who has no legal interest in the land acquired even though he may be dependent on it for his livelihood is even more pitiable, for he does not even have the right to receive any compensation for the havoc wreaked by the acquisition.

This begs the question, to what avail are the constitutional guarantees – the right to settle anywhere in the country, the right to conserve one's culture, the right to follow the occupation of one's choice and the right to enjoy life and personal liberty? These are all fundamental rights that have been constitutionally guaranteed, subject to the state's power to reasonable restrictions on the exercise of these rights in the interests of the general public. The last few years have witnessed the expansion of the scope of Article 21 which guarantees the right to life and personal liberty. The Indian Supreme Court has in several cases held that the right to live is not merely confined to physical existence but included within its ambit the right to live with human dignity and all that this entails, such as adequate nutrition, clothing, shelter and education.

The various legal loopholes in the rehabilitation policies are that the approach to such a vital issue has been piecemeal. All the policy directives are in the nature of guidelines that the concerned government departments have to keep in mind while executing a new project. The displaced have no legal right to demand that these guidelines be adhered to and implemented.

The Socio-Economic Aspects of Rehabilitation

A scrutiny of these directives reveals that there is no uniformity with regard to the people who are entitled to be rehabilitated, the nature of compensation offered, the civic amenities and the facilities to be made available at the new site. One can say that there are as many policies as there are projects. A few lacunae of these policies are presented below.

It is the landholders who are regarded as displaced persons and consequently entitled to such compensation and relief as may be available under the policy in question. In this respect, the policies of the State Governments appear to be based on the principle of the Act of 1894; that only persons who have a direct (owners, joint holders, as in the case of the Hindu Undivided Family) or indirect (a tenant or a mortgagee) interests are considered to be entitled to compensation for the acquisition of their land. In the case of the Sardar Sarovar Project, the Gujarat Government in its rehabilitation policy has decreed that every major son of the landed oustees, agricultural labourers, encroachers, co-sharers who had attained the age of 18 years on 1 January 1987, would be treated as a separate family.[30]

Agricultural labourers who do not own any land but who earn their livelihood principally by manual labour on agricultural land have been regarded as displaced persons. But other categories of labourers like artisans and craftsmen do not appear to exist in the eyes of policy makers. Another group that is neglected by the policy makers is that of women. A scrutiny of the definition of displaced person/oustee read in conjunction with 'family' reveals that in many cases an adult woman who is either unmarried, separated, divorced or abandoned and who does not hold any land in her own right is neither considered to be a displaced person nor part of the family of such a person. Consequently, she is not entitled to any relief. The pre-existing gender inequalities are further aggravated by the depletion of natural resources.

The decline of forests and village common grounds make women who collect fuel and fodder to travel longer distances, thereby extending their time and energy. Such degradation also reduces the women's income from gathered items and affects cattle dependent livelihoods also. The extra hours needed for gathering fodder, cut into the crop production time which affects crop incomes. Moreover, fuel wood shortages have adverse nutritional effects as people try to economize. As the women observe, 'it's not what is in the pot that worries you but what is under it'.[31] Nutritional deficiencies have direct health consequences. The large scale use of chemical fertilizers, with the resultant pollution of rivers and ponds affect women more because of the nature of their tasks. Population displacement arising from the submergence of villages due to large dams or from large scale deforestation disrupts the social support networks with kin and other villagers, built up especially by women. These networks provide small loans of food and cash or labour exchange to tide through periods of shortage. Their disruption usually goes unnoticed in cost-benefit exercises of large irrigation schemes. The rehabilitation programmes associated with such projects seldom enable the recreation of such social security networks. Since the women used to gather food and medicinal items from forests, they had a vast knowledge of the various properties of the plant species. The material base of these knowledge systems is destroyed. In a sense, the mega projects create not just a crisis of sustenance for the dispossessed and women; it is also the loss of knowledge critical for generating sustainable livelihood systems.[32]

A song by Daya Pawar, sung by the Dalit women in Maharashtra, captures the anti-life force of the dammed river which irrigates commodity crops like sugarcane while women and children thirst for drinking water.

As I build this dam
I bury my life.
The dawn breaks
There is no flour in the grinding stone
I collect yesterday's husk for today's meal
The sun rises
And my spirit sinks.
Hiding my baby under a basket and hiding my tears
I go to build the dam.
The dam is ready
It feeds their sugarcane fields
Making the crops lush and juicy
But I walk miles through forests
In search of a drop of drinking water.
I water the vegetation with drops of my sweat
As dry leaves fall and fill my parched yard.[33]

Most policies contain provisions for allotment of alternate agriculture land and house sites to families whose land has been acquired for the project. The basis on which this alternate land is allotted is generally the area of the land lost. Such a policy ignores the fact that submergence of farm land starkly affects the work opportunities for landless agriculture labour and that such families also need to be rehabilitated. Therefore, it may be more justifiable to take as the point of departure the pre submergence asset ownership structure of the displaced and build a system of relief around it.

The alternate land is allotted in one of the following ways. The government allows the oustees to search for and find their own land, gives them cash support in accordance with the entitlement of the family at the time of purchase; or it creates a land pool from government agricultural lands as well as farm lands likely to be sold by farmers in adjoining villages, negotiates the price with the owners and then offers such land to the oustees at a price determined by it. The policy of offering cash grants and leaving the oustees to find land for themselves is not conducive to the interests of the displaced as it is difficult for individual oustees to negotiate for competitive prices. This is particularly the case of tribals who tend to get caught in the clutches of exploitative land owners, lawyers and moneylenders as they are not accustomed to a monetary economy. Further, the assets held by the oustees are generally under valued by the assessing authority, whereas the value of the assets in the neighbouring areas where the oustees want to shift is inflated. Thus, cash grants do not help them in securing alternative land. Generally, the alternative land offered by the government is generally poorer in quality than that which has been acquired and may not even be a viable holding.

The nature of available land is constant and invariable, which leads one to question the 'land for land' policy. The number of those whom the land has to support and the number of those who desire to acquire land is increasing constantly. Hence, there will be time when it will not be feasible to provide the stipulated amount of land or perhaps any land at all to displaced persons.

The people who are displaced by a project are seldom relocated as communities. It takes place on an individual basis for it is easier to pay individual households and allow them to take care of themselves. Scant attention is paid to prepare the oustees for integration into the new communities. The socio-psychological dimensions of displacement are ignored and the callous bureaucracy further compounds their misery. Studies conducted on the rehabilitated villages reveal that the tribals have a 'marriage circle' consisting of several neighbouring villages. Being forced to resettle outside this circle is very traumatic for them.[34] To illustrate, many oustees of the Ukai Dam built on the river Tapti, learnt about the relocation only when the trucks arrived to carry away their belongings. The only choice they had was to accept Rs. 450 and disappear, or else face forcible eviction.[35] Hence, it is necessary to carry out in-depth sociological and anthropological studies to find out the requirement of the oustees. Without understanding the cultural and psychological bonds of the tribal or peasant, rehabilitation is bound to be a failure.

There is no authority or department at the state or at the central level that deals exclusively with the formulation, implementation and monitoring of rehabilitation programmes. While the projects are executed by the irrigation, power, mining, forest or other departments, the rehabilitation aspect is handled mostly by the revenue departments in the states. As for the actual implementation of the rehabilitation schedule, the field level machinery is adhoc, sporadic and lacking in expertise to formulate programmes and monitor their working.[36]

There are three main reasons why resettlement efforts are so often faulty.[37]

(*a*) Lack of an appropriate resettlement policy.

(*b*) The government resettlement machinery is ill equipped.

(*c*) The subordinate position of the oustees in the Indian social hierarchy due to their low caste and weak economic strength implies that they have very little economic and political bargaining power to exert *vis-à-vis* the state and other interest groups.

In the absence of any pre-project consultation with the community regarding the decision to vacate the dam site, the relocation process commences with the receiving of the land acquisition notice. As stated earlier, the Land Acquisition Act of 1894 empowers the government to acquire any land for public purpose in exchange for cash compensation. Land is a private property of the legal owner(s), generally the household head. The government deals with the individual owner and not the entire village. The Act thus raises certain basic issues. Firstly, all residents without land are excluded. Landless labourers, artisans, share croppers, tenant farmers and people living on collection of forest produce who constitute more than 50 percent of the population in any village are not entitled to any compensation. Second, very few cultivators have proper legal deeds of ownership. Hereditary usufruct rights are not recognised. Third, loss of common village property resources like grazing grounds are not compensated. Fourth, the land value is calculated as on the date of the gazette notification and interest is paid only from the date of taking possession up to the date of payment of full compensation. The Act does not take it into consideration the escalation of the market value between the time of notification and the date of actual possession. Moreover, to avoid a higher incidence of court fees, land transactions are often fictitiously recorded, far below the real market price. This results in low compensation as the official prices are under valued. Fifth, cash paid to people ignorant of the monetary economy leads to undesirable consequences. The cash compensation for land is grossly inadequate to buy new land, not to speak of indemnifying loss of employment or disruption of livelihood. The Common Property Resources (CPRs) are the first casualty of many development resources. The decline of CPRs can take three forms. (1) Physical loss of resources such as the submersion of grazing land by a newly constructed dam or covered by roads or buildings. (2) Deterioration of physical productivity of resources as revealed by degradation of pastures or forest lands. (3) Reassignment of usage and property rights as indicated by transfer of CPR lands to private ownership.[38]

In the history of the tribal use of resources, there is no strong evidence of the rights of ownership in the modern exclusionary sense. The absence of clear and simple rights offers ample scope for exploitation. 'The tribal people are losing their lands along the new arteries of communication and being incessantly pushed back from wherever new opportunities are arising. They are being squeezed out or forced to flee on their own, firstly as their lands are acquired by new establishments and then in the face of successive waves of migrants who begin to pour into these areas and spread out. The enclaves are emerging as islands of affluence and authority where the tribal has no place and can only creep in to occupy the substratum of the new socio-economic system'[39]

Concluding Remarks

The prevalent ideology of exclusive development has forged links between the state and external technology and capital to manipulate resources at the cost of the under privileged people.[40] As an alternative, new social movements in India are converging around a vision of participative and transformative development. The government is a supportive control agency and justice, equity and sustainability are the defining principles of inclusive development strategies. The Indian state has abdicated its central role in ushering in social transformation. As Rajni Kothari has observed, it has lost its role of a catalyst in the development process and dominant position in the realm of public welfare.[41] The public realm has been taken over by the techno-managerial structure of a corporate kind and public institutions are privatized.

Development as a concept and ideology has a wide spectrum of meaning and interpretation. It is a protean, multi-dimensional process leading to a desired and desirable change brought about by the masses themselves. It is a participatory process, which makes them self reliant in the end. Instead of a linear view, it has to be viewed in terms of the different environment needs of a people, i.e. in a non-linear perspective. However, such visionary ideas are only a footnote in India's development planning. They can make the whole development process more humane, participative, and understandable through the willing participation of the people themselves. Ultimately, development is the satisfaction of basic needs, especially the poorer segments of the population. It is the encouragement of the indigenous self-reliance, both in terms of using local raw materials and by invoking social participation and control. What is also essential is harmony with the environment to ensure long term sustainability of the development process. One needs to ponder that just because the present paradigm of development has secured international acceptance it is no proof of its universal sustainability. It only indicates how effective its rhetoric of development is and for whom?[42]

NOTES AND REFERENCES

1. An Officer at the Kevadia Resettlement Colony of the Sardar Sarovar Colony. Quoted by A. Kothari & R. Bharatari, 'Narmada Valley Project, Development or Destruction', *Economic and Political Weekly*, June 2-9, 1984, p. 916.
2. On a recent trip to Gangotri, we happened to visit the Tehri Dam site. The local people are unanimous that they have been shortchanged. The water and electricity are benefiting the plains. Many senior people still come to the submerged old Tehri town and shed copious tears at the destruction of their way of life. Any kind of protest has been stifled by the state's money and muscle power.
3. Rajan Gurukkal, "Ecological Perspective of Development", K.P. Joy, (ed.), *Eco-Development and Nature Conservation* (New Delhi: AIACHE, 1994), p. 71.
4. *Ibid.*, p. 74.

5. Madhav Gadgil, "Cultural Evolution of Ecological Prudence", *Landscape Planning*, 12, FAO Symposium, Amsterdam, 1985, pp. 285-299.
6. M.K. Prasad, "Conservation with People's participation", K.P. Joy (ed.), *Eco-Development and Nature Conservation* (New Delhi, AIACHE 1994), p. 41.
6. *Ibid.*, p. 74.
7. 'Progress Palls Kathmandu's Idyllic Setting', *Globe and Mail*, 19/12/1983.
8. Cheryl Payer, "World Bank, A Critical Analysis", *Monthly Review Press*, New York, 1982.
9. The Anti-Slavery Society for the Protection of Human Rights, London, 1985.
10. T. Hoffman and B. Johnson, "World Energy Triangle: A Strategy for Cooperation", *International Institute for Environment and Development*, Massachusetts, 1981, pp. 25-3.
11. B.K. Tyagi, "Malaria Spreading Rapidly in Rajasthan Desert Area", *The Hindu*, Coimbatore, 26/12/1995.
12. J. Bandhopadhyaya, "Political Ecology of Drought and Water Scarcity", *Economic and Political Weekly*, 12/12/1987.
13. S. Singh, "Evaluating Large Dams in India", *Economic and Political Weekly*, 17/3/90, No. 11.
14. K. Mankodi, "The Political Economy of Irrigation", *Lokayan Bulletin*, Delhi, 1985, Vol. 3, No. 4-5.
15. V. Ratna, "Irrigation in Colonial India, A Study of Madras Presidency", *Economic and Political Weekly*, May, 5-12, 1989, No. 30.
16. *Yojana*, "Water for Development, Government Guidelines", 26/1/95.
17. B. Das, "Tale of Woe in Urban Gujarat", *The Indian Express*, Ahmedabad, 19/5/05.
18. Vidyut Joshi, *Rehabilitation: A Promise To Keep; A Case of the Sardar Sarovar Project* (Ahmedabad: Tax Publications, 1991), pp. 55-56.
19. V. Joshi, *op. cit.*, p. 58.
20. P.A. Raj, *Facts: Sardar Sarovar Project* (Gandhinagar: Sardar Sarovar Narmada Nigam Ltd, 1995).
21. Quoted by Gayatri Singh, 'Dams and Other Major Projects', Report of a Workshop, Delhi, 1988, p. 92.
22. For arguments for a system of balanced and complementary land use of forests, refer, B.D. Dhawan, 'Big Dams Under Attack', *Economic and Political Weekly*, May 20, 1989, No. 20 and Sharad Kulkarni, 'Forests, Law versus Policy', *Economic and Political Weekly*, April 22, 1989, No. 16.
23. Mathew Areeparampil, PRIA, Delhi, 1987, p. 84.
24. C.R. Reddy, "Watch on the River", *The Hindu*, Sunday, September, 24, 1995.
25. Geeti Sen, (ed.), *Indigenous Issues, Peoples of India, Attitudes to the Environment* (New Delhi: Sage, 1992), p. 274.

26. A. Kothari and R. Bhartari, "Narmada Valley Project: Development or Destruction", *Economic and Political Weekly*, June 2-9, 1984, p. 916.
27. E.G. Thukral, *Big Dams, Displaced People* (New Delhi, Sage Publishers, 1992), pp. 19-21.
28. Kalpavriksh, The Narmada Valley Project, A Critique, April 1988.
29. Thukral, *op. cit.*, p. 155-7.
30. Raj, *op. cit.*, p. 36.
31. Bina Agarwal, "Feminist Environmentalism or Ecofeminism", *The Hindu Survey of the Environment*, 1995, p. 40.
32. Bina Agarwal, *op. cit.*, p. 41.
33. Quoted by Vandana Shiva, *Staying Alive* (New Delhi, Kali for Women, 1988), p. 55.
34. Kothari and Bhartari, *op. cit.*, p. 915.
35. PRIA, *People and Dams*, Report of a Workshop, New Delhi, September 1987, p. 37.
36. Recommendations of the Committee on Rehabilitation of Displaced Tribals due to Development Projects, Ministry of HomeAffairs, Government of India, 1985.
37. PRIA, *op. cit*, p. 21.
38. Robert Anderson and Walter Hubber, *The Hour of the Fox; Tropical Forests, the World Bank and the Indigenous People in Central India* (New Delhi: Vistaar Publishers, 1988), pp. 125-13.
39. Bharat Dogra, "Tribal Discontent, Timely Warning", *Economic and Political Weekly*, April 7, No. 14, 1990.
40. Iqbal Narain, *Development Politics and Social Theory*, (ed.), 'On Development', New Delhi: Sterling Publishers, 1989.
41. Rajni Kothari, *Rethinking Development, In Search of Human Alternatives*, see Introduction (New Delhi: Ajanta Publications, 1988).
42. Rajan Gurukkal, *op. cit.*, p. 72.

19

Agenda Against Social Exclusion: Democracy, Development and Citizenship

AVINASH KUMAR

In order to know how Muslims and dalits in post-independent India were thrown at the margins, it is indeed important to discuss the problems of identity, but perhaps equally important is to inquire about their development profiles. After India became independent, we almost had forgotten to look into the factors how these communities had lost out in terms of development, particularly the Muslims who had started living in closed private domain, more due to the victimization by their own religio-political leadership. There is a close link between democracy, development and citizenship, especially when we are trying to understand the kind of exclusion and marginalization that the communities have been facing since independence. The claim of being *democratic* is true only when *development* is inclusive of *citizens* from all the existing different communities, when development comes with the *right to equality* for all citizens and when there is an equal distribution of the developmental benefits among citizens of all communities. This chapter will focus on two studies that for the first time helped to change the discourse on 'discrimination and exclusion' in India.

The Indian democracy in the present decade has witnessed an unspeculated change in its secular politics. In the year 2004 the larger section of the electorate rejected the polished 'Shining India' slogan and it placed Sikh as the Prime Minister in Dr. Manmohan Singh and an Italian-born woman as the chairperson of the ruling United Progressive Alliance in Sonia Gandhi. Dr. APJ Abdul Kalam (since 2002) was already there as the President who is a Muslim and then in January 2007 it also got the first Scheduled Caste at the pinnacle of judiciary as the new Chief Justice of India in K.G. Balakrishnan. All this gives a very flattering picture about India as a flourishing democracy, but there are major deficiencies in our being a nation yet. Foremost among these is the discrimination and exclusion practiced against the fellow Indian citizens on several accounts, viz. because being a religious minority or being from a community 'scheduled' in the Indian Constitution. The form of discrimination and exclusion has reached to such an extent that they are not even secured of their right to life and livelihood. Episodes like Gujarat carnage and Khairlanjee massacre[1] are darkening the horizons of the growing and booming India continuously.

Realizing one of these deficiencies, the Government of India in the year 2005 appointed a high level committee[2] under Justice Sachar to prepare a report (discussed in detail in the next section of this chapter) on the social, economic and educational status of the Muslim community in India. It was with a purpose to identify areas of 'development deficit' in the social, economic and educational sphere of the Muslim community and specify areas where the 'intervention by Government' was urgently required. The committee reported,

> Since independence, India has achieved significant growth and development... However, not all religious communities and social groups have shared equally the benefits of the growth process... While the perception of deprivation is widespread among Muslims, there has been no systematic effort since Independence to analyze the condition of religious minorities in the country.[3]

Yoginder Sikand, one of the most widely read scholar on Islam and Indian Muslims observes that much has been written on the political history of the Indian Muslims, in particular on the life, times and legacy of various Muslim rulers who controlled large parts of India for centuries.[4] Yet, relatively little research has been done on the history as well as contemporary social and economic conditions of 'ordinary' Indian Muslims.' Glancing through the modern history, one easily finds that the British invaders considered Muslims as potential rivals in the beginning. And therefore they followed a policy of preference to Hindus over Muslims in the administrative positions and in several other works in the British India. However, it was only in the late nineteenth century where they felt the need to rediscover its relation with the Muslim community to counter the growing influence of the Indian National Congress. Then they started spotting individuals among the Muslim community who could side with them against the Indian National Congress (INC). Unfortunately, they found some who aligned with the British for the development of education among the community. But the intention of the British was not that simple, and ultimately led to the partition of the country in 1947.

However, partition brought in more problems for the Indian Muslims than creating solutions, says Haṣan Kamal:[5]

> Muslims who migrated to the newly created nation were from the upper and middle strata of the society. Those left were from the marginalized section of the community. Few left from the elite circle, completely detached themselves from the masses. This deprived Muslims of the leadership and thus the socio-economic condition of the Muslims never gained attention in the independent India

This gap in the leadership was filled in by the religious ulemas and clerics who always kept coining the religio-cultural issues rather than the socio-economic developmental concerns of the community. They kept the community confined within the issues like Muslim Personal Law, tripple *Talaq* (divorce), purdah, demanding minority status of the Aligarh Muslim University, etc. On the other hand the state too acted in the similar fashion. After independence, it instead of creating opportunities for the community for proper integration into developmental process started in 1959 giving 'Haj subsidy' to the community. In fact, none of the two parties did ever try to look into the issues of education, unemployment, poverty and under representation of Muslims in elected bodies, etc.

In the late 1970s a Minorities Commission was set up (by the first non-Congress Government at the centre) to evaluate the minorities' status in India. In its resolution dated 12.01.1978 the Ministry of Home Affairs (Government of India) mentioned,

> Despite the safeguards provided in the Constitution and the laws in force, there persists among the Minorities a feeling of inequality and discrimination... The Government of India ... is of the firm view that effective institutional arrangements are urgently required for the enforcement and

implementation of all the safeguards provided in the Constitution, in the Central and State laws and in the government policies and administrative schemes enunciated from time to time.[6]

However, the Congress Party after coming back into power in 1980 side-lined this Commission. It appointed a separate 'high powered panel', known as Gopal Singh Committee. On 14 June 1983, this panel submitted a 118-page 'Report on Minorities' containing extensive data on the participation and performance of minorities in education and employment.[7] But, for an unduly long period this report remained a closely guarded secret despite demands for its release. And even when it was made public, no action was ever taken on any of its recommendations.[8] On the other hand, when individuals like Shah Bano tried to break the barriers of the imposed personal religious laws of the community, the response of the Indian state was worth disappointing.[9]

It was only in the late 1980s and early 1990s that few Muslims in Maharashtra could make a successful attempt in the form of Muslim OBC movement that ultimately could bring in some major changes in the state laws.[10] However, the success of the movement could not make any large impact beyond the boundaries of Maharashtra. Even within the state, the result could not last for long. Sharing his experience Faqruddin Bennur[11] said:

> With the help of the OBC movement we successfully brought out the people of Maharashtra out from the identity specific issues and made them think about their development. But Gujarat 2002 has brought us back to day one. All our efforts have gone in vain. We are afraid now. People have started going back to the days of politics of identity. Self protection has once again become a prime concern for us. In instances like Malegaon and Bombay blasts we are targeted purposefully. We are booked under false charges and tortured for days and sometimes even months. The attitude of the administration has worsened day by day. We don't know where to go.

The concept on modern workplace came into being when the British came to India with their advanced technological skills and established mills and industries. The population therefore started segregating in these places and later they developed into cities. Despite the fact that it provided the space to break the traditional Indian village system of rigid caste hierarchy, the practice of caste based inequality remained visible. Gail Omvedt [12] observes:

> Untouchable workers…had lower-paid jobs… Because of feelings about untouchability, dalits were excluded from the higher-paying weaving department, where thread that broke had to be held between the teeth.

The word 'dalit' which actually means 'oppressed' person is a self-constructed and accepted nationwide identity of the scheduled castes community of India. However, it has acquired a new cultural connotation to mean 'those who have been broken, ground down by those above them in deliberate and active way.'[13] Dalits which comprise about one-sixth of the Indian population is the 'only underprivileged community that are treated as an entity beyond human intercourse and whose mere touch is enough to cause pollution.'[14] Although, the Indian Constitution under Right to Equality abolished 'untouchability' and forbid its practice in any form, a study carried out by Action Aid[15] in the year 2001-02, of 565 selected villages across 11 states demonstrated that:

> Untouchability is not only present in all over rural India, but it has survived by adapting to new socio-economic realities and taking on new and insidious forms...the study shows the systematic ways in which Dalit subordination is reproduced- in the public as well as the private sphere.

Discrimination is extended to all aspects of life: whether in education, employment, health, security, property rights and all aspects of women's rights. The caste system in India had divided the economic rights and obligations of the society on the basis of birth. It did not give the freedom to practice occupations of one's own choice to every individual or community. While all prestigious occupations were reserved for the upper castes, the dalits were forced to remain confined to perform only the menial services. In the definitional terms of Amartya Sen these rightly qualifies as 'unfavourable exclusion' and 'unfavourable inclusion'.[16] British tried to make inroads into the caste structure, but they remained only permissive rather than compulsive. They attempted to discourage and break the practice of untouchability but did not bring compulsive laws, as in the case of the abolition of *Sati* or child marriage. B.R. Ambedkar while criticizing the British policies said:

> Exploitation was not only economic but social. But, the British government could not sympathize with the living forces operating in the Indian society, was not charged with its wants, its pains, its carvings and its desires, was inimical to its aspirations... the Government of India dared not abolish the caste system... Progress involves interference with the existing code of the social life and interference is likely to cause resistance.[17]

However, some degree of success in creating a positive climate of change by the British was necessarily achieved. Later, the government of Republic India added the required compulsive characteristic to abolish untouchability in all forms. In the last six decades, although it has helped to decrease the degree of rigidity in the caste system, yet it continues to remain in the organizational (structural) and social (psychological) set up of the society in terms of both laws and customs. Explaining the structural existence, Darshan Rattan Ravan,[18] an important leader of the Balmiki community from Punjab said:

> The Municipal Act has worked against our community. It blocked our development and kept us attached to the traditional occupation of scavenging. Our people started getting secure jobs without any education and therefore they did not feel the need of making any effort to get themselves or their children educated. In the city of Ludhiana where we have several colleges and a university and all possible facilities for education, only two students from the Balmiki community could qualify to be doctors in more than 30 years. This mentality of depending on the Municipality service... is the biggest challenge for us.[19]

In terms of custom one can remember the notorious case of the Allahabad High Court judge who had his courtroom ritually purified (with Ganga-*jal*) because his predecessor had been a dalit.[20] *The USA Today*[21] on 5th of July 2006 carried a story of a dalit:

> As a young village school teacher, Hansraj Dugal would bring sweets to share with his colleagues at tea time. They remained uneaten. Not one of the other teachers would

'pollute' themselves by touching the sweets of an untouchable, he said. That kind of treatment drove Dugal, 45, to leave the village for the relative anonymity of New Delhi. He changed the last name of his children to try to conceal their low-caste background. Proudly describing their school honors, he hopes they can get through life without the benefit of quotas. 'I want to save my children from such discrimination,' Dugal said.

This is not the story of Dugal alone. There are many dalits who chose to live with a hidden identity. In the 1970s it was widely argued that the awareness of caste had undergone a particularly profound change in the arena of the modern workplace and the modern nation-state, but when India adopted the liberal capitalist frame in the 90s, it was seen to it that the old feudal system does not pass on economic benefits down the line to the lowest strata.[22] The new policy of modernization and development had curtailed the role of the state and prioritized the market. With the increasing role of the 'private' bodies where efficiency is considered to be the guiding policy, one hoped that the discrimination would cease to exist. This was an essential desire because the private sector in India was not obliged to be bound by any policy of protective discrimination alike the state. However, it proved to be far from reality. Therefore, a need was felt that the policy which has governed the allocation of places in higher education, public employment, and government itself should be extended to the private sector.[23] The private sector reacted strongly to it with a claim that they work in neutral manner and access to job and other markets is therefore determined by merit and efficiency alone.[24] Not only that, the business and academic leaders also warned that if quota system is introduced in the private sector, it would erode India's competitive advantages in a global economy. 'The only way we can compete with global players is by hiring best-in-class people from India and the rest of the world,' said Azim Premji, chairman of software outsourcing giant Wipro, 'We are an organization that requires selecting people on merit'.[25]

However, there was no study that could speak of this discrimination and exclusion faced by the dalits in the urban market in the post-globalized era. There was sufficient empirical evidence to suggest that discrimination exists, the latest being the study by Action Aid,[26] but it was limited to the rural sector. It was with this purpose that the researchers at Indian Institute of Dalit Studies (IIDS),[27] Delhi, decided to conduct a study that could find the discriminating patterns experienced by dalits (and Muslims) in employment and wages in the modern, formal sector of India's economy.

Indian Muslims: Education and Employment Status

The Indian Muslims, taken as a whole, rank among the most marginalized communities in India in terms of various social, economic and educational indicators.[28] But it is beyond the scope of this section to analyze all those indicators. The purpose here is to discuss the educational and job status of the community. The Sachar Committee Report mostly concentrated on the current status but it also presented some temporal contexts wherever needed. Below mentioned are some relevant indicators highlighted in the report:[29]

- The literacy rate among Indian Muslims is much below than the national average.[30]
- More than 25 per cent of children in the 6-13 years age group have either never attended school or have dropped out (Despite the fact that the increase in enrollments since 1990-2000 has been the second highest[31] among the Muslims: (65%). This percentage in the age group of 23 years and above is even worse. More than half the population is illiterate.
- Among all socio-religious communities (henceforth SRCs) Muslims had the least mean years of schooling. It was calculated that on an average a Muslim child goes to school only for three years and four months.
- Primary education seems to be the major hurdle for school education.
- Only 17 per cent of those 17 years and above have completed matriculation.
- Only 4 per cent of those 20 years and above have a degree of graduation or diploma. (Only 6% of the total Indian graduates are Muslims and the technical degrees at 18 years and above among Muslims is almost non-existent. The disparity in graduates between Muslims and all others has been widening since 1970s.)
- Only 3.3 per cent of the total number of students in the various Indian Institutes of Technology is Muslims, and the

corresponding figure for Muslim students in the Indian Institutes of Management is as low as 1.3 per cent.
- Only 2 per cent of Muslims are post-graduate.

The points can be increased further with the state level details. However, what it indicates clearly at the national level is that the gap between Muslims and other communities rises as the level of education rises. According to the report the committee had found that 'a community specific factor for low educational achievement is that Muslims do not see education as necessarily translating into formal employment'.[32] And therefore in its attempt to analyze the variety of factors that contribute to the level of education attainment, they first targeted to its relationship with the economic status. The two very important findings that they reported were:[33]

- Despite the fact that the probability of Muslims completing graduation is lower than for all other SRCs, the unemployment rates among the Muslim graduates are the highest.[34] It was specifically in urban areas and for males.
- The percentage of graduates in poor households pursuing post-graduate studies is significantly lower for Muslims *vis-à-vis* other SRCs.

As expected, the results showed that economic status has a very large, positive and significant impact on education attainment. However before we move on to discuss the factors that shape the economic status of the community, we need to look at some more factors that determine the educational status of the community. The report said that:[35]

- Muslims are at a larger disadvantage at the higher secondary level. The chances of completing higher secondary education are the lowest for Muslims in both rural and urban areas and for both males and females. (This presumably becomes the reason for a much lower size of Muslim population eligible for higher education.)
- Contrary to the popular conception that a large proportion of Muslim children study in Madarsas, the committee found that the only 3 per cnet of the Muslim children in the age group of 7-16 were enrolled in Madarsas.[36]
- However, the fact of the matter is that Schools beyond the primary level are few in Muslim localities... Many a time

Madarsas are the only educational option available to Muslim children, especially those belonging to the poor.

- Of all the villages having no facility of educational institutions nearly 20 per cent are those with Muslim population between 10-40 per cent.

Akhtarul Wasey, the head of the Department of Islamic Studies at the Jamia Millia Islamia, New Delhi in an interview with Yoginder Sikand says:

After all, the Government has done little, if at all, for Muslim education right from 1947 onwards, and instead of opening schools in Muslim areas, it is setting up more and more police stations there. And if there is some literacy among the Muslim masses, it owes much to the efforts of the ulema, who, despite facing numerous hardships, provide free education to literally millions of poor children through the madrasas… it is the madrasas that have kept the language alive.

As can be understood from the above, Indian Muslims have not been provided any targeted government and private action supporting their educational progress and from the schemes that were open to all, they have not been able to reap any advantage. The committee felt that, the positive impact of education crucially depends upon the existence of market (employment) opportunities. Without economic returns to education provided in the form of a higher probability of getting employment or earning higher income, investment in human capital formation will not occur. Before India opted for an open market, it was only the reasonable representation of various communities in government sector employment that generated confidence among them. They saw it as a means of participatory governance. The committee therefore, then attempted to find the percentage employment of the community in the government sector. But the report found that:[38]

- Muslims are heavily under-represented in all levels of government service.
- Most Muslim government employees are employed at the lower levels. But even in group 'D' employment (which requires only a low level of education), the share is only about 5 per cent. Their share in this category of jobs is even less in Central PSUs.

- Muslim presence at Group 'C' level is less than 5 per cent and even lower (2.5%) in public sector banks. Across categories, Group 'C' has the largest number of employees and officers who normally establish mass contact during the course of employment are generally from this category.
- Indian Railways employs only 4.5 per cent employees belonging to the Muslim community. Besides, almost all (98.7%) Muslim railway employees are positioned at lower levels; with only 1.3 per cent employed as Group 'A' or Group 'B' officers.
- The Postal Department, too, shows that Muslims are represented more in lower level positions than higher level positions. The maximum share of Muslims is in Group-D whereas their share in Group-A is just 3.8 per cent.
- In the University[39] employment Muslims are just 3.7 per cent in the teaching faculty and 5.4 per cent in non-teaching staff.
- In bank employment the representation of Muslims is as low as 2.2 per cent overall (just 1.7% at higher levels and 2.5% at lower level positions).
- In the central Public Sector Undertakings[40] employment Muslims have an abysmal representation at all levels. They are only 2.3 per cent in higher managerial and 2.8 per cent in middle managerial positions. Amongst lower level positions or as workers they constitute 3.9 per cent.
- In none of the all-Indian civil service cadres, the share of Muslims exceeds 5 per cent.
- In the private sector, too, Muslim representation is extremely low, there being very few Muslim-owned large industries.
- Only about 13 per cent of Muslim workers are engaged in salaried jobs (both in the public and the private sectors

The committee had requested all the States to furnish employment data for all their departments and PSUs. But only 12 states responded with some data, still fewer gave complete information. On the basis of the information provided by these states the committee came up with surprising figures of Muslim representation in various state government departments, viz. Education, Health, Home, Transport, Judiciary and State Public Service Commission and state level PSUs. However, the chapter is not considering those figures because the data analyzed was not of all states and therefore is only indicative. But the most important message that one cannot afford to miss from the state level analysis is:

> In no state,[41] and in no department of the state does the level of Muslim representation in employment exceed or even match their share in that state's population, not even in Jammu and Kashmir, where they form the clear majority of the state's population.

The community has shown 'signs of definite decline' since independence but more importantly the report brings out the fact that the Muslim community has failed to gain any benefit, rather the government has failed to share the fruits with the community, gained from the economic development that the country has witnessed in the globalized years. On the reverse, there has been a sign of decline in the development indicators after mid 1990s. According to Sikand, 'While economic 'liberalisation' and the withdrawal of the state have created new spaces for Non-Governmental Organisations (NGOs) to enter, particularly in the fields of education, health and provision of other basic services, few NGOs have included Muslims in their work, either as staff or as beneficiaries'.

Caste based Economic Discrimination in Job Market

The concept of 'economic or market discrimination' in the developed countries is seen in respect to race and gender, but in Indian context it adds to it the factors of caste and religion too. According to Sukhadeo Thorat,[42]

> The labour market discrimination refers to the situation of unequal treatment of the workers, possessing the same education, training and employment experience or productivity level in hiring or in wage payment, but differing in some non-economic personal characteristics associated with race, sex or caste... [it] thus manifests situations which involve exclusion or outright restriction on entry in market and/or 'selective inclusion' with unequal treatment in participation in various markets.

The research conceived by IIDS started with a hypothesis that discrimination is no longer an issue in the Indian labor markets, particularly in the formal, private sector, and at the end proved that the hypothesis was wrong. The study came out as a serious evidence of continued discriminatory barriers in the formal, urban labour market even for highly qualified dalits and Muslims felt that the natural operation of the market may not be sufficient to correct this inefficiency in labour allocation. The research was both quantitative as well as qualitative. Some of the major findings of the research that will be discussed here are:

- Low caste and Muslim applicants who are equally or better qualified than high caste applicants are significantly less likely to pass through hiring screens among employers in the modern, formal sector in India.[43]
- Managers bring to the hiring process a set of stereotypes that make it difficult for very low caste and very high caste applicants to succeed in the competition for positions.[44]
- Equally qualified dalit and non-dalit cohorts (limited to three central universities[45] in the national capital), who enter the labour market at the same time experience divergent outcomes in the labour market. Dalit students are far less likely to find jobs in the private sector.[46]

The first finding was the result of field experiment where the researchers replied to job advertisements in major English dailies sending[47] three applications to each call – as an upper caste Hindu applicant, as a dalit and as a Muslim. The larger findings of the study were:

- The odds of a positive outcome for an under-qualified high caste applicant applying for a higher-level job were statistically significantly lower than the odds for a high caste applicant with an appropriate qualification.
- The odds of success for an under-qualified high caste applicant were not significantly different from the odds of success for an appropriately qualified dalit.
- Having a high-caste name considerably improves a job applicant's chances of a positive outcome, but if a high caste applicant lacks the requested credential, his chances of success are considerably reduced.
- The odds of a positive outcome for an over-qualified dalit applicant (a dalit with an MA applying for jobs that required only a BA) were larger than the odds for a qualified dalit but were smaller than the odds ratio for a BA qualified high caste applicant.

- Since these outcomes occurred at the very first stage of the process, the caste and communal discrimination in the overall hiring mechanism was therefore evident.

The other attempt of the researchers at IIDS was rather qualitative that provided an insight into the mindset of the employers of the modern, formal sector in India. The researchers although cautioned that 'one cannot extrapolate from the data... that the patterns of un- and under-employment of stigmatized group in India be laid fully at the feet of discriminatory actors, acting either consciously or unconsciously on stereotypical expectations to overlook or eliminate qualified workers', yet they were not far from accepting that 'merit' was not the only watchword of the employment decisions as claimed by the private sector.[48] The study found that to ask questions on issues like 'family background' and involve other 'stereotypes' in the selection process may amount to indirect ways of discovering caste and practice discrimination and exclusion of the historically disadvantaged castes and communities of the country.

The third and the last finding that this section is concerned with was the role of caste in post-university employment expectations. In a nutshell the researchers found that social and cultural capital matter a great deal in the urban, highly skilled, formal and allegedly meritocratic private sector jobs, where hiring practices are less transparent than they appear at first sight.[49] The study confirmed the earlier mentioned finding by Jodhka and Newman that involving issues of family background are actually the indirect ways of discrimination on the basis of caste. A case study of a dalit student proved that everything[50] from his regional origins to his parental occupation was an issue in his interview to bar his entry in a private firm.

Call for An Inclusive Society

India today is struggling to bring a balance the contradiction between the superhighways and the slums. It has at one hand the task of modernizing its airports for the bourgeois and on the other to facilitate the basic amenities necessary for livelihood of the poor. While one India is singing the songs of modernity, the other India is suffering from cruel atrocities. The Scheduled Castes, Scheduled Tribes, socially and educationally backward classes, and the minorities still continue to remain next to the bottom economically and struggle for their survival.

After the Indian independence the Constitution took formal cognizance of the problems of SCs/STs, but still a larger part of the deprived population were left behind. Today nearly after six decades it realizes that mere provisions would not work for the uplift and sustainable development of the population at the margins. There was however, a need to bring a change in the pattern of discussing the problems of the socially excluded and marginalized sections of the society. The two studies discussed in this chapter proved to be the pioneer in that direction. The following section is an attempt to explain this claim.

Patterns of socio-economic inequality everywhere in the world is based on the older system of stratification, but the case of India being a diverse and unique multicultural nation becomes more complex. The Indian state's effort to redress the historically deeply-rooted institution of caste inequality in the form of protective discrimination did not include Muslim Dalits (and Christian Dalits) and they were denied these facilities simply on account of their religion, despite the fact that in many cases their conditions are, in fact, worse than those protected under the scheme. And whenever any attempt was made to redress their grievances, it was either termed as 'minority appeasement' or resisted by those upward in the hierarchical ladder. One reason perhaps, as discussed in the first section, is that the politics of the population and the attempts made by the state was revolving around the issues of identity and religion.

One (the Hindu right-wing) may condemn the Sachar Committee report as yet another step of minority-appeasement,[51] and the study conducted on labor market discrimination can still be said as a premature judgment, but the data that these studies have brought out has successfully cleared many myths and broken many stereotypes (already discussed in the above sections). In the democratic framework and with development (instead of identity) as its prime agenda the Sachar Committee has shifted the discourse on Muslim question from 'community rights' to 'citizenship' (the unit). The focus of the Sachar Report on the issue of development with significantly reformulating and incorporating ideas like sustainability, and the questioning of economic growth at any cost, has given a chance for the State to modify its approach towards the Muslims in a fundamental way. In the words of Surinder Jodhka, a political sociologist:

> From 'communities' with specific cultural histories and self-identities with clearly marked out boundaries, the Muslims of India are transformed in a population, identified and described through a language that primarily belongs to the state. This language of classification then also makes them available to the development agencies for an engagement which is different from the old language of identity and recognition... The Sachar Committee Report...also generates a new mode of mobilization among the different Muslim communities of India and provides them with a new language with which they can engage with State very differently.[52]

It has set the context in which the conditions of the Muslim community need to be assessed. It not only acquitted itself with data, but conclusively established that without affirmative action for Muslims, it would be impossible to harness India's social and economic potential and build an inclusive social order that respects diversity and plurality. It clearly prioritized an aggressive promotion of education, creation of employment opportunities, special recruitment drives in government and police services, and several other measures of Muslim empowerment. [53]

The dalits under the policies of 'protective discrimination' (PD) felt little safe until 1990s. With the liberalization of the economy the debate on the impact of PD underwent a change. While some argued for extending the reservations into the private sector, some opposed it vehemently. In a recent attempt by the state to extend 27 per cent reservation for the Other Backward Classes (OBCs) in higher education led to several days' long street protests and hunger strike by the so-called upper caste educated professionals. However, there was no serious attempt to provide with an actual understanding of the prevailing situation in the urban job market, that has been practicing discrimination silently under the name of meritocracy and efficiency. This study on labor market discrimination conducted by IIDS has proved to be an eye-opener for all including the judicial system of the country. The observations and the empirical evidence of the study are so surprising and strong that any policy decision over the debate on extending reservations (or not) or some form of affirmative prescriptions for the private sector cannot afford to ignore it. It was perhaps with this realization that the Supreme Court had to pronounce the judgment on 27 per cent reservation for the OBCs in higher education as affirmative action. And, for the first time in the plan era, in December 2007, the National Development Council accepted the approach to Eleventh Plan with 19 per cent of the total plan outlay devoted to education to make it more inclusive.[54]

Both these studies have invented a new language and that too supported by empirical data has lessened the chances of its opposition. With focus on 'democracy (the structure), development (the agenda) and citizenship (the unit)' prodded by these studies, a 'programme of empowerment *with a* grand inclusive agenda' has already begun. The 2007-08 and 2008-09 budgets have granted exclusive scholarships to deserving Muslims, increased allocations for the 'minority development and finance corporation' and the 'Maulana Azad education foundation'. In addition to that the financial year (2008-09) budget had also allocated:

- An increased amount of Rs. 500 crore from that of the last financial year to the Ministry of Minority Affairs.
- A multi-sectoral development plan for each of the 90 minority concentration districts will be drawn up at a cost of Rs. 3,780 crore. The allocation in 2008-09 will be Rs. 540 crore.
- A pre-matric scholarship scheme with an allocation of Rs. 80 crore next year.
- A scheme for modernizing Madrasa education with a provision of Rs. 45.45 crore.
- 256 branches of public sector banks had been opened until December 2007 in districts with substantial minority population. 288 more were targeted to be opened by March 2008 and many more in 2008-09.
- Continuation of the exercise of recruiting more candidates belonging to the minority communities to the Central Para-Military Forces.

However, the real success lies in the actual implementation of the recommendations made by the Sachar Committee. Nearly four years after the release of the Sachar Committee report, its implementation is still debated. Political commentators say that the steps taken by the Finance Minister are modest, even paltry. Very little of the promise has been translated into action. The United Progressive Alliance (UPA) has really summoned up the political will to implement the Sachar report, especially its recommendations for affirmative action in favor of Muslims.[55] Abusaleh Shariff, who was the Member Secretary to the Sachar Committee, feels that the Sachar Committee recommendations were aimed at effecting systemic changes in institutional functioning and improvement in governance, which are essential to enhance the inclusiveness of the marginalized communities. But the poor performance of the Ministry for Minority Affairs is shocking; it has failed to deliver any noteworthy service. He further adds that the ATR presented by the Ministry of Minority Affairs on the Sachar Committee recommendations, the context of Muslim focus is missing and is fraught with confusion and misinformation.[56]

After so much of critique, the government now has accepted the two recommendations made by the Sachar Committee seriously - creation of National Data Bank (NDB) and formation of Assessment and Monitoring Authority (AMA). The NDB on SRCs shall collect all relevant statistical information on various aspects like social, economic and educational status of Muslim community of India, while the AMA will 'evaluate the extent of development benefits which accrue to different SRCs' through various programmes.[57] In the month of May 2008, the Government of India constituted both AMA and NDB as steps towards realization of the dire need to take the minority issue seriously. A society with 'greater social cohesion and less exclusion' is a precondition for better economic performance and the attempts made by the two studies are a big way forward in this direction.

NOTE AND REFERENCES

1. Four members of the Bhotmange family, Mahar Buddhists in the village Khairlanjhi in Bhandara district of Maharashtra, were killed in full view of the entire village on 29 September 2006. Mother Surekha, daughter Priyanka (19 years old), son Sudhir (17) working in a town nearby and blind son Roshan (18). (report prepared by Dr. Babasaheb Ambedkar Research & Training Institute, Department of Social Justice, GoM & Centre for Equity & Social Justice, YASHADA, Commissioned by Nodal Officer, SC-ST (PoA) Act, 1989, November, 2006).
2. Henceforth SCR 2006.
3. *Ibid.*
4. In personal to the author.
5. The leader of All India Muslim All Backward Class (AIMABC) organization in a recorded interview to the author during his study on the Muslim OBC movement as a part of the 'Religions and Development' research programme.

6. http://ncm.nic.in/ (last accessed on 30 May 2008). The Minorities Commission was renamed as the National Commission for Minorities.
7. Report obtained from the National Commission for Minorities, New Delhi.
8. More sadly, on the name of minority empowerment, on May 11, 1983 (even before the Gopal Singh Committee submitted its report) it announced a 15-point programme which did not even mention a single recommendation for improving the educational and economic status of the community.
9. Asgar Ali Engineer in an recorded interview with the author shared that he had led several delegations to the then Prime Minister of the country requesting not to annul the judgment, and the PM had assured them so, but ultimately he surrendered before the orthodox voices (the author was on a field trip during his study on the Muslim OBC movement as a part of the 'Religions and Development' research programme).
10. This change is also visible in the Sachar Committee Report that indicates that in the literacy rate by social groups the Muslims have performed better in the past decades and even in the percentage who completed graduate schools Muslims stand higher than SC/ST community in Maharashtra.
11. One of the think tanks of the Muslim OBC movement in a recorded interview with the author at Solhapur. (the author was on a field trip during his study on the Muslim OBC movement as a part of the 'Religion and Development' research programme)
12. Gail Omvedt, *Seeking Begumpura* (Pondicherry: Navyana Publishing, 2008).
13. Eleanor Zelliot (1978), 'Dalit – New cultural Context of an Old Marathi Word', in C. Maloney (ed.), *Language and Civilaization Change in South Asia*, vol. XI, Contributions to Asian Studies, 1978, pp. 77-97.
14. Preface of *The Untouchables: Who Were They and Why They Became Untouchables?* by Dr. B. R. Ambedkar.
15. The study was brought out in the form of a book. Ganshyam Shah, Harsh Mander, Sukhdeo Thorat *et al.*, *Untouchability in Rural India* (New Delhi: Sage Publication , 2007).
16. Amartya Sen, 'Social Exclusion: Concept, Application and Scrutiny', Working Paper, Social Development Paper No. 1 (Bangkok: Asian Development Bank, June, 2000).
17. See Gail Omvedt, *Seeking Begumpura* (Pondicherry: Navyana Publishing, 2008).
18. In a recorded interview to the author. Balmikis are listed as the scheduled caste community in Punjab, and the author was there on a field trip during his study on the Balmiki Movement as a part of the 'Religions and Development' research programme.

19. S.S. Jodhka and Avinash Kumar, 'Internal Classification of Scheduled Castes: The Punjab Story', *Econmic and Political Weekly*, October 27, 2007.
20. Ghanshyam Shah, Harsh Mander, Sukhdeo Thorat *et al.*, *Untouchability in Rural India* (New Delhi: Sage Publication, 2007).
21. http://www.usatoday.com/news/world/2006-05-07-caste-barriers_x.htm (last accessed on May 23, 2008.
22. For details see K.S. Chalam, *Caste Based Reservations and Human Development in India* (New Delhi: Sage Publication, 2007).
23. Sukhadeo Thorat and Katherine Newman, 'Caste and Economic Discrimination: Causes, Consequences and Remedies' *Economic and Political Weekly*, October 13, 2007.
24. S.S. Jodhka and Katherine Newman, 'In the Name of Globalization: Meritocracy, Productivity and the Hidden Language of Caste', *Economic and Political Weekly*, October 13, 2007.
25. http://www.usatoday.com/news/world/2006-05-07-caste-barriers_x.htm (last accessed on May 23, 2008.
26. In 37 percent of the villages, untouchability was practiced in the physical distribution of wage payment—SCs received wages in cash or from a distance so that the dominant caste dispensers of wages could avoid physical touch with the SCs. In about 30 per cent of the villages there was discrimination between dalit and non-dalit students and in more than 20 per cent of villages the seating arrangements in public schools were separate and the arrangement for drinking water was different. In about one third of villages SCs were excluded from employment for construction of houses and in a sizable number of villages the SCs were forced to carry on their traditional occupation – considered to be unclean and polluting (G. Shah, Harsh Mander, Sukhdeo Thorat *et al.*, *Untouchability in Rural India*, New Delhi, Sage Publication, 2007).
27. In collaboration with Princeton University, USA.
28. For details see Mohammed Haroon, *Muslims in India: Their Literature on Education, History, Politics, Religion, Socio-Economic and Communal Problems*, New Delhi: South Asia Books, 1990.
29. SCR 2006.
30. However the state level presents a better picture for Muslims. In as many as 10 out of the 21 selected states literacy rates among Muslims are higher than the state average. These include Jharkhand, Karnataka, Maharashtra, Andhra Pradesh and Gujarat (See Appendix Table 4.1). Such estimates, however, can be deceptive and hide the low levels of attainment among specific groups. In quite a few of these states higher aggregate literacy rates are associated with low urban literacy levels among both males and females (SCR 2006, p. 53).
31. The highest increase in enrollment rate is among SCs/STs: 95%, *ibid.*, p. 57.
32. SCR 2006, p. 15.

33. *Ibid.*
34. 16.7 per cent among poor and 25.6 among non-poor. *Ibid.*
35. *Ibid.*
36. One reason for the misconception that the majority of Muslim children are enrolled in Madarsas is that people do not distinguish between Madarsas and Maktabs. While Madarsas provide education (religious and/or regular), Maktabs are neighborhood schools, often attached to mosques, that provide religious education to children who attend other schools to get 'mainstream' education. Thus, Maktabs provide part-time religious education and are complementary to the formal educational institutions. The common belief that a high proportion of Muslim children study in Madarsas stems from the fact that they are actually enrolled in the local Maktabs. As emphasized, such local Maktabs provide not a substitute, but a supplementary educational service. In Kerala, for instance, more than 60,000 Muslim students study in both 'mainstream' institutions and Maktabs at the same time. Since private and Government aided schools do not teach Urdu adequately, children have to be taught to read the scriptures at home. Some children are taught to read the Holy Koran by their parents, relatives or by private tutors. In many cases, especially in low and medium income families, parents do not have the time or ability to teach their children themselves. Micro-level studies show that such parents admit their children to maktabs, in addition to secular schools. *Ibid.*, p. 78.
37. Posted on Two Circles.net, on April 27, 2008.
38. SCR 2006.
39. The Committee received data from 129 Universities and 84 Colleges.
40. Information was received by the Committee from 154 Central PSUs which employ about 6.88 lakh people.
41. The Committee data from 12 states where Muslim share in total population is 15.4 per cent shows that their representation in government jobs is only 5.7 per cent.
42. Sukhadeo Thorat, 'Remedies against Market Discrimination: International Experience' in Sukhdeo Thorat, Aryamma *et al.*, (eds.), *Reservation and Private Sector: Quest for Equal Opportunity and Growth*, New Delhi: Rawat Publications, 2007.
43. Sukhadeo Thorat and Paul Attewell, 'The Legacy of Social Exclusion: A Correspondence Study of Job Discrimination in India' *Economic and Political Weekly*, October 13, 2007.
44. Jodhka and Newman 2007.
45. Delhi University, Jawaharlal Nehru University and Jamia Millia Islamia
46. Ashwini Deshpande and Katherine Newman, 'Where the Path Leads: The Role of Caste in Post-University Employment Expectations', *Economic and Political Weekly*, October 13, 2007.

47. A total of 4808 applications were made to 548 job advertisements over 66 weeks (Thorat and Attewell 2007).
48. Jodhka and Newman 2007.
49. Deshpande and Newman 2007.
50. Deshpande and Newman 2007. The study quotes the student:
Explain where you belong to [I was told]. I said I am from Orrisa. So how did you come here to Delhi?...He asked me so many questions about my caste, my family...First he asked me, if you are from Orrisa, why don't you settle down there...Then he asked: tell me about your background, what does your father do? I told him I come from a very poor background. My father was a farmer, he died recently. Now my mother is there, my elder brother is there. I am very much responsible for my family, so I want to earn some money.
The director went on to imply that someone from his background should be applying elsewhere and conveyed the student that:
You people are struggling for life, so you are not that competent, [he told me].
51. Christophe Jaffrelot, 'Positive discrimination for the Muslims of India? The reception of the Sachar Committee report by the Sangh Parivar', presented at a seminar on 'democracy, development and citizenship' at Jawaharlal Nehru University, New Delhi on February 8-9, 2008.
52. Professor of Sociology at CSSS/JNU, speaking at a seminar on 'Religious Communities and Development' organized at Jawaharlal Nehru University on 27 March 2007.
53. Praful Bidwai, 'Not by Haj Subsidies Alone' *Frontline*, Vol. 24, Issue 24, December 08-21, 2007.
54. K.S. Chalam, 'Inclusive Education and Eleventh Plan', *South India Journal of Social Sciences*, Vol. V, No. 2, 2007.
55. See Bidwai 2007.
56. Abusaleh Shariff, 'Sachar Committee Report and Pending Promises' *The Hindu*, November 17, 2007. He explains: 1. It recommends geographic targeting— 90 minority districts identified to provide 'basic amenities and employment opportunities.' Only about half of the districts have Muslims, and then what these basic amenities are is not specified. Only about 30 per cent of Muslims are covered in this approach, and the question is: what happens to the remaining 70 per cent, spread all over India? 2. Further, the ATR refers to a 'substantial Muslim population.' It does not clarify whether this refers to 90 selected districts. In my judgment, the 'substantial Muslim population concentrations' must be defined at the level of the taluks and blocks and not at the level of the districts, confined to only 90 districts. Given the advantage of decentralization through the panchayats, the taluk-block level focus will help reach out to the maximum number from the deprived communities. It is important that the Sachar Committee highlighted status of Muslims in a comparative perspective, but the ATR refers to 'Minorities,' thus diluting the Muslim focus. 3. It is

shocking that the ATR is silent on the need for universalisation of education. Besides, no mention is made about promoting higher education among Muslims. A strategy must be evolved to determine what mechanism will be used, and how it will be used, to improve the representation of Muslims in the Central and State administrations, and in public sector undertakings.

57. SCR 2006, p. 239.

Index